NORFOLK R
THE POOL L

PAUPER PALACES

STUDIES IN ECONOMIC HISTORY

Editor:
Professor F. M. L. Thompson
Bedford College
University of London

PAUPER PALACES

NORFOLK

ANNE DIGBY

Homerton College
Cambridge

ROUTLEDGE & KEGAN PAUL
London, Henley and Boston

First published in 1978
by Routledge & Kegan Paul Ltd
39 Store Street,
London WC1E 7DD,
Broadway House,
Newtown Road,
Henley-on-Thames,
Oxon RG9 1EN and
9 Park Street,
Boston, Mass. 02108, USA
Printed in Great Britain by
Redwood Burn Limited, Trowbridge & Esher

British Library Cataloguing in Publication Data

Digby, Anne
    Pauper palaces.—(Studies in economic history).
    1. Public welfare—England—Norfolk—History
    2. Poor—England—Norfolk—History
    I. Title   II. Series
    362.5'09426'1   HV249.E9N/   78-40412
    ISBN 0 7100 8784 5

CONTENTS

v

vi   Contents

ILLUSTRATIONS

PHOTOGRAPHS

MAPS

FIGURES

TABLES

PREFACE

Just as Oliver Twist has come to represent the pauper, so the workhouse has come to symbolize the Poor Law. These images of the modern
system of English poor relief reflect popular mythology rather more
than historical reality. Over-simplifications have also been generated by historians who until recently have tended to accept the
formal framework of the Poor Law as if it represented not just the
theory of how poor relief was administered but also its practice.
This study seeks to de-mythologize the Poor Law by attempting to
differentiate image from reality and theory from practice. Although
the analysis is formally based on the single county of Norfolk, it
is hoped that this book will make a contribution not only in the
field of local history but also in helping to create a fresh method-
ological perspective on the Poor Law.

New approaches have been developed during the last few years by
historians and economists working on the Poor Law, and this study
of the Poor Law in Norfolk is the first extended analysis in which
these are combined. A significant change of focus in work on the
Poor Law has come from an appreciation that variations in poor relief at the local level were so extensive and widespread that they
threw doubt on the validity of looking mainly at the Poor Law from
the traditional standpoints of either national legislation or central administrative regulations. A second development, which resulted from this shift of emphasis from centre to locality, was that
abstractions of national pauperism were supplemented by a more intensive study of individuals and of the interrelationship of administrators with paupers. With this growing interest in the experience
of individual paupers, poor law studies might claim to be part of
the new social history, in which history was written from below out
of a concern for people who were too ordinary to have attracted
much attention from earlier historians. Another product of the
different weight that has been placed on local experience in analysing the history of poor relief was that greater prominence has
been given to the economic, social and political context in which
the Poor Law was administered.

Norfolk was an interesting area in which to do this kind of con-
textual study. The pressures that moulded the practical administration of the Poor Law during the nineteenth century were illustrated

particularly clearly in the effect that the intractable problem of
surplus labour in the county's economy had on the distribution of
poor relief. This was also shown, though to a lesser extent, by the
influence that the disturbed condition of local rural society, and
the highly politicized state of Norwich life, had on local poor law
administration. In this kind of study the formidable difficulties
of relating developments in the relief of the poor to the economic,
social and political history of the locality were reduced by the
existence of a wealth of source material on the Norfolk Poor Law.
These rich sources also made the county an appropriate area in which
to study the interaction of the policies of local relief administrators with those in London in the period after 1843. The thrust of
central policy was blunted by the strength of regional traditions
in poor relief and the most distinctive of these traditions was that
of the East Anglian pauper palaces.

It is my pleasure to thank the many people with whose help this
book has been written. I welcome this opportunity to thank Professor R.H. Campbell whose penetrating criticism has helped shape this
analysis, and whose support has encouraged me during eight years of
research activity. Fruitful lines of investigation have been suggested by Professor A.W. Coats and I am grateful to him for his comments on Chapter 11. Chapters 1, 8 and 9 have benefited from the
perceptive points made by Dr M.A. Crowther, and Chapters 7, 10 and
12 by those of Dr P. Searby. I appreciate the way that many other
friends have either stimulated discussions that have caused me to
modify my arguments, or given me technical assistance of varied
kinds. As editor of the series in which this volume appears, Professor F.M.L. Thompson has given me much valuable advice. Any deficiencies that still remain in this study are, of course, my own
responsibility.

Archivists, librarians and museum curators have made a notable,
if hidden, contribution to this volume by their informed advice and
their patient assistance and I would like to express my appreciation
for their help. I also want to record my gratitude to Homerton
College, Cambridge, for giving me a term's study leave to complete
this book. Finally, I wish to thank Mrs E.W. Butt for the meti-
culously drawn maps, plans and graphs that she has produced for
this volume, Mr T.R. Robinson for help with photography, and Mrs
P. Osbourn for deciphering my manuscript and converting it into
such a neat typescript.

Grateful acknowledgment for permission to reproduce material is
made to Mrs E.L. Perrott (Photographs 16, 20); Norfolk Museums Service, Lynn Museum (Photographs 1, 2, 13; Figures 13, 14); Norfolk
Area Health Authority (Photographs 18, 19); Norfolk County Council
(Photographs 10, 14, 15; Figures 3, 4, 5); Norfolk Record Office
(Figures 1, 2, 6, 7, 12); Norfolk Federation of Women's Institutes
and the Boydell Press, Ipswich for the extract on page 160. The
originals of Figures 10 and 11 are in the custody of the Public
Record Office.

A.D.

CHAPTER 1

PERSPECTIVES

The East Anglian poet, George Crabbe, described in lines that have
since become famous the transformation that had occurred during the
late eighteenth century in the local administration of poor relief:
(1)

> Your plan I love not, — with a number you
> Have placed your poor, your pitiable few:
> There, in one house, throughout their lives to be,
> The pauper palace which they hate to see:
> That giant-building, that high-bounding wall,
> Those bare-worn walks, that lofty thund'ring hall!
> That large loud clock, which tolls each dreaded hour,
> Those gates and locks.and all those signs of power;
> It is a prison with a milder name,
> Which few inhabit without dread or shame.

Crabbe was born and brought up in east Suffolk in the period between
1756 and 1779, when local incorporations for the relief of the rural
poor were being set up there, and so he was able to supply an informed and critical comment on them.(2) The reforming movement also
spread into Norfolk, where there occurred between 1764 and 1785 a
parallel movement to group country parishes into local incorporations
and to erect in each a house of industry in which to relieve the poor.
While there were scattered rural and urban incorporations in other
parts of the country, the fourteen rural incorporations of East
Anglia represented, by the beginning of the nineteenth century, the
largest compact area to have initiated local poor law reform and so
to have departed from the national relief policies of the Old Poor
Law which had continued since the Elizabethan period.

The houses of industry in the East Anglian incorporations were
regarded as prisons by many of the labouring poor because they deprived the poor of their traditional social right to be relieved in
their own homes. Yet, paradoxical though it may seem, Crabbe was
reflecting contemporary local opinion when he called these houses
of industry not only prisons, but also pauper palaces. The buildings were constructed on an extensive scale and had a monumental
style. The most impressive example was probably that at One-House,
in the Stow Incorporation in Suffolk, where the classical archi-
tecture of the building was so imposing that local gentlemen were

1

outraged because it outstripped that of their own more modest
country houses.(3)   Houses of industry were equally grandiose in
Norfolk, where over £40,000 had been spent by the five rural incorporations on their houses of industry.   These buildings reflected
local pride in introducing a significant reform in the system of
relieving the poor and in developing a notable experiment in social
welfare.   The humane intentions of the reformers were blazoned forth
in the inscriptions on the Suffolk houses of industry at Melton,
and also the Norfolk one at Rollesby.   The latter stated:
> For the Instruction of Youth
> The Encouragement of Industry
> The Relief of Want
> The Support of Old Age
> And the Comfort of
> Infirmity and Pain.

Although the East Anglian incorporations were only partially successful in achieving these aims, their achievements were considerable, and not least in replacing the squalid misery of the parish
poor house by a more organized and comfortable welfare system.   In
1775 Crabbe had been appointed as surgeon to the Aldeburgh poor
house, and his first-hand experience of the wretchedness to be found
in such an unreformed institution was described in 'The Village',
a poem published in 1783.   Later, in 1810, he published 'The
Borough', where a quite different picture was given of the material
wellbeing of the paupers' lives in the local houses of industry:(4)
> Be it agreed — the Poor who hither come
> Partake of plenty, seldom found at home;
> That airy rooms and decent beds are meant
> To give the poor, by day, by night, content:...
> I own it grieves me to behold them sent
> From their old home;   t'is pain, t'is punishment,
> To leave each scene familiar, every face,
> For a new people and a stranger race.

Crabbe's distinction between the material superiority of life in
the house of industry when compared with that of the labourer's own
home, and the psychological deprivations of institutional life, was
a perceptive one.   It was valid not only for houses of industry
under the Old Poor Law but also for the new union workhouses which
were erected as a result of national reform in the New Poor Law of
1834.

In East Anglia it was the local incorporating movement of the
eighteenth century, and not the national reform in the Poor Law
Amendment Act of 1834, that made a decisive break with the Elizabethan basis of the Old Poor Law.   The New Poor Law of 1834 aimed
to amend local relief practices and to impose a uniform national
system through the central supervision of local administrators by
a board of Poor Law Commissioners in London, who were assisted by
a mobile poor law inspectorate.   East Anglia was among the first
areas to receive the attentions of the central administration; the
inspectors (or assistant commissioners, as they were called at the
time), began work in Suffolk, and later moved on into Norfolk. In
their public reports the assistant commissioners condemned the heavy
pauperism and high poor rates of the area, and deprecated the practice in the local incorporations of using outdoor allowances rather

than indoor relief in the houses of industry. The East Anglian
incorporations had failed in some cases to realize their twin objectives. They aimed to provide a liberal system of relief in the
houses of industry for the weaker members of society, and also to
provide economies for the ratepayers, by setting the able-bodied
inmates of the house of industry to profitable work. Financial
disillusionment meant that long before 1834 there had been a widespread resumption of relieving the poor in their own homes by means
of outdoor allowances. The East Anglian incorporations, to judge
from the assistant commissioners' public utterances, were a fertile
ground on which to sow the seeds of the New Poor Law, since the
local practice of outdoor relief contrasted so markedly with the
emphasis in the 1834 act on indoor relief in workhouses for the
able-bodied poor. Privately, the assistant commissioners acknowledged that the houses of industry of the Suffolk incorporations
'afford such excellent means of applying the proper test at once,
that, perhaps, the most extensive and earliest proofs of the cor-
rectness of the principles on which the new law is founded will be
derived from this county'.(5) This was not because the relief
arrangements of the East Anglian incorporations needed reform —
as their public reports suggested — but because many of the poor
law practices of the local incorporations had anticipated the policies of the 1834 act. The assistant commissioners recognized that,
where the incorporated areas of Suffolk and Norfolk were concerned,
the New Poor Law was not new at all, but a repetition of earlier,
local reforms.
     The assistant commissioners were correct in their assessment
that the administrative arrangements needed to introduce the New
Poor Law could be quickly established in East Anglia. By 1837
the geography of the New Poor Law had been set up through grouping
parishes into unions; 15 unions had been formed in Suffolk and
18 in Norfolk, while the remaining 5 rural East Anglian incorporations, which had refused to consent to their own dissolution were,
in practice unions in all but name. In workhouse-building the
tradition of the pauper palaces continued. In Norfolk, 12 new
union workhouses were built between 1835 and 1839, at a cost of
£75,000. Here, outdoor allowances were administered more strin-
gently in accordance with centrally determined regulations, and
expenditure on poor relief had dropped by 40 per cent by 1840. In
that year the Poor Law Commissioners thought their best administered counties were Norfolk and Kent.(6)
     The relative ease with which the New Poor Law was introduced
into East Anglia was similar to that in some other localities,
such as Tyneside or Northamptonshire; in each of these areas success had depended to a considerable extent on the tact and flexibility of the assistant commissioners in their handling of local
gentlemen. But whereas in Northamptonshire the assistant commissioners had leaned over backwards to meet the desire of the local,
landed gentry to align the boundaries of poor law unions with those
of their estates, in Norfolk the assistant commissioners were able
to balance the conciliation of the gentry against the need to accommodate within the new structure the existing poor law administrative arrangements of local incorporations and Gilbert Unions.
(7) They were able to achieve this because of the strong desire

of the Norfolk gentry and clergy to see the new law introduced.

This support for the New Poor Law seems at first to be a puzzling phenomenon because the 1834 act re-introduced policies for the indoor relief of paupers. These had already been tried and found to be inadequate in the Norfolk rural incorporations, where there had been a widespread movement to replace indoor relief with outdoor allowances in the decade before the Poor Law Amendment Act of 1834. The successful introduction of the New Poor Law in East Anglia would be more readily comprehensible either if these policies provided continuity with reforms that had been recently established in the 1820s (as was the case in Nottinghamshire), or if the more stringent relief policies of the 1834 act contrasted sharply with local regional practice (which was the case in much of southern England), and hence promised hard-pressed ratepayers some alleviation of their economic burden.(8) Neither interpretation is adequate by itself to explain the rapid adoption of the New Poor Law in Norfolk. The key to its successful introduction lay in the values and attitudes of the propertied classes, while the later history of relief administration can be clarified only by looking at the interests of the farmers, who took over the management of the poor from the gentry and clergy.

Norfolk property-owners collaborated with central administrators in introducing the New Poor Law into the county because they found the punitive, class element in this legislation congenial, and welcomed the more rigorous relief system as a means of disciplining the labouring poor. The highly disturbed state of East Anglia, which had experienced widespread rioting in 1816, 1822 and 1830, had convinced local property-owners that an increasing number of disloyal labourers existed who were involved in frequent riots, machine-breaking and acts of incendiarism. Earlier sympathy for the labourer's deteriorating situation and an understanding of the economic causes of low wages and under-employment, which forced a recourse to poor relief, were gradually replaced by a moral explanation in which the labourer was held responsible for his poverty and his protests in popular disturbances were regarded as disloyalty, which needed corrective discipline. Norfolk gentlemen and clergymen who had set the standard for a humane administration of relief under the Old Poor Law had become sufficiently disillusioned with the state of the poor by the 1830s to welcome the 1834 act, and to co-operate with the assistant commissioners in introducing it into the county. They supported the system of pauper education, which was highly developed in Norfolk union workhouses after 1834, because they liked its aim of rehabilitating the children of the poor by making them into useful and industrious members of society. It provided a microcosmic view of their expectations about the wider effects of the New Poor Law on Norfolk which they hoped might, in the long term, convert the disloyal, bad poor into good, useful members of local society. In the short term, however, many gentlemen withdrew gradually from an active involvement with poor law administration, since this was concerned with the undeserving poor, whose actions had excluded them from the paternalistic concern of their social betters. Increasingly, the propertied classes confined their attention to the good, deserving poor who lived on their estates and whose loyalty and industry were rewarded by regular employment, charitable help and the provision of model cottages. Their own earlier responsibility in helping to create these two classes of poor, either through developing a system of 'close' and 'open' parishes or through charging high farm rents which fostered low agricultural wages, was conveniently forgotten. The Norfolk gentry were active initially in the administration of the New Poor Law, since they wished to be involved in the first important decisions about union boundaries and workhouse building, but thereafter they failed very often to exercise their right as justices of the peace to sit as ex officio members of Norfolk boards of guardians. This diminution of gentry activity in Norfolk after the first few years of the New Poor Law was comparable to that in Durham. It contrasted with that in Northamptonshire, where the landed magnates and the gentry were unusually active during the 1830s in the administration of the 1834 act. However, the motivation of the Northamptonshire and Norfolk gentlemen guardians was similar in wishing to increase social control over the poor.(9)

The elected guardians on Norfolk boards were more consistent in their attendances at board meetings, and control of relief policies therefore passed to the farmers, who made up four-fifths of their number. Farmers, as occupiers of land, on which 80 per cent of the Norfolk poor rate was levied, were the principal payers of the poor rate. It is hardly surprising that they were vigorous supporters of the 1834 act when it is seen that expenditure on Norfolk poor relief in each of the three years from 1832 to 1834 amounted to over £30,000 annually, a figure that had been exceeded only once before, in 1818 (see Figure 8 below). Farmer-guardians welcomed the prospect of reduced poor rates through a downward revision of relief payments after 1834, since the cost of poor relief per head of Norfolk population had been very much higher than the average for England and Wales in every year since the beginning of the century. In 1834, the year in which the Poor Law Amendment Act was passed, Norfolk relief expenditure formed the sixth highest county figure, amounting to 15s 9d per head of county population, compared with an average figure of only 9s 1d for England and Wales (see Table 3a below). In the opening years of the New Poor Law the farmer-guardians of Norfolk implemented the rigorous relief regulations of the central Poor Law Board, outdoor allowances to the able-bodied labourer were reduced, and poor rates fell. With more difficult years for local agriculture in the 1840s than in the 1830s came a reversal of their relief policies by Norfolk farmer-guardians, who now concluded that outdoor allowances to the labourer were cheaper than indoor relief in the union workhouse.

Relief administration in rural Norfolk reflected local economic conditions. The battered state of the nineteenth-century Norfolk economy gradually eroded the sense of social responsibility felt by propertied groups towards the labouring poor, and the earlier sense of mutual interest and connection between different groups in society became progressively attenuated. By the mid-nineteenth century Norfolk farmers were prepared to pursue aggressively their own sectional economic interests because of their own more precarious financial position. In the eighteenth century Norfolk agriculture had been famous for its improving landlords and innovating farmers, but by the mid-nineteenth century its farming had been eclipsed by that of

east Scotland as the key centre of progressive agriculture. The
squeeze on agricultural profits that had resulted from the lower
grain prices after 1815 had hit Norfolk farmers hard since their
rents remained relatively high, while for farmers in clay areas
other costs also remained obstinately large. Demographic pressures
exacerbated this situation — the population in Norfolk grew from
273,479 in 1801 to 442,714 in 1851. By the early nineteenth century
Norfolk opinion had become convinced that an intractable problem of
surplus labour existed in rural areas. While traditional ideas of
social responsibility by the propertied towards the poor dictated
that everyone should be kept from starvation, the less affluent
condition of agriculture indicated that this must be achieved more
cheaply than before. Farmers resolved this dilemma by maximizing
employment for the labourer but also by paying him low wages which
then had to be supplemented by poor relief. The administration of
poor relief by farmers who dominated poor law administration in the
parish vestry before 1834, and in the guardians' board room after
1834, resulted in a confusion of public social policy with private
economic interests. As such, this study of Norfolk relief policy at
the local level gives support to a general analysis of the Poor Law,
and particularly the New Poor Law, as a class measure.(10)

From the second to the sixth decade of the nineteenth century it
was common for the Norfolk rural labourer to have his low farm wages
supplemented by poor relief in the form of outdoor allowances. Under
the Old Poor Law these were given more openly as 'allowances in aid
of wages', but in the 1840s, when the regulations of the New Poor
Law began to be quietly subverted by farmer-guardians, allowances
were given ostensibly 'in aid of sickness'. The subsidization of the
private farm labour bill by public poor law funds was one of the most
obvious elements in the interdependence of poor law administration
with the rural economy. Norfolk farmers wanted to maximize employment for the labourer through a mixture of poor relief and wages
because of the seasonal disparity in their demand for labour. Norfolk was a great corn-growing area, and the need for labour during
harvest time was much greater than at other times. Social policies
designed to maximize employment during the slack months of the farming year were organized by farmers, who through their dual control
of both the labour market and poor law administration were able to
organize labour allocation schemes. Under the Old Poor Law these
were organized on a parochial basis and took the form of roundsmen
schemes and labour rates, while under the New Poor Law the poor law
union became the geographical unit for a ticket system and the guardians' board room acted as the local labour exchange.

While economic attitudes permeated social policy in the administration of the rural Norfolk Poor Law, non-economic attitudes conditioned the farmers' wage and employment policy. The latter was
particularly obvious during the first years of the New Poor Law, before the farmer-guardians had learned to exploit the loopholes in
the central relief regulations in order to continue with their traditional practice of giving outdoor relief to the able-bodied
labourer. At this time farmers were conscious that, if as employers
they did not provide employment for the labourer, they would as
ratepayers have to finance unremunerative expenditure on giving relief to the man without work, and, what was worse, they would have

to provide expensive indoor relief in the union workhouse. Differential wage and employment policies were developed at this time
which discriminated in favour of the married man who was given the
opportunity to obtain higher earnings. This was because it would be
much more costly to relieve the married man with a dependent family
in the workhouse than it would be to relieve a single man in the
same predicament. To a very limited extent the requirements of social policy also limited the Norfolk farmers' use of machinery in
the early nineteenth century. However, in this as in other matters,
the limits of social policy were circumscribed by economic considerations, and by the need for farmers to keep a healthy profit margin
between the prices they received for farm produce and their costs.
The balance of criteria was complex since wages were a cost that the
farmers bore as employers, while relief was a cost that they subscribed to as ratepayers. The changing relief policies of the farmer, as a Norfolk poor law administrator, were essentially an attempt to square the circle, by taking into account conflicting economic factors in the formulation of a social policy that was responsive to the state of the local labour market. Much of this Norfolk analysis was also valid for other rural areas in the eastern
counties.(11)

   The interrelationship between the rural Norfolk economy and local
poor law administration also pivoted on poor law finance, and hence
on the distribution of poor rates among rural ratepayers. Until
national reform came in the 1860s poor relief was financed on a
parochial basis. This gave the Poor Law a fragile economic foundation, since it meant that the poorest and most populous villages
with the most paupers had to pay the highest poor rates, while
smaller, more prosperous villages had comparatively low poor rates.
Numbered among the former were 'open' parishes and among the latter
were 'close' parishes. 'Close' parishes were so named because, unlike 'open' parishes, they were closed to fresh settlement. New
residents were discouraged through a restriction on cottage supply,
because residence might lead to additional poor law settlements
being made. Settlements conferred the right to parish poor relief,
and hence might potentially lead to an increase in the rating burden
on local occupiers. A bitter, if subdued, civil war was fought between the 'open' and 'close' parishes of rural Norfolk which resulted
in there being an artificial distribution of cottages in relation to
the needs of local employers. Labourers who had been forced to live
in 'open' parishes might have to walk several miles to and from
their work in neighbouring 'close' parishes. Their own standard of
living was depreciated and their employer probably suffered through
lowered labour productivity. In the Docking area of north-west
Norfolk, where the system had developed to the point where one-third
of the villages were 'close' parishes, dissatisfaction at the system's undesirable socioeconomic consequences led to a local reform of
rating and settlement. The Docking Union was the first in the country
to utilize the clause in the 1834 act, which allowed it unilaterally
to replace the parish by the poor law union as the unit for rating
and settlement, and thus to anticipate by nearly 20 years the general, legal change that occurred in the Union Chargeability Act of
1865. Beneficial results followed from the Docking experiment, and
fears that employment would diminish and pauperism increase when the

employer no longer had such a direct interest in finding a man work
in order to keep him off the parish poor rate were proved to be un-
founded. This was because by the mid-nineteenth century the local
labour market in west Norfolk was beginning to change; a labour surplus was turning into a shortage as a result both of high migration,
which reduced the supply of labour, and of improved farm cultivation, which increased the demand for it. The Docking reform provided a good example both of the local origin of much general development in poor law administration, and of the interplay of the Poor
Law with the economy.

Economic explanations for general changes in the administration
of the Poor Law have become more common recently and more particularly so on the topics of poor law allowances, and of settlement and
rating. Blaug has argued that, at the national level in the period
before 1834, low wages and under-employment produced a policy of outdoor allowances. The Norfolk evidence that has been mentioned would
support such an analysis.(12) These interpretations are, of course,
at odds with the contemporary viewpoint, which was most powerfully
expressed by the Royal Commission on the Poor Laws of 1832-4, in its
argument that it was allowances that produced low wages. Both the
theoretical argument of McCloskey and the evidential analysis of
Baugh suggest that Speenhamland allowances before 1834 should be
seen as an income subsidy (where relief was given in response to
need), rather than as a wage subsidy (where relief was given in response to labour supplied). Norfolk evidence supports to some extent
the view that allowances were income subsidies. It also provides
some corroboration of Baugh's stress on the importance of the changing shape of the poverty problem, with three constituent trends in
poor relief in the period between the 1790s and 1834.(13) A different dimension has been given to the argument by Holderness in
looking at the geographical shape of the poverty problem in his work
on the national distribution of 'close' and 'open' parishes. Together with the regions of the East Riding of Yorkshire and the east
Midlands, that of west Norfolk (which has been discussed above),
was an area that had the highest proportion of 'close' parishes,
having one-third or more of its townships in this category. Since
the Poor Law Amendment Act of 1834 failed to modify substantially
the system of rating and settlement that had contributed to the
'close' and 'open' parish systems, economic conflicts between parishes continued from the Old to the New Poor Law era. In predominantly rural areas like Norfolk the rating battle was fought mainly
between 'open' and 'close' parishes in the countryside, and there
was comparatively little of the urban—rural conflict over rates,
which as Rose has shown was such an important feature of the New
Poor Law in the more urbanized and industrial North of England.(14)
The only area in Norfolk where this urban—rural struggle occurred
was in Norwich, and here it also took on the features of the 'close'
and 'open' parish contest, with nearby rural villages apparently
acting as 'close' parishes and Norwich being seen as an 'open'
parish.

The economic problems of Norwich were even more intractable than
those of rural Norfolk by the mid-nineteenth century. The earlier
prosperity of Norwich had been based on its textile manufacture of
high-quality worsted material, but during the first half of the

nineteenth century its predominance in this field was steadily undercut by West Riding manufacturers. By the 1840s long-term structural
unemployment had been superimposed on the previous pattern of short-
term cyclical unemployment during trading slumps. Although a small,
mechanized factory-based industry remained, which gave employment
to a small proportion of the city's population in making high-
quality mixed stuffs of wool and silk, the decline of the Norwich
worsted industry adversely affected not only the economy of the city
but that of surrounding country areas as well. This was because the
Norwich worsted manufacturers, during the eighteenth and early nineteenth centuries, had been dependent on domestic handworkers in the
Norfolk villages, at first for spinning, and later for weaving. This
had alleviated the problem of rural under-employment, as had migration to Norwich from country areas. During boom periods in the second and third decades of the nineteenth century people from Norfolk
villages had been attracted into the city by the rapidly expanding
employment opportunities. Even in bad times the hope of casual
employment and the liberal provision of poor relief and charitable
help attracted rural migrants to Norwich. Between 1811 and 1821 Norwich population increased by 35 per cent, or nearly twice the national population growth of 18 per cent, while in the following decade
the city's increase was 22 per cent compared with a national average
of 16 per cent. Thereafter, population growth in Norwich was much
slower as the economic difficulties of the textile industry increased. The decline of this staple industry had precipitated an
economic crisis in the city by the 1840s.

In 1847 half the population in Norwich was under the contemporary
poverty line in so far as payment of their poor rates was excused.
By 1848 one-fifth of the inhabitants were, in fact, paupers and were
receiving relief from the poor law guardians. The extent of poverty
and the pressure on poor law administration was so great that relieving officers were unable at times even to record the relief that
had been given. The most critical years were those between 1846 and
1849 when, to the problems arising from the decline of the textile
industry, was added the financial impact of the Poor Removal Act of
1846. This act gave a practical right to poor relief to destitute
people in Norwich who had resided for five years previously in the
city, even though they did not possess the legal poor law settlement which had earlier been the only basis of entitlement for poor
relief. Norwich ratepayers were among those in England who were
worst hit by this piece of legislation, because as a result of the
earlier high immigration into the city many additional people could
now claim poor relief. About half the rise in outdoor allowances in
the late 1840s was a result of the 1846 act. It added about £4,000
annually (or about one-sixth), to the city's poor rate bill.

The increased numbers receiving poor relief in Norwich, and the
distinctive policies of the Norwich guardians, led to a local ratepayers' revolt against the huge burden of the city's poor rates and
to a reform of the Norwich poor law administration, which brought
it under the regulations of the New Poor Law in 1863. Unlike most
other areas in Norfolk, the city of Norwich had not come under the
provisions of the Poor Law Amendment Act of 1834 because its poor
law administration was laid down by a local act of incorporation of
1712. The clauses in this, and succeeding, local acts gave the

Norwich guardians substantial independence from the newly established central board in London, whose strategy for imposing the New
Poor Law in the city could therefore only be one largely consisting
of bluff or persuasion. Even these weapons were soon abandoned, because it was felt that if the New Poor Law became an important issue
in the volatile politics of Norwich, the agitation would spread to
rural Norfolk, and might overturn the new administrative arrangements that had been implemented there so successfully. So the Norwich guardians were left more or less alone by the central poor law
administration after 1834 and were able to continue with their traditional policies of relieving the poor.

The Norwich Court of Guardians was highly politicized; every
issue in the mid-nineteenth century was seen in party terms. The
erection of a workhouse that was adequate to the needs of the city
was delayed until the 1850s because neither party faction wanted to
incur the political odium of having introduced an effective workhouse test to the city. The Norwich guardians administered mainly
outdoor allowances and were concerned to maintain a flexible system
of poor relief which balanced the need for humanity to the poor with
that of economy to the ratepayer.   But with the economic crisis
of mid-century, the guardians were unable to conciliate the ratepayers sufficiently, and were overwhelmed by a ratepayers' coup
d'état in 1863. It was local initiative and not central power that
introduced the provisions of the New Poor Law to Norwich at that
time.

In considering the balance of power between the central poor
law board in London and local guardians, the contrasting evidence
from different regions furthers the continuing debate on the nineteenth-century revolution in government. In the context of poor law
administration, the impact of state intervention in the regions seems
to have depended very much on specifically local factors. Where
the inspectorate as the agents of central government were successful in introducing the New Poor Law expeditiously, as in rural Norfolk or on Tyneside, their accomplishment should be seen as a product both of their own administrative efficiency and political
skill in utilizing local connections and influence on the one hand,
and on the other hand of the desire of social groups in the local
area to implement the new reform.(15) Where this willingness was
not present, as in Norwich, the West Riding of Yorkshire or Lancashire, relief at the local level showed strong elements of continuity between the Old and the New Poor Law eras. Here, the attempts
by the central poor law administration after 1834 to introduce a reform of relief were mainly unsuccessful.(16) To some extent the
existence of local poor law legislation could strengthen the independence of local administrators, as was the case in Norwich; but
that this by itself was not a sufficient explanation is shown by the
Coventry Incorporation, which was also under local act but which,
because of different local circumstances, belatedly accepted the reforms of the central poor law board.(17)

In looking at the impact of state intervention at the local level,
it is essential that the argument should be concerned not only with
the administrative arrangements of the Poor Law, but with the question of how far relief practices approximated to those laid down in
centrally determined regulations. The extension of the analysis in

this way transforms one's perception of the impact of central administration on a local area like Norfolk. Whereas there was a marked
contrast between rural Norfolk, with its model administrative arrangements which had been laid down under the 1834 act, and Norwich, with
its individual and independent poor law administration, there was a
similarity in the relief policies that had been adopted by each area
by the late 1840s. These consisted predominantly of outdoor relief,
and were therefore a deviation from the policy of the central poor
law board, which was trying to restrict the allowance system and
replace it by indoor relief to the able-bodied labourer. The super-
session in areas nominally under the 1834 act of central poor law
regulations by a locally determined relief policy was not uncommon.
The experience of Shropshire was similar to that of Norfolk in that
by the late 1840s there was little difference between the relief
policies of local incorporations and of new poor law unions. Outdoor
relief to labourers, given ostensibly in aid of sickness, was found
by the 1840s not only in rural Norfolk unions but in many other
rural areas in the southern part of England, and was also found in
Wales.(18)   Northern manufacturing areas in Lancashire and the West
Riding also continued to give outdoor allowances to the able-bodied
after 1834, through motives which combined economy, humanity and a
desire for political independence. In regions suffering from economic depression during the 'Hungry Forties', local guardians were
particularly likely to try to save money by adapting the relief
regulations of the Poor Law Commissioners to suit the needs of the
local economy, and in this respect the experience of an urban and
industrial area such as County Durham was not unlike that of an
agricultural area like rural Norfolk.(19)

The substantial autonomy of rural poor law guardians in Norfolk
in pursuing their own outdoor relief policies continued into the
second half of the nineteenth century. The problem of relieving
the able-bodied labourer became less intransigent as the local
labour market tightened, as a result both of improved agricultural
cultivation in the third quarter of the century and of heavy population migration from the county. By the last quarter of the nineteenth century the continued population exodus had resulted in an
ageing population in Norfolk, and the relief of the aged and infirm (rather than of the able-bodied labourer) became the chief
headache for poor law guardians in the Norfolk countryside. In
spite of the agricultural depression at this time, the wages and
employment of the Norfolk farm labourer remained relatively good
until the 1890s. When problems did develop in the relief of the
able-bodied labourer then recourse was had to the traditional social policies that have been described earlier. The nature of the
poverty problem therefore changed in Norfolk during the second half
of the century but the heavy burden of pauperism remained. During
this period the percentage of pauperism per head of Norfolk population was consistently higher than the national average (see
Table 3b below). More significantly, the Norfolk figures showed
only a weak reflection of the downward national trend. In the
1890s Norfolk had the greatest weight of pauperism in any area which
in these years averaged 4.5 per cent of the population. And in
the county league table of poor relief expenditure per head of population, Norfolk in the 1890s stood third behind London and Here-
fordshire.

The intractability of the problem of pauperism and the persistence of economic difficulties in Norfolk during the nineteenth century meant that local expedients that promised economy to ratepayers were the preferred solution in the determination of relief policies. Both the indoor relief system of the old poor law incorporations and that of the new poor law unions were abandoned as a means of relieving the able-bodied labourer because they conflicted with the farmers' economic preference for supplementing low wages by outdoor allowances. Both the house of industry before 1834 and the union workhouse after 1834 were used increasingly only to relieve the economically useless members of society. Since there were insufficient numbers of children, old people and sick or infirm people to fill those institutions, the pauper palaces of East Anglia became, from an administrative or financial point of view, palatial white elephants. Looked at from a humanitarian standpoint, their history is more complex.

The shadow of the workhouse touched many people's lives. It even loomed over the man who had been master of the Norwich workhouse for ten years. William Corfield wrote to beg assistance from the Norwich Court of Guardians in 1835:(20)

That in consequence of your petitioner being dismissed without sufficient previous notice, from the office of master of the workhouse he is quite destitute, and without pecuniary means to get into any trade or business, having lived up to his income.

Your petitioner therefore humbly prays that the guardians will be pleased to take his case into their consideration and assist him with a sum of money in order that he may get into some trade and thereby get a livelihood which will prevent his becoming an inmate of the house of which he was the late master.

The wheel of fortune had turned full circle, and within a few months Corfield's comfortable economic circumstances had vanished, leaving him with the prospect of pauperism. This illustrated the economic insecurity in which many lived at this time, although most were in much humbler circumstances. The actual number of people who became paupers was relatively small in comparison with the population as a whole. In 1840 1 in 12 nationally, and 1 in 10 in Norfolk, were in receipt of relief, while by 1900 the figures had declined to 1 in 40 of the population in England and Wales and 1 in 25 of the Norfolk population. However, many more people saw the workhouse as a possibility, an ultimate degradation, to which they might be driven by their state of extreme poverty. Booth's survey in London in 1887 indicated that over 30 per cent of the population had means that were insufficient to support them, while Rowntree's later survey in York produced corroboration of this extent of poverty, with 28 per cent of the population having an income inadequate for their maintenance.(21) The major cause of poverty and pauperism were large families, low or irregular earnings, widowhood, sickness and old age. Many were forced therefore to seek poor relief at the most vulnerable points in their lives, and as a result of this the psychological impact, the stigma of pauperdom, was felt keenly.

Yet the gap between the poor's perception of life in the workhouse and the reality of the experience was extremely wide in a country area such as rural Norfolk. Here, the local poor hated and

feared the advent both of the houses of industry in the eighteenth
century, and of the union workhouses after 1834. Each period had
its share of terror-stricken rumour and Bastille literature which
dwelt on the death or ill treatment of those unfortunates incarcerated in the house. There was resistance to the introduction
of both these revised relief systems in East Anglia. Indeed,
opposition to the New Poor Law by the rural Norfolk labourers was
much greater than that suggested by general studies where the focus
of interest is generally provided by the more organized and concentrated opposition of the anti-poor law movement in northern
England.(22) But greater familiarity with an indoor system of
relief tended to blunt the edge of popular apprehension in Norfolk. In the 1830s the labouring poor in the areas with local
incorporations wished to retain the humane regime of the houses
of industry, which they now valued, although earlier they had regarded these institutions as prisons.

However, the union workhouses of the New Poor Law in Norfolk did
not introduce such a harsh regime as the labourers had feared. Indeed, in the early days of the New Poor Law the material standard
of living of able-bodied paupers in Norfolk workhouses in terms of
diet, accommodation and clothing was better than that of the independent rural labourer, although this was offset by the psychological deterrent of workhouse classification which split up the
family. In any case, there were generally few adult able-bodied
labourers in the country workhouses of Norfolk, and of these only
the unmarried mothers and the vagrants received a treatment that
could be characterized as a deterrent one. The children and the
aged, who were present in considerable numbers, were treated as a
rule with humanity and consideration by the poor law guardians and
their officers. In the mid-nineteenth century pauper children in
Norfolk workhouse received an education that was better in certair.
respects than that which could be obtained by rural children in
the county. Only the needs of the sick poor in Norfolk workhouses
were neglected until the second half of the century, and this was
in marked contrast with the outdoor medical relief system which
was organized much more quickly and efficiently. In the treatment of indoor paupers the practice of Norfolk guardians differed
considerably from that laid down in central regulations. Norfolk
guardians were in the van of progress where pauper education was
concerned, and they anticipated by many years the liberalization
in policy towards the aged; but they lagged behind in the treatment of the sick, and simply ignored the regulations governing the
relief of both the able-bodied male and the vagrant for most of the
century. The practical autonomy of the Norfolk guardians in the
administration of relief gave them freedom on the one hand to pursue liberal and humane policies, and on the other hand to follow
penny-pinching and harsh policies. The relative humanity of much
Norfolk practice when compared with that of central policy contrasted to some extent with the experience of many other unions,
where the Poor Law Commissioners were the agency of either restraint or enlightenment, against abuses which were generated by
local guardians.(23)

After 1834 the practice of Norfolk poor law administrators therefore owed comparatively little to the policies laid down by the

central administrators.   The relief measures of local administrators, before and after 1834, were produced mainly by balancing
the economic interests of Norfolk ratepayers and employers against
the traditional ideas of social responsibility which had been developed earlier by the propertied classes towards the poor.   It is
by reference to these contemporary ideas, rather than by modern
concepts of social welfare, that the relative humanity of Norfolk
relief practices should be judged.   And these ideas must themselves be placed in the context of the social and economic life of
Norfolk.

CHAPTER 2

ECONOMIC AND SOCIAL LIFE IN NORFOLK

The vitality of Norfolk's economic and social life during the
eighteenth century attracted visitors to the county, but drastic
changes in the locality during the next century meant that out-
siders in this later period often penetrated this insular area
only to catalogue its decline. At the beginning of the nineteenth
century Norfolk agriculture was pre-eminent and was famous for its
innovating character while Norwich was still a major centre of the
worsted industry. Socially and culturally county life mirrored the
buoyancy and self-confidence of the local economy; Norwich intellectual life was as vigorous as that of Edinburgh, while county
society was still enlivened by a resident gentry and by the ani-
mated social life that flourished in country houses. But by mid-
century farmers in east Scotland had taken over Norfolk agricul-
turalists' pioneering role while manufacturers in the West Riding
had become supreme in the worsted industry. It was at this time
that a growing number of Norfolk gentlemen preferred to spend much
of their time outside the county, and their absence from the county
gave Norfolk rural society a neglected, if not a moribund, character. Before the end of the nineteenth century the See of Norwich
became known as the 'Dead Sea', an ironic comment which encapsulated the overriding impression given by this area. The decline in
the economy of this, England's fourth largest county, provided the
context for changes in the local relief of the poor during the
nineteenth century.
    Norfolk was predominantly a rural county, and most of its 740
parishes were villages whose fortunes were bound up with local
agriculture. Although Norfolk is often thought of as a uniformly
flat county, there is considerable variety in its landscape and
also in its soil. These soil regions dictate different patterns of
farming, and in the nineteenth century there were broadly five differing agricultural areas within the 1,234,884 acres of the county.
The most barren region was south-west Norfolk, an area of poor
sandy soils which sustained only sheep walks and rabbit warrens,
and where little improvement was possible, except in the provision of fir belts to break the wind. This was an area of game preservation by the landlord and of poaching by the labourer. To the
north of this, beyond Swaffham, lay the improved farming area of

west Norfolk where a naturally weak, light soil had been transformed by good farming practice. Manuring, marling and, later,
artificial fertilizers had put the soil in good heart, and this
was maintained by continuous cultivation and by the famous Norfolk
husbandry with its annual rotation of crops. This was the classic
area of Norfolk farming, where innovation had been fostered by progressive landlords such as Townshend of Raynham or Coke of Holkham,
and where the boundaries of cultivation were continually being expanded either through land reclamation from the sea or from the enclosure of wastes and commons. There was high farming in west
Norfolk by the mid-nineteenth century; a high input gave a high
output, and profitable farming with improved cultivation meant expanding employment opportunities for the rural labourer and his
family. This tighter labour market led to some dissatisfaction
with the restrictive effect of the settlement laws of the Poor Law
and to their reform in 1847 in the Docking Union in the north-west
of the county.

In west Norfolk, as in the third region of north-east Norfolk,
there was a close interconnection between arable and pastoral farming, and with a trend towards more stock-fattening and sheep-rear-
ing. But unlike west Norfolk, the farming in the north-east was
in a relatively static state of cultivation in the late eighteenth
and early nineteenth centuries, since it had had a good standard of
mixed farming for many generations and there had also been an early
enclosure of land. While the agricultural commentator, Arthur
Young, gave greatest emphasis to the fresh agricultural glories of
the west, those of east Norfolk were championed by the pen of William Marshall. Marshall also noted the changes that were going on
in the next farming area, the eastern marshland, where drainage
mills in the south of the area had created valuable farming pasture. Whereas there was some steam drainage of the land between
Norwich and Yarmouth, this was of much greater importance in the
Fens in the far west of the county. Here far-reaching changes in
drainage, and a comprehensive control of the flow of water between
levels, had made the alluvial soils into a fertile farming area.
Lush pastures were also found in the Waveney Valley, which formed
the southern boundary of the fifth farming region of south and mid-
Norfolk. Here there was mixed farming on stiff loams or clays which
provided more difficult farming conditions with less employment for
the labourer and a greater dependence on poor relief.(1)

Early travellers often approached Norfolk through this region
having taken the road from Ipswich to Norwich. Indeed, access to
the county in 1800 was easy only from the south because of the wet,
inhospitable fens to the west, and the treacherous 90-mile coast
to the east and north. These geographical factors gave Norfolk
life distinctiveness and even an insularity. Once inside the
county, however, road and river transport systems were good. The
light soils and flattish terrain of much of the area made for an
excellent natural road system so that there was little need for
improvement by turnpike trusts. In 1800 turnpike roads centred
principally on the trading centres of Norwich, Yarmouth and King's
Lynn, while even 40 years later, at the dawn of the railway age,
there were still under 5,000 miles of turnpiked roads in Norfolk.
In 1844 the Norwich—Yarmouth railway line was opened, and a year

later Norfolk was linked with a wider rail network through the
opening of the Norwich-to-Brandon line which connected up with
the Ely, Cambridge and London line. An alternative route to London,
which was 12 miles shorter, came in 1848 with the Norwich, Ipswich
and Colchester line. The five railway companies that were operating in the region joined together as the Great Eastern Railway in
1862. By this date nearly all the major towns in the county were
part of an extensive rail network. There was a notable further
expansion in the north of the county later on, and the Great Eastern's practical monopoly was broken by the formation in 1893 of the
Midland and Great Northern Joint Railway, which took over smaller
companies operating in this area.(2) The impact of the railway
was to facilitate the migration of the Norfolk labourer to other
areas and hence to reduce the problem of surplus labour which had
earlier been such an intractable issue in the administration of
rural poor relief. The railway system also provided a fast, if
expensive, means of transporting agricultural goods to market and
hence accelerated the decline of the north Norfolk ports.

The annual value of corn exported from the Norfolk ports of
Lynn and Yarmouth together with the smaller north coast ports,
was estimated at over £1 million at the end of the eighteenth cen-
tury and this increased still further during the next half-century.
Exports included wheat, barley, malt, flour, oats, potatoes, beans,
peas and rye. King's Lynn was the most important sea port in Nor-
folk. It had a hinterland which embraced the basin of the Great
Ouse where navigation had been improved with the completion of the
Eau Brink Cut in 1821. Importing coal from the Northumberland and
Durham fields and exporting corn, wool and some manufactured goods,
Lynn was vulnerable to the wide fluctuations in the corn and coal
trades. The resulting variations in employment posed problems for
poor law administrators in the relief of unemployed labourers.
However, its malthouses, breweries and range of manufactures, when
added to the importance of its Tuesday and Saturday markets for the
surrounding rural area, made the economy of Lynn more soundly based
than that of the smaller ports on the north Norfolk coast. The
trade of Wells, Cley and Blakeney in exporting corn and malt and
importing coal, timber, rape and linseed cakes was already declining in the early nineteenth century, and received a mortal
blow with the advent of the rail system.(3) The faltering economy
of these ports (and especially of Wells) was reflected in the difficulty with which the poor rates were collected from the town's ratepayers at this time. This illustrated the basic weakness in the
finance of the Poor Law before the 1860s, which was that with a
parochial unit of rating a parish in economic difficulties found
itself with an increased amount of poverty to relieve from rates
levied on local ratepayers who had a decreased amount of wealth.

Yarmouth was second only to Lynn as a Norfolk port and had a
similar trade in corn and coal. In both towns poor law administrators faced similar problems in the large amount of casual employment, vagrancy and illegitimacy that were common in a port at this
time. Not surprisingly, neither Lynn nor Yarmouth managed to formulate coherent or successful sets of relief policies to deal with
these intractable social problems. In both towns, not only did
poor law administrators face difficult social problems, but they

also found that the Poor Law became involved in political controversy. In King's Lynn, the Poor Law entered the political arena
when there was a dispute over the compilation of the poor rate
books. The franchise in a municipal election was dependent on the
payment of poor rates, and in 1839 the Tories, who had lost the
municipal election, accused the Liberal Party of cooking the rate
books in conjunction with Liberal overseers. This kind of activity
was common in other Victorian towns such as Leeds, Liverpool, Sal-
ford and Preston. A different, but not uncommon, politicization
of the Poor Law occurred in Yarmouth in 1839. The desperation of
the Tories at failing to overthrow the Liberal control of the Yarmouth Board of Guardians during the annual election of guardians
led to complaints of electoral malpractice. First, there was a
Tory complaint that the Liberal officers had not distributed voting
papers to ratepayers and owners with Tory views, and then, when
arrangements had been made for additional voting papers to be distributed to meet their complaint, the Tories complained of the im-
propriety of the additional distribution and concluded that the
election was an irregular one! In this case the political conflict
was engendered by disagreement over the use of poor relief, with
the Tories representing themselves as the friends of the poor
against the Whigs who had built a union workhouse.(4)
    Yarmouth was a local market centre, a coastal resort, a centre
of silk manufacture and a focus for the valuable herring and mackerel fisheries. Mackerel fishing took place from April to July and
in the 1840s was worth £14,000 annually to the town. At this time
20,000 barrels of salted, cured herrings were exported each year
with another 60,000-70,000 barrels produced annually for the home
market. The herring fishing took place in October and November
when the town's population expanded dramatically as men from surrounding country districts left the land to become fishermen, while
Scottish girls came down to clean and gut the herring ready for the
fish to be salted and smoked in local curing houses. Yarmouth was
at the centre of a flourishing river and coastal trade which was
carried on in beautiful, large-sailed East Anglian wherries. Before
1833 Yarmouth was also the out-port for Norwich, but in that year
the completion of the Norwich and Lowestoft Navigation led to rivalry with Lowestoft for the trade of Norwich.(5) This competition was
short-lived because the advent of the railways in the 1840s tended
to reduce the amount of water-borne freight from Norwich.
    Norwich was not only a manufacturing town but also a marketing
and commercial centre for much of rural Norfolk. The city's weekly
cattle and sheep market grew from a small size in the early nineteenth century to one of the largest in the country by 1900. Although the flourishing markets and corn halls in the smaller towns
in the Norfolk countryside provided for some of the commercial needs
of their local farming communities, substantial business was reserved for the much larger corn exchange and provision market in
Norwich. The crowded state of this provision market was only the
most visible sign that Norwich was the commercial centre of the
region. Not only did farmers coming to market generate commercial
business in Norwich, but the growth of financial institutions in
the city was itself intimately connected with the agricultural fortunes of the area. The relationship by marriage of Quaker families

in Norwich and London linked the brewing interests of the latter
with the farming connections of the former, and led to local finance
for malting the fine Norfolk barleys. A notable by-product of one
local Quaker family's mercantile interests, that of the Gurney's,
was the foundation of the Norwich and Norfolk Bank in 1775. This
developed a network of branch banks throughout Norfolk before being
amalgamated in 1896 with the joint stock bank of Barclay and Co.
Ltd.(6)

By the mid-nineteenth century commercial vitality in Norwich
was overshadowed by the much greater industrial decay caused by the
decline of the city's textile industry. This affected not only Norwich but the economy of surrounding rural areas as well, because
Norwich manufacturers had employed domestic workers in country areas
in east Norfolk. While Norwich had experienced short periods of
depression in the eighteenth century, it was not until the second
quarter of the nineteenth century that long-term structural unemployment was added to short-term cyclical unemployment. Because of
successful competition by worsted manufacturers in the West Riding
of Yorkshire, first spinning in the 1820s and then weaving and
finishing in the 1830s and 1840s became depressed. After the 1850s
only a small weaving industry, making high-quality mixed stuffs of
worsted and silk (and especially the world-famous fillover shawls),
survived from this once major industry.(7) The resulting unemployment caused such widespread destitution that sufficient relief from
the city's poor law guardians was forthcoming only because of the
enlightened system of a common poor rate by which wealthier parishes
in Norwich subsidized the poorer ones.

One of the casualties in the decline of the Norwich textile industry was Thomas Martineau, whose business in making bombazines
was harmed by the financial crisis of 1826 and which was wound up
in 1829. His daughter Harriet was forced to make her own living
and did so with spectacular success as a writer of stories which
illustrated the laws of political economy. Within a few years
this little deaf woman (accompanied invariably by a large ear trum-
pet) was being acclaimed by London society. She rejoiced at the
freedom that the capital offered her in contrast to what she felt
was the provincialism of Norwich life at that time. Harriet Martineau wrote a story called 'Cousin Marshall' which featured the
defective operation of the Old Poor Law and drew on the experiences
of her elder brother Henry, who had become a Norwich poor law guardian in 1830. It was published in her 'Illustrations of Political
Economy', which attracted the attention of Lord Brougham, the Lord
Chancellor, who visited Miss Martineau and persuaded her to write
more about the Old Poor Law. She was given access by the Government to the evidence, as yet unpublished, that was being assembled
at that time by the Royal Commission on the Poor Law. Her four
stories, 'Poor Laws and Paupers Illustrated' came out in 1833 and
1834, and were successful in helping to educate public opinion and
prepare the way for the Report of the Royal Commission and the ensuing Poor Law Amendment Act of 1834.(8) This New Poor Law had
little immediate impact on the poor law incorporation in Harriet
Martineau's home town, because of the protection that local poor
law legislation had given it.   It was not until 1863 that Norwich
adopted the 1834 act after a reappraisal of the local relief system

had been precipitated by the industrial crisis of the middle of
the century.

The economic stagnation of these years had been replaced before
the end of the century by a limited prosperity in Norwich which had
resulted from a reconstitution of the city's economy. Unemployed
skilled workers from the textile industry were recruited into the
boot and shoe trade. At first this was organized on an outworking
basis, but as mechanization increased after the 1860s it became
progressively factory-based. In 1901 the boot and shoe trade was
the largest employer in Norwich, and was followed in order of importance by food and drink manufacture, the clothing trade, building, conveyance, engineering and printing. Side by side with the
more regularly employed workers in these industries and trades were
a large number of casual labourers, who picked up a poor living
from work in the markets and elsewhere. Neither the poor law administration nor the many charitable organizations in Norwich worked
out a satisfactory social policy of dealing with them.(9)

The liberality of the charity and relief administrators was said
to be one cause of the migration of poor people from the surrounding countryside into Norwich during the nineteenth century. By the
second half of the century such mobility was part of a more general
depopulation of the English countryside. The population of rural
areas in Norfolk fell during each decade after 1861 and declined
from 273,000 to 245,000 between 1861 and 1901. However, the overall trends in demographic data for Norfolk did not always approximate to the national pattern. Norfolk population grew relatively
slowly during the nineteenth century and increased at little more
than half the average growth rate for England and Wales. The two
rates of growth were not dissimilar for the first three decades of
the century, but county population grew at only half the speed of
national population in the next two decades between 1831 and 1851,
while it actually decreased by 2 per cent between 1851 and 1861.
Norfolk was not alone in experiencing a decline in population at
this time; two other rural counties had done so previously between
1841 and 1851, and there were ten other counties that experienced
population decline between 1851 and 1861. For the remaining four
decades of the century Norfolk population grew very slowly at the
rate of only 1 or 2 per cent each decade compared with the 12-14
per cent average decennial growth rate for England and Wales.

During the second half of the nineteenth century population
losses from Norfolk through net migration to other places amounted
to half the natural increase in the county population. The major
migratory movement from East Anglia was a comparatively long-dis-
tance mobility to London, with smaller movements to northern mining
and manufacturing areas and especially to the Durham coalfield.
During the agricultural depression in the late nineteenth century
many agricultural labourers left the Norfolk countryside, and
their numbers decreased by 10 per cent between 1871 and 1891. Of
course there had been considerable mobility by the rural labourer
before this time; many had gone to work in local brickyards,
joined the fishing boats during the herring season or gone to
work in the Staffordshire breweries during the winter when work was
scarce on the East Anglian farms. Others had gone off during boom
times to work on rail construction or in the iron or coal industries

of the Midlands and North.(10)   While much of this earlier mobility
had not formed a permanent exodus of labour from the county, yet by
1900 the Norfolk farmers were becoming resigned to young men pre-
ferring better paid employment in the towns to a life of poverty and
hard work on the land.   Since west Norfolk was less densely populated, labour mobility created greater anxiety among employers there
than in the east of the county.

The impact of the Poor Law on labour mobility and on population
size has generated a great deal of analysis and discussion, while
the defectiveness of the available data has prevented firm conclusions from being made.   The Malthusian linkage of the old poor law
system of outdoor allowances with an increase in the size of population, and contemporary assertions that the New Poor Law had led to
prudential restraint by the labourer, cannot be either confirmed
or denied because of the small and conflicting amount of Norfolk
evidence available on birth, marriage, illegitimacy and death rates
at this time.   However, the 1834 act did increase population mobility from the county in the short term through poor law-sponsored
migration and emigration schemes.   Traditionally, the settlement
laws of the Poor Law (by which the right to poor relief was restricted to those who had a poor law settlement in a parish), have
been thought to have inhibited population mobility.

Modern research on Norfolk and other areas suggests that these
laws of settlement and removal had only a minor restrictive effect
on the labourers' mobility.   In Norfolk there was little use by
poor law administrators of their legal power to remove migrants
back to their original parish of settlement once they had become
chargeable to the parish where they lived.   Also, a system of certification operated in Norfolk until the middle of the nineteenth
century, by which poor law administrators in the parish of settlement from whence the migrant had come gave a certificate to him
which acknowledged his legal settlement and promised to send relief to him should this prove to be necessary while he was living
elsewhere.   After 1834 this formal system of certification was supplemented by an informal network of non-resident relief, by which
parishes agreed to relieve their settled poor who resided in another
parish.(11)   Not every parish allowed migrants to live in the village in case they acquired a new settlement there.   Those that discouraged immigration and kept down the number of resident poor were
the 'close' parishes, while those that permitted residence were the
'open' parishes.   Gradually, during the late eighteenth and early
nineteenth centuries, this situation created an artificial distribution of population in relation to employment in certain areas
of Norfolk.

Although the settlement laws were blamed for creating a war
against cottages through encouraging the restriction of cottage-
building in 'close' parishes, the widespread shortage of cottages
in rural Norfolk had other causes.   Where cottage-building involved
a satisfactory standard of accommodation, it did not provide an
economic investment for the landlord, because the rent that could
be paid by a low-paid rural labourer gave an inadequate return on
the initial capital expenditure.   Rent was the single largest item
of expenditure for the labourer and was typically £4 a year, although it might be as low as £2 or as high as £6.   By the mid-

nineteenth century the traditional one-up-one-down was giving way
to the model cottage with two rooms on each floor. In the 'open'
parishes particularly, the labourer's need for housing encouraged
speculators to convert older buildings into squalid accommodation
for which a high rent was charged. Even in well-built cottages the
labourer's wife counted herself fortunate to have a supply of water
available from a nearby well, or to have an oven. Inside the cottage furniture was sparse and consisted of essentials such as a
table, chairs, beds and a chest of drawers. Perhaps a touch of
substance was given by a clock, a piece of china, or candlesticks
which had been handed down from a more affluent generation.(12)

Agriculture formed the largest single occupational group in
Norfolk until 1861 and labourers made up four-fifths of those employed in farming. Agricultural labourers included not only the
more regularly employed and higher paid team man who lived in a
cottage on the farm, but also the day labourer, who lived in a
rented cottage in the village and was employed on a daily basis, and
the casual labourer, who was employed intermittently to meet peak
periods of farming activity at hay or harvest time. As the most
typical employee on the farm, the Norfolk day labourer concerns us
here. At the end of the eighteenth century the Norfolk farm labourer was more highly paid than in many other areas and his energy and
hard work were praised by contemporaries:(13)

> There is an alertness in the servants and labourers of Norfolk,
> which I have not observed in any other district ... and if he go
> to mow, reap, or other employment, his habit of activity accom-
> panies him.... That the Norfolk farm-labourers dispatch more work
> than those of other counties is an undoubted fact.

During the nineteenth century the wage rates of the Norfolk agricultural labourer increased more slowly than the national average
for the farm worker. It is interesting to see how this change from
a relatively high paid worker to a low paid worker had come about.

Theoretically, the day wages of the Norfolk farm labourer were
related to the price of wheat, and since whaten bread was the staple
commodity in his diet this should have protected him against changes
in his real standard of living. But in practice wages were dictated
more by social assumptions about what was needed to provide a subsistence income, and this led to a deterioration in real wages after
1814. Farmers in a locality agreed on the going rate for wages
and there was strong social pressure to conform to this. When wheat
prices rose and real wages declined, then the Norfolk farmer preferred not to give a rise in money wages because they might be difficult to lower again. He chose other alternatives; either the
cottage rent was subsidized or, more commonly, perquisites in the
form of food, fuel or a garden plot were provided. Perquisites
merged into charitable help such as subscriptions for a clothing
club or the provision of sustaining food for a sick member of the
family. Alternatively the farmer (who was as influential in the
parish vestry under the Old Poor Law as he was in the guardians'
board room under the New Poor Law) might use poor relief as a supplement to farm wages. This balancing by the farmer of the alternative cost of wages against poor relief was a necessary concomi-
tant of the surplus labour problem in rural Norfolk. Here, the
predominantly arable farming meant that under-employment existed

during most of the farming year and this tended to depress the
level of day wages. The Norfolk labourer had no incentive to work
hard since his industry would not be rewarded in an overstocked
labour market. This was because the farmer's usual concern was to
employ as many as possible in order to keep down the poor rates,
rather than to employ the skilled man at higher wages. Exceptionally, at harvest time there was a tight labour market and the Norfolk labourer was able to show the real quality of his skills and
energy and reap his reward for them. The high harvest wages (of
between £5 and £7) earned by the Norfolk labourer when compared
with low day wages (which usually amounted to between 9s and 11s per
week) illustrated clearly the economic impact of this surplus labour
problem before the 1860s. After this the pressure from a tighter
labour market together with that from agricultural trade unionism
helped to increase wages. These reached a peak during the 1870s
with day wages that amounted to 13s weekly and with harvest wages
of £8, but which more commonly were 11s or 12s per week with a
harvest payment of £6 or £7.(14)

In the mid-nineteenth century the low wages paid to the Norfolk
labourer resulted in a poor diet. Even in the 1860s the amount of
money spent each week by an adult worker in rural Norfolk was estimated at only 2s 0½d, or half the amount of a Northumbrian worker.
It was the lowest amount to be found in any agricultural county at
this time. However, the Norfolk labourer's wife was noted for her
economical housekeeping and the way in which a nutritious meal was
conjured out of a few ingredients. A typical cheap meal for a
growing family was provided by a vegetable stew enlivened by a
few scraps of meat or bacon and made more substantial by the addition of Norfolk dumplings. Good wheaten bread was the staple food
of the labourer's family in the county. Once a week there was
butcher's meat, or bacon from a home-reared pig, while in coastal
areas there might also be herrings. These were supplemented by
turnips, onions, potatoes, cabbages and apples grown on a garden
plot or allotment. Some tea and sugar, but very little milk or
eggs were consumed, and butter, lard or cheese were almost lux-
uries.(15) The effect of this low standard of diet was to make
the dietaries in use in union workhouses in Norfolk superior to
those of the independent labourer.

Household budgeting was a desperate affair when wages for the
Norfolk agricultural labourer might fall as low as 8s a week as
they had done during the 1840s and early 1850s. Wet or frosty
weather meant a further diminution of income since the labourer
when employed by the day could be laid off at the convenience of
his employer. The high prices of the village stores soon made a
hole in the budget when foodstuffs, soap or candles were bought.
In the 1840s a Norfolk labourer's family with three children and an
income of 10s a week might lay out the money on: 3 stones of flour
at 6s 6d, ½ cwt of coal at 6d, 1½ oz tea at 4½d, ½ lb soap at 3d,
¾ lb sugar at 4½d, ½ lb candles at 3d, butter and cheese to the
value of 8d and 1d towards other dry goods, which left 1s 0d towards the family's clothing and any other contingencies. Rent
came from harvest earnings and medical assistance from the Poor
Law.(16) If money ran out before Saturday, when wages were paid,
then recourse was had to neighbours. This kind of mutual assis-

tance also operated during more serious misfortunes.

There were additional sources of income to supplement the man's wage although by mid-century some of these were shrinking. In west Norfolk, where farmworkers' wages were traditionally a shilling per week higher than those in the east of the county, there were also better opportunities for the wife and children to be employed in field work. Women could earn from 6d to 8d a day while children earned from 2d to 8d according to their ages and capabilities. (Children below the age of 10 contributed little to the family income except in valuable gleaning which followed the harvest.) In east Norfolk the earnings made by the labourer's wife in outwork for the Norwich worsted manufacturers had all but disappeared by the 1850s. Another addition to the household economy was the acquisition of a rabbit for the pot. The Norfolk labourer had tended to regard this as a traditional right but it was now becoming a hazardous operation. Although the tenant farmer connived at poaching because he resented the damage done by ground game, stricter game preservation by the landlord led to conflict with gamekeepers. By mid-century there was also a battle of wits with the village policeman. Enclosure of wastes and commons affected half the villages in the county between 1790 and 1870 and in some cases the poor suffered because inadequate compensation was given for the previous common rights of grazing or fuel collection. Fishing remained as an additional resource in coastal areas, although poor law administrators after 1834 were less willing to give temporary loans to the labourer's family to tide them over until the six to eight weeks of the herring season had finished, and the man's wages were paid.

The margin of income over expenditure was therefore precarious for the Norfolk labourer and his family during the nineteenth century although the rise in wages after 1860 brought some alleviation. Only after harvest was there some cash in hand, and so large items of expenditure, such as that on the cottage rent or on boots and shoes, were made at this time. Dependence on the Poor Law, on charitable assistance or on friendly societies resulted from lack of work, the growing infirmity of age or sickness. In poverty-stricken areas typhus, diphtheria and scarlet fever were often present; rheumatism and ague were to be found in the marshlands; consumption or scrofulous diseases were fairly widespread; while periodic outbreaks of smallpox or cholera aroused widespread alarm. Although the boards of guardians in rural Norfolk were unenthusiastic about their growing responsibility for public health and therefore did not develop preventive medicine, nevertheless the curative medical services provided by the poor law administration for the outdoor poor were good ones. For the farm labourer with four or five children recourse to the poor law doctor was automatic at least until the second half of the century, because low wages meant that he was unable to afford a subscription to a friendly society.

In the early nineteenth century Norfolk belonged to a group of a dozen rural counties where the growth of friendly societies had been notably slow. Although figures concerning friendly societies can be little more than estimates in this period, it would appear that in 1815 Norfolk had only 1 in 25 of the population as a member of a friendly society compared with an average for England

and Wales of 1 in 8. At the beginning of the century there were estimated to be 401 societies with 14,080 members in Norfolk. These
local societies consisted of small groups of men who ran an independent association with its own rules and finances which made payments to members in times of sickness or for funerals. Financially
precarious, these were often short-lived. There were however exceptions, such as the Attleborough Club, which was established in
1840 and had built up a capital of £2,000 by 1873. Nationally,
there was a growth in the number of friendly societies after 1834.
This had pleased the administrators of the New Poor Law, who attributed it to the stricter regulation of relief which had encouraged
the labourer to be more independent, to develop foresight and to
provide for future contingencies. But labourers resented the practice of the boards of guardians, who followed a ruling of the Poor
Law Commission in 1840 that no preferential treatment should be
given to members of benefit clubs, and who deducted from the standard poor relief allowances to the sick and aged the sums that the
recipient had already received from his friendly society. The
thrifty felt that they were penalized, since even if they had not
made contributions to a benefit club their total income would still
have been the same.

There was no friendly society established on a county basis in
Norfolk as there was in Essex or Cambridgeshire, and this may have
been because of the rapid growth in Norfolk of the affiliated orders of friendly societies during the mid-nineteenth century. The
Independent Order of Oddfellows was the first to penetrate the
county in the period after 1835. Already by 1845 they had 48
lodges in Norfolk and this number had doubled by 1875. In agricultural areas the Ancient Order of Foresters was more important. It
made rapid progress in the county between 1845 and 1865 since it had
low subscription rates which the rural labourer was increasingly
able to afford because of higher wages at this time. The Foresters
also made it easy for existing local societies to affiliate. By
1902, when Norfolk had the highest county membership within the
Foresters, as many as 61 out of every 1,000 Norfolk people were
members. Of course, friendly societies were important in urban
areas too, and by the early twentieth century about half the adult
male workers in Norwich were members of a friendly society. The
great value and attraction of the friendly society was the provision that it made for a local medical practitioner to treat members during sickness instead of application having to be made to the
poor law medical officer. This expansion of friendly societies in
Norfolk was only the most notable illustration of a widespread
growth in self-help, which included the organization of many local
burial clubs, a co-operative distribution society and a short-lived
Trustees Savings Bank.(17)

Reliance on poor relief by the labourer was reduced by his own
self-help and also by other people's charitable assistance. Charity
might take the form of private assistance or be derived from a formal endowment. Voluntary charity from the propertied to the poor
was widespread, as can be seen by the account books of gentry house-
holds in the county. Indeed, under the Old Poor Law, in cases
where a landed proprietor owned an entire parish, no distinction
had been made between private charitable assistance and the statutory

poor rate. On occasions of extreme social distress, voluntary private charity was supplemented by a public subscription. For example, a public fund was opened to assist the widows and orphans of fishermen who were lost off the Norfolk coast in the gale of 28 May 1860, and relief funds were opened in Norwich, Yarmouth and King's Lynn during the hard winter of 1886-7.(18) More regular assistance to the poor was provided by the substantial endowed charities of Norfolk. By 1843 the income from these came to £36,522, and, when account was taken in 1868 of improved income, to £50,487. Two-fifths of this endowed charity was distributed in Norwich. Whereas in Norwich three-fifths of the endowment income went to support almshouses, their inmates and pensioners and little over one-tenth to dole charities, in rural Norfolk nearly half the endowed charity was of doles. Typically, these provided for periodic distributions of bread, coals, blankets or material for sheets and clothing.(19) Even at the end of the nineteenth century the Charity Commissioners lamented that most charities were doles in rural Norfolk in spite of their attempts to have a more constructive use made of endowments. A lack of co-ordination in the administration of charity and of poor relief in Norfolk was revealed in an analysis made in the early twentieth century.(20)

Earlier, the agricultural interest had attempted to encourage the independence of the labourer and to reduce his dependence on poor relief through the formation of agricultural associations. In 1831 the Launditch Society, the first of these associations, was formed to give rewards for good conduct and industrious habits among cottagers, servants and labourers. Prizes included those for labourers who brought up large families without compromising their independence. For example, in 1835 second-class prizes were awarded to 'James Futter of North Elmham, James Boldero of Gressenhall, and Charles Craves of Worthing, for supporting a family of five children under 12 years of age, without ever receiving any relief from the parish, the former three sovereigns, and the two latter two sovereigns each.'(21) Gentlemen congratulated themselves over the increased good feeling between social groups which had resulted from this kind of paternalism. An older method of assisting the rural labourer was through the provision of allotments or plots of garden ground amounting to a quarter or half an acre in extent. By 1833 Norfolk approximated to the national average in that two out of five parishes made some provision for these. Further progress was slow in Norfolk because of hostility by some farmers to an activity which they felt would detract from the productivity of the labourer on the farm. Enclosure of common land had earlier increased the number of allotments because these were given in compensation for the loss of the labourers' common rights. But compensation was not always adequate, as in the notorious enclosure of Swaffham Heath in 1868, when the labourers' allotments were sited on poor ground which was situated inconveniently a mile and a quarter from the town.(22) This kind of activity had helped to radicalize the rural Norfolk labourer by the 1870s when his social independence was shown by his participation in agricultural trades unionism and his activity in village politics.

An earlier indication of independent attitudes was the adoption by many rural labourers of a more democratic form of religion. Pri-

mitive Methodism entered the west of the county from Lincolnshire
in the 1830s and spread rapidly among the labouring classes. By
the time of the religious census of 1851 15 per cent of the attendances at Sunday services and 35 per cent of the places of worship
in Norfolk belonged to this faith. The census indicated how strong
Dissent had become in Norfolk, since by this time there were almost
as many Dissenting places of worship as Anglican parish churches,
and nearly as many non-Anglican worshippers on Census Day. Nationally, there was concern that it was in the rapidly growing urban,
industrial areas that the Church of England was losing ground, but
this was also evident in the predominantly rural area of Norfolk.
This was hardly surprising, since for many years the Norwich diocese had languished, and clerical absenteeism had flourished under
Dr Bathurst. Aptly labelled by a modern scholar as an eighteenth-
century anachronism, the bishop's death at the age of 93 made possible the appointment in 1837 of Edward Stanley. An active and enlightened reformer, Bishop Stanley was concerned about the widespread absenteeism in west Norfolk and insisted on his clergy residing in their parishes.(23) He also gave a lead on a number of
matters of social concern, including that of pauper education, but
his untimely death in 1849 meant that his impact was necessarily a
limited one. Although by this time religious rivalries were strong
in Norfolk, the religious contention found in the poor law administration of some other areas was avoided by Norfolk boards of guardians. They appointed an Anglican chaplain for the union workhouse
but allowed Dissenting ministers to visit members of their congre-
gation who were in the workhouse.(24)
    A popular Norfolk handbill suggested in 1836-7 that, rather than
shipping ordinary paupers to North America in the Poor Law Commissioners' Emigration Scheme, it would be preferable to get rid of
the rich paupers — the Anglican clergymen. Anti-clericalism was
already strong in the county as had been shown in 1830 by the wage
and tithe riots in south-east Norfolk. Farmers, embittered by
high and rising tithe payments (which they regarded as a continuous
tax by the clergymen on other people's hard work), had encouraged
the labourers to intimidate the Anglican clergyman so that he would
reduce tithes and enable the farmer to pay higher wages to the labourer. In contrast, the incumbent regarded tithes as the first tax
on the land and resented attempts to reduce his rights. He felt
threatened too by the continual erosion of his central place in the
village community. In the 1820s and 1830s the writings of the Rector of Little Massingham, C.D. Brereton, illustrated this by his
passionate attacks on external agencies — such as an active magistracy, the board of guardians or the rural police — which he felt
had emasculated the autonomy of the parish under the paternalistic
regime of the Anglican clergyman.(25) However, the parson was
able to maintain a substantial influence over village affairs in
the mid-nineteenth century through his activity in National Schools,
and his work as a charity trustee or a poor law guardian. But his
traditional assumptions were increasingly challenged because of
the changing religious and social nature of the Norfolk village.
The growth of Dissent tended to polarize issues between Church and
Chapel. Sometimes the controversy was aroused by specifically religious issues, such as the hostility to the parson's power before

1880 to stop a dissenting minister from conducting a burial service
in the village churchyard. At other times it represented a challenge to the social paternalism of the Anglican clergyman, as when
Norfolk labourers who were householders, insisted after 1869 on exercising their right to vote at parish vestry meetings.

> The ideal village is a happy valley, where a simple people are
> living sweetly under the paternal care of a gracious landowner,
> benevolent, open-handed, large-hearted, devout.... Parson and
> Squire work together in perfect harmony.... This is the ideal
> village. How different are the real villages.

So wrote the Rev. Augustus Jessopp, Rector of Scarning, whose nos-
talgia in 1909 for a lost rural idyll was equalled only by the ir-
ritable and arrogant sensibility with which he regarded the parson's
life in a Norfolk rural community. His disillusioned comments on
the Norfolk labourer are perhaps understandable since he had had
his windows broken by Nonconformists when the Charity Commissioners
were reforming Scarning village school during 1883-4.(26)

Jessopp's opinion on the gulf between ideal and reality, where
the relationship of the parson and squire were concerned, was also
the view of the Rev. William Andrew. Made vicar of Ketteringham in
1835, Andrew was both religious enthusiast and a man dedicated to
good works. In this small parish of under 300 people the parson's
independent mind and vigorous ministry soon challenged the paternalistic authority of the new squire, Mr J.P. Boileau. Boileau had
bought the estate in 1836 but did not take up residence at Ketteringham Hall until 1838. Even after this date the Boileaus, like so
many other gentry families in Norfolk, were often absent from their
estate. This did not prevent the squire from regarding his word as
law in Ketteringham, an attitude that soon led to disputes between
parson and squire. Boileau was both liked and feared by his villagers, since although he was generous to them he kept a close control over their lives. Model cottages were built and moderate rents
were charged, employment and wages were good on the estate, and
there was an efficient village school. In return the villagers were
expected to behave well; cottagers were not allowed to take lodgers
and parents had to send their children to school until the age of 12
or they were not found employment later on. The village, together
with its villagers, was regarded as his property.(27) This traditional assumption was still widely held by gentlemen who were proprietors of close parishes in Norfolk at this time.

County society was dominated by the landed gentry in Norfolk.
There were more than 200 estates consisting of more than the 1,000
acres that had come to define the rank of the gentleman. Of these
only 11 comprised more than 10,000 acres and these were located
mainly in the west of the county. Few Norfolk estates therefore
qualified their owners for the rank of landed magnate. Prominent
among them, however, were the Marquis Cholmondeley of Houghton Hall
with 16,995 acres, the Marquis Townshend of Raynham Hall with 18,129
acres, and the Earl of Leicester of Holkham Hall with 43,024 acres.
Only 19 per cent of the land in Norfolk was included in these very
large estates compared with an English average of 24 per cent. A
much higher than average proportion of land fell into the category
of the gentry estates (of between 1,000 and 10,000 acres), with
37 per cent in Norfolk compared with only 29.5 per cent for English

counties as a whole. The proportionate division of land among
smaller landowners in the county was that 13 per cent was held in
estates of 300 to 1,000 acres, 11 per cent in estates of 100 to
300 acres and 12 per cent in those of 1 to 100 acres. This was
not dissimilar to the average for English counties where the respective figures were 14, 12.5 and 12 per cent.(28)   Only a minority of landowners farmed their own land and most farms were worked
by tenant farmers.

The reputation of Norfolk farming had been made by the larger
farmers, yet the typical farmer in the county had a smaller acreage.
Returns of farms (of over 20 acres) in the census of 1851 indicated
(although with some imprecision) that one in two Norfolk farms were
under 100 acres, one in three of 100 to 300 acres, and fewer than
one in seven of between 300 and 1,000 acres. Only 89 out of 4,938
farms in the county were of over 1,000 acres and only eight of
these had more than 2,000 acres. Land tenure was regionalized, with
larger farms let at more moderate rentals by larger proprietors in
west Norfolk, and smaller landowners letting small farms at higher
rents in the east of the county.

But whatever the locality, the Norfolk farmer was not slow to
air his anxieties and grievances. The reports of boards, committees and commissions on the state of agriculture during the nineteenth century give the impression that the farmer in Norfolk always felt himself worse off than could be accounted for by the
available evidence. This was partly the result of a psychological
hang-over from the golden days before 1814 which had conditioned
the farmer's attitudes. Then they had benefited from high agricultural prices, and from farm rents which lagged behind the increase in profits, whereas after 1814 the position was reversed
and prices fell faster than rents. In 1816 and 1821 Norfolk farmers complained of the fall in agricultural prices which had occurred after the end of the Napoleonic Wars and the resultant increased
burden of poor rates and other taxes. Farmers felt that they bore
an unduly heavy share of this taxation burden in relation to other
members of the community. By the 1830s many Norfolk farmers were
pulling out of depression; some large landlords had reduced rents,
tithes were not always demanded in full, and poor rates had fallen
after the introduction of the New Poor Law. But on the heavier
soils of south Norfolk the more difficult farming conditions meant
that costs remained high in relation to the lower postwar prices
and profits. It was here that there was greatest subversion of the
New Poor Law by the farmer-guardians who administered it, and who
wished to keep relief expenditure down so as to keep poor rates low.

The 1840s, 1850s and 1860s included many years of relative prosperity for the Norfolk farmer. In spite of this the practices that
had developed in the years of stringency in the postwar depression
were continued as a means of coping with under-employment in the
countryside. Low wages were paid to the Norfolk labourer, and these
did not improve until increased labour mobility had created a tighter market after 1860, when higher wages were needed to retain
labour. There was a large seasonal variation in demand for labour
by the Norfolk farmer because of the predominantly arable farming.
Norfolk was part of the granary of England, and in 1866 had the
seventh-highest county acreage under corn. With the series of bad

harvests after 1874, and the contemporary slump in wheat prices
which was caused by cheap imported grain, Norfolk farming became
depressed again. Even those local farmers who kept beef cattle
or sheep were impoverished at this time by the prevalence of animal disease, while their distance from the market put them at a
disadvantage because of the high freight rates charged by the Great
Eastern Railway Company. As the depression deepened in the 1880s,
so the farms with the poorest soils in the Breckland and in south
Norfolk were abandoned, let rent-free or taken in hand by the landlord. Landowners were the class worst hit by depression, since even
on farms with good soils rent reductions of a quarter had to be made
between 1874 and 1894. Farmers benefited to some extent from lowered rents, from reduced local assessments to the poor rate and
from national legislation which in 1896 had rated farm land at half
its value. But economies still had to be made in labour costs by
converting land from arable to pasture, which reduced the need for
labour, and eventually by reducing the labourers' wages.(29)

The relative prosperity of Norfolk agriculture was crucial to
the administration of the local Poor Law. It affected the farmer's
ability to pay the poor rates, of which he was the principal contributor. It shaped his employment policies and therefore influenced the numbers of unemployed labourers seeking poor relief. Central to the farmer's concerns in his role of poor law administrator
was the complex problem of surplus labour. This was felt most
keenly when demand for labour was less buoyant during 'agricultural
depressions':— to a marked extent in the period after 1815, and
to a lesser extent after 1880. Between these two periods the problem had been alleviated by migration. This mobility had also revealed the underlying regional disparity in the supply of labour
that existed in the different population densities of east and west
Norfolk. Already by mid-century, population mobility had contributed to a labour shortage in some areas of west Norfolk where
improved farm cultivation at this time had also increased the demand
for labour. As a result a tight labour market had been created
which existed throughout the year. This was quite distinct from the
seasonal shortfall that was experienced in most areas of east Norfolk only during the peak demand for labour at harvest time. For
essentially, the surplus labour problem of many areas in east Norfolk was rooted in the arable agriculture of the county where a
seasonal disparity in the demand for labour meant that under-employment occurred during two-thirds of the farming year. But superimposed on this broad regionalized pattern was tremendous local variation. The most obvious variation occurred in the different experiences of 'close' and 'open' parishes. The labour-deficient
'close' parishes had a resident population that had been artifi-
cially restricted to a point where it was insufficient to meet the
demand for labour from local farmers. In the 'open' parish there
was sufficient labour to meet employers' requirements both in the
home parish and in neighbouring close parishes. However, the localized nature of demographic change, arising from fluctuations in
birth, marriage and death rates, produced considerable variations
in the state of the labour market even between neighbouring villages.
Many Norfolk villages fell into neither the category of the 'close'
parish nor that of the 'open' parish. The state of the labour

market in rural Norfolk was therefore a product of complex changes
in labour supply and demand.   The impact of these changes was also
to alter the shape of the poverty problem and to mould the dimensions of poor relief both under the Old and the New Poor Law.

CHAPTER 3

LOCAL REFORM BEFORE 1834

The different social and economic conditions of east and west
Norfolk had led to regionalization in poor law practice by the
early nineteenth century (see Map A). In east Norfolk there was
a stronger economic incentive for innovation to be made in the Poor
Law since owners and occupiers of land had more moderate resources
with which to finance the requirements of social policy in a more
densely populated countryside. In this area too there were more
resident clergymen and gentlemen to interest themselves in the
question of how best to relieve the poor; and they were able to
initiate and support notable innovations in the local administration of the Poor Law.

An increasing range of local alternatives in the administration
of the Old Poor Law were possibly by 1800 because a series of permissive general laws and local acts for the relief of the poor had
been grafted on to the Elizabethan bases of the Old Poor Law. The
original statutes of 1597-8 and 1601 had laid down a national
framework in that the employment of the able-bodied poor, the relief of the impotent poor and the correction of the idle were to be
financed and administered by individual parishes. Several areas
soon appreciated that the parish was too small to achieve administrative efficiency or financial economy in the management of the
poor. Nowhere was the departure from the Elizabethan basis of the
individual parish as the unit of poor law administration more striking than in East Anglia. By 1834 one-third of the parishes in Norfolk had formed themselves either into incorporations under local
act or into unions under Gilbert's Act. Local legislation enabled
parishes to form incorporations which would both administer the Poor
Law economically (through the profitable employment of the able-
bodied poor in workhouses) and also administer the Poor Law humanely (through the provision of specialist facilities for the treatment of the impotent poor). Another alternative was Gilbert's Act,
a permissive piece of legislation passed in 1782, which allowed
parishes to combine together in unions to provide a poor house which
would act as an asylum for the impotent poor.

Norfolk was heavily unionized before 1834 in that it had one in
ten parishes in a Gilbert Union and one in four parishes in an incorporation under local act. The considerable extent to which the

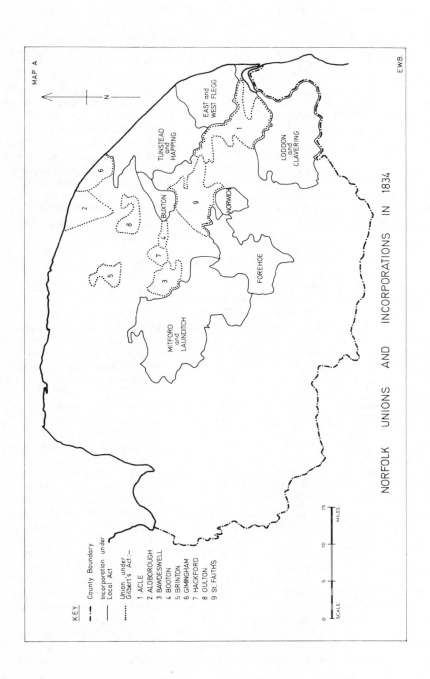

MAP A

N

TUNSTEAD
and
HAPPING

EAST and
WEST FLEGG

LODDON
and
CLAVERING

BUXTON

NORWICH

FOREHOE

MITFORD
and
LAUNDITCH

EWB

NORFOLK   UNIONS   AND   INCORPORATIONS   IN   1834

KEY

County Boundary

Incorporation under
Local Act

Union under
Gilbert's Act:-

1 ACLE
2 ALDBOROUGH
3 BAWDESWELL
4 BOOTON
5 BRINTON
6 GIMINGHAM
7 HACKFORD
8 OULTON
9 St. FAITHS

SCALE

0   5   10   15

MILES

county had departed from the more usual parochial administration of
the Poor Law suggests the very active interest taken by the Norfolk
gentry and clergy in the relief of poverty. Even Parson Woodforde
took time off from his well-laid table in March 1787 to visit the
Gressenhall House of Industry in his local Mitford and Launditch
Incorporation. There the Rector of Weston Longville found 'a very
large building at present tho' there wants another wing. About
380 poor in it now, but they don't look either healthy or cheerful,
a great number die there, 27 have died since Christmas last.'(1)
Such a gloomy view was unusual in 1781, although hostility to the
local incorporations was to become more widespread in Norfolk in
the years before the general reform of the Poor Law in 1834. It is
interesting that in spite of local criticism of these incorporations some of these East Anglian innovations in the management of
the poor were to be more generally influential because of the impact
that they had on the national format of the New Poor Law. However,
this chapter and the ones that follow suggest that both before and
after 1834 the preferred administrative solution to the relief of
poverty at the local level in Norfolk alternated between centralized
control in an incorporation or union, and decentralized control in
the individual parish.

I   LOCAL INCORPORATIONS, UNIONS AND PAUPER PALACES

At the beginning of the nineteenth century about half of the parishes
in Norfolk had access to a workhouse; one in seven had a parish poor
house, one in ten a Gilbert Union house and one in four a pauper
palace or house of industry in a local incorporation.(2) Of these
the incorporated house of industry was a direct ancestor of the union
workhouse of the New Poor Law, and the administration of poor relief
in the incorporations influenced the Poor Law Commissioners' regulations for the unions instituted under the Poor Law Amendment Act of
1834.
   The existence of five Norfolk and nine Suffolk rural incorporations meant that East Anglia was the most heavily incorporated part
of England by the early nineteenth century. More than a century
earlier the desire for a frugal administration of the Poor Law had
led nationally to the establishment of urban incorporations of
parishes which could provide a pauper manufactory or workhouse on
a scale allowing for the profitable employment of the poor under
professional management. The Bristol experiment of 1696 was soon
imitated by other towns, including Norwich in 1712, and in the second half of the eighteenth century by rural areas in East Anglia,
the Isle of Wight and Shropshire. Shropshire, with one in five of
the county's parishes included in five small incorporations, was
second only to East Anglia in its heavily incorporated character.
The parishes in the Suffolk hundreds of Carlford and Colneis were
the first rural area to be incorporated by local act of Parliament
in 1756, and 14 other Suffolk hundreds were incorporated during the
next 23 years into 9 unions, which included over half the parishes
in the county. The incorporating movement in east Suffolk spread
into Norfolk, and the hundreds of Loddon and Clavering in south-
east Norfolk were united under local act in 1764. The impulse to

1   Front and 2 rear view of silver badge worn by the Beadle of the
King's & Lynn Guardians in the eighteenth and nineteenth centuries.
It depicts St James the Great holding his pilgrim's staff and
supporting the town arms.

reform was checked temporarily in the 1760s by the disturbances
caused by the poor's hostility to the changed methods of poor relief in Suffolk incorporations in 1765. Opinion in Norfolk itself
was divided over the desirability of local incorporations, and a
project of the years 1770-2 to pass a general enabling bill through
Parliament that would have allowed any hundred in Norfolk to erect
a house of industry failed to attract sufficient local support. A
bitter propaganda war was fought in Norfolk over the next incorporation in the county, that of Mitford and Launditch in 1775. But
the reforming tide grew in strength and other areas in the county
were incorporated with much less social friction; East and West
Flegg in 1775, Forehoe in 1776, Tunstead and Happing in 1785, and
Buxton in 1806.(3)

> In the incorporated hundreds, the houses of industry ... are
> all of them built in as dry, healthy, and pleasant situations,
> as the vicinity affords; the offices ... are all large, con-
> venient, and kept exceeding neat; the work-rooms are large,
> well-aired, and the sexes are kept apart, both in hours of work
> and recreation.... The interior of these houses, must occasion
> a most aggreable surprise, to all those who have not before seen
> poverty, but in its miserable cottage, or more miserable work-
> house.

This vindication of the houses of industry in Suffolk came from
Thomas Ruggles, a former opponent of the incorporations who had

altered his opinions after visiting them in the 1790s. He concluded that the East Anglian incorporations could be justified because they reduced expenditure on the poor, and because the houses
of industry preserved the health and improved the morals of the
inmates. A few years later F.M. Eden, in his classic study of the
poor, took a more critical look at these East Anglian incorporations and found that some local people felt that already they were
not fulfilling the aims of their founders. His account of several
of the incorporations in both counties demonstrated their common
origin, since the rules, dietary and government of the Norfolk
houses of industry were almost identical to those in Suffolk. Indeed, there were visits by directors and guardians of newly established incorporations to more established ones; in October 1776 a
group from the recently formed Flegg Incorporation set out to visit
other houses of industry that were already in operation to see how
they were furnished and run.(4)
     The Norfolk incorporations aimed to balance the interests of
the poor in a humane system of relief with those of the ratepayers
in an economical administration. In 1775 Parliament passed an 'Act
for the better Relief and Employment of the Poor within the Hundreds
of East and West Flegg in the County of Norfolk'. The preamble
stated the purpose of the legislation:
     Whereas the poor within the hundreds of East and West Flegg,
     in the county of Norfolk, are very numerous, and are maintained
     at great expence: and whereas the granting proper powers for
     the government and regulation of the poor in the said hundreds
     and providing a place for their general reception, will tend to
     the more effectual relief and assistance of such as by age or
     infirmities are rendered incapable of supporting themselves, to
     the better employment of the able and industrious, to the cor-
     rection of the profligate and idle, and to the education of the
     poor children.
These objectives echoed those of Loddon and Clavering, the first
Norfolk incorporation, which had been set up in 1764.(5) Attention
is here concentrated on the Flegg Incorporation since the manuscript sources for its first years have survived whereas this is
not the case for the Loddon and Clavering Incorporation or any of
the other Norfolk incorporations. The Flegg act gave the management of the poor to guardians, who were either justices of the peace
or who possessed an estate worth £30 a year in the hundred, or
alternatively, who occupied land worth £80, or who had an estate
worth £200 in the county. At an annual meeting in July the guardians chose 24 acting guardians by ballot to administer the affairs
of the incorporation for the coming year alongside 24 directors.
These were to serve for three years, one-third retiring each year,
and being replaced by election from the guardians. Of the 48
directors and acting guardians active in any year, 12 would serve
in each quarter and of these two directors and two acting guardians
were designated each month to form themselves into a weekly committee for routine business. Important decisions would be referred
to the quarterly meetings. Fines were imposed if directors or
guardians did not attend meetings. These administrative arrangements were, with variation in detail, the common pattern for the
Norfolk incorporations.

For the INSTRUCTION of YOUTH
The ENCOURAGEMENT of INDUSTRY
The RELIEF of WANT
The SUPPORT of OLD AGE
And the COMFORT of
INFIRMITY and PAIN

3   Rollesby House of Industry, East and West Flegg Incorporation

The Flegg guardians met first on 2 May 1775 and spent the next
two years making careful arrangements for the reception of the poor,
who were therefore not received into the newly built house of industry until 15 July 1777.   Twenty-two acres of land on Rollesby
Common was obtained, a plan for a house of industry was drawn up
by a Mr John Green for a payment of £5 5s, and an estimated expenditure of £2,300 was authorized for the building.   The incorporating act of 1775 had laid down the broad specifications for such a
building.   It should include a hospital for the aged and infirm,
an infirmary for the sick, a separate place for lunatics, provision
for children too young to work, and accommodation for the reception,
maintenance and employment of the poor who were able to work.   When
the building was completed, the humane ideals of the incorporation
in relieving the different categories of the poor were inscribed
over the entrance for all to see: 'For the Instruction of Youth /
The Encouragment of Industry / The Relief of Want / The Support of
Old Age / And the Comfort of / Infirmity and Pain.'   In July and
August 1777 the parish overseers in the Flegg hundreds brought to
the house of industry the poor who were, in the words of the local
act, 'incapable of providing for themselves'.   Of the 89 original
inmates, whose ages ranged from 11 weeks to 96 years, half were
under 20 years of age and one-third over 60.   This kind of age distribution, with its heavy weighting towards the extremes of youth
and age, was to become a familiar feature both of the East Anglian
houses of industry and also of the union workhouses after 1834.
The needs of all kinds of poor people were liberally provided
for in the house of industry at Rollesby.   The thoughtful attention
to every aspect of the paupers' comfort and the concern for sub-

stantial quality in their environment made this truly into a pauper
palace. The guardians and directors were careful to specify that
the bedsteads, stools, chairs and tables should be constructed in a
sound workmanlike manner and made of properly seasoned wood. The
niceties of clothing were detailed in instructions to suppliers
down to the linings of the men's waistcoats, the buttons on the
boys' breeches and the provision of wooden, rather than leather,
soles on the shoes of women and older girls. Officers were appointed to take care of the poor. Inside the house of industry a governor and matron at £40 a year were in charge of its routine management, while a chaplain at £25 per year instructed the children and
other inmates in the principles of the Christian religion, and also
baptized infants and buried the dead. A surgeon was appointed to
look after the sick (whether they were indoor or outdoor paupers),
to supply medicines and to perform surgery and midwifery, for a
salary of £40 per annum. In the summer of 1777 the 19 acres of
land round the Rollesby House were ploughed and harrowed ready for
the male paupers to begin their farmwork, and spinning wheels and
wool were bought for the women and girls to spin wool for a Norwich
manufacturer. Finally, insurance was taken out which amounted to
£2,000 for the buildings and the same again for its furnishings and
working-capital.(6)

The Flegg Incorporation, like several other East Anglian incorporations, was financed in part by a tontine scheme, which was a
form of life annuity which increased in amount as other subscribers
died. Of the £6,000 authorized by the Flegg local act, £2,500 was
in fact raised, by 25 shares or bonds of £100 each, in a tontine
scheme:(7)

A nominee for each share on whose life the interest of the sub-
scriber to such share shall depend and as the nominees or lives
fall in, the shares and interest depending thereon shall vest
in the subscribers or names of the surviving nominees.

There was no shortage of shareholders, who found it an irresistible
method of satisfying their gambling instincts while salving their
consciences by subscribing to a good, charitable cause. In the
Forehoe Incorporation the entire capital was raised in a tontine
scheme, and 110 shares of £100 each raised £11,000 in 1776-7. The
initial interest was 5 per cent per annum, but by 1800, when there
were only 85 shareholders still alive, the interest had been raised
to 6.4 per cent, and by 1836 their numbers had been further reduced
so that interest was then 15.3 per cent.

A Norfolk incorporation that preferred to raise its capital by
other means, and found it more difficult to do so, was Mitford and
Launditch, which at first paid 4 per cent annual interest, but was
forced to raise this to 4.5 per cent, on indentured loans of £100
each which were made between 1776 and 1796. Not only did the act
of incorporation authorize the very large sum of £15,000 to be
raised (although only £13,700 was borrowed through indentured loans),
but the Mitford and Launditch Incorporation also had to repay its
loans promptly. Between 1782 and 1801, £3,700 was repaid, a further
£3,200 was paid back by 1805, and another £4,000 by 1808, leaving
£2,800 still owing when the sole surviving account book closed.

The mode of finance chosen by each incorporation was to have important consequences. It may be conjectured that the intense dis-

satisfaction evinced by the ratepayers in the Mitford and Launditch
Incorporation, which nearly forced its early disincorporation, was
linked to the necessity to repay its loaned capital. The Loddon
and Clavering Incorporation, which was financed in a similar way,
managed to clear its repayments by 1786 but had borrowed only
£7,000.(8)

4   Gressenhall House of Industry, Mitford and Launditch Incorporation

    The major cost for the five rural Norfolk incorporations was the
purchase of land and the erection and equipping of the houses of
industry, which amounted to over £40,000. The largest of these
pauper palaces was that of Gressenhall in the Mitford and Launditch
Incorporation. It had been designed on a symmetrical plan in which
an elegant entrance block, built in a classical style, was to be
flanked by a linear block and wing on each side of a central courtyard. But before this grandiose scheme could be realized funds ran
dry, and the block and wing on one side of the courtyard were never
built. Another monumental building was the Wicklewood House of Industry in the Forehoe Incorporation, where classical symmetry was
achieved in a rectangular block which had a central feature consisting of a pedimented entrance. Rather less imposing in scale was
the Heckingham House in the Incorporation of Loddon and Clavering,
although the building itself was substantial, and was ornamented
pleasantly by blind arcading. The few remaining buildings of the
Smallburgh House of Industry in the Tunstead and Happing Incorporation suggest that this had buildings of an agreeably functional
simplicity. Planned on a more domestic scale was the Rollesby House
of the Flegg Incorporation, that was built in a rather severe classical style which was enlivened only by the portico over the entrance,
and above that by the inscription with the objectives of the incorporation.

5 Wicklewood House of Industry, Forehoe Incorporation

6 Heckingham House of Industry, Loddon and Clavering Incorporation

The paternalistic sense of responsibility which the propertied felt towards the poor at this time is illustrated clearly by the idealistic objectives of the Flegg inscription. Their pride in setting up a notable experiment in social welfare resulted in the erection of impressive buildings in which to develop a humane system of relieving the poor. Self-esteem in each locality required also that these large and prominent buildings should enhance the landscape. Once a prestigious building had gone up in one area local jealousy dictated that the next house of industry should be at the very least of a comparable standard, and preferably of a superior one. The experimental nature of the buildings also delivered the guardians into the hands of those who built them, and it is possible that local architects and builders saw a good opportunity to make their name by erecting a grandiloquent building which exceeded the rather vague specifications that had been laid down. In several of the incorporations the tontine method of financing encouraged liberality in building because the cost of paying for these large houses of industry was effectively transferred from the local ratepayers to the subscribers. Once the directors and guardians of the incorporations under the Old Poor Law had established that ostentatious buildings were required in which to relieve the poor, the guardians in the new poor law unions after 1834 felt that they must carry on the tradition. Competitive rivalry was also present, and since some unions had the grandiose buildings of dissolved incorporations to act as their union workhouses, so other unions felt that they had to erect notable buildings in their own locality. The tradition of the pauper palaces found new life, but the less affluent circumstances of the 1830s dictated that some compromises should be made. Norfolk union workhouses after 1834 tended to have imposing entrances embellished with pediments, towers or turrets while the remainder of the building was erected in a plainer style.

The difference between the houses of industry of the Old Poor Law and the union workhouses of the New Poor Law was not so much one of architectural style as the provision, in the former, both of more highly developed welfare arrangements for the impotent poor and of measures for the productive employment of the able-bodied poor. The illustrated plan of the Smallburgh workhouse (Figures 1 and 2) is the only one of the Norfolk houses of industry to have survived. The plan dates from after 1834, but despite the re-christening of the yards and certain of the rooms to comply superficially with the New Poor Law, it remains almost entirely a plan of an Old Poor Law house of industry. It shows that there were six cottages for the aged poor. Old people were treated indulgently, as this entry in the Smallburgh House of Industry Book for 1793 suggests: 'The Banns of Marriage were published in Smallburgh Church on Sunday last, the second time, between John Browne, aged 74 years belonging to Horning and Ursula Jolly aged 65 years belonging to Tunstead. N.B. They are both paupers in the House.'(9) Married on 16 September 1793, they were presumably given one of these cottages. Alternatively, they might have had one of the 31 family rooms that were provided in the Smallburgh House for the use of both impotent and able-bodied poor. There was ample provision for the sick or infirm in the sick room, surgery and infirmary wards for men and women; although not all of these rooms were sited intelligently in relation to the manu-

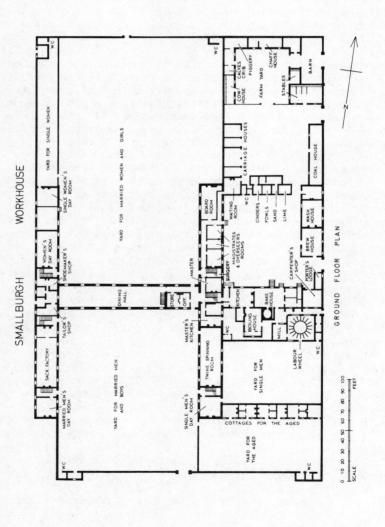

Figure 1   Smallburgh Workhouse

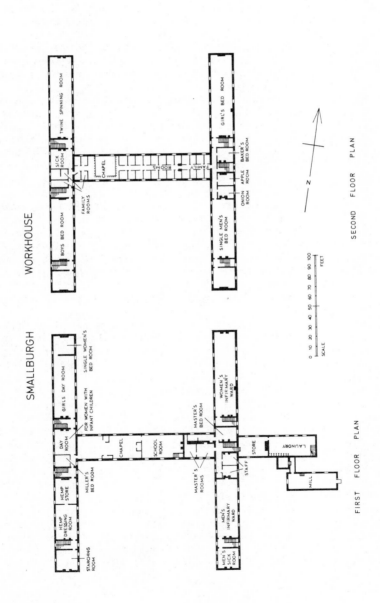

Figure 2   Smallburgh Workhouse

facturing processes that went on in the House. The careful arrangements made for those who were ill is suggested by this minute by
the Governor in 1793:(10)

> Mary Ann Green aged 22 years from Tunstead was this day delivered
> of two illegitimate children — having a very difficult labour I
> wrote for Mr Dix [the Surgeon] who attended. She was delivered
> of the first, a female by the Midwife of the House, which was
> born dead and the other, a male, by Mr Dix which is alive.

Those paupers needing surgery were taken to the Norfolk and Norwich
Hospital, a voluntary hospital, to which the Smallburgh Incorporation subscribed, while the mentally ill went to the Bethel in
Norwich. Unlike the houses of industry in the Flegg or Loddon and
Clavering Incorporations, the Smallburgh House does not appear to
have had a pest house to isolate infectious cases, such as those
suffering from smallpox, although it would have been necessary to
provide some means of segregating them from the other inmates.

The able-bodied poor in the Smallburgh House were put to productive labour which was designed to inculcate industrious habits, to
make the house of industry self-sufficient where possible, and to
make a profit for the incorporation which would offset the costs of
the paupers' maintenance. Men were employed on the farm of 24
acres where wheat, oats, clover, potatoes, turnips, peas and other
garden produce were grown. Some cows, pigs and hens were also kept.
Produce was used in the house and any surplus was sold. The compact
farm buildings were efficiently designed and are still in use. They
are virtually all that remains of the buildings today. Under the
supervision of a miller, corn was ground on a labour wheel in the
mill (which was treated as a task of work and was not a form of
punishment) before being baked into bread by a baker in the bakehouse. Malt and hops were bought to make beer in the brew house
and a brewer was employed to make a decent product. In the early
days of the incorporation the women spun wool for a Norwich manufacturer and the children spun hemp yarn. Later there was productic
of nets and sacks.

As early hopes of profit evaporated, however, the emphasis in thi
as in other incorporations shifted to developing industrious habits
among the poor. The industrious poor in Norfolk incorporations received rewards in the form of small sums of money. In the Smallburg
Incorporation the lazy were reprimanded: 'The Boy Summers, the Governor apprenticed to hemp dressing, continued very idle.... Something should be done with this boy to prevent his ruin. Reprimanded.'(11) If reprimands were ineffective then punishments en-
sued. For serious offences there was 24 hours' solitary confinement
with only bread and water to sustain the culprit. Less heinous
crimes resulted in the culprit being given bread and water instead
of a nice hot dinner of meat on the days when this was served in the
dining hall.

The liberal dietaries, and the poor accounting methods in use for
supplying the needs of the Norfolk houses of industry with fuel or
clothing, had attracted hostile comment from ratepayers before the
end of the eighteenth century. Although the Norfolk incorporations
had been set up on a common pattern not long before 1834, much di-
versity had developed among them. The administrations of the two
incorporations that have been described in greater detail, those of

Flegg and Tunstead and Happing, continued to be run in a relatively efficient and economical way. Among the other three rural Norfolk incorporations, that of Loddon and Clavering was undoubtedly the most neglected, corrupt and disorderly by the time of the New Poor Law. Yet in its early days, in the 1770s, its administration had been of a high standard, which had combined an efficient and humane system of relief to the poor (especially during the smallpox epidemic of 1773-4) with financial accountability to the ratepayers. The inspectors, appointed by the newly instituted, central poor law administration after 1834, found that the paupers at the Heckingham House in this incorporation had plenty of licence to pursue their own inclinations. The first inspector, Sir Edward Parry, was actually assaulted by the Heckingham paupers, while his successor, Dr James Kay, was more circumspect and found much good copy to include in a hostile report on the Norfolk incorporations. On Sundays, the Heckingham paupers were allowed their freedom, he reported sourly: (12)

> The paupers had made abundant provision for the enjoyment of this license; it was found profitable to erect two beer-shops in the immediate neighbourhood, which were usually crowded with paupers on this day. The women had boxes in the neighbouring cottages containing dresses, which, as soon as they were released, they exchanged for workhouse garb, and thus, attired in a more attractive style, flaunted about the neighbourhood with the young men.

Like Bumble, who later attributed Oliver Twist's spirited behaviour to his meat diet, Kay could well have blamed the spirit of the Heckingham paupers on their lavish dietary. A comparison of the dietary in use in Heckingham when it was part of an old poor law incorporation with that adopted in 1836 when it was put under the New Poor Law indicated that male paupers in 1836 had only 70 per cent of the amount of solid food given earlier. Breakfast and supper were not dissimilar, consisting mainly of bread and cheese; but dinner, the main meal of the day, differed considerably because the number of meat meals was cut from four to one each week and beer was no longer supplied. Women paupers had a particular grievance, since under the regime before 1834 it was assumed that their appetites were as large as those of the men, whereas under the second dietary of the Poor Law Commissioners they got less meat at dinner, and butter instead of cheese at other meals. Paupers in the Heckingham House of Industry ate well before 1834 and were given 250 ounces of solid food per week, which was much better than the 168 ounces of a soldier, or the 122 ounces of an agricultural labourer. (13) This superiority in diet was matched by other aspects of the lives of the paupers in the rural Norfolk incorporations. Material comfort was associated with the humane spirit in which the Norfolk houses of industry were run, and in which references to the inmates as 'the family' accurately reflected the atmosphere there. When Crabbe had earlier christened the East Anglian rural houses of industry as 'pauper palaces', he had drawn on his unusual depth of knowledge and sympathy for the poor of the area. It had proved to be an apt title.

While the rural incorporations of Norfolk were based on a common pattern, the urban Incorporation of Norwich stood apart from them and had greater similarities with those that had been established

in other towns such as Bristol or Exeter at about the same time. It
was the thirteenth town to apply for a local act, and this took
effect in 1712 when the Court of Guardians, consisting of the most
important members of Norwich Town Corporation together with 32
elected representatives, took control of the poor law administration.

The original act had stressed that indigent, idle, disorderly
people, together with children under the age of 16, should be put to
work in the workhouse, but lax administration gradually converted the
Norwich workhouse into little more than a comfortable lodging house.
In 1788 the paupers had three beef dinners a week at each of which
everyone had 18 ounces of meat. A reforming guardian, Dr Rigby,
estimated that it would have been cheaper to feed the paupers at a
cook shop or public house. In 1805 Rigby found that conditions had
again reverted to their earlier unreformed state. In the same year
James Neild toured the workhouse with Rigby and compared it unfavourably with those of King's Lynn and Aylsham which he had also
visited. He wrote a devastating report in the 'Gentleman's Magazine' in which he described the squalid, overcrowded, unhealthy and
inhumane conditions in St Andrew's workhouse. The Court of Guardians as a whole viewed the report as overdrawn and were complacent
about their administration so that things continued in much the
same way.(14) In 1826 there was another bout of adverse publicity
on the workhouse in the local press, which graphically described it
as 'a scene of *filth, wretchedness* and *indecency*' in which paupers
gnawed food from their hands, bedding was verminous, and inmates
were mixed together indiscriminately. The disclosures of an ineffi-
ciently managed workhouse were accompanied by accusations of a corrupt administration of relief. This led to revised local acts in
1827 and 1831 which converted the Court of Guardians into a democratic body, while reorganization of committees and more precisely
defined duties for officials produced a more responsible administration. Re-invigorated by these reforms and protected by its local
legislation, the Norwich Guardians were able, as Chapter 7 indicates, to ignore the provisions of the 1834 act.

Although the criticisms levelled at the Norwich Workhouse by
contemporaries indicated that a necessary balance of efficiency
with humanity was not achieved there, yet evidence from some other
areas in England suggests that workhouses were successful in meeting the social needs of their locality. In these areas, as in the
rural Norfolk incorporations, indoor relief systems were much better than has sometimes been supposed.(15) The humane administration of the East Anglian pauper palaces, where the minutes referred
to inmates as 'the family', was not a purely regional phenomenon.

The combined objectives of humanity to the poor with economy for
the ratepayers, which characterized the local acts that instituted
the rural East Anglian incorporations, was also exemplified in Gilbert's Act of 1782. This was a permissive act which parishes could
adopt if they wished. Since it was very much cheaper to set up a
Gilbert Union of parishes than to seek incorporation under an expensive local act of Parliament, Gilbert's Act slowed the incorporating
movement in Norfolk. Only one old-style incorporation of hundreds
was created in the county after 1782, and this was that of Tunstead
and Happing in 1785. Its local act echoed Gilbert's Act in its provision that the justices could order the parish officers to direct

occupiers to find work for the unemployed poor. The major amending
act of 1801 for the Mitford and Launditch Incorporation also made
a similar provision in that the justices could direct the parish
overseers to secure work at fair wages for the poor outside the
house of industry. The case of the Buxton Incorporation is interesting in showing the interaction of incorporations and unions in Norfolk. This started as a Gilbert Union of three parishes in 1801 but
was enlarged into an incorporation of nine parishes under local act
in 1806, when deviations from Gilbert's Act were specified in the
local legislation.(16) Its indeterminate character means that it is
equally valid to describe it as a Gilbert Union under local act or
as a local incorporation under Gilbert's Act.

Map A (see p. 33) indicates how the later Gilbert Unions complemented the earlier incorporations, since both were concentrated in
a striking fashion in east Norfolk with the unions being created
in the areas between the incorporations. There were three phases
of support for Gilbert's Act and two of these also saw the institution of local incorporations. The first came in the 1780s with a
handful of parishes included in the Gilbert Unions of Brinton in
1783, Bawdeswell in 1785 and Booton in 1786, which was paralleled
by 41 parishes included in the Tunstead and Happing Incorporation in
1785. A lesser impulse came in 1792, when a few parishes were
formed into the Gilbert Unions of Acle and Oulton. The third and
major period of reform occurred in the years 1801-8. In 1805 a much
larger number of parishes were included in the Gilbert Unions of
Aldeborough, Gimingham and St Faith's, and the Acle Union was also
expanded. In the following year the Buxton Union of 1801 was enlarged and re-established as the Buxton Incorporation under local
act, and in 1808 the Hackford Union was created. Applications by
additional parishes to join existing Gilbert Unions continued
until 1834, when over 70 parishes were to be found in the nine
unions.(17) This was a similar number to those in the counties of
Lincolnshire, Kent or Sussex, but far fewer than in the counties
of Leicester, Nottingham, Derby or York.

II THE REVERSION TO THE PAROCHIAL SYSTEM

In the final years of the Old Poor Law many parishes in local incorporations and under Gilbert's Act were virtually indistinguishable in their poor law administration from any other Norfolk parish.
A Norfolk landowner and magistrate described Hindolveston in 1834
as a parish that claimed to be under Gilbert's Act but in which the
poor house was occupied by homeless families, the governor of the
poor house worked as a farm servant of the clergyman, and the poor
law guardian and visitor no longer relieved the poor.(18) Dis-
enchantment with the Norfolk incorporations had led to a resumption
of the parochial system in Mitford and Launditch between 1801 and
1829, in Tunstead and Happing after 1824, and in Forehoe after 1833,
while similar moves were narrowly defeated in East and West Flegg
in 1830, and in Loddon and Clavering shortly afterwards. By 1834
the supposed benefits of a centralized control of relief in several
of the incorporations had been rejected in favour of a revived
parochial administration of outdoor allowances, which was thought to

provide a flexible and cheap system of relief to suit the economic
conditions of the area.   But the parishes still had to finance an
expensive central house of industry, and in doing so they got the
economic disadvantages of both a parochial and a centralized system.   It is interesting to analyse why this came about.

Profound disillusionment had followed when the formation of local
incorporations had failed to produce a decline in the poor rates.
The palatial scale of the houses of industry had encumbered the incorporations with debt from the beginning.   The local act for the
Flegg Incorporation authorised it to raise £6,000, that of Loddon
and Clavering £7,500, Tunstead and Happing £10,000, Forehoe £11,000
and Mitford and Launditch nearly £15,000.   Most of this money was
spent on the pauper palaces.   The expectation that the able-bodied
poor in the East Anglian houses would make a profit by their labour
is the manufactories, which would more than cover the costs of their
maintenance, was not to be fulfilled.(19)   The high standards of
living of pauper inmates inside the pauper palaces, the generous
system of medical relief and the inefficient accounting systems
could result in expensive and wasteful management which was often
inadequately checked by the oversight of the directors and acting
guardians.   In attempting to achieve the twin objectives of the incorporations of humanity to the poor and economy to the ratepayers,
the balance had swung too much towards the first aim and a backlash
from local ratepayers was predictable.

The earliest dissatisfaction in Norfolk occurred in the 1790s in
the Mitford and Launditch Incorporation about increasing poor
rates,   and a fixed rating quota which assessed parochial
contributions on the average rate for the seven years preceding
1775, the date when the incorporation was set up.   A revised local
act in 1801 resulted, in which there was a fixed parochial contribution to the establishment charges of the house of industry, but
with an additional charge for each pauper sent there.   With this
came, in practice, a replacement of the central direction of relief
by directors and guardians with a decentralized control by parish
overseers, who made little use of indoor relief in the Gressenhall
House.   Discontent continued and led in 1825 to a public meeting to
consider the disincorporation of the two hundreds.   This meeting
decided on a less drastic solution of economic and administrative
reform.(20)

'And whereas inconvenience and increase of expense in the management of the poor has arisen from the said establishment, without any
adequate beneficial result, either to the poor themselves or to the
greater number of the parishes composing the incorporation', stated
the 1826 Act of Dis-incorporation of the Loes and Wilford Incorporation in Suffolk.   Disappointment at the failure of the incorporations
to achieve economy with humanity in the administration of the Poor
Law had therefore been even more intense in Suffolk than in Norfolk.
Earlier, it had prevented the Act of Incorporation of the Hundreds
of Hartismere, Hoxne and Thredling from being put into practical
operation in 1779 and had led to discussion about the dis-incorporation of the Samford Incorporation before 1800.(21)   Discontent in
both counties was rooted in a sense of financial grievance, but was
intensified by a general but amorphous impression that, in spite of
great expense for the ratepayer, society was being harmed by the

creation of a pauperized peasantry.

The inflexibility of fixed systems of rating assessments and contributions to the central establishment created a pervasive sense of injustice among the constituent parishes in the incor- porations. However, when this produced enough local concern to justify the expense of another local act of Parliament to revise the rating system, the opportunity was also taken to decentralize the administration of poor relief. The revised act of 1824 for the Tunstead and Happing Incorporation rated each parish only for its own poor and devolved the management of relief on to the parish overseer. In the Forehoe Incorporation nine years later, the fifth in a series of modified local acts instituted a new parochial rating quota, and also resulted in the central committee of guardians and directors being demoted to a mere appeals committee, to whom the poor might appeal against the relief administration of their parish overseers. Discontented ratepayers in the Flegg Incorporation tried unsuccessfully in 1830 to get a new local act 'on the plan now exist- ing in the adjoining Hundreds of Tunstead and Happing'. An explo- sive situation had been created in the Loddon and Clavering Incor- poration by the 1830s because there had been no modification of the original rating quotas of 1764 and the minority of parishes that lost financially under this system were consistently out-voted on the issue of reform by the majority who benefited from it.(22)

Supporting the trend towards a decentralization of the relief ad- ministration in the incorporated parishes was the increasingly un- fashionable character of indoor relief for the able-bodied in a central house of industry. This was already apparent in Gilbert's Act of 1782, which had specified that work was to be found outside the poor house for the able-bodied labourer. The use of the poor house in Gilbert Unions for the impotent poor reinforced a tendency in the hundred or so other Norfolk parishes (which had established a workhouse under an act of 1723) to use the workhouse as a poor house for the infirm, aged, orphaned and sick. After 1815, when the postwar agricultural depression led to a deterioration of the real wages of the rural labourer, there was a widespread use of outdoor relief to bring his income up to subsistence level. Poor law allowances, which were sometimes systematized into a scale based on family size and bread price, spread rapidly in this period. In the 1820s and 1830s particularly, they were supplemented or re- placed by outdoor employment schemes financed by the poor rates. One in three villages operated a roundsman scheme in the 1820s, and in the 1830s one in five used a labour rate.

The use of increasingly complex relief policies in the closing years of the Old Poor Law stimulated a more vigorous and sophisti- cated parochial administration in Norfolk. Many parishes, and par- ticularly the larger ones and those in the east of the county, took advantage of the permissive Select Vestry Act of 1819, which allowed them to appoint either a permanent salaried official (the assistant overseer) or a parish committee (the select vestry) to provide a continuous oversight of poor law affairs. Between 1820 and 1834 an average of 70 parishes in the county had appointed select vestries. This reform was most popular in 1828, when 91 parishes were managed by a select vestry, but their numbers had dwindled to only 47 by 1834. The select vestry was a more transitory reform than that of

the assistant overseer, but it was effective in restricting allowances and checking rising poor rates. Assistant overseers were
frequently appointed when labour rates were introduced or when, as
the village of East Rudham explained, it was 'rendered necessary
by the increasing trouble and difficulty of parish business'. In
the years 1820 to 1834 an average of 80 parishes had an assistant
overseer, and in 1832 when labour rates were legalized there was a
peak total of 104.(23) Parishes took a lot of trouble over the
management of outdoor relief, which formed the main business of
parochial administration, but under-utilized and neglected the parish poor house. This appeared to one critical observer to be only
a 'receptacle of age, vice, disease, and infirmity' by the end of
the Old Poor Law era.(24)

Reforms in the administration of the Poor Law in the late eighteenth and early nineteenth century had reduced the power and authority of the Norfolk justices of the peace. In the incorporations
under local act their authority was replaced by that of the directors and acting guardians, although of course these might themselves
be magistrates. The Select Vestry Act of 1819 had restricted the
magistrate's power to order allowances, and the tendency to replace
allowances by employment schemes in the 1820s and 1830s had in any
case made the justice less prominent in poor law affairs. It is
true that the justice still retained very extensive legal powers
over parishes in Gilbert Unions and in all those outside the incorporations. He had a general supervisory oversight over parochial
administration in selecting officials, auditing accounts, regula-
ting poor houses, authorizing removal and bastardy orders and
granting relief.(25) But an increasingly hostile public opinion in
the county, which blamed the magistracy for the growth of the allowance system, inhibited local justices from the practical exercise
of these powers.

By the end of the old poor law era parishes in Norfolk had tried
out the available spectrum of poor law policies from the bold innovation of incorporating hundreds for a common poor law management to the transitory adoption of the latest fashionable remedy by
single parishes. Increasingly, contemporary opinion and practice
emphasised the value of piecemeal reform based on the individual
parish. A member of the Norfolk Magistrates Committee on the Rural
Poor in 1831 defended its lack of specific or large-scale remedial
measures in its report with a statement that is typical of local
opinion at that time. 'The fact was, any plan intended for the
whole kingdom would be found utterly impracticable; the object
of the committee was to have every parish to [sic] adopt the measures most suited to its own views.'(26) The virtual sovereignty
of each parish in determining on its own methods to relieve the
poor shows the difficulty of generalizing about the administration
of the Poor Law in a county as large as Norfolk. Two parishes,
those of Shipdham and Edgefield, will be taken as examples of the
varied poor law policies in use at this time, and also of the relative failure of the two generalized plans of reform (those of the
local incorporations and of the Gilbert Unions), to solve the socioeconomic problems of Norfolk parishes.

Shipdham was a large village with 1,889 inhabitants in 1831 and
was divided into two townships, each of which had its own overseers.

Although it was included in the Mitford and Launditch Incorporation,
it made little use of the central house of industry, and between
1830 and 1834 spent only 14 per cent of its relief expenditure on
indoor paupers. Instead it preferred a system of outdoor allowances. In the same period 55 per cent of its expenditure was on
permanent weekly allowances to the aged, widows and children, and
another 25 per cent went on temporary allowances to the sick and
unemployed. The able-bodied poor were employed on the roads or on
a roundsman-cum-labour rate scheme. They were also given money to
seek work in the Fens and in Northamptonshire, or to go harvesting
in Lincolnshire. The administration was vigorous and efficient,
and loans were given on an unusual scale. Yet only 4 per cent of
the relief expenditure went on loans or employment schemes; the
expensive House of Industry at Gressenhall was under-utilized; and
the parish relied predominantly on a hand-to-mouth administration of
dole allowances. The basic reason for this was that half the population was engaged in agricultural pursuits and there was insufficient farm employment available locally. A surplus labour problem
is suggested by migration at the beginning of the new poor law era;
in 1836 44 people migrated to Leeds with assistance from the Shipdham
poor rates.(27) With substantial under-employment in Shipdham, the
administrators of the old poor law could only try out a variety of
palliatives to relieve the labourer. They were unable to alter the
basic cause of his distressed condition.

The extent of the surplus labour problem in Edgefield, a parish
under Gilbert's Act, defeated all the administrative innovations
in the local management of the Poor Law. It showed the difficulty
of implementing the act's direction that work should be found for the
able-bodied. Edgefield had a population of 774 in 1831 and seven out
of every eight families worked in agriculture. Local farmers were
badly hit by the postwar agricultural depression after 1815, and this
produced a vicious spiral of reduced employment and rising poor
rates, which resulted in only one-third of the population being in
employment and poor rates of over 23s an acre by the 1830s. A labour
rate was tried but was a failure because the small occupiers and the
tithe-owner did not employ their quota of labourers. Wages for agricultural labourers were fixed by agreement at successively lower
levels — 12, 9, 6 and finally 4s in 1833 — in an attempt to employ
all the poor. The parish then made up the wages to a subsistence
level by a subsidy from the poor rates. G.B. Ballachey, who was the
resident gentleman in the parish and who took an intelligent interest
in the Poor Law, felt that the distress of the farming interest and
the extent of unemployment in Edgefield and its neighbourhood was so
bad as to 'threaten almost universal pauperism'. In 1836 this small
village sent the amazing total of 123 emigrants, or one-sixth of the
population, to North America, and financed it from the poor rates
and the contributions of local landowners. Even with this stupendous
effort the surplus labour problem continued to bedevil the administrators of the New Poor Law, as it had already defeated the ingenuity of administrators under the Old Poor Law.(28)

III   FROM THE OLD TO THE NEW POOR LAW

The establishment of rural incorporations under local act had involved a trial within the county of many of the features of the New
Poor Law before their enactment in 1834.   These included both the
union of parishes rated for a common workhouse, in order to provide
for the indoor relief of the able-bodied, and the administrative
device of elected representatives who supervised permanent salaried
officials by means of committees.   The Webbs concluded that this
combination of an elected body who supervised officers pioneered
the typical form of English local government machinery, while the
principal features of the incorporation also provided the basis
from which the Poor Law reform of 1834 was constructed.(29)
     The Poor Law Commissioners, whose authority was established by
the Poor Law Amendment Act of 1834, were clear that they could
learn a great deal from the experience of the East Anglian incorporations.   Their instructions to their assistant commissioner,
Charles Mott, who was sent post-haste into Suffolk to investigate
the incorporations under local act were sufficiently revealing to
be worth quoting at length:(30)

> Sir, It appears from the evidence taken before the late commis-
> sion of enquiry that the money raised for the relief of the
> indigent and the progression of pauperism in the hundreds of
> Suffolk which are incorporated is less than in the parishes of
> the hundreds which are unincorporated....
>   You are requested to examine and report:
>   1st As to the general management of the incorporated
> workhouses: as to the defects which exist there and the reme-
> dies applicable
>   2dly As to the general management of the business
> of the incorporations; and the grounds of the discontents of
> the parishes incorporated and the means of removing it.
>   And generally to report upon any points which you may
> conceive to be conducive to the immediate objects of the Board
> in this mission, which objects are, to ascertain from the ex-
> perience of existing unions the precautions to be taken in the
> formation of new unions or useful suggestions to be adopted es-
> pecially as to the employment of the able bodied and as to the
> mode of keeping accounts and also to place the old unions in a
> more effective state.

The Poor Law Commission were advised by Mott swiftly to form the
Suffolk incorporations into new poor law unions, so that the benefits could 'be immediately shown as an example to the country at
large'.   His colleague, Sir Edward Parry, who was assisting him,
and who later introduced the New Poor Law to Norfolk, gave the game
away still further by describing their task as persuading the incorporations 'to commit suicide'.   It is arguable that a certain
sleight of hand was in progress whereby the Poor Law Commission
planned to take over the old poor law machinery of the East Anglian
incorporations and use it to suggest that the supposedly 'New'
Poor Law was an instantaneous success.   This policy of disincorporation worked well in Suffolk because it took the incorporations
by surprise.   But Sir Edward Parry thought that this had given the
Norfolk incorporations 'the alarm, and from the first moment of my

entering this county they have been keenly alive and suspicious'
about plans to form them into new poor law unions.(31)   These
Norfolk incorporations were to be a more serious impediment to
the imposition of the New Poor Law than had been the case with
their Suffolk counterparts.

CHAPTER 4

THE IMPACT OF NATIONAL REFORM AFTER 1834

The strong localism of Norfolk, with its tradition in poor law administration of relief in pauper palaces, made the county after 1834 an apparently unpropitious place in which to introduce a national measure for the reform of poor relief. The county was declared to be part of England where 'the circulation languishes' and 'life manifests itself less vigorously', by the energetic Dr Kay who, with Sir Edward Parry, introduced the New Poor Law to Norfolk. (1) After a closer acquaintance with rural society in the county, they found a surprising amount of support for the Poor Law Amendment Act. Local property-owners helped to introduce the national reform because they saw it as a means of social discipline for the poor. To this support from the gentry was added that of the farmers, who as occupiers of land paid most of the poor rates. They hoped that the 1834 act would succeed where local reform had failed, and that poor law expenditure and poor rates would be cut. Rapid progress was made in introducing the New Poor Law to Norfolk; the county was carved up into poor law unions, and union workhouses were built. But by the 1840s a local reaction occurred. There was a belated recognition of the irrelevance of the 1834 act and an appreciation that, although poor law administration was in theory centralized in London, yet in practice it was controlled in Norfolk. Older, local ideas about the relief of the poor could then be reasserted in the new era.

What were the administrative and relief principles of the New Poor Law contained in the Poor Law Amendment Act of 1834, which Dr Kay, as the agent of the central board, was implementing in Norfolk? The Benthamite principle of national uniformity in the treatment of each category of destitute people was to be achieved through a central authority which would regulate the work of local administrators devoid of discretionary power. The able-bodied poor, who were the central preoccupation of the reformers of the Poor Law, were to receive relief only in a workhouse, where their life was to be made less eligible or less attractive than that of the ordinary, independent labourer. This deterrent was aimed at discouraging the merely poor from seeking relief, because only the truly destitute would accept poor relief in the unappealing conditions of the union workhouse. Since it would be too expensive for a single parish to

build and staff a workhouse, parishes were to be grouped into poor
law unions. The new poor law administration therefore consisted of
a bipartite structure. A central board of commissioners framed
and enforced regulations and were assisted by assistant commissioners (later called inspectors), who acted as their agents in the
localities. Each local union of parishes had a board of elected
guardians which was served by permanent, salaried officials.

I   THE FORMATION OF THE NEW UNIONS

Much of the administrative format of the New Poor Law in Norfolk was
not new at all but owed a lot to previous experience and the Old
Poor Law. In Norfolk, the national administrative objective in
forming poor law unions of a uniform size was modified by the prac-
ticalities of accommodating both the existing local administrative
structure of the Old Poor Law and the personal views of influential
landowners. In contrast to Northamptonshire, a county with an unusual concentration of peers and landed magnates, the assistant commissioners, Sir Edward Parry and Dr James Kay, did not give priority
to the views of the landed gentry in Norfolk, so that poor law boundaries did not necessarily coincide with the limits of estates or
mark off existing deference communities.(2) They were able to enlist the support of many of the landed gentry for a reformed administration of the Poor Law while subordinating their individual interests to a more general strategy. Local interests were conciliated
only to the extent necessary to facilitate the implementation of a
reformed administration of poor relief.
     The county was unionized swiftly. Table 1 shows that eighteen
unions were formed between 1835 and 1837. Most of the early unions
were created in west and south Norfolk, where the absence of incorporations under local act or of Gilbert Unions gave the assistant
commissioners a relatively free hand in grouping parishes into
unions. The sequence of unions formed under the first commissioner,
Sir Edward Parry, was a rather haphazard one. As he had to go to
Brancaster on the north Norfolk coast to sort out a bitter conflict
over the parish accounts between the overseers and the clergyman, he
took the opportunity to get the local gentry to consent to the first
new poor law union in Norfolk.(3) This was the Docking Union, which
consisted of parishes in the hundreds of Smithdon and Brothercross,
and which was instituted on 1 August 1835. The hundred was the
ancient local governmental unit which also served as the unit for
petty sessions and as such was the obvious geographical basis for
the new unions. Meetings of local owners and occupiers of land were
called in groups of hundreds and addressed by an assistant commissioner who explained the purpose of the Poor Law Amendment Act of
1834. Typically, he would stress the highly pauperized state of the
local parishes, the heavy burden that therefore devolved on the ratepayers who made up his audience, and the financial savings that the
New Poor Law would effect. The meeting would be chaired skilfully
by a prominent local landowner who supported the measure, and influential magistrates would act as the proposer and seconder of a
motion that the area should be brought under the 1834 act. Some
months would elapse in which the assistant commissioner would

TABLE 1   Norfolk unions and incorporations after 1834

Union or incorporation	Date instituted as union	Acreage	Population in 1831	Average poor law expenditure in 3 years before formation of union	No. of parishes	No. of guardians or directors***
Aylsham	Apr. 1836	68,123	19,351	20,391	46	47
Blofield	Oct. 1835	44,178	9,851	5,816	32	41
Depwade	Apr. 1836	72,681	24,768	24,008	43	53
Docking	Aug. 1835	101,136	15,376	16,840	36	53
Downham	Aug. 1836	83,687	16,016	11,083	34	35
Erpingham	Apr. 1836	69,178	20,024	16,532	49	53
*Flegg	-	29,087	7,210	-	20	24 (24***)
*Forehoe	-	37,834	13,473	-	22	38 (24***)
Freebridge Lynn	Nov. 1835	78,775	11,489	8,952	32	36
Guiltcross	Nov. 1835	44,585	11,873	10,833	21	24
Henstead	Dec. 1835	43,358	10,739	10,231	37	38
King's Lynn	Sept. 1835	5,499	13,370	9,220	2	21
Loddon and Clavering	May 1836	59,401	13,680	6,494	42	44
Mitford and Launditch	May 1836	105,239	27,694	26,684	60	64
*Norwich	Oct. 1863	4,325	60,505	37,040	44	42
St Faiths	Jan. 1836	48,304	11,126	10,525	30	33
Swaffham	Aug. 1835	81,200	12,321	12,197	28	41
Thetford	Dec. 1835	79,592	16,198	9,850	32	43
*Tunstead and Happing**	Oct. 1869	62,607	14,424	37,040	41	46
Walsingham	Apr. 1836	87,342	20,866	21,497	50	53
Wayland	Sept. 1835	51,063	10,643	9,450	25	30
Yarmouth	Mar. 1837	1,510	21,115	6,605	1	16

*   Incorporation under local act of Parliament.

** This became the Smallburgh Union in 1869.

Sources: Annual Reports of PlC and PLB. 'Return on Poor Law Unions', PP, 1869, LIII.

attempt to accommodate the interests of major local landowners who
wanted their property within a given union, and when the boundaries
were fixed the union would be declared. As a result, union boundaries often deviated from those of the hundreds.

While conciliation of the landed gentry was an important consideration, the assistant commissioners did not give it pride of place
in their strategy. The treatment of Thomas William Coke (created
Earl of Leicester in 1837) may be taken as a critical case. Politically he was very influential, and his Holkham estate of 43,000
acres was far larger than any other in the county, but he found that
his views on unionization were only of secondary interest to Parry
and his successor, Dr Kay. Parry remarked, 'I should prefer taking
Mr Coke on the flank to facing him too directly at the outset', and
did not consult him over the formation of the Docking Union whose
boundary ran along the Holkham home park itself.(4)   Kay did seek
Coke's approval for the unions he had drawn up in the eastern part
of the Holkham estates but only after he had already designated them
on the basis of the practical availability of existing workhouse
accommodation. In spite of the fact that the Holkham estate was inconveniently divided between five unions, Coke gave his support to
the New Poor Law and agreed to be the chairman of the Walsingham
Board of Guardians. A parallel case was that of Sir W.H.J.B. Folkes
of Hillington, a smaller landowner, who was M.P. for the Western
Division of Norfolk from 1830 to 1837. Folkes substantially helped
Parry in making possible the formation of the King's Lynn and Docking Unions, and also agreed to become the first chairman of the
Freebridge Lynn Union, but his own requests to Parry on union
boundaries were not met.(5)

The Gilbert Unions 'are beginning to come very much in my way',
wrote Sir Edward Parry during his first few months of union formation.(6)   These delayed his work, although they did not provide a
permanent constraint, because their moribund condition meant that
the officers in almost all the Gilbert Unions were more than ready
to consent to a dissolution of the union. First came the dismant-
ling of the Acle, St Faith's and Booton Unions after the necessary
legal consent of two-thirds of the guardians had been obtained.
This made possible the formation of the Blofield and St Faith's
Unions under the 1834 act. In the spring of 1836 there was a unanimous consent to the dissolution of each of the Aldeborough,
Bawdeswell, Oulton, Gimingham and Hackford Unions under Gilbert's
Act and also the Buxton Union under local act. This facilitated the
creation of the new poor law unions of Aylsham and Erpingham (see
Maps A, p. 33, and B, p. 58).

> The commissioners will however perceive that I have extended to
> the utmost limits the Aylsham and Erpingham Unions, in order to
> diminish the need of new workhouse accommodation in this district,
> and I shall endeavour to make the arrangements in the Walsingham
> Union as economical as possible.

This revealing comment by Dr Kay, in his report to the Poor Law
Commission in March 1836, suggests that the most important criterion
in his formation of unions in north-east Norfolk was the location of
existing workhouse accommodation. This explains his apparently
cavalier carving up of hundreds, and his division of landed estates,
in order to form the new units of poor law unions. He stated that

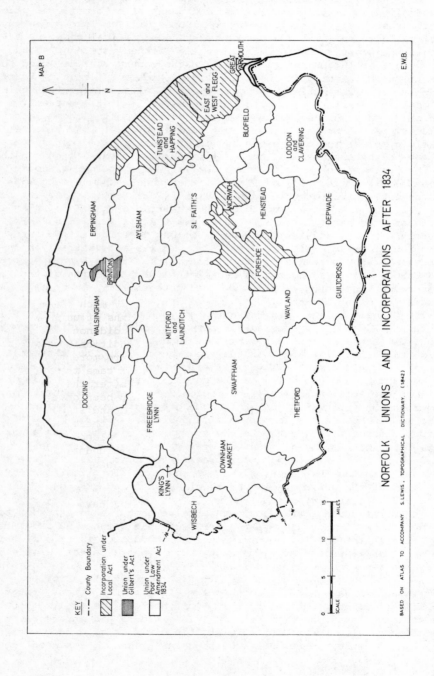

MAP B

KEY

County Boundary

Incorporation under Local Act

Union under Gilbert's Act

Union under Poor Law Amendment Act 1834

NORFOLK UNIONS AND INCORPORATIONS AFTER 1834

BASED ON ATLAS TO ACCOMPANY S. LEWIS, TOPOGRAPHICAL DICTIONARY. (1842)

E.W.B.

the Aylsham Union was based on the South Erpingham Hundred containing
the Oulton and Buxton poor houses, which were 'capable of containing
600 persons and are well adapted to be applied as tests of pauperism
when classified'. The Erpingham Union was based on the North Erpingham Hundred which contained the Gimingham and Sheringham poor houses
of the Gimingham and Aldborough Unions under Gilbert's Act. These
'will admit of classification at very slight expense'. Since they
would house some 400 paupers, the accommodation was thought by Kay
to be sufficient for a larger area, and half the Holt Hundred was
also included in the new poor law union of Erpingham. 'These
arrangements leave the remaining part of the Hundred of Holt together
with a part of the Hundred of Gallow, and the whole of the North
Greenhoe Hundred to constitute the fourth new union under the name
of the Walsingham Union.'(7)

The major problems in the formation of new poor law unions were
the incorporations under local act which, by April 1836, when 14
Norfolk unions had already been created, still remained undissolved.
Sir Edward Parry had been quick to visit the incorporations in the
summer of 1835 to test their attitude to the 1834 act. He had set
the Blofield Union up rapidly 'from the circumstance of its being
almost entirely surrounded by the Incorporated Hundreds, to which it
is of importance to show, as soon as possible, the particular good
effects of better management under the new system'.(8) This decision
to form unions in the interstices of the incorporations meant that,
even if two-thirds of the directors and acting guardians gave the
necessary legal consent to an incorporation's dissolution, its existence had pre-determined the geographical limits of the new unions.
Of course this provided another reason for departing from the
boundaries of the hundreds in forming unions.

Both assistant commissioners made the dissolution of the incorporations their priority and as late as July 1836 Kay had a misplaced confidence that he would achieve the dis-incorporation of
them all. The Norfolk incorporations were suspicious of the commissioners because they had seen their earlier activities in the Suffolk
incorporations. Kay forced the reluctant directors and acting guardians of the Loddon and Clavering Incorporation to consent to a dissolution in May 1836 by threatening to expose their financial inefficiency. In the same month the weak Mitford and Launditch Incorporation, which had considered dis-incorporation a decade earlier, also
consented to its own dissolution. Its house of industry was so large
that additional parishes were added from the Eynesford Hundred when
it was formed into a new poor law union. Signatures in favour of
dis-incorporation were collected from the directors and guardians of
the Forehoe Incorporation but at the last moment the dissolution fell
through. This was because of the political hostility of the influential Tory family, the Wodehouses, who reminded local landowners
and occupiers, of the £1,500 they had so recently spent in 1833 in
improving their incorporation through a new local act. The incorporations of East and West Flegg and Tunstead and Happing were relatively
efficient and economical in their administration and saw no reason
to alter their traditional methods of managing the poor.(9)

By the late summer of 1836 the assistant commissioners saw little
point in unnecessarily arousing political hostility to the New Poor
Law by attempting to force the dissolution of the remaining local

incorporations. It was more convenient to concede the appearance
of independence, but win the substance of their aims, by converting the incorporations into unions in all but name. The directors
and acting guardians of the Norfolk incorporations were persuaded
to accept the Poor Law Commission's rules and regulations concerning the relief of the poor. This promised welcome savings to the
ratepayers in the incorporations, while their election of the incorporated body of guardians and directors, together with the existing area of the incorporation, remained subject to local control. By March 1837 the remaining three rural incorporations had
accepted this compromise and a few years later they were indistinguishable in their relief administration from the newly formed
unions.(10) Indeed, the Reports of the Poor Law Commission publicized this by printing the accounts of the rural Norfolk incorporations with those of the unions formed after the 1834 act, and not
among the accounts of areas under Gilbert's Act or local legislation.   This was a striking success for the commissioners because
the New Poor Law, with its centralization of relief administration
and its emphasis on relief in the workhouse, appeared to be a
reversal of the existing trend towards parochially administered
outdoor relief in the Norfolk incorporations. Only two areas remained substantially independent of central authority and the provisions of the 1834 act. The Brinton Union under Gilbert's Act
remained a tiny old poor law oasis in north Norfolk because the financial interests of the Astley family made them block its dissolution. Its insignificance meant that the central Poor Law Board
forgot its existence, and it was not until 1869 that the Board
utilized summary powers it had had since 1844, and added the Brinton
Union to the Walsingham Union.(11) A more formidable challenge was
presented by the Norwich Incorporation, which continued in existence
until local ratepayers forced its dissolution in 1863.
   In the urban centres of Norwich, King's Lynn and Yarmouth and in
the old incorporated areas, the New Poor Law became a bone of political contention, and this both delayed and obstructed the formation of new poor law unions. The King's Lynn Union was not only
riven with political faction between Whigs and Tories, which led to
a vigorous pamphlet war, but also there was a deep-seated hostility
between the two constituent parishes of St Margaret's, and All
Saints in South Lynn. It was only through the good offices of a
local landowner, Sir William Folkes, that the new poor law union in
Lynn was formed in September 1835. King's Lynn resented its loss
of autonomy in the administration of poor relief under the New Poor
Law. Pride in a local system of poor law administration had earlier been shown by the fine silver badges that were made for the
beadle of the guardians of St Margaret's Parish in the eighteenth
century. An independent spirit therefore characterized the deal-
ings of the Lynn Board of Guardians with the Poor Law Commission
after 1834. Yarmouth was belatedly constituted a union in its own
right in March 1837 after the failure to dis-incorporate the neighbouring Flegg Hundred had made an additional poor law union necessary. Its political experience was similar to that of the Norwich
Incorporation in that the local Whigs were tarred with the odium of
the national Whig party in having brought in the revised regulations of the 1834 act. The Tories challenged the returns of guard-

ians' elections and managed to carry resolutions at the board of guardians deploring the centralization of the New Poor Law. The activities of the Tory magistracy in the undissolved incorpora- tions, in the disincorporated areas of Loddon and Clavering and Mitford and Launditch, and in the neighbouring unions of Blofield and Henstead also made hazardous the operation of the newly formed unions.(12)

In the establishment of the geography of the New Poor Law in the unions, priority went to convenience of formation and operation, rather than to the utilitarian principle of uniformity of size. Unions had to be sufficiently large to offset narrow interests in the administration of poor relief and to defray the cost of union officials, but sufficiently small to allow a detailed administra- tive control. In Norfolk the largest rural unions were more than twice the size of the smallest while urban unions were much smaller still (see Table 1, p. 56). However, the exclusion of a rural hin- terland from urban unions in Norfolk prevented the collision of eco- nomic interests on boards of guardians that was experienced in York- shire and Lancashire, where urban and rural areas were included in one union.(13) The assistant commissioners' attention to local interests, and the impediment presented by the existing incorpora- tions, meant that one-third of the Norfolk rural unions had no central market town, as the Poor Law Commissioners had planned, where guardians and parish overseers would have found it conven- ient to attend meetings. The union, or poor law, county of Norfolk also differed from the geographical county in that the Downham Mar- ket and Thetford Unions contained parts of Cambridgeshire and Suffolk while the Cambridgeshire Union of Wisbech included several Norfolk parishes. (The Wisbech Union was administered as part of the poor law county of Cambridgeshire and is therefore excluded from this study.) Poor law unions that straddled counties were the re- sult of a very casual attitude to county boundaries by the assistant commissioners. Belatedly, Parry met Kay in November 1835 'for the purpose of dove-tailing' the unions of Norfolk and Suffolk together. But Alfred Power's creation of unions in the Cambridgeshire Fens went on independently of parallel efforts inside Norfolk so that here there was considerable local dissatisfaction and some reshuff- ling of union boundaries.(14) There was far more time available to form the new poor law unions in East Anglia than there was to be in the North of England, where the commissioners started work only in 1837, and where they had to form the unions before the Registration Act became operational. As a result, Norfolk unions were smaller, more convenient units, and the attention paid to local interests meant that a stable structure was created, which survived intact until the changes were brought about by Workhouse Amalgamation Move- ment at the turn of the century. The movement aimed to rationalize the over-generous provision of accommodation for indoor paupers by amalgamating unions and reducing the number of expensive union work- houses that had been built in the early years of the New Poor Law. In Norfolk the Guiltcross Union was dissolved in 1902 and its par- ishes added to the Thetford, Wayland and Depwade Unions.

II   UNION WORKHOUSES

The Poor Law Commission published standard plans of workhouses in
their first reports in order to give some guidance to local guardians on the type of accommodation that was required in a new poor
law union workhouse. However, the four architects who designed
workhouse buildings in the county (within the different size and
financial specifications of the local boards of guardians) provided quite distinctive architectural styles and interpreted these in
varied building materials. The original plans of Norfolk workhouses have apparently not survived, with the single exception of
Thorold's elevations and section of Walsingham workhouse. These
are illustrated and show a front elevation, and behind this, at
right angles to the front, an elevation across the workhouse yards.
The illustrated section through the central octagon (with its dining room) is itself at right angles to the elevation across the
yards, and runs parallel to the front elevation. In Figures 3-5
are reproduced three of the plans, those of Depwade, Henstead and
Downham Market, drawn up by Norfolk County Council of the poor law
institutions that they took over at the end of the new poor law era
in 1930.

7   Docking Union Workhouse

    John Brown, the Norfolk county surveyor, designed several work-
houses in East Anglia between 1835 and 1839 which included those for
the Docking, Henstead, Blofield and Yarmouth Unions. They were
built in brick and slate in a style that used classical proportions
and detail and that commonly featured either a classical pediment
or late-classical, pedimented gables. The Docking Workhouse, with
its linear plan in which a three-storied central block was flanked

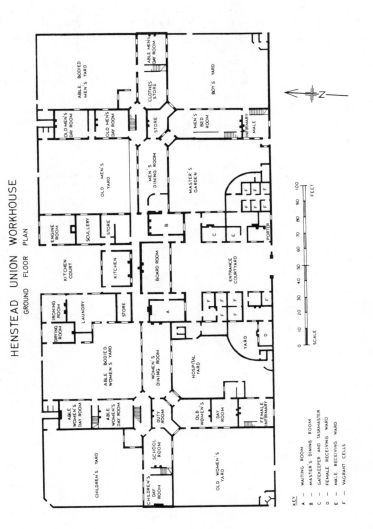

Figure 3   Henstead Union Workhouse

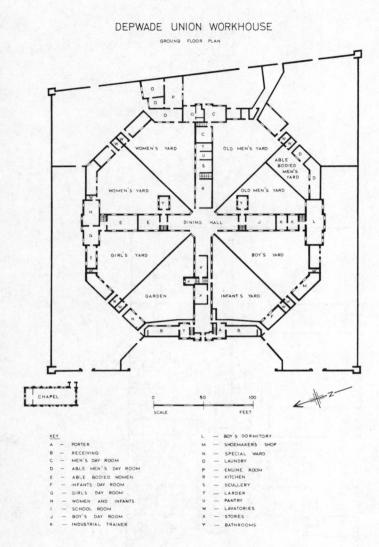

DEPWADE UNION WORKHOUSE
GROUND FLOOR PLAN

KEY

A — PORTER
B — RECEIVING
C — MEN'S DAY ROOM
D — ABLE MEN'S DAY ROOM
E — ABLE BODIED WOMEN
F — INFANTS DAY ROOM
G — GIRL'S DAY ROOM
H — WOMEN AND INFANTS
I — SCHOOL ROOM
J — BOY'S DAY ROOM
K — INDUSTRIAL TRAINER

L — BOY'S DORMITORY
M — SHOEMAKERS SHOP
N — SPECIAL WARD
O — LAUNDRY
P — ENGINE ROOM
R — KITCHEN
S — SCULLERY
T — LARDER
U — PANTRY
W — LAVATORIES
X — STORES
Y — BATHROOMS

Figure 4   Depwade Union Workhouse

8   Depwade Union Workhouse

9   Walsingham Union Workhouse

on each side by long two-storied wings each with a central pedimented gable, was the largest to be built at this time in Norfolk. The
Docking guardians had commissioned a building whose style was a
faint, but humble, imitation of Holkham Hall, the seat of the local
magnate. Henstead and Blofield Boards of Guardians also employed
Brown, although they economized by utilizing the same linear grid-
iron design by him.

    William Thorold used a similar octagonal plan for his brick work-
houses with pedimented gables in both the Depwade and the Walsingham
Unions in 1836-7. The Depwade building was on a more grandiose
scale (see Figure 4). In 1836 he designed the Thetford workhouse,
which was to be built in brick with a cruciform plan focusing on a
central, pedimented entrance block. At this time too he planned
the Wayland and Guiltcross buildings, although their early demolition has left their architectural style unrecorded. Thorold produced little work in East Anglia so that these workhouses were his
most substantial local achievement.

    While Brown and Thorold worked within the classical tradition,
their more famous rival, W.J. Donthorne (a founder member of the
Royal Institute of British Architects), designed in the Tudor style.
This style was only just becoming fashionable for institutional
buildings. His earliest workhouse building at Swaffham has been
knocked down, and the style of his next workhouse, in the Freebridge Lynn Union, was condemned by Pevsner. To the less critical
eye, this Gayton building appears pleasantly non-institutional with
its small size and its use of local carstone faced with lighter
brick. He followed this in 1836-7 with a larger workhouse in the
Elizabethan style at Downham Market, which again used the warm brown
carstone as the main building material and an open, linear grid-
iron plan. Donthorne was also involved in the second phase of
Norfolk workhouse construction in the middle of the century. He
used the same ideas in the Aylsham and Erpingham Unions in 1849 and
1851. Both were designed in the Tudor style although the Erpingham
workhouse was a cut-price version of the larger and more grandiose
Aylsham building. Aylsham was the most impressive union workhouse
in Norfolk, and was designed on an extended cruciform plan, with a
splendid entrance block, in which four polygonal towers framed a
lofty board room which was lighted by a huge transomed window. Donthorne's designs for his entrances and board rooms were increasingly
ambitious; the simplicity of Freebridge Lynn had evolved into twin
flanking turrets in Downham Market which were then elevated into
four dignified towers at Aylsham. The Aylsham workhouse is remi-
niscent of nearby Blickling Hall. This suggests that Donthorne's
architectural speciality, which was designing country houses, had
also informed his designs for workhouses. As such, his designs
formed the most obvious continuation of the pauper palace tradition
begun by the local incorporations in East Anglia during the previous
century.

    The later urban workhouses in Lynn and Norwich were designed by
Medland and Maberley. The former was an agreeable building in a
broadly Tudor style which was constructed in dark orange brick with
contrasting cream brick ornamentation. A massive new workhouse was
completed in Norwich in 1859 and demolished, without regret, exactly
a century later. Even in the 1860s its three-storey main building,

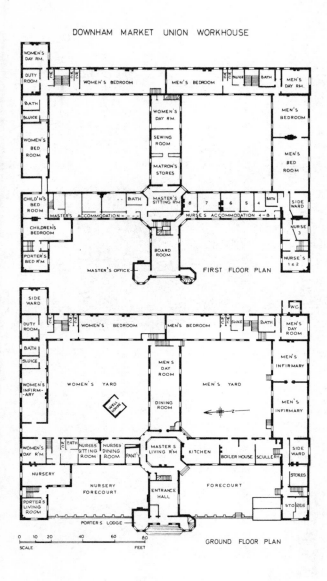

Figure 5   Downham Market Union Workhouse

10   Downham Market Union Workhouse, shortly before demolition, c. 1967

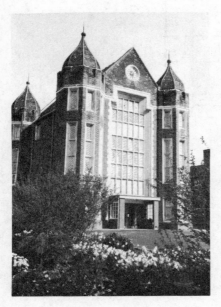

11   Aylsham Union Workhouse

built round a central space encased by railings and open to the
roof, was described as being 'very like that of a prison'.   It
was the only building in Norfolk to conform to the stereotype of
the Victorian workhouse. With this, workhouse building in Norfolk
virtually ceased except for the erection of chapels or infirmaries
in some unions and the adaptation in others of the existing fabric
to provide for growing social needs such as sick wards.(15)

12   King's Lynn Union Workhouse

   Union workhouses in Norfolk were substantial, even impressive,
buildings, yet their isolated sites indicated the ambivalence with
which nineteenth-century society viewed them. They were placed on
the very edge of a market town in the few cases where this was the
focal point of the union, or in many instances they were built deep
in the countryside. Norfolk boards of guardians found some difficulty in acquiring suitable sites because nobody wanted a workhouse
on their doorstep. In the Walsingham Union, Sir Charles Chad had
incurred unpopularity because, as an absentee landowner, he had
not always borne his fair share of responsibility in employing the
poor, and the local farmers acting as guardians welcomed the opportunity to even the score by siting the union workhouse near the
gates of his park.   Chad thought a workhouse next to his fine seat,
the Elizabethan Thursford Hall, 'would be greatly prejudicial to my
interest'. He managed to enlist the good offices of Dr Kay, the
assistant poor law commissioner, who was anxious not to have the
Norfolk gentry antagonistic to the New Poor Law. Kay got the local
magnate, Coke of Holkham, to use his influence with the Walsingham
guardians, who grudgingly accepted Chad's offer of land in Great
Snoring as an alternative site for the union workhouse.(16)   In the
Aylsham Union the guardians belatedly decided to build a new work-

house, chose their site and had erected the building in 1849, when
they were astonished to find that the local miller demanded that
they should pull down their fine building. Mr Soames owned a wind-
mill next to the site and complained that the new buildings stopped
the breeze from turning the sails of his mill. But he failed to
take his case to law as he had threatened to do, and having less
influence than Chad was unable to get any redress from the administrators of the Poor Law.(17)

    The scale of the public building programme that the erection
of 12 union workhouses from 1835 to 1839 involved was a massive one
which cost over £75,000 (see Table 2). The most ambitious workhouses were those in the Docking and Depwade Unions, which each
cost over £9,000, while even the most modest union building came to
over £4,000. Not surprisingly, therefore, there was some resistance
to such expenditure which would burden the local ratepayers with the
repayment of loans for years to come. In south Norfolk, where small
farmers on heavy clays were feeling the economic pinch, the farmer-
guardians in the Guiltcross and Wayland Unions dragged their feet
on the workhouse question and Parry, the assistant commissioner, became worried as the Poor Law Commission had no legal powers to compel them to build a new workhouse. 'The farmers are too stupid to
see anything but the immediate expense', he irritiably remarked.(18)
In the 10 unions and incorporations that did not build a new workhouse in the opening years of the New Poor Law, only the five areas
that could utilize one of the substantial houses of industry built
in the eighteenth century by the local incorporations were free
from central pressure to build an entirely new workhouse. It took
25 years of continuous persuation by the central poor law board to
persuade four of the remaining unions to build new accommodation at
a cost of £62,000. Only the St Faith's Union stood firm and continued to use a rat-infested, overcrowded and inadequate building
at Horsham St Faith's which had earlier served only half as many
parishes in its role as a Gilbert Union poor house. The administrative inconvenience of utilizing small Gilbert poor houses at
Buxton and Oulton forced the Aylsham guardians to build a single
central workhouse at Aylsham in 1849, while the neighbouring Erpingham Union found parallel difficulties in using the Sheringham
and Gimingham poor houses, and erected a new union building at West
Beckham in 1851. In the urban areas of Lynn and Norwich party
strife meant that neither faction when ascendant in the guardians'
board room dared to incur the odium of building a new 'Bastille'.
It was not until the 1850s, when increasing pauperism forced the
issue in Norwich and the old Lynn workhouse collapsed in a spectacular manner, that the issue was decided.

    In King's Lynn the guardians had continued to use the St James
Workhouse which was centred on a medieval building that had earlier
been a chapel at ease to St Margaret's Church. Reports of subsi-
dence in the 80 feet high central tower had been received since 1824
but had not been acted upon by the local poor law administrators.
In the summer of 1854 the buttresses began to come away from the
walls, and on the morning of Sunday, 20 August 1854, mortar began
to fall, and the tower clock stopped at a quarter to eleven. The
workhouse master fetched the local clockmaker, William Andrews, who
according to Lynn tradition started his repair work in the customary

TABLE 2   Norfolk workhouse accommodation after 1834

Union or incorporation	Existing workhouses			New workhouses		
	(I) Utilized at	(II) For the period to	(III) Which gave accommodation in 1842 for	(I) Built at	(II) At a cost of £	(III) Which gave accommodation for
Aylsham	Buxton	1849	200	Aylsham	12,000	600
Blofield	Oulton	1849	85	Lingwood	5,810	250
Depwade				Pulham St Mary	9,700	400
Docking				Docking	9,125	450
Downham				Downham	5,360	250
Erpingham	Sheringham	1848	300	W. Beckham	8,200	500
*Flegg	Gimingham	1851	100			
	Rollesby		270			
*Forehoe	Wicklewood		450			
Freebridge Lynn				Gayton	5,146	150
Guiltcross				Kenninghall	4,805	300
Henstead				Swainsthorpe	6,200	250
King's Lynn	St James	1856	260	Exton Rd	13,100	420
Loddon and Clavering	Heckingham		600			
Mitford and Launditch	Gressenhall		477			
*Norwich	St Andrews	1859	-	Heigham	29,000	1,200
St Faith's	St Faith's		162			
Swaffham				Swaffham	7,125	405
Thetford				Thetford	5,375	300
*Tunstead and Happing	Smallburgh		800**			
Walsingham				Gt Snoring	5,900	250
Wayland				Rockland	4,128	250
Yarmouth				Yarmouth	7,100	350

* Incorporation under local act of Parliament

** A misprint. A more likely figure is 300

Sources: Annual 'Reports' of PLC and PLB; Report of J. Walsham, 16 Sept. 1842, MH 32/79, PRO.

13   St James Workhouse, King's Lynn. Ink and wash by E. Edwards, c.1820

manner, by aiming a stout kick at the clock mechanism. At this
point the tower collapsed, killing Andrews and John Cana, one of the
inmates, and burying for several hours a second pauper named Wil-
liams together with Thurlow Nelson, the master of the workhouse.
This was a surprisingly low injury rate as there were 160 paupers
on the workhouse books at the time. The guardians were fortunate
in being absolved from blame at the inquest. As the tower had
knocked a 70 feet gap in the surrounding buildings the workhouse was
unsafe for use. Unsuccessful attempts were made to send paupers to
nearby union workhouses and so temporary accommodation in the town
had to be used until the new workhouse in Exton's Road was completed
in 1856.(19)

     Union workhouses were novel buildings, and in the first years
after their opening there were frequent minor building adjustments
to alter doors and windows and to reallocate the use of rooms, in
order to make more efficient the scheme of workhouse classification under which different categories of paupers were separated
from each other. This suggests that architects and guardians were
fumbling to articulate the philosophy of the New Poor Law in the
concrete terms of the workhouse building. Modifications to existing houses of industry, in order to convert their structure into
one in which the workhouse regulations of the Poor Law Commissioners
could be implemented, also cost the ratepayers money. In the Smallburgh and Rollesby houses these alterations were minor and at
Rollesby they included dividing walls in the yards and a screen in
the dining room to separate men from women. But at Gressenhall the
specifications to the builder were so vague that the cost exceeded

the estimate of £1,500 by a further £3,300. Heckingham House was
damaged by fire in April 1836 (when paupers protested at the regulations of the Poor Law Commissioners being imposed upon them), and
the repairs cost £3,000.(20) These alterations, extensions and
modifications to workhouses cost £25,000 in the first 35 years of
the New Poor Law's operation. Expenditure in Norfolk on workhouse-
building and on various alterations during the mid-nineteenth century came to the colossal total of £163,000.

Underlying the obvious differences in individual style and plan
of these Norfolk workhouses was an overall similarity in function,
since each building was designed to give separate accommodation for
different categories of pauper. These were old or infirm men or
women, able-bodied men or women aged 16 years of age or over, boys
or girls aged 2 to 15 and infants.(21) Each workhouse had separate
airing or exercise yards, with adjacent day rooms and on occasion
dining rooms, and above them sleeping quarters for each class of
pauper. This necessarily imposed a geometric pattern of divisions
upon the building. The workhouse was split down the middle into
male and female quarters and with the women's accommodation placed
near the children's nursery and schoolroom.· At the front of the
building were the porter's room; the receiving wards (where new
arrivals were bathed, had their hair cropped, and where they were
dressed in workhouse uniform); and (built later) the vagrant cells
for the tramps and casual poor. Placed near the outer perimeter
were the bakehouse, laundry, storehouses, workshops and earth
closets. Water closets and fixed baths were provided later on,
separate buildings being often added for this purpose. Some workhouse buildings focused on a central octagon. This provided strategic accommodation for the master of the workhouse, which gave him
a clear view over the exercise yards and quick access to most parts
of the building. Alternatively, the communal dining room (which
might double as the chapel in the early years) occupied this central
position, because it was a room to which paupers of all categories
needed access from their own quarters. Behind this was the kitchen
wing and, in front, the entrance hall and board room. The latter
was part of the building that was used the least but ironically it
formed its most ostentatious and imposing architectural feature. It
was isolated from the rest of the workhouse, having its own entrance
or staircase and a lofty window looking outwards over the countryside.

In building and equipping a union workhouse the guardians were
poised uncomfortably between economy (to defend the ratepayers'
interests) and expenditure (to provide adequate maintenance for
the poor). They economised — by choosing a site with good brick
earth from which to make their basic building material; by sharing
architects plans with other unions; and by getting much of the furniture and fittings made by local joiners. The furniture provided
for the workhouses was functional; long forms, stools and tables
together with a stove for heating were placed in day rooms, dining
hall and schoolroom; while the sleeping quarters had iron bedsteads and straw mattresses. But expenditure mushroomed beyond
their initial estimates in spite of these economies because of un-
foreseen problems of design, which led to alterations, delayed
schedules and increased labour costs. A minor additional cost was

PARTICULARS OF EXPENCES

INCURRED IN ERECTING

A UNION WORKHOUSE,

CAPABLE OF RECEIVING 250 PAUPERS,

AT GREAT SNORING,

IN THE WALSINGHAM UNION,

COMPRISING 50 PARISHES.

	£.	s.	d.
Paid Purchase Money for Land - - -	151	5	0
Conveyance of Land - - -	29	1	8
W. Thorold, Architect - - -	309	7	6
Allen Paul, for Watching - - -	9	2	0
Clerk of Works, Wages - - -	106	19	6
Advertisements - - -	6	2	6
Making Drains and Labour - - -	52	12	3
Mr. Bunn, Amount of his Contract - - £4330 0 0			
Ditto, Extra Work and Gravel - - - 677 7 2			
	5207	7	2
Hot Water Apparatus - -	174	4	0 -
Joiner's Fixtures, viz.:—Tables, Shelving, Cup-			
boards, Water Closets, &c. - -	194	14	5
Iron Bedsteads, W. Horsley, as per Contract	161	9	0
Playford, Tent and other Bedsteads - -	26	1	6
Ditto, Chairs and other Furniture - -	59	12	0
Fane for Cupola - - - -	4	14	6
Varley, for Turret Clock - - -	53	0	0
Spice, Ironmongery, Tin, and Copper Ware	124	8	3
Earthenware - - - -	10	0	4
Thermometers - - - -	0	15	0
Total Cost - -	£6680	16	7

Amount Borrowed by the Board on Security of the Poor Rates of the respective Parishes in the Union, of the Exchequer Loan Commissioners, to be paid by Twenty Instalments of £300 a Year, with Interest at £4 per Cent.

In the First Instance the Loan was Advanced on Condition to be Paid in Ten Payments of £600 a year, with Interest at £5 per Cent.: but the Board Memoralised the Exchequer Loan Commissioners, and they Reduced the Interest and Extended the Time for Payment as above stated.

MATCHETT, STEVENSON, AND MATCHETT, PRINTERS, MARKET-PLACE NORWICH.

Figure 6   Expenses of Erecting Walsingham Union Workhouse

that of paid watchmen who guarded the half-finished workhouses against the guerilla attacks of the poor. For example, the initial estimate for the Walsingham workhouse was £5,900, but the actual cost was £6,680 (see Figure 6). This pressurized the guardians into re-negotiating their loan from the Exchequer Loan Commissioners (which was made on the security of the poor rates) from a 10-year repayment scheme at 5 per cent interest to one of 20 years at 4 per cent. Pressure on boards of guardians to reduce the short-term financial burden on ratepayers was intense. This was because, under the 1834 act, union expenditure (of which the workhouse loan was an important constituent) was shared among the parishes in the union on the basis of the relative levels of expenditure on poor relief in each parish. Those villages with most poor and the least ability to pay were therefore charged the most for the union building. In the Docking Union, for example, Anmer paid only 10s 9d a year towards the annual loan charge of £455 while Docking paid £48 2s 8d. (22)

III   THE ADMINISTRATORS

Although the Poor Law Commission had been remarkably successful in establishing unions and workhouses in Norfolk, it found that the quality of poor law administration in the county was determined not so much by the standards set by its own centralized administration, as by the practices of elected guardians and their salaried officials in each local union. The central board possessed a few coercive powers. These were the sanction of enforcing an order against a recalcitrant board of guardians in the courts (which was a threat never implemented against a Norfolk union), and the ability of the auditor to disallow expenditure incurred illegally by the guardians (which proved to be effective only as a means of curbing the more blatant acts of local independence). These weak powers of compulsion in enforcing centrally devised regulations meant that it was the inspectorate that had the crucial role in acting as the central board's persuasive agent with local administrators. This was important in getting unions formed, workhouses built and reformed relief policies adopted. Centralization in the relief administration after 1834 was a convenient fiction to which public lip service was paid by the inspectors, while they acknowledged privately that effective power lay in the localities.(23) The degree to which the illusion coincided with reality depended to a large extent on the personalities of the individual inspectors. They had minimal powers to keep local guardians on a steady course, and relied on inspiring in Norfolk boards of guardians a professional adherence to abstract principles which was underpinned by personal respect for the inspectors themselves. Individual inspectors varied in their ability to analyse this situation and to act upon it.

Sir (William) Edward Parry was a renowned Arctic navigator and explorer whose talents Whig patronage sadly misplaced in making him in 1835 the first Norfolk poor law inspector. His bluff, authoritarian approach and appeals for support to a central authority, which did not possess the necessary power to help him, soon created intractable difficulties, and his resignation in the spring of 1836

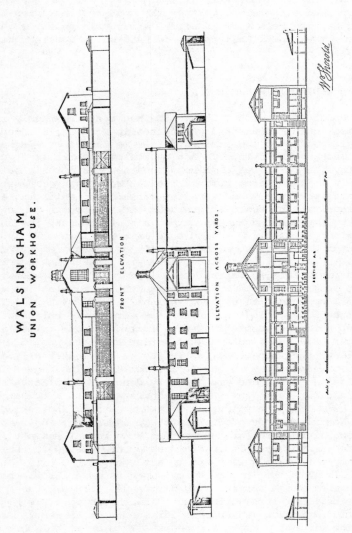

Figure 7   Elevations and Section of Walsingham Union Workhouse

on the grounds of ill health came opportunely. In contrast, his
successor Dr James Kay, possessed the necessary drive, eloquence
and political agility to implement the New Poor Law in the county
with a surprising facility and speed between 1836 and 1838. This
was because he possessed considerable powers as an administrator,
and also because his doctrinaire attachment to the principles of
the New Poor Law was tempered by an intelligent pragmatism in its
practical implementation. His ambitious self-confidence meant that
he acted on his own initiative; often he merely informed the Poor
Law Commissioners of his current strategies rather than acting as
their subordinate agent. Indeed, his ideas on migration, emigration and education helped to shape the policies of the central
board itself. Both George Clive (1838-9) and Edward Twisleton
(1838-42) helped to consolidate the framework of Kay's administration. (Twisleton also found the time to write an excellent analysis on the condition of the East Anglian poor in 1842, which was
published in a volume of local reports which accompanied Edwin
Chadwick's 'Report of an Inquiry into the Sanitary Condition of the
Labouring Population of Great Britain'.)

Twisleton's experienced successor, Sir John Walsham, was a very
steady, conscientious administrator who kept his district one of
the more efficient areas in the country. A declining number of
inspectors in the 1840s meant that the size of the poor law district under a single inspector increased. As a result Walsham
could visit a Norfolk union only once or twice a year compared
with the half-dozen visits of Dr Kay earlier. Walsham's experience, derived from the length of service in the eastern region
from 1842 to his retirement in 1868, earned him the respect of local
guardians. It is arguable that because of this respect he gained a
greater adherence to central policies in Norfolk unions than might
otherwise have occurred. He continued the tradition of involving
himself closely in pauper education and also had an enthusiasm for
workhouse ventilation for which he designed his own scheme which
was sufficiently efficient to be adopted by many unions.

An interest in the health of workhouse inmates was continued by
H.B. Farnall, who was exiled to inspect the unions of the eastern
counties in 1870. This was a punishment for his over-involvement
in the Association for the Improvement of Workhouse Infirmaries when
he was poor law inspector for the more important metropolitan area.
But increasingly in the second half of the century the inspectorate
were administrative beasts of burden; their role reduced to an end-
less form-filling which stultified any individual initiative or
interest. However, the eastern counties were fortunate in the 1880s
and 1890s in having Messrs Lockwood and Preston-Thomas among their
inspectors. They were perceptive about the subordinate relationship of the local poor law administration to the regional economy
and their accurate analyses made an interesting contrast to the
earlier over-optimistic reports of Dr Kay. He had believed erro-
neously that the Poor Law would have the power to change socioeconomic conditions in the countryside.(24)

Walsham commented that 'it has been my practice ... to work, as
far as possible, through the boards of guardians', and that the
guardians had the responsibility for the detailed management of the
workhouse and of the relief and account books.(25) How efficiently

and conscientiously did the Norfolk boards of guardians fulfil this trust? During the early years of the New Poor Law the full board of guardians met once a week (or in harvest time once a fortnight) to see to the routine business of the union. Later, a meeting once a fortnight proved to be sufficient. Their business included the appointment and oversight of officials, acceptance of tenders, correspondence with other unions on questions of settlement and removal, approval of accounts and interviews of individual applicants for relief in the presence of the relieving officer. Meetings took up the greater part of the day, except at the very beginning of the union when there were extensive reviews of relief cases in every village, and business took up several days in the week. In the first year of operation attendances by elected guardians at Norfolk weekly board meetings averaged one out of every two meetings, while that of justices of the peace who could attend as ex officio guardians were less good and averaged one in three boards. This experience contrasted with that in Northamptonshire, where the interest of the landed magnates and gentry in the New Poor Law was exceptionally strong and resulted in the ex officios attending half the board meetings, a record that was exactly comparable with that of the elected guardians. However, this was in the first year of the New Poor Law and it is possible that interest declined there later on. Certainly in Norfolk, as in Durham, the active involvement of the landed gentry, acting as ex officio guardians, decreased once the initial important decisions had been made.(26)

The stultifying boredom of routine business soon decimated attendances and particularly those of landed gentlemen who were ex officio members of the board. The least motivated boards like Freebridge Lynn and St Faith's sometimes failed even to achieve a quorum of guardians. (To encourage attendances the latter voted themselves refreshments during the meeting at the ratepayers' expense, but this failed to pass the strict eye of the auditor.) By 1859 seven guardians were present at an average board meeting in the Docking or Swaffham Unions, out of a possible attendance of 53 or 41 guardians respectively. In the neighbouring Mitford and Launditch Union, where there was an unusually good attendance of ex officios, the typical board meeting had a higher attendance of 20 out of 64 guardians. The management of the union therefore devolved on to a handful of interested regulars, who were frequently farmers, together with a few clergymen and magistrates. Often these were the guardians who represented close parishes where an unusually careful oversight of the affairs of the poor was maintained in order to keep down the poor rates. The office of guardian was both onerous and unpopular and there was little competition for the job. Indeed, in small parishes few people would possess the electoral qualification to stand as a guardian, since in Norfolk unions this comprised a rental or a property valued at £35 or £40 per annum. Elections were rare in rural Norfolk because the principal owners and occupiers agreed among themselves who should stand each time. Even if elections occurred this small group of influential people could generally determine the electoral result, since guardians under the New Poor Law were elected by plural voting, which was based on the ownership and occupation of property. If an efficient defender of the ratepayers' pockets was found, then he continued as parish

guardian for many years and in the Erpingham Union service of 30 or
40 years was not uncommon.(27)

The character of individual unions varied a great deal; from
the stringent efficiency of Aylsham and the humane good sense of
Mitford and Launditch, Wayland or Guiltcross to the inefficiency
and financial economies of Erpingham or St Faith's. Certain boards
pioneered new ideas and stimulated other boards into adopting them,
which was a practice encouraged by the collaborating habit of neighbouring Norfolk unions. This practice of formal and informal col-
laboration helps to explain why administrative practices that had
originated in the local incorporations under the Old Poor Law were
often adopted by the newly formed unions under the New Poor Law.
As a result of this the regionalization of poor law practice, which
had earlier been so obvious, was gradually eroded after 1834, although the traditions begun by the pauper palaces in the old poor
law incorporations of east Norfolk were more generally influential
in the new poor law unions in that region than in those situated
in the west of the county. The guardians in Norfolk unions were
at first less bureaucratically organized than the local incorporations had been before 1834,, but as time went on the practice of
forming small committees to deal with specialized items of business
increased in the new unions. At the start of the New Poor Law a
typical union would have a workhouse visiting committee and a finance committee, and to these were later added committees for nuisances, rate assessment and school attendance. In some unions additional committees were formed to deal with the subjects of education, emigration, tenders, bastardy or pauper employment. In 1856
the Aylsham guardians were the first in Norfolk to adopt the enlightened practice that was beginning to spread nationally at that
time when they allowed a 'Ladies Committee' to visit women in the
workhouse. Other unions in the county later imitated this practice,
although it was not until 1893 that the Local Government Board
sanctioned it.

The visiting committee was responsible for regular supervision of
the workhouse and its management by officials. In the early days
of the New Poor Law guardians took such duties seriously. One of
the earliest reports of the Docking Visiting Committee indicated
that they had examined the new workhouse fittings with minute parti-
cularity and that this had led them to condemn a stove as unsafe and
a laundry pulley as inefficient. Inquiring of each inmate whether
they were comfortable, they found that the men wanted more potatoes
with their meals and that the women whose infant children slept with
them needed extra blankets. They discovered small boys to be wear-
ing their own clothes, 'there not being any workhouse clothes small
enough'. They were intrepid enough to sample the soup that was
simmering in the kitchen and found it 'tasted very good'. By the
1840s this kind of interest was diminishing, and an inspector criticized several unions for inadequate workhouse-visiting. However,
the guardians were sufficiently alert to uncover at least some of
the misdemeanours of their officials. Two examples from 1842 will
suggest the variety of abuses which occurred. The Loddon and Clavering guardians caught up belatedly with their workhouse master
who had substituted cheap broth for cheese in the paupers' dietary
for the previous 12 months, and not content with such peculation had

also kept bees and run greenhouses stocked with plants as commercial
sidelines. He was dismissed. But the master of the Gimingham workhouse was merely reprimanded by the Erpingham guardians for his continued pimping activities. An aggrieved woman inmate complained to
the visiting committee, 'how hard she thought it that she should be
separated from her husband and that another woman named Hazell of
Hempstead should be shut up with him'. This workhouse master was
found to have not only condoned the breaking of the workhouse rules
of classification that separated men from women on several occasions,
but to have made the workhouse a convenient road to adultery!(28)

The central board was often an inadequate bulwark against the
independent-minded policies of local guardians, and the latter
provided a haphazard check on the activities of their salaried officials. The number and cost of officers in Norfolk Unions steadily increased; the 323 officers of 1846 had risen to 457 by 1851,
and the salary bill had also increased from £14,793 to £18,107.(29)
Each union had a clerk to deal with the books and legal proceedings,
a master and matron to superintend the workhouse, a schoolmaster
and schoolmistress to teach the children, a porter to control entry
to the workhouse, a chaplain to preach a Sunday sermon and catechize
the children, one or two relieving officers to distribute outdoor
relief, several medical officers to care for the needs of the sick
poor and, later in the century, nurses to care for pauper patients
in the workhouse. Their multifarious duties, which were laid down
by the central board, meant long hours of work for which local
guardians paid ungenerous salaries. In spite of this, hundreds of
officials in Norfolk gave years of devoted service. Breaches of
trust did occur, but in the majority of cases these involved financial embezzlement or material peculation (which harmed the ratepayers), rather than harshness or cruelty to the paupers. However,
there was some criticism of the relieving officers' and medical
officers' treatment of the poor and this is included as part of a
discussion on the relief given to different types of pauper in
Chapters 8 and 9.

The misdemeanours of Norfolk poor law officials were regarded
with a sterner eye by the central poor law administration than by
local guardians. Norfolk guardians tended to defend their officers
against external criticism and often to retain them against the
wishes of the administrators in London. To some extent this was because guardians were aware that if they sacked an officer they were
unlikely to get a better replacement at the meagre salary that they
offered. A more influential reason was that local administrators
were increasingly confident that they could run the Norfolk Poor
Law in their own way and with little external interference. Beneath
the apparent orthodoxy of poor law management (circumscribed by the
returns of paupers relieved and money spent on particular purposes
which Norfolk unions provided punctiliously for London), there was
considerable room for unorthodox manoeuvre. A good example of this
hidden subversion came in the Norfolk outdoor relief system of the
mid-nineteenth century, with its use of tickets and relief ostensibly in aid of sickness, which is analysed later in Chapter 6.
This kind of activity fell outside the coercive authority of the
central board since auditors could not disallow expenditure that was
apparently legal. But it fell within the preventive responsibility

of the inspectors. 'Without poor law inspectors the machinery of
the poor law department would scarcely work at all', wrote one
inspector of Norfolk unions.(30)   However, the twice-yearly visit
of the inspector to a local union was a perfunctory check on local
initiative, and was sufficient only to keep the appearance of Norfolk practice in a broad conformity with London's policies. Cum-
bersome bureaucratic machinery permitted Norfolk guardians substantial autonomy.

Independence in the local administration of poor relief at first
produced a creative response to the problem of Norfolk pauperism.
But by the 1870s the huge challenge posed by the able-bodied pauperism had passed and poor law administration in the county became
a matter of routine. Local resistance to change was suggested by
the few Poor Law Conferences that were held in East Anglia at this
time when compared with those of other regions. Reports of those
held in Norwich in 1875, and in Ipswich in 1883, indicated a complacent attitude by local guardians towards the prevalent system of
outdoor allowances, and a conservative approach to new ideas, such
as the relief of pauper children by boarding out or through the establishment of cottage homes.(31)   In 1894 a reform of the Poor Law
offered the prospect of ending the old type of relief administration. In that year the monetary qualification for election to the
office of guardian was removed, the franchise lowered, and the ex
officio membership of justices of the peace on rural boards of
guardians was ended. But in Norfolk the 'new' boards of guardians
who were elected after 1894 were remarkably similar in social composition and attitude to the 'old' boards, although there was an
increase in the number of women guardians. The experience of the
Erpingham Union was atypical in having several working-class representatives elected to the board of guardians after 1894, who strove
to raise the standards of relief to the poor even if this emptied
the ratepayers' pockets. In most areas of rural Norfolk the agricultural labourer could not afford to give up his wages in order to
act as a poor law guardian, even if he had wished to hold the office. There had been little progress made in this direction by the
time that major reform of the administration of poor relief was considered by the Royal Commission on the Poor Laws of 1905-9.(32)

The evidence given by Norfolk guardians and poor law officials
to this Royal Commission indicated that local poor law administration was continuing along well-worn channels. Outdoor relief was
given whenever possible. The workhouse was the almost exclusive
preserve of the aged and infirm (who were unable to look after
themselves any longer), the feeble-minded, a few 'bad' characters
and some unmarried mothers.(33)

> In truth, to whatever extent it may be brightened and rendered
> habitable, one cannot pretend that a workhouse is a cheerful
> place. The poor girls, with their illegitimate children creep-
> ing, dirty-faced, across the floor of brick; the old, old
> women lying in bed too feeble to move, or crouching round the
> fire in their mob-caps...; others vacuous and smiling — 'a
> little gone', the master whispers; others quite childish and
> full of complaints.... The old men, too, their hands knobbed
> and knotted with decades of hard work, their backs bent, their
> faces almost grotesque.... It is not the place that is so

82 Chapter 4

melancholy, it is this poignant example of the sad end of life
and all its toilings.
This was a description of Heckingham Workhouse in 1898 by the writer H. Rider Haggard, who had himself previously served as a poor
law guardian in this Loddon and Clavering Union.(34) Heckingham had
been erected 130 years before this as the first pauper palace
in Norfolk. Like Crabbe in his earlier picture of the East Anglian
pauper palaces, Rider Haggard emphasized the pathos of the inmates
in a poor law institution. But sympathy for the indoor pauper
needs to be tempered by a recognition of the generally humane administration of the Norfolk workhouse, and balanced too by an appreciation of the cost of this relief to local ratepayers.

CHAPTER 5
POOR RATES AND SETTLEMENT

For more than two centuries a civil war was waged between the separate parishes of England and Wales. The military commanders were
the owners and occupiers of land, their adjutants were the parish
overseers, and the casualties in the front line were the labouring
poor. Strategy was dictated by the complex provisions of the laws
of settlement and rating, and was directed to minimizing the poor
rates that financed poor relief through reducing the number of poor
people in the parish. The victors in this long drawn-out contest
were the small, 'close' parishes and the losers were the heavily
populated, 'open' parishes. In the open parishes, particularly, a
second struggle took place inside the parish, in which hand-to-
hand combat was joined between the inhabitants over the relative
share of the high poor rates each should pay. Paradoxically, poor
rates that had been instituted for the relief of the poor fell most
heavily on the impoverished, and the provisions of the Poor Law
Amendment Act of 1834 tended to worsen this situation where poverty
rather than property was taxed. In spite of the vast sums involved
in the collection of the poor rates, this unfair and precarious
system was not effectively reformed until the 1860s, when legislation established a systematic method of assessing property and extended the geographical unit of taxation from the parish to the
poor law union. The delay in reform had serious consequences, since,
although high poor rates had been an important cause of the reform
of 1834, the financial weakness and injustice of the rating system
resulted in subversion of the New Poor Law.

Conflicts between Norfolk parishes and ratepayers, in which each
attempted to shift their rating burden to others, were the product
of heavy poor law expenditures in the county.(1) In 1775-6 expenditure on the Norfolk poor had amounted to £64,171, and this had
risen to an average annual expenditure of £94,670 in the years
1782-5, and to £175,764 by 1802-3. During the nineteenth century,
Norfolk had both a higher expenditure on the relief of the poor per
head of county population, and a higher proportion of paupers to
population, than the national average (see Table 3a and b). The
immense burden of local pauperism reflected the difficulties of a
regional economy hard hit by the decline of its major industry, the
Norwich textiles industry, and suffering from periodic agricultural

TABLE 3a   The per capita expenditure on poor relief in Norfolk
and England and Wales, 1803-47

Year ending at Easter * or Lady Day	Norfolk		England and Wales	
	s	d	s	d
1803 *	12	5	8	11
1813 *	20	0	12	8
1818	20	0	13	3
1821	15	7	11	7
1824	14	5	9	2
1831	15	4	10	0
1832	16	3	10	2
1833	16	3	9	9
1834	15	9	9	1
1835	14	0	7	7
1836	11	10	6	5
1837	9	1	5	5
1838	8	7	5	5
1839	9	10	5	9
1840	9	3	5	11
1841	8	10	6	0
1842	8	11	6	2
1843	9	2	6	5
1844	9	2	6	1
1845	9	7	6	1
1846	10	0	5	11
1847	10	0	6	3

Sources: Figures for Norfolk taken from R. Taylor, The Development
of the Old Poor Law in Norfolk, 1795-1834 (University of East
Anglia MA thesis, 1970), 156, for the years 1803-32, and from 'Poor
Rate Returns' and the Annual 'Reports' of the Poor Law Commissioners
thereafter. Figures for England and Wales from Webb, 'Poor Law History', Pt 2, 1038-9.

TABLE 3b   The percentage of pauperism on population in Norfolk and
England and Wales, 1851-1901

Year ending Lady Day	Norfolk	England and Wales
1851*	6.3	5.3
1861	7.0	4.4
1871	6.7	4.6
1881	4.4	3.0
1891	4.5	2.6
1901	4.0	2.4

*   Until 1857, poor law returns referred to the geographical county
and after 1857 to the (poor law) union county of Norfolk.

Sources: Figures for Norfolk based on population figures in 'Census
Enumeration' and poor rate returns in Annual Reports of Poor Law
Board and Local Government Board. Figures for England and Wales
taken from Webb, 'Poor Law History', Pt 2, 1041-2.

depression. This situation suggests a precariousness in poor law
finances in that increased liabilities in the form of relief to
the unemployed were matched by the decreased assets of those who
paid the poor rate. However, poor law finances were far more secure in a rural area than in the urban, industrian North of England.
In Norfolk and surrounding rural counties four-fifths of the poor
rate was levied on land, and so until the end of the period there
was a fairer correspondence between rated property and the wealth
of the area. In contrast, in the North poor rates did not adequately tax industry, the real wealth of the area, and poor relief rested on a fragile financial basis. This also produced bitter conflicts on northern boards of guardians over the light rating of
industrial, compared with agrarian, property because the poor law
unions there included both rural and urban areas. In Norfolk urban-
rural hostilities were rare (except for a brief period after 1846),
because the large towns formed their own separate poor law unions
from which the rural hinterland was excluded. Poor rates and relief
expenditures in both agricultural and non-agricultural areas reflected the state of the harvest, and years of poor harvest with
high wheat prices resulted in high relief expenditure. In the early
nineteenth century particularly the fluctuations in poor rates and
relief expenditure in both England and Wales and Norfolk coincided
with those of wheat prices (see Figures 8 and 9). While all poor
law statistics were defective to a greater or lesser degree, those
that involved sums of money, as in figures of poor rates or relief
expenditures, were a great deal more reliable than those dealing
with numbers of paupers. The marked rise in the amount levied in
poor rates as the century progressed was less the result of rising
expenditure on poor relief than of the increased number of extra-
neous charges placed on the poor rate. These charges, which varied
to some extent between local governmental areas, might include expenses of public vaccination, population registration, police, asylums, highways, elementary education and miscellaneous minor
services.(2)

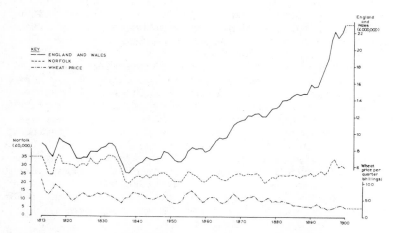

Figure 8   Poor rates levied in Norfolk and England and Wales,
1813-1900

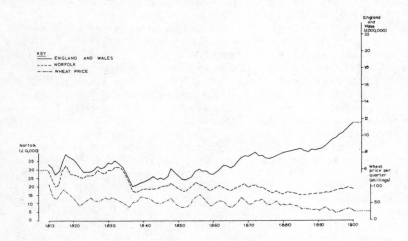

Figure 9   Poor relief expenditure in Norfolk and England and Wales, 1813-1900

I   RATING POVERTY TO RELIEVE PAUPERISM

Comparatively high poor rates in Norfolk led to attempts to rate even the impoverished for the relief of the poor. A poverty-stricken man wrote in great distress to the Poor Law Commissioners in 1837 to protest against the assessment of the poor to the poor rate in the Norfolk town of Wymondham: 'the poor can never pay it. I am sure I cannot and if it is to be enforced by distraining the few things that ... we have, which with many are but very few indeed, what is to become of us?' He raised the very real social problem of the extent to which the independent poor could be taxed to support those dependent on poor relief without impoverishing them so much that they became paupers themselves. This situation had arisen because by the nineteenth century the parish poor rate had departed from the Elizabethan practice of taxing all the inhabitants of a parish according to their general ability to pay. Instead, the poor rate was levied only on the occupiers and was based on the annual value of their immovable property in the form of lands and buildings. The advisability, or indeed the practicability, of assessing small houses or tenements to the poor rates was a perpetual bone of contention during the nineteenth century. In fact, the poor could by an act of 1814 be excused from paying poor rates if their inability to pay was proved before two justices. However, it was common practice in the county before 1834 for parish overseers themselves to exempt the poor of the parish. Norfolk justices, like those in Dorset, did not take their legal duty of annually auditing the poor books very seriously before the 1830s. If they did trouble to look at the parochial accounts they merely rubber-stamped the overseer's excusals.(3)

The Poor Law Amendment Act of 1834 brought both a stricter audit and a local magistracy made hostile to the Poor Law by the act's reduction of their powers over the administration of poor relief. The justices exercised their remaining powers with greater rigour and at first reduced the number of poor excused from payment of the poor rate. In the Henstead Union, where exemption of the poor had been virtually automatic, the parish overseers now had to prove an individual's destitution to the justices, and this selective excusal caused envy and discontent among the poorer inhabitants of the area. A still harsher attitude was taken by the neighbouring Blofield magistracy, who expected all except paupers to pay poor rates. The system was exposed to ridicule by the magistrates in the Harling division of the Guiltcross Union who, as an expression of their hostility to the reformed poor law, expected even paupers to pay the poor rates to finance their own relief! The North Lopham overseer, who had the responsibility for rate collection, grew desperate at the justices' refusal to excuse the destitute he nominated, and gazed bleakly at a prospect of expensive summonses, and seizures of the possessions of the indigent which would produce only old clothes and bedding. The Guiltcross Guardians confronted a nightmare situation where the union workhouse would eventually overflow with poor who had been made penniless by the operation of the New Poor Law itself. Eventually a solution was found, and a compliant friend to the reformed Poor Law, the Honourable and Reverend Edward Keppel, was nominated to the magistrate's bench for the sole purpose of authorizing poor rate excusals.(4)

The vexed problem of rating the needy tenant produced a variety of more or less unsatisfactory solutions but in practice it was increasingly recognized that the working classes could not be assessed to the poor rate. The real difficulty lay with properties of an annual value or rental of under £6, and legislation of 1819, which circumvented this problem of rating poor occupiers by assessing the owners instead, only dealt unhelpfully with properties with a value of *over* £6. Poor law administrators had little option but to continue with, or even to extend, a policy of excusing the poor from their rates. In the Swaffham Union excusals amounted to £400 in 1836, and in the Docking Union to £4,600 in 1849. The parishes in the Docking Union excused all occupiers with a rental of £4 or £6 (or exceptionally £8), and therefore exempted all labourers from paying the poor rate. This meant that 40 per cent of the properties in the Docking Union, which were liable for assessment, were excused payment. The loss of revenue involved in excusing the poor occupier was so considerable that seven Norfolk boards of guardians petitioned Parliament on the problem during 1837 and 1838. It is not surprising that when legislation came in 1850, which gave powers to rate owners rather than occupiers of houses with an annual value of under £6, Norfolk parish overseers greeted it with enthusiasm. Within a year more parishes in Norfolk had adopted its provisions than in any other county, and by 1866 over half of Norfolk parishes were operating it. But some parishes abandoned the experiment, and this may have been because rating the owners of cottages merely led to a corresponding rise in the rents charged to the poor. In this case poor tenants would be worse off since they were now effectively paying the poor rates whereas previously they

had been excused them. On the other hand, a very generous policy
of excusals for the poor ratepayer could produce hardship and
resentment among the moderately well off, as in Yarmouth, where
there were only 1,100 ratepayers but 5,000 inhabited houses.(5)

Until the 1860s the poor rate, which had been instituted for
the relief of the needy, remained not so much a tax on property as
on poverty itself. The basis of rating for the relief of the poor
had been castigated as 'in the highest degree uncertain and capri-
cious' by the Royal Commission in 1834, but it had failed to advocate substantial reform. The 1834 act had retained parochial
rating and each parish in the new poor law unions had the cost of
the relief given to its poor charged to its separate account. This
expenditure, averaged out over three years, was then used to cal-
culate the share that each parish made to the new common fund of the
union. This fund financed general expenditure on such items as the
cost of the workhouse or the salaries of the officials. Effectively therefore, the poorest parishes were doubly penalized, since
those with many paupers were charged large sums for their relief,
and then had to pay a high proportion of the common fund because
of this. This injustice was compounded at the beginning of the New
Poor Law by the almost inevitable unfairness of the original assessments to the common fund. These were made on the basis of an average of the poor rate for the three years ending in 1835 and were
constructed by the assistant poor law commissioners from figures
supplied by the parishes. But the accounts of many parishes were
so badly kept that their cryptic and haphazard entries were difficult to decipher and interpret, and on the rarer occasions when they
had been sufficiently well kept for the new poor law auditor to
follow them he was astounded by their inaccuracies.

'This will speedily undo all a board of guardians can effect',
fulminated the Chairman of the Loddon and Clavering guardians in
1839.(6) He was complaining about the use of highway rates by
parishes in his union to finance the relief of the poor in the
opening years of the new poor law era. In the St Faith's Union
too, this practice continued to be used extensively into the 1840s
as a way of reducing the parish poor rate and therefore the establishment charge. Employing the poor on the roads and paying them
from the highway rate was also cheaper than paying for expensive
indoor relief inside the union workhouse. The same motive led to
a parallel, but more short-lived, practice in the use of private
rates to supplement the wages of agricultural labourers with large
families by financing gifts of flour. Private rates were used by
farmers in heavy land parishes when they had been hit hard by lower
corn prices. Consequently, they saved money, both through the payment of below-subsistence wages, and by substituting cheap private
relief for the costlier public relief of the low-paid labourer in
the union workhouse. However, private rates offered a less serious
challenge then highway rates to the operation of the reformed Poor
Law because there was no compulsion on ratepayers to contribute
and so they tended to be ephemeral.(7)

II   'CLOSE' AND 'OPEN' PARISHES

The deadliness of the battle between Norfolk parishes over their
relative share of financing poor relief is best revealed by the
differentiation in the poor rates themselves. In 1847 the lowest
Norfolk parish poor rate was Os ½d in the pound while the highest
was 12s 4d, while in 1861 the inequality had been only slightly reduced to a minimum rate of Os ¾d against a maximum parish rate of
6s 5¾d. These startling contrasts in the relative burden of financing poor relief in Norfolk had come about mainly through the
exploitation of the laws of settlement. Parish ratepayers and
poor law officials were dedicated to reducing the poor rate by
shifting the poor law settlement, and therefore the chargeability,
of poor persons to other parishes. By the nineteenth century the
settlement laws had become a complex body of intricate legislation
which offered a challenge to the parish overseer similar to that of
a present-day accountant confronted by the modern tax system. The
creation of parochial settlement by which the poor man had a legitimate claim to relief in the parish where he had a settlement was
the practical product of the Elizabethan act of 1601 which had made
the parish into the financial unit of poor law administration. By
1834 there were many grounds, under either common or statute law,
by which a settlement could be gained, including: serving an apprenticeship; holding a parish office; an annual hiring; possession of a substantial estate or buildings; renting a tenement if
the occupier had certain additional qualifications; and payment of
the parish poor rate. The most common ways by which settlements
were gained were by parentage, by birth and, in the case of women,
by marriage.(8) The Poor Law Amendment Act of 1834 scarcely
altered a situation that was crying out for reform. It ended only
settlements gained either by serving a parish office, by yearly
hiring, by sea apprenticeship, or by renting a tenement unless a
year's poor rate was also paid.(9) So the basis for inter-parochial
struggle and disputed legal cases was as rich in possibilities at
the beginning of the New as it had been under the Old Poor Law.
     The struggle between Norfolk parishes was polarized between what
contemporaries termed 'open' and 'close' parishes (according to
whether they were open or closed to new settlements), and in which
the 'close' parishes' gains were the 'open' parishes' losses. Typically, a 'close' parish had a small population and either one, or a
very few, landed proprietors who could exercise a careful supervision over poor law management. But contemporaries used the term
loosely and emotively, as is apparent if named 'close' parishes are
analysed for structure of land ownership, housing provision and
population size. Exaggerated ideas of their numbers flourished, but
the Norfolk guardians' own lists of 'close' parishes suggest a lower
proportion of one-quarter to one-third of the total in the worst
affected areas. A modern estimate made on the basis of social
structure, housing provision and the density and growth of population suggests a range of from 17 per cent in south-east Norfolk to
40 per cent in the north-west of the county. The west of Norfolk
had one-third of its parishes as 'close' parishes and this high proportion was exceeded only in the Wolds of the East Riding and an
area in east Leicestershire, Rutland and west Lincolnshire.(10) The

proprietors of 'close' parishes tried to minimize or reduce the
number of poor law settlements within their village and if possible
to shift them to other townships. Before 1834 farmers in a 'close'
parish had to be very careful not to create a new settlement by
hiring a farm labourer for a full year. In the south Norfolk
parish of Larling, for example, the farmers' leases included a
clause requiring a payment of £50 for each settlement made through
their 'default or omission' up to a total penalty of £200. Nine
miles away the 'close' parish of Threxton safeguarded itself by the
more usual method of demanding from any labourer who came to work
there from another village a certificate recognizing his chargeability to his parish of settlement. The two proprietors of Threxton were Thomas Barton and Lord Clermont, and although they were
on extremely bad terms with each other they managed to reach agreement on the vital issue of keeping down the poor rates. Their policy of reducing poor law settlements apparently included binding
out the children of the parish in apprenticeships to a Staffordshire
manufacturer, although apprenticeships over such a long distance
were rare in early nineteenth-century Norfolk.(11)

Most settlements were made through parentage, marriage or place
of birth so that the energy of the poor law administrator in the
small parish was directed mainly at restricting cottage building.
As early as 1774 Arthur Young described the consequences of the law
of settlement for the supply of cottages:(12)

By forcing every parish to maintain not the resident, but the
settled poor; and by disenabling the poor from settling where
they please, you give a strong and effective motive to very many
people to do everything in their power against population, by
raising an open war against cottages. The landlord and the
farmer have almost equal motives to reduce the number of poor
in their parishes.

This process became so much an accepted part of the social scene
in Norfolk that it received little attention by contemporaries
until the single dramatic stroke of the Poor Removal Act of 1846
effectively completed the work of the administrators in 'close'
parishes. This piece of legislation, which was eventually held to
be wholly retrospective, gave irremovability, or a de facto new
settlement, to the poor after they had lived in a parish for five
years. Those poor who had been forced by the shortage of housing in
a 'close' parish to reside in an 'open' parish now became chargeable to the poor rates of the latter. It would be interesting to
be able to quantify the burden that was transferred from 'close' to
'open' villages by the 1846 act, but this is not possible because
the legal muddle over its provisions, which lasted until 1848, made
chaos of the relevant parochial accounts, and by that time the irremovable poor had become a charge on the common fund of the union.
This addition of the irremovable poor to the common fund slightly
lightened the rates of the 'open' parishes, but since they were
the heaviest contributors to the fund, the 'close' parishes still
retained substantial financial gains.

The outburst of indignation that the 1846 act provoked led to
wild accusations of cottage destruction in the 'close' parishes,
but these can hardly be accepted as no authenticated examples were
ever given. The evidence of Norfolk guardians to an inquiry by the

Poor Law Board into this problem gave illuminating examples of men
mouthing contemporary platitudes, whose eloquence was halted sud-
denly by the obvious need for substantiating evidence, which they
realized they could not supply. The Reverend Edward Postle, vice-
chairman of the Loddon and Clavering Board of Guardians, said that
the 1846 act was unsatisfactory because:

>   an absolute premium [was] offered to individuals to rid their
>   parishes of burdens then and thereafter by pulling down cot-
>   tages, or, at any rate, not building such.... I cannot say I
>   know of any gross case of pulling down cottages; but *without*
>   *doubt* the five years' residence will *tend to it*.

John Wright, who was a Thetford guardian, and was himself the proprietor of the 'close' parish of Kilverstone, from which he had
acquired a monomania on the subject of settlement, was the man most
likely to be able to produce examples of cottage destruction if
these had occurred. Yet he tamely ended his evidence on 'close'
parishes by stating that 'in these parishes the cottages have in
many instances been destroyed; at any rate they have not been increased according to the wants of the farms'. Indeed, it is a
testament to the intellectual naivety of G.A. a Beckett, who compiled the report on the laws of settlement for the area that included Norfolk, that he should have accepted the available evidence
with a credulity that was much greater than his more experienced
colleague Robert Weale, who investigated the South and Midlands,
and thought that complaints about the 'close' parishes benefiting
at the expense of the 'open' parishes had been unduly magnified.

The most nefarious action that can be laid at the door of the
proprietors of 'close' parishes in Norfolk was their purchase of
land in a neighbouring parish. This was subsequently rented to
the poor of their own village so that they would gain a new settlement by means of either renting a tenement or paying a poor rate.
(13) But more widespread and effective in the long run was the
deliberate policy of restricting the number of cottages in a 'close'
parish by omitting to build new ones as population increased, and
by failing to repair old ones. The results of this policy can still
be seen in the empty, rolling landscape of west Norfolk, where the
'close' parishes are easily distinguishable by the small numbers
of well built, model cottages blessed with neogothic decoration and
tidy cottage gardens, which cluster in semi-feudal dependence near
the gates of the hall.

'Open' parishes complemented 'close' parishes in having a larger
population and a more fragmented land ownership. The labourers
who were unable to find a cottage in their own 'close' village
tended to gravitate to a neighbouring village which was open to
newcomers and where they could at least put a roof over their heads,
even if the rents were high. The larger size of the 'open' parish
made it difficult to keep a careful supervision over settlements,
and the self-interest of many of the inhabitants also militated
against this. Tradesmen, publicans, small artisans and gang-masters
invested their savings in cottages which they let out at high rents.
This speculative investment produced cottages with a number of fundamental defects: 'Thinness of external walls, small size of rooms,
want of ventilation, and on the ground floor brick or tile instead
of wooden floors, and sometimes windows which cannot be opened, and

want of fire-places in sleeping-rooms.'(14)   A rent of £5 was
charged for a badly built, insanitary cottage that might perhaps
have had £50 spent either on its erection or in the conversion of
existing buildings into tenements. But these cottages met the real
social need of the tenant. The owners also gained more as landlords in their income from rents than they lost as ratepayers in
contributing to the higher poor rates, which might result from the
new settlements acquired by the tenants residing in their cottages.

III REFORM

When parishes bribed their poor with premiums to go away and gain
a new settlement while labourers perjured themselves to obtain one,
the Norfolk situation was obviously ripe for reform. The Docking
Union in west Norfolk was the only new poor law union in England
and Wales to attempt a bold reform, by using the clause in the 1834
act that allowed a board of guardians, by unanimous vote, to adopt
union rating and settlement. This reform was an institutional
response to the changed condition of the labour market in west Norfolk, where high labour mobility had worried local farmers who
wished to increase employment in order to improve the state of cultivation. Local shortages of labour had resulted from the unusually
large number of 'close' parishes in the area, where one in three
villages was closed to fresh settlements. This had also produced
striking inequalities in the rating burden, and by 1844 the oppressed parishes, with the support of the poor law inspector, were demanding that fresh rating averages should be made which would relieve them of their unduly heavy share of the establishment charges
of the Docking Union workhouses. The gains made by 'close' parishes
as a result of the 1846 act exacerbated the situation and in June
1847 the Docking Board of Guardians decided on the unprecedented
step of union rating and settlement. It was felt that this would
improve cottage provision and hence help labour supply. Reduced
labour migration would ensue when the labourer realized that his
standard of living had improved through the provision of cottages
near to his work.(15)
     The chairman of the Docking Board was Mr H. Blyth, himself a
proprietor of a 'close' parish and an early opponent of reform who
had, however, recognized belatedly the social and economic injustices of the system of 'close' and 'open' parishes. It was his
enthusiastic support of union rating and settlement that eventually
overcame the faint-hearted among the guardians, and the lukewarm
response to projected reform of the Poor Law Commission in London.
Blyth provided an illuminating description of the distribution of
cottages in the Docking Union:(16)

     There are nine parishes ... the exclusive property respectively
     of one proprietor.... In each one of these parishes the system
     has been quietly acted upon, more or less, of avoiding the ex-
     penses of maintaining the poor as much as possible by reducing
     or keeping down the number of cottages. In Barmer, Broomsthorpe,
     Waterden, there are not more than two cottages each; the labour-
     ers required to till the land residing respectively for Barmer
     in Syderstone, for Broomsthorpe in Rudham, for Waterden in South

Creake, in Tring and Burnham Deepdale.... These are all proofs
that the dislike to build or maintain cottages have in close
parishes driven the labourers who till the soil to more distant
residences. These residences are found, secondly, in our larger
villages or towns, such as Docking, Burnham, Creaknorth, Creak-
south, Snettisham. In these places are small freeholders and
copyhold estates, the owners of which have found the building of
cottages a most profitable investment; and *that alone* being their
object, they have paid no attention to the convenience necessary
to make these comfortable or even healthy residences. In one
part of Docking there is a large collection of houses, apparently
20 or 30, built all together, without one bit of garden-
ground.

This unusual severity of the system of 'close' parishes in the Docking Union helps to explain why the guardians unilaterally adopted
the reform of union rating and settlement and anticipated by nearly
20 years the provisions of the Union Chargeability Act of 1865,
which brought this about for every union in England and Wales.

Union rating and settlement became effective in Docking on 25
March 1848 and the economic results of the reforms were beneficial.
A detailed report by a Docking Guardians' Committee in 1850 compared pauperism in the union between 1848 and 1850 with that of the
preceding two years and decided that the decline in pauperism had
justified their brave reform. There had been 822 fewer paupers in
the workhouse, and the cost of indoor relief had been reduced by
£312. This had been parallelled by 306 fewer cases of outdoor relief with a consequent saving of £2,558. The number of able-bodied
men in the workhouse had fallen by 49, applications by able-bodied
men on account of sickness were also reduced by 58, while an additional 20 able-bodied men who accepted tickets for entry to the
workhouse had not used them. The committee admitted that these
results had been helped by unusually good farm employment in 1848
but that this had been offset by numbers of men returning home after
working on railway construction. Local Jeremiahs (who reflected
typical, contemporary attitudes) had prophesied that without parochial settlement, which gave local ratepayers an interest in employing the inferior or old labourers, such men would not find work.
In the event, these 'half-men' continued to be employed. The cost
of poor relief declined faster in the Docking Union than in surrounding unions, with a decrease of 11 per cent between 1846-8 and
1856-8 compared with 2 per cent in seven neighbouring unions. By
1860 the Docking Guardians noted proudly that requests for relief
by the able-bodied had fallen by two-thirds since 1848 and relief
on account of sickness to the able-bodied by a half.(17)

Considerable interest was shown in the Docking experiment and
not least by the guardians of the neighbouring Mitford and Launditch
Union, who were used to making the running in the management of the
poor and therefore viewed the reform with a somewhat jealous eye.
They wondered whether to follow suit and set up the inevitable committee to make a report on the question. The committee's report
in 1851 noted the 5 per cent greater reduction in expenditure in
Docking compared with Mitford and Launditch since 1848, and commended the freer market for labour and the beneficial effects on
cottage supply that would follow from union settlement. Against

this they felt that, with fewer 'close' parishes in Mitford and
Launditch than in Docking, their problems were less acute; that
there were difficulties in finding a fair rating basis for parishes
to make their contributions to the union's common fund; and that
interest in the poor might decline if parochial settlement was
abolished. The full board of guardians thought that more decisive
arguments were necessary to justify a reform of this importance,
and the Mitford and Launditch Union retained their existing system.
Certainly, a reform of this magnitude raised fresh problems, as the
Docking Guardians discovered. Their reform had perpetuated any
rating injustices that already existed, because it continued to
assess each parish to the common fund (which was to finance poor
relief in the union) on the basis of the proportion in 1846 that
their expenditure on the poor bore to the total expenditure in the
union.(18) This retained the fundamental weakness of the Poor Law
Amendment Act in taxing poverty rather than property, and meant
that 'open' parishes with considerable numbers of poor and a high
poor rate continued to pay a large contribution to the common fund.
Also, without the national reform in rating in 1861, the lack of
provision for a changing basis of assessment in the Docking common
fund might have produced the inequalities and bitterness that had
been engendered earlier in the Loddon and Clavering Incorporation.
Here, parochial chargeability in the 1830s had been based on proportions fixed in the original act of incorporation of 1764, which
had first established common rating and settlement in the incorporation.(19)

In the Incorporation of Norwich, an unusual system of common
rating actually taxed property and wealth, rather than poverty, for
the relief of the poor. This radical rating system had been included in the original act of incorporation of 1712, which had been
designed, according to a later governor of the Court of Guardians,
'to relieve the poor parishes, and to throw a greater burden on the
rich ones'. Ironically, this had come about after an earlier failure to rate one parish for the relief of another. All the parishes
in the city contributed to the poor rate in proportion to their
share of the total rateable value of the incorporation and not on
the basis of expenditure on their own paupers. This progressive
system of local taxation (which anticipated a national system based
on rateable values by 150 years) involved considerable transfers
of wealth between the parishes. A calculation made in 1846 suggested that, if parish rating was to operate, with each city parish
responsible only for its own poor, then a rich parish like St Michael
at Plea or St Peter Mancroft would pay poor rates of only 0s ½d in
the pound, while an impoverished parish such as St Martin at Oak
would pay 4s 8d. Given the parochial outlook in this period, it
seems surprising that such a generous financial system operated without criticism in a city that was in economic decline arising from a
failing textiles industry in the mid-nineteenth century. The Clerk
to the Norwich Guardians explained this when he said that 'the
parochial system would be *quite* impracticable in Norwich, the number of poor in some of the parishes being so large that the necessary funds for their support ... in those several parishes could
not be raised.' He went on to say that the rating system had gone
on for so long that a common interest in the poor had been created

in all areas, and that ratepayers thought of the city as one parish.(20)

A more usual viewpoint by the propertied classes in the nineteenth century, and one that delayed the much needed reform of the rating and settlement laws, was that described by Dr Hunter in 1865. After conducting an inquiry into rural labourers' cottages, he concluded that ratepayers looked 'on the people as a surging fluid anxious to find its own level, and ruinous wherever it comes. To give it vent will be to render their beloved estate uninhabitable, and to eat it up with poor rates'.(21) The proprietors of close parishes in Norfolk shared these assumptions, and since they had most to lose from any changes in rating or settlement were always the keenest defenders of the status quo. They looked on their parish as their own possession, were indignant at its compulsory inclusion in a poor law union, and viewed any outside intervention over matters of poor relief as interference with the sacred rights of private property. It is fascinating to notice that some of the most assiduous and conscientious administrators of the reformed Poor Law, like H.E. Blyth in Docking, T.B. Beevor in Wayland and Rev. J. Fellowes in Henstead, were proprietors in 'close' parishes, who had earlier petitioned for their respective properties to be excluded from the new poor law unions,because their existing economical management of the poor could not be improved upon by the new arrangements.(22) Once their parish was included in the new union they became guardians and attended the board with great punctiliousness in order to defend their parish's privileged position of few paupers and a low poor rate. Their belief that a dilution of the parochial system would lead both to wasteful and negligent administration of relief, and to a failure by local property-owners to employ the local labourers, was widely held in the county. Sir James Graham's unsuccessful proposal in 1844 to restrict the ground of settlement to birth or parentage and to confer irremovability on the poor after five years' residence provoked repetitious resolutions from Norfolk boards of guardians. They were afraid that this reform would lead to unemployment and wholesale cottage destruction.

This local reluctance to adopt a larger unit than the parish for settlement and rating was more than just a weak reflection of national opinion but was based on knowledge hard won from previous experience. It has been argued earlier, in Chapter 3, that in the rural Norfolk incorporations before 1834 there had been a widespread resumption of a parish-based administration of the Poor Law after what ratepayers had felt to be a failure to achieve an economical relief policy by a centralized administration, which had acted on behalf of the constituent parishes.

A generation of timid tampering with the law finally established union rating and settlement on a national scale by 1865, but this came about less through intellectual conversion than through force of circumstances. The influential Report on the Poor Laws of 1834 had rejected a larger unit of rating or settlement than the parish, and had thought a national rate would be objectionable in principle and would in practice increase pauperism and the poor rates. But a change in sentiment came in 1846 as part of the political deal that gave landlords compensation for the Repeal of

the Corn Laws. Although the Poor Removal Act was not too revolu-
tionary in its actual proposals, by implication it raised issues
that inevitably opened the door to later, and more decisive, reform. The act gave irremovability or a de facto new settlement to
a poor person once he had lived in a parish for five years. Bad
drafting in the act, compounded by poor legal advice to the Poor
Law Board, produced grotesque muddle in the administration of relief for two years. When the legal fog lifted the towns in Norfolk
were horrified to find that large numbers of country poor who had
been living in urban houses were now the town's financial responsibility. In rural areas 'open' parishes also lost out to 'close'
parishes.(23) The consequences of the act caused a rapid conversion of Norfolk opinion from parochial to union settlement. Insi-
diously, gradualist reform brought this about. The Irremovable Poor
Act of 1861 gave irremovability after three years' residence, and
the Union Chargeability Act of 1865 gave irremovability after one
year's residence. The latter conferred a de jure new settlement
after three years' continuous residence in a single parish and finally replaced settlement in a parish by that in a union.
    Side by side with changes in settlement came rating reform. In
1847 Bodkin's Act minimized the financial changes of the 1846 act
by making the irremovable poor a charge on the common fund of the
union, and this temporary piece of legislation was renewed annually
until 1865. Between 1848 and 1865 the cost of vagrants, of urgent
relief to the non-settled poor and of the sick and lunatic poor all
became charges on the common fund of the union. The logical conclusion was reached in the Union Chargeability Act of 1865 which made
all relief chargeable to the common fund and which therefore established union rating. This removed the worst of the financial injustices between parishes. After the act more Norfolk parishes
had increased than decreased rating expenditures, which suggests
the disproportionately heavy burden previously borne by the minority.(24) Financial disputes between parishes were reduced but
those between unions continued. The Wisbech Union was incensed
that recently drained land near the Wash was to be added to the
Holbeach, and not the Wisbech, Union. They protested that this
neglected 'the obvious principle that the poor rates collected over
any area of land should be applied to the maintenance and relief of
the poor who supply the labour for such area or district'.(25) With
the increased mobility of the second half of the nineteenth century,
the union was almost as arbitrary and inadequate a unit of rating
and settlement as the parish had been earlier.
    In the Irremovable Poor Act of 1861 occurred the most radical
change in the financing of the Poor Law during the nineteenth century. This introduced rateable value and not past expenditure on
poor relief as the basis of each parish's share of the union's common fund. In the following year, unions had to appoint guardians
to Union Assessment Committees, who were to work with parish overseers to prepare valuation lists of property as a basis for contributions to the common fund. Their lengthy task is some indication
of the inadequacies of the previous rating systems.(26) By the
1860s rates were levied only on immovable property in the form of
lands and tenements, and assessment was based on the annual rental
of the property, and expressed as so much to be paid in the pound.

In Norfolk rates had commonly been made on half, two-thirds, or full (rack) rental, while in Norwich it had been assessed on 90 per cent of the rack rental. Assessments were made by the overseer who might find his unenviable job made more difficult by parishioners who refused to tell him their rental. Boards of guardians had powers unanimously to order a new valuation to be made. If they failed to do so sufficiently often to reflect changing property values, an explosive situation built up in the union, as occurred in the Docking Union in 1843. More acute problems of financial in-justice were later raised by the union assessment committees, which, like Norfolk boards of guardians, were dominated by farmers. The property that these assessment committees had to value was predomi-nantly farmland, and it is probable that there was some discrimi-nation against other categories of rated property as a result of this. During the agricultural depression of the late nineteenth century they made ad hoc deductions in the rateable value of land. For example, between 1881 and 1894 the rateable value of farmland in four of the unions in Norfolk was reduced by a quarter.(27)   In 1896 the rates of all farms were reduced by the Agricultural Rates Act, by which agricultural land was to be rated at half its value and the Exchequer was to pay the remitted half. This was the cul-mination of a series of actions designed to relieve the localities of rates assessed on property, by a central subsidy financed by national taxes on income.(28)

IV POOR RATES AND AGRICULTURE

This help to the farmer, who was the principal contributor to the poor rates, had come too late to prevent socioeconomic conflicts in Norfolk caused by the farmers' attempts to shift his economic lia-bilities to others. This had happened most obviously between 1815 and 1834 when agriculture was relatively depressed. Then, farmers had found it more difficult financially to pay high poor rates, while psychologically they resented the rating burden more than they had done in better times. In the decade before the Poor Law Amdnd-ment Act of 1834, 79 per cent of the poor rates in Norfolk were as-sessed on land, compared with 67 per cent in England and Wales. Only 17 per cent of the county's poor rates came from houses and a mere 3 per cent from mills, factories and other industrial property. This meant that the unusually heavy burden of pauperism in Norfolk was financed mainly by the farmer and that the poor rates formed an exceptionally large part of the Norfolk farmer's costs. An esti-mate of 1831 found the cost of the Norfolk poor per acre to be 4s 1½d compared with an average English cost of only 3s 7¼d.(29) Farmers in the county reacted to this burden by trying to transfer their costs to others.

In the early nineteenth century Norfolk farmers emerged for the first time as a separate force in county politics, pursuing their own economic interests with a singlemindedness that suggested a growing sectionalism in local society. During the Napoleonic Wars the farmers had paid a disproportionately heavy share of taxation. Although the malt duties and property tax had been abolished in 1816, the farmers in the postwar period felt an increased real burden of

taxation because of the decline in agricultural prices. A Norfolk
farmer complained in 1816 that the poor rates 'press far heavier on
farmers than at the dearest periods, for the plain reason, *then*
they had the means to pay them, *now* they have not'.(30) Of course,
farmers were also concerned about their income and agitated about
the effect of the currency and the regulation of trade on agricultural prices, but their main complaint was about 'taxes' (including
poor rates), which formed such a heavy item in their costs. Their
sense of economic grievance emancipated them from the tutelage of
the Norfolk landowners. They organized themselves as a distinct
political group and held their own county meetings in 1822-3 and
1829-30 to protest against the high level of taxation.(31)

The divisiveness that economic pressures had fostered in county
society was fully revealed in the stark confrontation of interests
during the Norfolk agrarian riots of 1830-1. Since they felt themselves to be staggering under heavy poor rates, the farmers countered the agricultural labourers' request for increased wages and
poor relief with their own demands for reduced rents and tithes
from the landlord and tithe-owner. Rising tithes were very much
resented by the Norfolk farmer, who regarded them as a continuous
tax on the improvements he had made, and who therefore viewed the
tithe-owner with particular hostility. In 1830 the farmers of
south-east Norfolk offered increased wages to their labourers on
condition that their own tithes were reduced. In doing so they encouraged a series of vicious attacks by the labourers on the tithe-
owner. The farmers also demanded a reduction in rent from their
landlords to compensate them for their concessions to the labourers.(32) A leading Norfolk landowner, Lord Suffield, sadly observed
to the Prime Minister, Lord Melbourne, that during these disturbances there had been a widespread tendency 'to shift the burden
from our shoulders upon those of our neighbour', and complained that
the farmers had demanded 'an unreasonable abatement of both rent and
tithe'.(33)

A few years later Robert Wright, a Norfolk land agent, came to
an alarmist conclusion that unless 'there is an alteration in the
poor laws the property will be annihilated in many places'.(34)
But the small amount of available evidence does not suggest that
the high level of poor rates in the county forced landowners to reduce rents so much that it endangered agricultural capital. On
the other hand, neither does it indicate that Norfolk farmers were
generally oppressed by rents that were unreasonably high. Rents
in this predominantly arable area primarily reflected grain prices,
and only secondarily costs such as poor rates. In the war period
Norfolk rents had risen less than prices, to the farmers' advantage,
but in the ensuing period a continued demand for farms kept rents
buoyant, so that this item in his costs fell more slowly than the
farmer's income which was derived from the lower prices he received
for his produce.(35) In the very depressed year of 1822, when
wheat prices had fallen 60 per cent from their peak price of 1813,
landlords in Norfolk were forced, like those elsewhere, to give
rent rebates. Writing in this crisis year, Blaikie the famous
Holkham agent described the landlord's unenviable situation since
the low prices of agricultural produce left the tenant farmer with
no surplus funds to pay his rent.(36) Arrears of rent mounted, and

in spite of rent rebates there was an unusual turnover of tenants
on the Holkham estate. But the large Norfolk landowners treated
their tenants with sympathetic consideration in this difficult
period. Coke of Holkham had always charged moderate rentals, but
during the price fluctuations of 1813-24 he had not immediately
renewed a 21-year lease when it fell in but had continued it on a
year-to-year basis so that rent and income kept in step. Lord
Suffield also recognized the inequality of the rent burden imposed
by long leases in an era of changing prices. In 1829 he replaced
the terms on which his farms had originally been leased and equal-
ized the rents on his estate according to the relative value of
the occupations. Rents were therefore adjusted by the wealthier
landlord according to the farmers' ability to pay, and by the 1830s
many Norfolk farmers had adjusted their costs to the lower prices
and were in better financial shape. The Holkham rentals by 1833
had risen to their earlier level of 1820 and the increase gathered
momentum thereafter, with a 2 per cent rise to 1837 and a further
10 per cent rise before 1842. The smaller landlord could not afford
to be so generous with his tenants, and one local writer accused
Norfolk landlords in the early 1830s of beggaring their tenants by
high rents.(37) In this period farmers on the clay lands were
crushed between costs that remained obstinately high and falling
prices. The financial difficulties of the clay-land farmers in the
south of the county led them to circumvent the poor rate with
cheaper methods of relieving the poor by using the highway rate or
instituting private rates.

The vast weight of Norfolk pauperism, supported by a ramshackle
and anachronistic system of local taxation, produced a long drawn-
out economic struggle which eroded mutual loyalty and responsibility in local society. The landowners set the tone for a rapa-
cious defence of sectional economic interest when, as proprietors of
'close' parishes, they utilized the subtle convolutions of the laws
of settlement and rating to make decisive gains. The small value
that landlords set on social dependency in relation to economic
profit was also suggested by their very limited attempts to reduce
the rent burden which after 1815 adversely affected the farmers. The
farmers followed the example of their social betters and attempted
to shift their own heavy rating burden to the tithe-owner and landlord but with comparatively little success. However, in their dual
role as employers and poor law administrators the farmers were more
successful in reducing their economic liabilities. The poor suffered a double penalty, since as a result of the proprietors' action
some were forced to live in sub-standard cottages in 'open' villages
that were distant from their work, while the consequences of the
farmers' control of employment and poor relief were low wages, which
were supplemented by poor law allowances.

CHAPTER 6
POOR RELIEF IN RURAL NORFOLK

In 1834 the Royal Commission on the Poor Laws stated that under the Old Poor Law abuses in poor relief to the able-bodied had resulted in low wages and had created a temporary surplus labour problem. But in 1847 Edwin Chadwick, who had been an influential member of this Royal Commission, put forward an alternative interpretation when he suggested that the poor law was a response to, and not a determinant of, the rural labour market. He considered that, after the Poor Law Amendment Act of 1834, the poor law administration had been used as an instrument for rural employers' labour policies:

> Parish officers, were viewed by the labourers in their private characters as employers or owners rather than in their character as public officers, is I conceive in its degree applicable to the mode of administration carried out by means of tickets.... In all the unions where the ticket system was in use the guardians would necessarily be viewed as employers of labour; and the board a sort of trades union of employers.

The ticket system of the eastern counties was the most striking example of labour assignment policies under the New Poor Law. Seeing these policies in operation had led James Caird in 1851 to comment that he saw little difference between the allowances of the Old Poor Law and the labour allocation policies of the New Poor Law. This study of poor relief in rural Norfolk indicates that both before and after 1834 there was a combination of outdoor allowances and labour apportionment schemes which developed as a response to the county's agrarian under-employment. Surplus labour was not the temporary phenomenon suggested by the Royal Commission of 1834, but an important explanation of the 'Two Nations' of nineteenth-century England; the North, characterized by high wages and low poor rates, and the South, characterized by low wages and high poor rates.(1)

I SURPLUS LABOUR AND POOR LAW MIGRATION AND EMIGRATION SCHEMES

In 1831 a Norfolk committee of magistrates who had conducted an inquiry into the employment of the agricultural poor reported that more than one-eighth of the men in rural Norfolk were partly or totally unemployed. Returns from 426 parishes revealed that 2,714

out of 23,148 were without work. Surprisingly, the committee concluded that there was 'no material surplus of labourers beyond what
the cultivation of the soil might fairly be said to require'. The
main reason for this view was the seasonal fluctuation in labour
demand by Norfolk farmers. They required a reserve labour force of
under-employed men who could then be recruited during periods of
peak labour demand during haytime and, more especially, during harvest. The county was one of the great corn-growing areas in England;
in the earliest returns of crop acreage in 1866 it had 44.5 per cent
of its cultivated area under corn, which was the seventh highest
county total.(2) About half the harvesters were resident, regularly
employed labourers, but the others had to be recruited from part-
time, casual or migrant workers. By the nineteenth century the Norfolk farmer could rely on few migrant Celtic harvesters since they
rarely penetrated beyond the Fens. The supply of casual labour
recruited from workers in domestic industry was shrinking because
of the changes in the Norwich textile industry, which had converted
it by the middle of the nineteenth century into a small, factory-
based manufacture. The farmer had increasingly to rely on part-time
workers who were resident in Norfolk villages. He could never forecast accurately how many he would need because many more labourers
would be required during a dry season, when corn had to be cut
quickly after ripening, and when a heavy crop was badly laid.

A Norfolk proprietor wrote in 1835 that 'Many of the lower class
are clamorous for want of employment, and except during the harvest,
become during the great part of the year a dead weight upon us.'(3)
Norfolk farmers wanted a surplus of labour because they needed it
during harvest time, but they were less than enthusiastic about retaining it either by occasional employment or relief from the poor
rate during the rest of the year. Because of the conflict between
their requirements as employers and their liabilities as ratepayers,
the farmers were ambivalent towards surplus labour. Its true economic and social cost was brought home to them in the agrarian
riots of 1830-1, which had followed the lowering of farm wages and
rural poor relief during the postwar agricultural depression. Widespread local debate on the surplus labour problem resulted. This
was renewed in 1835-6 when it was appreciated that the provisions
of the New Poor Law meant that, instead of cheap and partial outdoor relief in their own homes, the under-employed would now have
to receive expensive indoor relief in the workhouse.

This anxiety resulted in a heavy but short-lived participation
by Norfolk villages in emigration and migration schemes which were
financed mainly by the farmers through the parish poor rate. Between 1835 and 1837 Norfolk villages sent out the astonishing total
of 3,354 emigrants under a scheme of the Poor Law Commission. This
was much the largest number sent by any county and was over half the
national total of 6,403 participants.(4) The returns sent by Norfolk
unions to the Poor Law Commission showed that the emigrants were almost exclusively agricultural labourers, although there were a few
village tradesmen or craftsmen such as butchers, tailors, black-
smiths, carpenters or bricklayers. Norfolk emigrants were generally
enterprising people who disliked being forced to seek poor relief
occasionally, rather than inadequate individuals habitually dependent on the Poor Law. Wright Thompson of Carlton-Forehoe wanted to

go to Canada because he had 'a large family and am quite unable to support them in this country'.(5) His parish was reluctant to finance him and so he petitioned the Poor Law Commissioners. So too did the poor of Attleborough in a similar situation, who were so desperate that they wrote five times between May 1836 and March 1837. The Attleborough petitioners were mainly agricultural labourers, whose wages when in work were only 9s a week, and who found work increasingly hard to get. They were 'willing to emigrate, with a good hope of bettering our situations in consequence of obtaining permanent employment for ourselves and families'.(6)

Emigration from Norfolk to Canada gathered momentum until it had become a feverish exodus by 1836-7. The emigrants sailed mainly from Lynn or Yarmouth and were joined by emigrants from neighbouring counties. In 1836 3,025 sailed from Yarmouth and 810 from Lynn, while in 1837 617 went from Yarmouth and 1,546 from Lynn. Norfolk parishes made sound arrangements for their emigrants' voyages and only one case of hardship was recorded, when the 'Venus', sailing from Yarmouth to Quebec, refused to land the passengers' baggage and also overcharged the emigrants' tax.(7) Parochial emigration under the provisions of the 1834 act continued at a diminishing rate until in 1870 the Poor Law Board dismantled its arrangements because it felt that emigration was no longer a useful means to reduce pauperism. Between 1834 and 1870 the annual reports of the central poor law administration showed that 3,650 of the Norfolk emigrants went to Canada and 388 to Australia. In addition nine emigrants went to the Cape in 1849 and 25 went illegally to the United States in 1836-7. The cost of these 4,072 emigrants was £21,685, so that Norfolk parishes made a good speculative investment, as this averaged out at about the cost of one year's poor relief for each participant. This emigration almost ceased after 1853. Between 1853 and 1870 there were only nine emigrants to Canada and four to Australia at a cost to Norfolk ratepayers of little more than £50.

Complementary to the Poor Law Commissioners' Emigration Scheme was their Migration Scheme of 1835-7 which was designed to reduce the labour surplus of southern, rural counties by sending labourers to northern, manufacturing areas which were short of factory hands. The Migration Scheme was centralized and two agents in Manchester and Leeds co-ordinated the requirements of northern employers for factory hands with those of southern boards of guardians anxious to reduce surplus labour. Dr Kay, the assistant Poor Law Commissioner for East Anglia, developed the scheme and in consequence nearly two-thirds of the 4,323 migrants came from this area. Suffolk sent the highest total of 2,128, and Norfolk the second biggest with 583 migrants. However, these official figures considerably understated the true extent of migration from Norfolk and confused independent and parochial migration. This was because the scheme occurred when administrative procedures were only just coming into existence during the creation of the poor law unions in the area. Because many of the Migration Agents' papers were later destroyed the figures cannot be cross-checked with a second source. Even the statistically minded Kay was unable to quantify East Anglian migration and stated that there had been 'an almost unobserved diffusion of the population'.(8)

Two-thirds of the Norfolk unions showed interest in the Migration Scheme and advertised it to the 'unemployed industrious poor' in handbills such as the one in Figure 10 for the Blofield Union. This indicated that northern factories were particularly keen to obtain adolescent labour and preferably that of girls. Since the typical potential migrants in Norfolk were an agricultural labourer and his family, there was some difficulty in placing applicants, and demand for situations outran the supply. Migrants from southern England were sent mainly to Lancashire with fewer to the West Riding of York- shire, Cheshire and Derbyshire. The pattern of Norfolk migration differed from this, since two out of three went to the West Riding and only one in four to Lancashire. Mr Muggeridge, the migration agent, explained that many Norfolk people went to Yorkshire because they could take advantage of the cheap steam shipping between Yar- mouth and Hull. Four Norfolk unions also arranged for single men to go to work on railway construction in the Midlands, where they earn- ed 2s 6d a day. However, the employment was relatively short-lived and many returned home again. A fifth union negotiated independently for jobs in factories in Sheffield and Wakefield. This poor law- sponsored migration also stimulated independent mobility. The most notable example was the successful work of the Rev. William Blackley of East Bradenham, who helped 130 migrants to the North of England. (9)

The extent of migration and emigration from Norfolk between 1835 and 1837 is quite extraordinary, since, as a local landowner re- marked, 'Norfolk men are proverbial for the difficulty with which they can be induced to move from the spot on which they were born; so much so, that it is a common observation in the army, that if one of them deserts, the first place to seek for him is at home.'(10) But this love of his native soil was countered by the fear of the new union workhouses that were being erected in the county at that time. In the Docking Union, where fear of the 'Bastille' was parti- cularly strong, emigration and migration removed 3 per cent of the population between 1835 and 1837 compared with less than 1 per cent over the county as a whole. Already by the end of 1836 393 emi- grants and 100 migrants had left Docking and there were sufficient numbers of Docking migrants for it to be worthwhile to organize a virtual wagon train for them to the North of England. This exodus was considered by the chairman of the Docking Union to have been 'most useful' in reducing pauperism and decreasing the amount of surplus labour. In the Swaffham Union, however, the labouring class was not so eager to move away, and the guardians' concern with a situation where the poor could not find employment for half the year made them want to compel them to migrate.(11) Although indus- trial depression had ended migration to the north by 1838, emigra- tion continued to provide a convenient means of reducing surplus labour, and more particularly during the late 1840s and early 1850s when agricultural depression increased rural unemployment. Emigra- tion was heaviest from the Docking, Aylsham, Erpingham and Walsing- ham Unions in the north of the county and from the Guiltcross Union in the south, which together provided two-thirds of the emigrants between 1834 and 1870.

Local attitudes to the exodus of labour remained ambivalent be- cause surplus labour was seen not only in quantitative, but also in

NOTICE

TO THE UNEMPLOYED INDUSTRIOUS POOR.

The Guardians of the Blofield Union, being desirous of finding work for the industrious and unemployed poor, hereby inform such persons that there is at present a great demand for labour in several of the manufacturing counties of England, and especially for large families of children, provided the greater part of them are above 12 years of age ; and *the more girls the better.*

The Wages given to families are as follows ;—and an agreement will be entered into for that purpose for a term of 3 or 4 years.

A labouring man, about .	12 Shillings per week.
A lad of 17 or 18 . .	8 ditto.
A boy of 16 . .	5 ditto.
A boy of 14 . .	4 ditto.
A girl of 15 to 20 or upwards	5s. 6d.
Ditto of 14 . .	5s.
Ditto of 12 or 13 . .	4s.
Ditto of 11 . .	1s. 3d.
	and schooling.

and increasing after the first year.

There is also an opening for girls who are orphans, or otherwise unprovided for, between the ages of 12 and 18, who may be bound as Apprentices to a Master who has not a large family of his own, and be employed under an agreement, the same as if they were his own children.

Every attention is paid to the religious and moral education of the younger children.

Application is to be made to the Guardian, Churchwardens, and Overseers, of each Parish, who will communicate with the Board of Guardians.

None but persons of steady industrious habits will be accepted.

H. N. BURROUGHES,

CHAIRMAN OF THE BOARD OF GUARDIANS.

October 21st, 1835.

PRINTED BY WILLIAM DURRANT PAGE, GENTLEMAN'S WALK, NORWICH.

Figure 10   Blofield Union Notice to Unemployed Industrious Poor

qualitative, terms. East Anglian ratepayers encouraged the worst
characters to emigrate and were dismayed when large numbers of good
workmen grasped this opportunity to vote with their feet. Coke of
Holkham stopped his financial assistance for emigration when it
emerged that it was the good labourers who were leaving his estate.
A more widespread equivocalness had developed by 1837 and this was
shown by the failure of an ambitious scheme to send emigrants to
Australia from the eastern counties. This plan, which was financed
by the Government of New South Wales, was to send the 'Orontes' from
Yarmouth with several hundred emigrants of good character. In the
spring of 1837 the local guardians were informed of the scheme,
and they found over 200 people (most of them agricultural labourers)
who were qualified and willing to emigrate. The majority of the 34
families came from the Norfolk unions of Guiltcross and Wayland.
But when the agent went to assemble the emigrants in the autumn he
found only three of the families prepared to emigrate; the harvest
of 1837 now promised good winter employment for them, while it had
also dimmed the spectre of surplus labour for the farmers. As a
result the 'Orontes' sailed from London with emigrants not from
East Anglia but from the south-east of England.(12)

II THE ALLOWANCE SYSTEM BEFORE AND AFTER 1834

Norfolk farmers were ambivalent about the problem of surplus labour
since, although they wanted a reserve of labourers to meet peak,
seasonal labour demands, they disliked the high level of poor
rates that resulted from such under-employment. They were fortunate in being able to resolve this conflict of interest by exploiting their position as poor law administrators to pursue a policy
with an economical alternation of poor relief and independent income for the labourer. While the changing dimensions of poverty
led to variations in the detailed form of relief, the overall policy remained constant. The centralized reform of 1834 foundered
because it provided an expensive and inflexible relief system which
failed to take account of the needs of the local labour market.
    Before 1815 allowances to the able-bodied in their own homes were
one of many types of English poor relief, and were found only in limited areas and as a response to a crisis situation of very high
bread prices. The extreme seriousness of the bread crisis of 1795-6
provoked local justices into encouraging the use of these allowances
and also a variety of other methods of relieving the poor. Those
in Oxfordshire and Berkshire promulgated a true Speenhamland scale,
which related poor relief to the size of the family and the price of
bread, while those in Hampshire and Buckinghamshire sanctioned relief in aid of wages.(13) In contrast to these county policies the
East Anglian magistracy left relief policy to local initiative. This
was because they were deeply involved in an active administration of
relief through their activities in the incorporations under local
act. The policies of these Norfolk rural incorporations give a
reasonable indication of the progress of allowances in the county,
because they had the most sophisticated administration of any local
relief authority and thus were the most likely areas to introduce
complex scales of allowances. In the hundreds of Tunstead and

Happing the incorporation subsidized a supply of cheap butter and cheese to the poor during the 1790s.(14) The Flegg Incorporation in 1795 extended and systematized into a scale based on family size an earlier policy of 1790, in which bread was sold to the poor at below-market prices. In the Loddon and Clavering and the Forehoe Incorporations Speenhamland scales were found between 1795 and 1815 in periods of very high bread prices.(15)

But the experience of a small parish like Castle Rising is perhaps more representative of Norfolk villages outside the local incorporations. Doles of food and reduced prices of necessities to the poor were achieved by a combination of private charity and subsidy from the poor rates. These remedies were used in the severe winter of 1789 and repeated in years of high bread prices like 1795-6 and 1800.(16) The Norfolk replies to a circular on relieving the poor, published in the 'Annals of Agriculture' in 1795-6, indicated a widespread use of these traditional remedies of subsidizing food and fuel to the poor. Much less common was a more generous provision of agricultural piecework or a modest increase in farm wages. Farmers were generally reluctant to raise wages in case they found it difficult to lower them later, and so preferred temporary relief in kind to tide the labourer over particularly difficult times.(17) The parish overseer also preferred to make ad hoc relief payments rather than the alternative of working out a complex scale of allowances to solve what was only a temporary difficulty.

The situation changed when lower wheat prices after the Napoleonic Wars led to agricultural depression and reduced farm wages and employment. Under-employment became a permanent problem, and many able-bodied labourers earned a wage that would not provide subsistence for their families. In Suffolk the allowance system had begun at the end of the eighteenth century but had operated only in periods of high corn prices until 1816-17, when farm wages fell below subsistence level and poor relief became a more permanent supplement to low wages. Falling wage rates and rising poor relief expenditure suggests that there was a similar growth in the allowance system in Norfolk after 1815.(18) A return of 1824 from 20 out of the 33 hundreds in Norfolk indicated that all the respondents gave allowances; two-thirds gave an automatic allowance to families, most commonly after the third child; while one-third gave allowances according to circumstances such as lack of work or insufficient earnings. Two Norfolk writers at this time considered that allowances were widely given in the county and attributed it to low wages and lack of agricultural employment. The rural riots of 1830-1 reinforced the Norfolk allowance system because they highlighted the labourer's wretched condition and resulted in more generous allowances being given to him. Further evidence on allowances was given by 41 Norfolk parishes who completed a questionnaire of the Poor Law Commission in 1832, although badly worded questions produced ambiguous answers which need to be treated with caution. The replies suggested that two-thirds of the parishes gave allowances that were linked to family size but that only one-third explicitly linked allowances to a scale that also included the bread price. This argument that allowances become a widespread and permanent method of relieving the able-bodied Norfolk poor only after 1815 receives support from a study of quantitative evidence

in three other rural counties in this period. In Sussex, Essex and
Kent per capita poor relief in terms of wheat price was steady until about 1814, rose from 1814 to 1820, and remained at a high
level thereafter. In these three counties it was not until the
1820s that poor law administrators saw chronic unemployment or surplus labour as a permanent problem to be met by systematized relief
scales. Both in East Anglia and south-east England, poor law allowances seem to have functioned as an income subsidy (in which relief
was dependent on need), rather than as a wage subsidy (in which relief was dependent on the labourer's effort).(19)

The Royal Commission of 1834 had seen the allowance system as a
cumulative process which increased the pauperism it had been designed to relieve. This conclusion has been challenged recently, and
it has been suggested that the Speenhamland system (defined narrowly
as allowances in aid of wages) was actually in decline before 1834.
(20) At first this recent argument appears to have little relevance,
since it has been argued that Speenhamland scales were more widely
used in the 1820s than they had been before. Also, the few attempts
to abandon allowances in Norfolk were short-lived, since they foundered either on the farmers' preference for paying low wages which
were made up from the poor rate, or on the difficulties of administering a labour rate. But although the incidence of Speenhamland
allowances was not decreased, they were given on a less generous
scale at the end of the old poor law era. A good example of this
was the Loddon and Clavering Incorporation, where the scale of
payments to the unemployed, able-bodied poor was halved between
1830 and 1835.(21) One may suggest that Speenhamland relief did
not 'snowball' to create the pauperism it was meant to relieve, as
the Royal Commission had asserted, while on the basis of Norfolk
evidence disagreeing with the argument that the allowance system
was in decline before 1834.

The Report of 1834 was substantially embodied in the Poor Law
Amendment Act of that year which was mainly concerned with relief
to the able-bodied poor. This class of pauper, although never
precisely defined, were to be de-pauperized by relief that would
make them less well off than the independent labourer who lived
off his own earnings. This was to be achieved by discontinuing
outdoor relief to the able-bodied in their own homes and offering
indoor relief inside a workhouse, where conditions would be such
as to deter any but the really destitute. This self-acting
proof of destitution was called the workhouse test. To implement
the 1834 act the newly formed poor law unions in Norfolk either
built new workhouses or utilized existing poor law institutions.
By 1839 all the Norfolk unions had sufficient workhouse accommodation for the workhouse test to be a practicable policy. The Norfolk guardians gradually reduced outdoor relief to the able-bodied
by offering relief inside the workhouse to successive classes of
poor, starting with the single man or woman and ending with the
married labourer with a large family. Dr Kay, the assistant poor
law commissioner for the area, had adopted a subtle policy by
which he encouraged the guardians to adopt these new poor law policies on their own initiative. The success of this East Anglian
policy was such that he was able to claim proudly that his unions
were 'universally greatly in advance of any orders issued' to them.

Only when the guardians had ended outdoor relief to the able-bodied
would he advise the Poor Law Commission in London to issue an Outdoor Relief Prohibitory Order. By 1841 all rural Norfolk unions
had received one. This restriction of outdoor relief in the county
was in advance of that in most other areas. In 1840 the Poor Law
Commissioners had singled out Norfolk and Kent as their best administered counties. Two years later able-bodied pauperism in Norfolk
was at the lowest level of any county in the eastern region.(22)
    The stringent provisions of the New Poor Law deterred the Norfolk
able-bodied poor from seeking relief in these early years. Little
more than a quarter of the people offered indoor relief in Norfolk
workhouses accepted it in 1835-6. The result of this understandable reluctance to enter the workhouse was that in the winter
months of 1837-8 only 6 per cent of workhouse inmates were able-
bodied, and in a similar period in 1838-9 only 8 per cent.(23)
The proportion of the able-bodied to the total of applicants for
relief was halved, from one in three in 1834 to one in six in 1839.
The economic result of this successful operation of the workhouse
test in the county between 1834 and 1840 was that expenditure on
poor relief fell from £306,787 to £181,058 and expenditure per head
of county population declined from 15s 9d to 9s 3d (see Table 3a, p.84).
    This restriction of outdoor relief to the able-bodied continued
until 1843. R.N. Bacon collected a reliable series of relief statistics of Norfolk unions for his 'Report on Norfolk Agriculture'
and these showed that, in the 14 unions where figures were available from 1837 to 1843, those receiving outdoor relief decreased
from 89 to 79 per cent of the total. From 1839 and 1843 the decline
in outdoor relief was greater in Norfolk than in England and Wales.
The restriction of outdoor relief to the adult able-bodied in the
same period Norfolk was even larger, while the comparable decline
in England and Wales was again smaller (see Tables 4a and b).

TABLE 4a Outdoor pauperism in Norfolk and England and Wales, 1839-47*

	Norfolk			England and Wales		
	Total nos relieved	Nos and % receiving outdoor relief		Total nos relieved	Nos and % receiving outdoor relief	
			%			%
1839	35,057	29,101	83.0	904,765	780,128	86.2
1840	31,076	26,217	84.3	955,224	818,632	85.7
1841	33,034	27,372	82.8	1,080,774	920,946	85.2
1842	34,876	27,987	80.2	1,208,032	1,019,578	84.3
1843	37,666	29,849	79.2	1,303,089	1,101,162	84.5
1844	41,255	33,150	80.3	1,249,682	1,054,462	84.3
1845	42,161	34,316	81.3	1,244,107	1,061,991	85.3
1846	40,938	33,057	80.7	1,145,679	974,106	85.0
1847	46,436	37,558	80.8	1,471,133	1,244,554	84.5

* Quarter ending 25 March.
Source: Annual Reports of PLC.

TABLE 4b   Adult able-bodied pauperism in Norfolk and England and Wales, 1840-6*

| | Norfolk | | | | England and Wales | | | |
	In-door nos	Out-door nos	Total nos	% Out-door poor	In-door nos	Out-door nos	Total nos	% Out-door poor
				%				%
1840	1,530	4,731	6,261	75.5	42,712	203,060	245,772	82.6
1841	1,891	4,971	6,862	72.4	54,021	231,069	285,090	81.0
1842	2,480	5,241	7,721	67.8	69,625	269,446	339,071	79.4
1843	3,271	5,827	9,098	64.0	83,898	309,589	393,487	78.6
1844	3,522	6,928	10,450	66.2	82,704	282,234	364,938	77.3
1845	3,501	7,108	10,609	66.9	74,094	281,032	355,126	79.1
1846	3,442	6,900	10,342	66.7	70,081	247,171	317,252	77.9

*Quarter ending 25 March.
Source: Annual Reports of PLC.

But by 1843 the successful momentum of the New Poor Law was checked and the trend in poor relief was thereafter reversed in Norfolk.   Until this time the reformed Poor Law had worked well because, as the Walsingham guardians remarked, 'it is well known that the present poor laws apply the test to the rate payer, as well as to the labourer, and every provident parish have [sic] endeavoured to keep especially all the men with families in employment.'(24)   This system broke down in rural Norfolk under the more difficult farming conditions of the 1840s.   The run of good harvests from 1842 to 1844 had led to lower wheat prices, while the prolonged drought in the summer of 1844 had led to low yields on spring corn and a failure of fodder crops.   The resultant agricultural distress with squeezed profits for the farmers meant less employment for the labourer (particularly in winter) and more recourse to poor relief.   The revival of parochial emigration in rural Norfolk in 1844 also suggests a renewed concern with the problem of surplus labour.   The retention of parochial settlement in the Poor Law Amendment Act meant that the economic choice facing occupiers in a parish was still the same as under the Old Poor Law — either a labourer was employed, or he was relieved.   A Norfolk observer rightly stated in 1843 that this situation made it impossible to enforce the Outdoor Prohibitory Order since it was 'like building a wall round a space which would contain only a given number, and the prohibitory order like attempting to force into it a larger number than it would contain.'(25)   With less employment leading to more applications for relief, the local administrators of the Poor Law turned to cheaper alternatives to the workhouse system.   Their action was not untypical, since in the neighbouring county of Lincolnshire subversion of the New Poor Law had begun even earlier in 1842.(26)

The poor law inspector for the area, Sir John Walsham, admitted that the rural boards of guardians were 'actuated by what they imagine to be their immediate interest' and were 'chiefly an association of farmers'.(27)   In rural Norfolk unions four-fifths of the poor law guardians were farmers, and this group dominated the

administration of the New Poor Law as in many areas they had controlled the relief administration of the parish vestry before 1834.
Since the farmers were also the main ratepayers, they were concerned to administer poor relief on as economical a scale as possible
and reverted to proven traditional methods to achieve this. While
the inspectorate were earlier able to supervise closely local relief
administration, the reduction in their numbers from 21 in 1837 to
nine in 1842 meant that a brief twice-yearly visit was the most that
was feasible at this time. The inspectorate themselves admitted
that the detailed administration of relief in the localities rested
with the guardians. Although the relief regulations of the New Poor
Law did not give discretionary powers to the guardians, the earlier
policy of Dr Kay in encouraging the local boards to take the initiative in implementing a reformed relief policy had reinforced the
customary view that administrators in the localities controlled relief to their own poor. A comment that revealed Norfolk guardians'
attitudes was made by Mr James Hartt of Billingford, who had been a
guardian of his parish, first under Gilbert's Act and then under the
Poor Law Amendment Act. In 1844 he thought that 'if discrecinery
[sic] powers be given to the guardain [sic] and proper persons be
sent as guardians [sic] to administer the law — I think there can
be do doubt of it working well.'(28)   In his sense the law did work
well, because the guardians were able to follow their traditional
practices and ignore an overworked inspectorate. The inspectors
were the agents of a central board which was without effective coercive power.

Local administrators therefore had both the economic motive and
the practical opportunity to replace the workhouse system of the New
Poor Law with customary policies of outdoor relief. After 1843 the
proportion of outdoor to total relief given to paupers in Norfolk
increased. However, the most significant statistics concerning relief policies are those for the adult able-bodied poor, since it
was outdoor relief to this category of pauper that the 1834 act had
aimed to stop. The term 'able-bodied' never received a precise definition from the central poor law administration, and in practice
this group of paupers probably embraced all but those too obviously
infirm or sick to earn a livelihood. In the period 1840-6 the adult
able-bodied paupers made up one-fifth of the outdoor poor in Norfolk.
There was an increase in the relative share of outdoor to total
relief given to the Norfolk adult able-bodied from 1843 to 1846 while
there was a small overall decline nationally in the same period. But
the decisive overthrow of the policies of the New Poor Law came with
the agricultural depression of the late 1840s and early 1850s. The
statistics for the period after 1847 are not exactly comparable,
because the figures that were issued by the Poor Law Commission for
the winter quarter were replaced by the Poor Law Board with statistics for 1 January and 1 July of each year. However, the trend is
sufficiently clear for this to be of minor importance. By 1849 the
percentage of outdoor relief to the adult able-bodied poor had risen
to 83.7 per cent in Norfolk and 87.7 per cent for England and Wales.
It continued at a high level thereafter with the proportion of outdoor relief given to the Norfolk adult able-bodied pauper increasingly approximating to that for the country as a whole. In the 1870s
the Local Government Board's crusade against outdoor relief reduced

TABLE 4c Adult able-bodied outdoor pauperism in Norfolk, 1840-6*

	Total nos relieved by indoor and out-door relief	Nos and % receiving out-door relief	%	Nos and % of those receiving outdoor relief because of:							
				Low wages			Unemployment			Sickness	
				(i) Total**	(ii) Males only	(iii) %	(iv) Total**	(v) Males only	(vi) %	(vii) Total	(viii) %
1840	6,261	4,731	75.5	1,121	(22)	23.6	186	(56)	3.9		
1841	6,862	4,971	72.4	1,177	(151)	23.6	266	(118)	5.3		
1842	7,721	5,241	67.8	1,183	(85)	22.5	122	(47)	2.3	3,143	59.9
1843	9,098	5,827	64.0	1,235	(188)	21.1	202	(69)	3.4	3,399	58.3
1844	10,450	6,928	66.2	1,326	(193)	19.1	355	(122)	5.1	4,234	61.1
1845	10,609	7,108	66.9	1,472	(159)	20.7	321	(97)	4.5	4,796	67.4
1896	10,342	6,900	66.7	1,528	(159)	22.1	255	(97)	3.6	4,448	64.4

*   Quarter ending March 25.
** Excluding dependent wives.
Source: Annual Reports of PLC.

its incidence nationally, but in Norfolk the share of outdoor relief
cases continued to rise, so that this now formed a higher percentage
of the total than that for England and Wales. While the proportion
of outdoor relief cases declined both in the country as a whole and
in Norfolk in the 1880s and 1890s, the incidence of relief given
outside the workhouse was larger in Norfolk than elsewhere at the
end of the century (see Tables 4c and 4d). The pattern of outdoor
relief in Norfolk is interesting because it shows the contrasting
experience of southern rural England (where the workhouse system had
been swiftly and successfully imposed only to be gradually subverted)
with the northern industrial areas (where the New Poor Law was not
effectively implemented until the 1870s.(29)

TABLE 4d The percentage of adult able-bodied paupers receiving
outdoor relief, 1850-1900

	Norfolk	England and Wales
1850s	82.1	86.7
1860s	83.8	87.0
1870s	86.4	83.4
1880s	75.9	77.8
1890s	76.2	68.2

Source: Annual Reports of PLB and LGB.

By 1856 the poor law inspector for east and south-east England
had conceded defeat over the relief regulations of the New Poor Law:
  With scarcely an exception, the tendency everywhere is to substitute out-door for in-door relief whenever the guardians may
  legally do so. The *exceptions* to the Prohibitory Order, as I
  have often been compelled to remark, are almost invariably
  treated as *rules*. Out-door relief *may* be given — *ergo* outdoor relief *should* be given.
This policy of quietly subverting the 1834 act continued, and 15
years later another inspector commented that the guardians in this
same area very readily availed themselves of the exceptions in the
Prohibitory Order which gave them discretion in administering relief.(30) The most useful exception for the rural guardians was
relief in aid of sickness or accident, because this was a form of
outdoor relief that could legitimately be given to the able-bodied.
The proportion of outdoor relief ostensibly given for sickness to
the adult able-bodied in Norfolk was much higher than in England and
Wales. The statistical returns given in the Annual Reports of the
Poor Law Commission show that between 1842 and 1846 the county proportion of relief in aid of sickness to total outdoor relief for the
adult able-bodied was 62.2 per cent compared with a national figure
of 50.6 per cent. However, before 1843 the Norfolk guardians administered relief in aid of sickness more sparingly than in surrounding counties, but in that year (which it has been argued marked a
turning point in relief to the able-bodied in the county) there was
a large increase in relief ostensibly given for sickness, and by
1844 this type of relief had risen to a similarly high level in
Norfolk.

A systematic use of relief ostensibly in aid of sickness as a
means to relieve the able-bodied more cheaply outside the workhouse
is suggested by the fact that in Norfolk, as well as in Suffolk, the
rate of increase of such relief was twice as high between 1842 and
1846 as it was in England and Wales. There were no East Anglian
epidemics that could have accounted for this startling increase.
Later figures available for the period from 1849 to 1859 in the
Reports of the Poor Law Board indicated a continued use in Norfolk
of relief ostensibly in aid of sickness, although at a slightly
lower level than in neighbouring counties. In Norfolk 19.2 per cent
of adult able-bodied paupers relieved outside the workhouse from
1849-59 were men who received it ostensibly on account of their own
sickness, and this rose to 25.7 per cent if men relieved because of
their children's sickness were added, and to 44.6 per cent if relief
on account of their wives' illness was included. Indeed, by 1847,
Edwin Chadwick, the secretary to the Poor Law Commissioners, had
concluded gloomily that guardians in the eastern counties were using
relief in aid of sickness for a wholesale evasion of the relief regulations of the New Poor Law:(31)

In Norfolk and Suffolk now, in large districts, I believe the
allowance system was let in upon the apparently small exception
of allowing relief to a poor family, on the occurrence of sickness to one of them. That was made the means of flooding the
unions or parishes with the allowance system; a man presented
himself for relief, and said he must have an addition made to
his wages; that he could not go on with those wages. The ordinary reply was, 'But the prohibitory order prohibits your having
relief in aid of wages.' But they went on to say, 'Have you got
none of your family sick?' 'No.' 'Think again?' 'Yes, there
is my boy has got a sore eye.' 'Well, you shall have an order
for medical relief for him, and an allowance on account of the
sickness of a part of your family.'

Rural guardians used relief ostensibly in aid of sickness as a
means of relieving low-paid, irregularly employed agricultural
labourers. This form of relief needed no justification to the central board in London, since it was an exception to the Prohibitory
Order; whereas this was not the case when relief was given, and
was stated that it was given, because of low wages or unemployment.
Outdoor relief given to the adult able-bodied poor in Norfolk on
account of low wages or unemployment remained at a low level, as
can be seen in the two periods of 1840-6 and 1848-59 when statistics were available in the reports of the central poor law authority.
In the first period of 1840-6 this type of relief on account of low
wages or unemployment formed only a quarter of that given, of which
4.0 per cent was due to unemployment and 21.8 per cent to low wages.
But these were figures for the adult able-bodied and concealed the
fact that most of this went to women (particularly to widows), and
only 3.6 per cent went to men impoverished because of low earnings
and irregular employment. It was significant too that the rise in
proportion of relief given to the adult labourer outside the workhouse in 1843-4 was accounted for less by relief stated to be given
because of low wages or unemployment, which the local economic
conditions would have suggested, but by relief given on the ostensible grounds of sickness (see Table 4c). In the second period of

1848-59 only 0.7 per cent of the adult able-bodied outdoor poor
in Norfolk were men who received it for reasons that included lack
of work. This very low proportion was similar to that in surrounding, rural counties.

III EMPLOYMENT SCHEMES UNDER THE POOR LAW

When the New Poor Law had been in actual operation for over a decade
in East Anglia, Edwin Chadwick concluded accurately that the 'abuses'
in the administration of the Poor Law were as great as they had been
before the Poor Law Amendment Act of 1834. He attributed this to:
(32)

> that part of the present poor-law which throws the burthen upon
> the occupiers of a narrow area, who endeavour ... to get back by
> fraud what is imposed upon them by force. In various ways they
> try to get relief, or a diminution of the rates; sometimes by
> undue exceptions to medical orders, sometimes by throwing their
> labourers on the highway rates, sometimes by subscription rates;
> and in various other ways the old abuse does prevail very
> largely....

It has already been suggested that the allowance system was as much
a feature of the New, as of the Old Poor Law, while public employment schemes under the New Poor Law included not only a continued
use of the highway rates to relieve the poor, but a modification of
the old poor law practices of roundsmen and labour rates in the
ticket system of the new poor law era.

The use of the highway or surveyor's rate to relieve the able-
bodied labourer was widely used in Norfolk before 1834 and was also
resorted to after 1834. In 1831-2 2,850 Norfolk men were relieved
by being employed on the roads (the third highest county total), and
a sum of £16,554 was paid from the poor rate to the parish surveyors
for this purpose. After the Poor Law Amendment Act it became cheaper for parishes to relieve the poor through the highway rate than
from the poor rate. This was because high parish relief expenditure
led to a correspondingly high contribution by the parish to the common fund of the poor law union. The use of highway rates to relieve
the Norfolk poor partly explains the rise in the county's highway
rates from £21,544 in 1837 to £34,527 by 1845. In 1845, £13,700 of
the surveyor's rate was spent on manual labour or a sum equivalent
to 8 per cent of poor relief expenditure. This use of the highway
rate to relieve the poor after 1834 was fairly common, being found
not only in neighbouring rural counties but also in the industrial
and mining areas of County Durham.(33)

Parallel to the use of the highway rate were private or subscription rates which were found in south Norfolk in the late 1830s.
These aimed to subsidize low real wages, caused by high corn prices,
with doles of corn financed by private subscription. This stopped
the labourer from having to enter the workhouse because of his below-
subsistence income, saved the farmer as employer from having to raise
money wages, and prevented the farmer as ratepayer from having to pay
for the expensive indoor relief of the labourer in the workhouse.
Unlike the highway rate, the private rate was a voluntary levy and
as such tended to be more short-lived.(34)

Before 1834 the economic pressure of surplus labour had led to more ambitious and organized schemes to employ the poor. Popular in the late eighteenth and early nineteenth centuries were rounds-men schemes, which often either developed into, or were supplemented by, labour rate schemes. For example, the Shipdham employment schemes from 1830 to 1835 had characteristics of both, while in Brockdish roundsmen were used to supplement a labour rate. Norfolk parishes attached no very precise meaning to the term 'roundsmen', but typically it involved labourers, termed 'roundsmen', tramping round the employers in the parish in search of work, their wages if employed being paid partly from the parish poor rate. A very rough idea of the use of roundsmen was given in returns of 1824 and 1832, which suggested a decline in their incidence from one in every three to one in eight Norfolk villages.(35) This declining popularity is accounted for by an increasing use of labour rates in the same period. The successful operation of labour rates in a few parishes like South Walsham and Great Dunham in the 1820s recommended them to many more villages when the rural disturbances of 1830-1 had led to a greater concern to employ the Norfolk labourer. About one-fifth of Norfolk villages were using a labour rate from October 1832 to March 1834 when such schemes had a legal sanction. Characteristically, a labour rate involved the allocation of set-tled, unemployed labourers among the employers or ratepayers in the village on the basis of their relative share of the acreage or the poor rate. Those who did not employ the requisite number at the wages that had been agreed upon had to pay a corresponding amount in a labour rate. The financial hardships that have been attributed to the labour rate were in practice often avoided in Norfolk parishes by excluding the poorer occupiers, and by giving a special basis of assessment to tithe-owners and to shopkeepers or trades-men.(36)

Labour allocation was also used in the new poor law era, and an interesting scheme was the ticket or certificate system, which was found in a quarter of the poor law unions in six counties in eastern England. It was similar to the labour rate in that it relied on a division of labourers in a parish, although this was based on a tacit, rather than formal, agreement. It shared with the roundsman system the practice of sending labourers round the local farmers in search of work, but with the difference that in the ticket system the labourers were in search of independent employment in which wages were not supplemented by money from the poor rate. Tickets, like earlier roundsmen and labour rate schemes, were a response to the continued existence of surplus labour in the area, but they did not directly evolve from them, as Chadwick asserted. One obvious difference between the allocation schemes of the Old and New Poor Law was that the ticket system operated not on the basis of the parish but on that of the poor law union, and that the board of guardians and not the parish vestry served as the labour exchange. (37)

The system was first publicized in 1844 in an inquiry by 'The Times' into incendiarism in East Anglia, which concluded that fires were a result of abuses in the administration of the New Poor Law. John Campbell Foster, the special correspondent in this inquiry, had earlier reported on the Rebecca Riots in South Wales, and must

be counted an experienced investigator, although his connection with
a newspaper that was an avowed opponent of the New Poor Law suggests
that he may have been predisposed to believe the worst of local relief administrators. On the ticket system he said, 'I believe this
practice to prevail generally throughout the counties of Norfolk and
Suffolk; and hence the distress and discontent, and the consequent
fires.'(38) Questions in Parliament led to placatory answers by Sir
James Graham, the secretary of state for home affairs, who said
that tickets were not used generally and that the Poor Law Commission would see that their use was discontinued. He had been briefed
by a report from Sir John Walsham who was the poor law inspector for
East Anglia. Disagreeing with Foster's view that tickets were common in Norfolk, Walsham thought correctly that they existed only in
the two east Norfolk unions of Blofield and Henstead. However, Walsham had his own reasons for minimizing both the incidence and the
economic implications of the ticket system. The publicity had
wrong-footed him, and he had had to admit to the Poor Law Commissioners that he was imperfectly informed of this practice which
operated over a sizeable part of his district. His inquiries were
conducted with circumspection through the clerks of the union, and
his final report on the ticket system contained the warning that it
involved ex officio guardians with social and political influence.
The Poor Law Commissioners, divided over policy and conscious of
their unpopularity and political weakness, wished only to smother
any adverse publicity. They must have been grateful for the diver-
sion of public interest from East Anglian incendiarism to the Post
Office Affair, which also centred on the hapless Graham, and which
followed the political dynamite of his admission that he had been
opening the mails. Mainly because of this, the Poor Law Commission
escaped the public inquiry that had been demanded in the Commons
and merely submitted to Parliament a brief analysis by Sir John
Walsham in a 'Report on Certain alleged Abuses in the Administration of the Poor-law in Norfolk and Suffolk'.

In Norfolk the ticket system had begun shortly after the beginning of the new poor law administration by the Blofield guardians
in 1836:

> The board now agreed that no application should be taken from
> any able-bodied paupers for relief for want of employment unless
> such paupers produce to the relieving officer a certificate from
> the several occupiers in their respective parishes of having
> applied to them for work.

Printed certificates were supplied by the union which stated that
'The day of ───── 18── we the undersigned inhabitants and occupiers
of the parish of ───── do hereby certify that ───── has applied
for work and that we are unable to supply them with it.'(39) Later,
standard certificates supplied to relieving officers were used, and
these had been produced as a result of the independent growth of the
ticket or certificate system in a second area. This had originated
earlier in the north Essex town of Saffron Walden in 1829, and the
old poor law practice had spread first to the other parishes that
were included in the new poor law Union of Saffron Walden in 1835,
and then to neighbouring unions in Cambridgeshire, Suffolk, Essex
and Hertfordshire. In some unions in this second area tickets were
used oppressively as a means of delaying or refusing relief to the

labourer, or of forcing him to accept employment at very low wages.
But in the Blofield Union there was little delay because the unemployed labourer received his ticket from the relieving officer
rather than from the board of guardians, and could therefore submit
his completed certificate at the next weekly board meeting. When he
had obtained the ticket the labourer went round the local employers,
who would sign the ticket if they had no work to offer, but who
might be reminded of the alternative cost of unemployment in relief,
and therefore provide a job. The Blofield guardians apparently
acted humanely, since they claimed that they never refused relief
to an applicant who had no ticket, nor did they deny relief if a man
had refused work at inadequate wages. But their actual practice may
well have been harsher, since the labourers' resentment against the
Blofield guardians was revealed by fires at their farms in 1844.(40)
    This organized allocation of labour was the response to rural
under-employment of farmers who dominated both local employment and
the administration of poor relief. The highly organized distribution of labour in the ticket system was the remedy for a particularly acute problem of surplus labour. The Blofield Union faced not
only agrarian under-employment but structural unemployment caused by
the decline of the Norwich textiles industry. In this context it
is significant that it was in 1839, a particularly depressed year
for Norwich manufacturers, that the certificate system spread from
Blofield into the neighbouring Henstead Union.(41) In other areas
in the county chronic under-employment in agriculture also led to
the machinery of the new poor law unions being used to control the
local labour market. In the Erpingham Union, where continued parochial emigration indicated a real surplus of labourers, the guardians' weekly board meeting acted as a labour exchange for the area.
The poor law inspector, Dr Kay, commented that the Erpingham guardians 'have undertaken to manage the union on the same shortsighted
economical principles as their own farms'. The guardians brought
news of jobs available in the parishes every spring, and the surplus labourers who had spent the winter in the workhouse were discharged to fill them. The labourers were prosecuted by the guardians if they applied for relief again after they had been found a
job at 'fair wages' and were liable to a month's imprisonment with
hard labour.(42) The guardians acted as both judge and jury since
the local justices who tried the case were themselves ex officio
guardians. In this situation an oppressive control of the labour
market could be established because the same men controlled the two
alternative sources of income for the labourer. The effect of this
dual control by farmers of employment and poor relief was to blur,
if not to eradicate, the distinction between private and public
policy.

IV   THE POOR LAW AND INDEPENDENT WAGES AND EMPLOYMENT

While economic attitudes permeated social policy in the administration of the Poor Law, non-economic attitudes produced by the social
implications of under-employment conditioned the Norfolk farmers'
employment policies. Labour allocation policies (whether these were
associated with the administration of the Poor Law or independent of

it) were designed to make farmers employ more men than they would otherwise have done. In the 1820s and 1830s spade husbandry schemes run by poor law administrators were parallelled elsewhere by those of private individuals.(43)   The public apportionment of the surplus labourers as parochial roundsmen or in labour rates or ticket schemes was found side by side with purely private agreements among occupiers or landlords to employ all the labourers in the parish. The New Poor Law made farmers even more conscious of the need to employ the labourer than had been the case under the Old Poor Law. As a west Norfolk farmer commented, 'now if a farmer has any feeling of shame he will not allow his parish to occupy a conspicuous situation before his *brother farmers* at the board of guardians.'(44) However, this desire to maximize employment was conditioned by the relative prosperity of agriculture and hence the economic ability of the farmer to pay the labourer, and was at all times a more obvious characteristic of the large owner—occupier and the wealthier tenant farmer. It was these farmers particularly who increased employment, after the Poor Law Amendment Act of 1834 had made the alternative cost of unemployment more expensive, by its attempt to restrict poor relief for the able-bodied to costlier indoor relief in the workhouse.

The workhouse test of the New Poor Law had been designed to reduce pauperism not only by its 'less eligible' conditions, deterring any but the destitute labourer from entering the workhouse, but also by the high cost of indoor relief, pressurizing the employers into providing sufficient wages and employment to give the labourer an independent subsistence income. What had not been foreseen was that this test on employers would produce differential employment policies. This was particularly important in the first years of the New Poor Law before it was appreciated that outdoor allowances to the able-bodied poor could be engineered within the framework of the reformed system of poor relief. While it cost twice as much to relieve a married man with a family in the workhouse as it cost to employ him, it was cheaper to relieve than to employ a single labourer. This worked advantageously for the married man, for whom the provision of day work became more regular and for whom there were more opportunities for higher earnings at piece work. His wife and children were also provided with more work on the farm, and the increased use of child labour struck contemporaries as one of the most obvious effects of the 1834 act. In contrast, the single man was the first to be laid off when work was short in wet or frosty weather and the last to be employed again. He customarily spent the winter in the workhouse along with a few married men whose laziness or independent spirit was also penalized in this way. The use of the union workhouse as a repository of surplus labour was most common among small farmers. As they paid a small proportion of the parish poor rate they were liable for only a minor fraction of the higher relief costs resulting from increased unemployment.(45)

Lack of quantitative data and emotive contemporary opinions make it difficult to assess how much the need to maximize employment in rural Norfolk retarded mechanization on local farms. A well-stocked labour market and the social desirability of providing winter employment for resident labourers meant that farmers in the

county were comparatively slow to adopt threshing machines. In 1792
none of the great corn farmers in Norfolk was using one, and in the
opening years of the nineteenth century few were in use. After 1814,
however, the relatively depressed state of agriculture meant that
older ideas of social responsibility by employer to labourer were
undercut by the increased economic pressures on the farmer. Mechanized threshing helped the farmer to get corn to market earlier
after harvest and so to obtain higher prices. East Anglia was a
centre of production for agricultural implements, and with two firms
in Norfolk and three in Suffolk the local farmers found it easy to
acquire from them the newer, portable threshing machines either by
purchase or hire.(46) The impact of this local adoption of threshing machines was felt even in west Norfolk, where under-employment
was a less serious problem. The overseers of Hilgay lamented in
1825:(47)

> The use of thrashing machines is very injurious to the interests
> of agriculture, by throwing a great number of labourers out of
> employment during the winter. The consequence is, that they
> contract a habit of idleness, and are a continual burthen on the
> poor rates; as instead of being paid by the farmer, they are
> paid by the overseer.

The effect of mechanized threshing on the surplus labour problem of
east Norfolk was greater and the hostility of the labourers there
was shown in the widespread breaking of threshing machines in 1816,
and again in 1822 and 1830. Their continued hostility suggests that
they thought that their livelihood had been damaged by the use of
threshing machines while the ritualized quality of some of the
machine-breaking also suggests that they had become a powerful symbol for the labourers of their deteriorating social condition in
this period.

Mechanization was certainly one cause of the mobility of the Norfolk poor in the 1830s. A party of Attleborough labourers who wanted
to join in the Poor Law Commission's Emigration Scheme in 1836 wrote:
'For the farmers are imployint the threshing machines and other mech-
inery so that there are from 6 to 12 of able men that are able to
work that cannot get imployint.'(48) A few years later east Norfolk
guardians thought that mechanized threshing was a principal cause of
the many applications that there had been because of unemployment.
(49) By the 1840s the threshing machine was used by virtually every
improving farmer in Norfolk to thresh wheat, although the flail was
still thought to be a cheap and efficient means to thresh barley.
A few of these larger farmers showed that they were conscious of the
surplus labour problem and modified the progress of mechanization on
their farms accordingly. Some had a portion of their corn threshed
by the flail while others used a hand-powered, rather than steam- or
horse-powered, threshing machine in order to maximize employment.
Others dibbled rather than drilled some of their wheat in order to
give work to women and children.(50) But by the mid-nineteenth century the comparative prosperity of Norfolk agriculture meant that
mechanization was a less serious threat to the employment of the
labourer. John Hudson of Castleacre, a typical high farmer, stated
that mechanization had actually increased the employment available
on his farm. He also said that he employed more men than were necessary, since he did not like to see men on the roads, and that the

poor rate would double if they were sent to the workhouse.(51)   Delayed or limited mechanization was therefore of smaller importance
in the attempt to maximize employment than labour allocation schemes
and relief in aid of wages.

'For the poor's rates of a country village fall principally on
the farmer; and if he does not employ the poor, he must support
them in idleness.' So wrote a correspondent of William Marshall at
the end of the eighteenth century in a discussion on the provision
of fieldwork for the poor in Norfolk agriculture. The organization
of women and children in agricultural companies or gangs was widely
used as an alternative to poor relief, both before and after the
Speenhamland period. From the 1760s the poor were employed in east
Norfolk to dibble or drop wheat, and the practice spread rapidly
because it was more efficient than broadcasting since it economized
on seed and also improved yields.(52) After the New Poor Law of
1834 the practice of dropping and dibbling corn became more widespread in order to provide employment, instead of relief, to the
poor. Since by this time drilled wheat was recognized to be more
efficient than dropping, this indicated a deliberate use of non-
economic methods to achieve socially desirable ends.(53) By the mid-
nineteenth century dropping was only one out of many tasks done by
women and children in Norfolk field labour. They were often organized in mobile public gangs to weed corn, clear stones, single
turnips, top and tail root crops and set potatoes for the farmers
in the neighbourhood. A survey of 1867 showed that 70 per cent of
the members of Norfolk gangs were women and only 5 per cent were men.
Gangs had been found before the new poor law era in Castleacre, but
they spread after 1834 to several other areas and by the 1860s were
found in villages over half the county, and particularly in the
west.(54)

'From these two causes, viz.,the excess of labourers in Castle
Acre and the defect of them in neighbouring parishes,sprung the
gang-system of employment.' With this statement Mr Denison, who
had investigated the employment of women and children in Norfolk
in 1843, firmly attributed the gang system to the artificial distribution of the population in the 'close' and 'open' parishes caused
by the settlement provisions of the Poor Law. Since later historians have also suggested a causal relationship between 'close' and
'open' parishes and the gang system, it is worth examining Castleacre, the supposed origin of the gang system, as a critical case to
test the hypothesis.(55) Denison stated that gangs went from the
'open' parish of Castleacre to work in the neighbouring 'close'
parishes of Southacre, Newton by Castleacre, Narford, Westacre, East
Walton, Gaytonthorpe, Weasenham, Lexham, Rougham and Sporle.

Castleacre was a good example of an 'open' parish. Fragmented
land ownership had led to a plentiful supply of sub-standard homes,
which were described as early as 1784 by a French traveller as being
'dirty and badly built, fit only for France'. By 1843 a third of
its poor had no settlement there. A resident described the village
graphically as 'the coop of all the scrapings in the county' because
its gang employment attracted all those whose bad character would
prevent them getting jobs elsewhere.(56) Abundant labour in Castleacre made it worthwhile for enterprising individuals to organize
several gangs of women and children who were sent to perform field-

work for farmers in neighbouring parishes. All these parishes
(listed by Denison) were 'close' parishes if the wider definition
of a concentrated land ownership is an acceptable criterion; but
if a more rigorous test on the basis of the adequacy of the resident population to supply the regular labour demands of local employers is used, then only three of the villages were 'close'
parishes.

Contemporaries thought that the gang labour of women and children was displacing male labour on Norfolk farms. An analysis of
employment in the area suggests that this was not the case. Only
in the three parishes of Southacre, Newton by Castleacre and Narford
was there an inadequate supply of resident male labourers for the
regular employment on the farms in the parish. In these three
parishes, landowners had restricted cottage provision so much that,
on a ratio of adequacy of one cottage to every 50 acres (which was
the yardstick of the local chairman of the board of guardians),
Southacre was deficient in 34 cottages, Newton by Castleacre in 10
and Narford in 25. Here, men were imported to work on the farms
from Castleacre and other parishes, although the latter were still
responsible for the relief of the labourer during unemployment,
sickness and old age. Obviously, the Castleacre gangs of women and
children were not only a product of the distribution of population
in 'close' and 'open' parishes, because in the majority of the
parishes they visited a displacement of resident male labour engaged in regular employment would have been prohibitively expensive
in poor relief. In the remaining three parishes of Southacre, Newton by Castleacre and Narford, imported male labour, and not gang
labour from Castleacre, was employed regularly. But the improved
cultivation of mid-nineteenth-century Norfolk required extra seasonal labour, which the small reserve of under-employed labourers in
the 'close' parishes could not supply, so the need was filled by
the mobile gangs of Castleacre. Only to this modified extent were
agricultural gangs a product of the 'close' and 'open' parish system created by the settlement provisions of the Poor Law.(57)

Shortly after the Poor Law Amendment Act had been implemented in
Norfolk, the poor law inspector Dr Kay reported to the Poor Law
Commission that the act had led to a 'substitution of employment
with sufficient wages for dependence upon the poor rates'. A
casual reading might suggest Kay thought that the New Poor Law had
increased wages, thus vindicating the 1834 Report which had stated
that an end to the outdoor allowances of the Old Poor Law would result in increased wages to the rural labourer. But he later clarified his position by stating that any increase in day wages was a
result of higher wheat prices, and that it was a more generous provision of piecework that had led to higher earnings and a greater
income.(58) All contemporary observers agreed that in the first
half of the nineteenth century changes in Norfolk agricultural wages
followed those in wheat prices. It was said that the weekly wage
rate was customarily one-third of the price of a coomb of wheat
(an East Anglian measure equivalent to two bushels), with wages
varying by 1s for about every 5s fluctuation in the price of wheat.

In theory, the standard wages—wheat sliding scale operative in
Norfolk provided for wages at 9s per week when wheat was 20-25s
a coomb, 10s when wheat was 25-30s, 11s when wheat was 30-35s and

12s thereafter, whatever the wheat price. Wages were not reduced
below 8 or 9s a week, which, on economic as well as customary
social grounds, was held to be a subsistence income. In practice,
however, wages were inelastic in relation to rises in wheat price,
so that, as Sir John Walsham commented in 1846, 'the increase in
wages consequent upon an increase in the price of corn bears no
kind of proportion to such increase'. This was because farmers
were afraid that they would not easily be able to lower wages when
a good harvest had lowered corn prices again.(59)

It was this reluctance to raise money wages sufficiently to
compensate for higher wheat prices that had led to the system of
poor law allowances in Norfolk. Nathaniel Kent had noticed that in
the 1780s and 1790s prices had increased faster than the cost of
labour in the county. Earlier in the chapter it was argued that very
few farmers were prepared to raise wages in the years of high bread
prices in 1795 and 1796 but preferred to compensate for the decline
in the labourer's real wages by subsidizing him through charity or
poor relief. This reluctance to maintain the labourer's income in
real terms continued as was shown by two sets of wages, one for east
Norfolk between 1806 and 1845, and the other for west Norfolk for
five-year periods from 1791 to 1845. These suggested that the farm
wages that were actually paid were lower in three out of four years
than those theoretically provided for on the wheat—wages scale,
which had been designed to guarantee a subsistence income for the
Norfolk labourer. This evidence supports Mark Blaug's thesis that
the authors of the 1834 Report were wrong in condemning the allowances of the Old Poor Law as leading to low wages, but suggests
instead that low wages resulted in allowances.(60) It also indicated that the 1834 act had a minimal effect on this situation in
Norfolk.

In rural Norfolk economic change rather than administrative reform shaped the system of poor relief. Variations in the wages
and employment of agricultural labourers, who formed the largest
occupational group in the county, were a major determinant of poor
law allowances and poor law employment schemes. Before 1814 agricultural prosperity and an acceptance of social responsibility by
the farmer towards the labourer resulted in adequate agricultural
wages. By the 1860s revived farming affluence meant that the farmer could afford to pay better wages, while the increased mobility
of the labourer gave him sufficient motive to do so, and so prevent
a labour shortage developing. But between the second to the sixth
decade of the century there was a widespread failure in Norfolk to
provide an independent subsistence income for the agricultural
labourer. Rural under-employment in this intervening period led
farmers in their capacity as poor law administrators to confuse the
private labour bill of the farm with the public poor relief of the
parish or union. Poor law allowances and employment schemes were
found to be a cheap alternative to wages for a reserve labour force
during the slack months of the farming year. In contrast to this
major impact that the economy had on the Poor Law in rural Norfolk,
the changing relief and settlement provisions of the Poor Law itself
were only a minor influence on the wage and employment policies of
the Norfolk farmer. The important influence that economic factors
had on poor law policy in the Norfolk countryside was also experienced in the major urban area in the county — Norwich.

CHAPTER 7

POOR RELIEF AND THE POLITICAL ECONOMY OF NORWICH, 1834-63

> Norwich, it is feared, has seen its best days as a place of
> commerce; and would appear to be in that painful state of
> transition from a once flourishing manufacturing prosperity to
> its entire decline, and must, ere long, revert to its original
> condition of a capital of an extensive agricultural district.
> A large portion of its inhabitants are therefore poor, their
> labour becoming daily lowered in amount and recompense....
> Neglect and decay are now conspicuous in the streets and
> quarters occupied by the working classes, so as to render them
> places of most dismal aspect.

This description of Norwich in 1844(1) revealed the impact on the
city of the decline of its staple, the textile industry. The city's
economic crisis during the mid-nineteenth century produced great
social changes which included the overthrow in 1863 of the system of
poor law administration that had been established in 1712. A central preoccupation of the Norwich guardians in the period from 1834
to 1863 was how to maintain a traditionally humane policy of relieving the poor, when the local ratepayers were feeling the financial pinch of industrial depression, and when the numbers of poor
were increasing rapidly.

There was substantial unemployment among Norwich handloom weavers
by the late 1830s. In 1839, a very depressed year, it was estimated
reliably that weavers were without work for one-third of their time
and that one-fifth of the looms were unemployed. Six years later
the 'Norfolk Chronicle' stated that three-quarters of the 2,000 to
2,500 outdoor paupers were unemployed weavers, and that they cost
the Norwich ratepayers over £300 each week.(2) The widespread dependence of the city weavers on poor relief was a result of the
economic difficulties of the textile industry, but these industrial
difficulties were themselves held to be partly a result of the costly administration of the Poor Law. William Stark, a Norwich textiles manufacturer, blamed the slow mechanization of the Norwich
industry on the administration of the Poor Law and on party strife.
(3)

Norwich life was pervaded with the party struggle between the
Whigs (the 'blue and whites') and the Tories (the 'orange and
purples'). The poor law administration of the Norwich Incorporation

was one of the main party battlegrounds; in the original act, which incorporated the parishes and hamlets of the city for the common relief of the poor in 1712, the municipal corporation had dominated the composition of the Court of Guardians. Guardians gradually came to view the poor rate as a supplement to their elec- toral funds, so that by the 1820s they were ordering poor relief to their nominees with almost no accountability, and poor law allow- ances became a fruitful method of buying votes in municipal elec- tions. In 1827 the high level of the poor rates caused a revulsion against this tradition and the Whigs won the municipal election in that year by attacking the guardians' administration. They went on to sponsor a revised poor law act for the city, which restricted the nominees of the Norwich Corporation to one-third of the guard- ians, and which allowed the citizens to inspect the accounts of poor relief. The large extent of the corruption that was revealed, and the refusal to implement a more frugal poor law administration by the guardians who had been nominated by the municipal corpora- tion, led to a further act in 1831 in which all the guardians were to be chosen by ratepayers. The electorate consisted of those who paid poor rates on properties with an annual value of £10 or more. (4) The electoral qualifications indicated the paternalistic char- acter of the reformed poor law system since those with more valuable property were given multiple votes in the guardians' elections.

The direct involvement of the Norwich Town Corporation in the work of the guardians had ended, but the close connection of poli- tics and the Poor Law continued, because it was impossible to insu- late any aspect of the city from party strife. A citizen commented in 1839 that 'The party spirit enters into everything; every insti- tution of the town is a subject of party election; it is like two towns in one, and acting in hostility against each other.'(5) The Poor Law continued to be an issue in both municipal and parliamen- tary elections in the city. On the board of guardians the appoint- ments of officials and the awarding of contracts were made on a party basis. Also, slipshod accounting made it possible for relief to continue to be administered to further political interests as well as the relief of poverty. A politicized Poor Law was found during the new poor law era in other urban areas in the Midlands and in the North of England, where guardians' elections, and in some cases poor law policies, involved a struggle between political parties.(6)

This tradition of a passionate struggle between the party fac- tions within the propertied classes was strengthened in the 1830s and 1840s by the turbulence of the ordinary people who responded violently when their income was threatened by the economic decline of Norwich. Mr Wilson, the guardians' accountant, commented that a man was forced into one party or another; neutrality was impos- sible. The Norwich guardians were polarized into party camps and both sides were prevented from introducing, or supporting, poor law reform by the threat of electoral defeat or physical violence. The high state of tension in the city is suggested by the guardians being careful to go about their daily business armed during the period when they were conducting a review of outdoor relief cases in 1836.(7) Dr Kay, the assistant poor law commissioner, compared Norwich to an angry boil which generated pus or corruption, and was

pessimistic about the imposition of the New Poor Law there.   He
commented sarcastically:(8)

> I hope all Norfolk will in a very short time indeed be completely
> subjected to the authority of the Commissioners excepting that
> pure city of Norwich, in which though the orders have not yet
> been burned by the common hangman, I have no confidence that my
> eloquence will *prevail above* the voice of faction.

But although the violence and corruption shocked the visitor to
the city, the Norwich citizens preferred their own customary methods
of conducting their affairs to any of the alternatives that the
central government attempted to impose upon them.   Its independent
temper had been shown in the extraordinary lengths taken to oppose
the Municipal Corporation Act in 1835.   Outside interference with
the local administration of the Poor Law by the Poor Law Commissioners, who were devoid of effective, coercive authority, was unlikely to succeed.   Indeed, early opposition to the powers of the
Poor Law Commission by the conservative M.P. for the borough, Sir
James Scarlett, had helped to bring this about because it had led
to a limitation of the powers of the central body in the committee
stage of the 1834 act.(9)

I   THE FAILURE TO IMPOSE THE 1834 ACT

Sir Edward Parry, the first assistant poor law commissioner to
attempt to bring Norwich under the Poor Law Amendment Act, was ham-
pered not only by the unpropitious political situation in Norwich
but by his own personality and ignorance of the law.   An upright,
sincere man with old-fashioned principles, Parry lacked political
guile and tactical flexibility.   He confronted the Norwich Court of
Guardians in December, taxing them with neglecting their duty, and being
determined to oppose a central authority.   He threatened that, although the Poor Law Commissioners were distant, yet their power was
effective.   Parry sincerely believed this, but in reality the Poor
Law Commission had restricted powers over an area protected as was
Norwich by a local poor law act.   These powers were clarified by a
later series of court cases involving disputes between places under
local act and the Poor Law Commission, in which it was decided that
local poor law acts were not complete codes of practice but merely
modified the general law in specified matters.   However, the local
acts for Norwich poor law administration were sufficiently comprehensive to give the city substantial protection from external interference while wider, political considerations suggested to the central authority that discretion was the better part of valour in
dealing with Norwich.(10)

A frontal assault on the city's administration of relief had
failed to bring about reform but had precipitated the Poor Law into
the central whirlpool of Norwich politics.   The Tory guardians had
left the Court of Guardians before Parry had finished addressing
them during his visit in December 1835, and a few days later a Tory
broadsheet was circulated in Norwich which attacked the Whigs for
supporting a Poor Law which oppressed the poor man.   The next Tory
production was entitled 'The Glorious Working of the Whigs!', and as
Figure 11 shows, it combined a party attack with a personal offensive

THE GLORIOUS WORKING

OF THE

WHIGS!

Jan. 2nd,   PRICE ONE PENNY.   1836.

Jack Straw & the Polar Star

GRINDING the POOR!

INDEED! SIR EDWARD you're not courteous,
In fact, your Language don't please half of us;
When *Gentlemen* have spoken, Sir, in court,
They seldom like to be *brow-beaten* for't;
Much less to be degraded lower still,
By hearing threat'ning hints of the *Tread-mill*;
And shall the honor'd Guardians of the Poor,
Be sent the Tread-wheel horrors to explore,
Because they dare to speak in their own Hall,
To advocate the cause of one and all ?
Or must they servilly stand still in awe,
And side with you like that old black *Jack Straw?*
Or else be sent to the Felon's Wheel,
Which makes *hard* hearts, e'en hearts of *flint* to feel!
C-mm-ss--n-r or not, SIR EDWARD P---y,
Than see you more—we'd sooner see Old Harry!

Thus much, Sir, for *Ourselves* we dare to plead,
And now, Sir, for our *Poor*—who stand in need
Of lodgings, raiment, food and every thing
That honest labour should to poor folks bring!

Why should the Whigs raise up their *Prisons* high
With gloomy fronts, and walls that reach the sky ;
Are such dark Dungeons to immure a band
Of *Rogues* and *Swindlers* that infest the land ?
"No!" some cry,—"They are for *one crime* more
The *crime* of being *old, infirm,* and *poor!*"
O Heaven! assist us how to make reply,
To such *cold, base,* and *selfish villany* !
What! trample on their *rights*, and herd them there
In close confinement—e'en to *speak* nor dare !
And the mis'rable creatures you would feed
With scanty pittances—ah! small indeed !
You say they're *Paupers*, that's indeed too true ;
But tell us, *Sir Edward*—Pray what are *You?*
Perhaps you think it right to domineer,
And drive your Measures by exciting fear?
Be *tame, kind,* don't *bully—Good Sir Ned*,
And show at once you've been humanely bred ;
Tell the base Whigs—*the Plund'rers of the Poor*.
To ope their *hearts*, and not the *Workhouse-door*.

To THE PUBLIC.—We are sorry to state, there is
Letter, signed "A Weaver," which appeared in
Weathercock) Dated Dec. 26.—"But let the gall'd
that in consequence of the Foul Abuse therein
Waggeries for the Whigs), that we have a
a short period.

not time at present to answer a truly contemptible
one of our Local Papers, (well known as *The*
jade wince!"—We beg to inform our Friends
levelled at our Thrifty Publication *(The*
for the Party concerned, which will appear in

Norwich: Printed by Davy & Berry, Albion Office, St. Andrew's.

FIGURE 11   The Glorious Working of the Whigs!

against Parry. He was drawn supervising a workhouse mill, which
ground the poor thin, above verses that included the lines:

INDEED! SIR EDWARD you're not courteous,
In fact, your Language don't please half of us;
When *Gentlemen* have spoken, Sir, in court,
They seldom like to be *brow-beaten* for't;...
Why should the Whigs raise up their *Prisons* high
With gloomy fronts, and walls that reach the sky;
Are such dark Dungeons to immure a band
Of *Rogues* and *Swindlers* that infest the land?
'No!' some cry — 'They are for *one crime* more
The *crime* of being *old, infirm*, and *poor!*'...
Tell the base Whigs — *the Plund'rers of the poor,*
To ope their *hearts*, and not the *Workhouse-door.*

In January 1836 Parry was unwise enough to assist the Relief Committees in their administration of outdoor relief to the poor and this
led later in the year to a broadsheet entitled 'Poor Law Starvation
Bill! A dialogue between a poor law commissioner and the paupers.'
(11) This opened with verses that referred to Parry as a 'pamper'd
up pensioner' who frowned on an applicant for relief and treated him
worse than a criminal, before going on to a searing dialogue in which
Parry said to the pauper:

don't you know that the Poor Law Bill order you to be separated
because your allowance of food will be so wretchedly small that
they are afraid you should eat each other ... give me a thief
before a pauper at any time, we can transport a thief for life,
and he is got rid of at once, but a pauper is an eye sore which
we can never get rid of except by slow degrees, [viz.] by starv-
ing him to death in our bastilles or workhouse.

Parry resigned on the ground of ill-health in the spring of 1836,
and his successor, Dr Kay, adopted a more circumspect policy. He
recognized that the lack of power of the central poor law authority
meant that persuasion, not coercion, was the only possible theoretical policy, but that the state of Norwich politics made this impossible to effect in practice. Also, that 'the partial success of
the resistance of the guardians of this court to the authority of
the commissioners, had excited the hope of attaining the like success in every corporation in the county, and had encouraged malcon-
tents in the various boards in a sullen and dogged opposition'.(12)
Kay therefore reversed Parry's policy in Norwich and left the city
to its own devices. He was also scrupulously careful in his handling of the Forehoe Incorporation and the Blofield and St Faith's
Unions because of their nearness to Norwich. Kay counselled his
successor George Clive to avoid any policy that could raise 'an anti-
poor law agitation in the City of Norwich which might interfere with
the well working of the unions in the county'.(13) After 1836,
therefore, the central poor law authority made no further attempts
at dis-incorporation in Norwich in case it upset the framework of the
New Poor Law in the county of Norfolk.

Minor clashes between the Poor Law Commission and the Norwich
guardians continued because the central administration was determined
to exercise its authority, in the interstices of the Norwich local
poor law act, on subjects where the independence of the local relief
administration was not protected specifically by its legislation.

For the next decade the Norwich guardians protested at the irres-
ponsible and expensive machinery of the Poor Law Commissioners.
They came into conflict with the central administration over a
range of issues which included the appointment of a workhouse master, the nature of workhouse regulations and the legality of the
separate establishments for pauper children in Norwich. The main
battlefield concerned the administration of relief in which the
central authority wished to impose a workhouse test, or failing
that to introduce outdoor relief in kind (i.e. in bread or flour),
and with a labour test for the able-bodied applicants for outdoor
relief.

'Our object is, to get a new workhouse built — and without this
one can do *nothing* in Norwich', was the accurate diagnosis of Sir
Edward Parry.(14)   The Poor Law Commissioners could not order a
new workhouse to be built, but under the 1834 act were dependent
on the consent of a majority of guardians or of rated owners and
occupiers. It was not until 1855 that the Norwich guardians agreed
to erect a new workhouse which was built at a cost of over £29,000
and was opened in 1859 with accommodation for 900 paupers. The
new workhouse was not the result of the persuasion of the central
administration, but rather the result of economic pressure from
high poor rates in an impoverished city, which forced a local reappraisal of the administration of relief. Before this date the
question of a new workhouse had always been treated as a political
issue and neither party wished to incur the odium of having supported it. St Andrew's, the old workhouse, was a medieval eccles-
iastical building which Parry referred to as 'this wretched old
workhouse' and a more tactful successor as 'a fair specimen of
ancient buildings not unskilfully adapted to the reception of four
classes of paupers' but which was 'not capable of being converted
into a workhouse which would stand a test of comparison ... with
a union workhouse'. Its accommodation, for only 380 paupers in a
city that had 62,344 people in 1841, was clearly inadequate and a
Norwich guardian estimated that rural Norfolk unions had five times
more workhouse provision in relation to population.(15) Not only
could able-bodied applicants for relief not be offered indoor relief
in the Norwich workhouse as the Poor Law Commissioners desired, but
the conditions within the workhouse were so far from being deterrent
that no self-acting test of destitution could be provided. By the
1830s St Andrew's workhouse had been changed from a house with all
the defects of the stereotyped mixed workhouse, which it had exhi-
bited in the 1820s, to a reasonably regulated establishment. But
living conditions there were still comfortable, as an assistant poor
law commissioner crossly pointed out when he said, 'I have never
seen bread of such fine quality in any other workhouse; it is equal
to any provided for my own family.' The Norwich guardians recognized this themselves when they wrote to a Norfolk union asking that
a Norwich pauper family should remain in the Swaffham workhouse and
not be removed back because 'the Norwich guardians believe it will
prove a greater punishment to be an inmate in the Swaffham Workhouse
than in the Norwich House'.(16)

Until the 1860s there was no effective workhouse test in Norwich,
so that the Poor Law Commissioners were unable to issue an order
prohibiting outdoor relief but had to content themselves with

attempts to make outdoor relief less attractive to the able-bodied
by offering it in kind instead of money, or by instituting a labour
test. The experience of Norwich poor law administration until the
1860s was therefore very similar to that of the urban, industrial
North of England, where the workhouse test had not yet been widely
adopted. Norwich was one of the few urban areas to receive a relief-
in-kind order in the 1830s. It ignored the first instruction of 1835
to administer one-third of outdoor relief in the form of flour or
bread and had the proportion increased to one-half for its disobed-
ience. But the victory of the Poor Law Commission was short-lived
because the guardians discontinued the reformed system after only
two years. The Poor Law Board again took the initiative with the
Outdoor Relief Regulation Order of 1852, which specified one-third
to one-half of outdoor relief in kind and a very small proportion
of relief in kind was re-introduced in the Norwich Incorporation.
Norwich did not come under the Outdoor Labour Test Order of 1842,
which was issued to many comparable urban, industrial areas. It
was included in the Outdoor Relief Regulation Order of 1852 which
specified that all able-bodied men relieved outside the workhouse
should be employed by the poor law authorities. The city joined in
the storm of protest from unions that received the order, and stated
that 'in times of sudden depression it would be impossible to find
employment for all the able-bodied paupers who might at such a time
be obliged to apply for relief.' The Poor Law Board was forced to
modify the order to these unions, and allowed guardians to retain a
greater discretion over outdoor relief.(17)

II   THE LOCAL RELIEF ADMINISTRATION

The complex apparatus of the Poor Law Amendment Act of 1834 therefore left the Norwich Incorporation with an unfettered discretion
in poor law administration, and the principles of the New Poor Law
were disregarded in favour of the three-fold concern of the local
guardians to administer relief in such a way as to be economical to
the ratepayers, humane to the poor and (therefore) politically ad-
vantageous to themselves. Overall, the concept of 'humanity' dominated the administration from the 1830s to the 1860s, but there
were periodic attempts at economy and the reduction of the bill for
outdoor relief. The Norwich guardians, while rejecting the comprehensive system of labour testing advocated by the central authority,
were forced to make ineffectual efforts to devise labour tests in
order to check fraudulent claims. By putting a pauper to work the
poor law authority prevented a man still in independent employment
from receiving relief in aid of wages. A product of the economical
reform movement, which had led to the revised local poor law acts
for Norwich in 1827 and 1831, was the recommendation by a Special
Committee of Guardians in 1834 that all able-bodied applicants for
relief should be set to work. As a result outdoor paupers came
into the workhouse to work alongside indoor paupers in the weaving
and hosiery factory and the shoemaking shop, and relief was discontinued if the work was refused. The expense of this test was
ironically the cause of its discontinuance in 1857. In 1848 when
there was widespread distress in the city outdoor institutions were

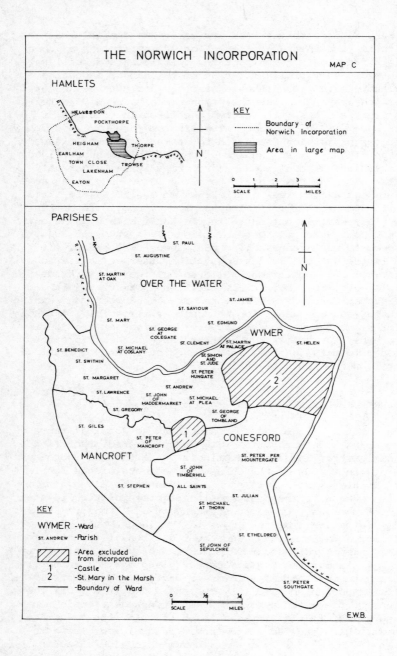

THE NORWICH INCORPORATION

MAP C

HAMLETS

HELLESDON
POCKTHORPE
HEIGHAM
THORPE
EARLHAM
TOWN CLOSE
TROWSE
LAKENHAM
EATON

River Wensum
River Wensum

KEY

.... Boundary of Norwich Incorporation

Area in large map

SCALE   MILES
0 1 2 3 4

N

PARISHES

ST. PAUL
ST. AUGUSTINE
ST. MARTIN AT OAK

OVER THE WATER

ST. JAMES
ST. SAVIOUR
ST. MARY
ST. EDMUND
ST. GEORGE AT COLEGATE
ST. CLEMENT
ST. MICHAEL AT COSLANY
ST. MARTIN AT PALACE
WYMER
ST. HELEN
ST. BENEDICT
ST. SWITHIN
ST. SIMON AND ST. JUDE
ST. MARGARET
ST. PETER HUNGATE
2
ST. LAWRENCE
ST. ANDREW
ST. JOHN OF MADDERMARKET
ST. MICHAEL AT PLEA
ST. GREGORY
ST. GEORGE OF TOMBLAND
ST. GILES
1
CONESFORD
ST. PETER OF MANCROFT
MANCROFT
ST. PETER PER MOUNTERGATE
ST. JOHN OF TIMBERHILL
ST. STEPHEN
ALL SAINTS
ST. JULIAN
ST. MICHAEL AT THORN
ST. ETHELDRED
ST. JOHN OF SEPULCHRE
ST. PETER SOUTHGATE

River Wensum
River Wensum

N

KEY

WYMER – Ward
ST. ANDREW – Parish
▨ – Area excluded from incorporation
1 – Castle
2 – St. Mary in the Marsh
—— – Boundary of Ward

SCALE   MILES
0   ⅛   ¼

E.W.B.

added as labour tests; men were employed in an oakum shop and
women in a knitting school. Again the short-term expense led to
the closure of the latter in 1857. Men were also employed in the
gravel pit and stone yard, and in cleansing or repairing the
streets. Others were asked to report twice daily to the Guardians'
Office to reduce the possibility of relief being given in aid of
wages.(18) This suggests that the varying employment devised by
the guardians could not absorb all the unemployed able-bodied applicants and that the labour tests must be considered as expensive
failures.

'Healthy able-bodied paupers may ... reasonably hope to obtain
out-door relief' in Norwich, commented the poor law inspector in
1844.(19) The failure to achieve a workhouse test meant that poor
relief in Norwich continued to be predominantly outdoor relief in
the new poor law era while the small scale of the labour tests gave
the guardians a wide discretion in its administration. The granting of outdoor relief was delegated to two guardians' committees;
the Monday Relief Committee had responsibility for the Mancroft
Ward and the Ward Over The Water, and the Thursday Relief Committee
was responsible for the Wymer and Conesford Wards, while the hamlets were apportioned between them (see Map C). A Norwich guardian
had unusually large powers in the administration of relief, because he had most of the powers of an overseer under the Old Poor
Law, and of a guardian under the New Poor Law. In Norwich, relief
was given very much according to the individual discretion of a
guardian, whereas in a Norfolk union the entire board of guardians
agreed on suitable relief after hearing from a relieving officer,
who had received the first notification of the relief application
and had researched into the veracity of the applicant's claim. In
contrast, in the city there was no prior warning of an application
and guardians worked individually, questioning applicants about
their circumstances before determining on whether relief should be
granted or refused. The city's relieving officers did not auto-
matically check out the applicant's tale of woe so that there was
no consistent test of the propriety of relief applications. While
this personalized system had its advantages in a prosperous economy,
the crisis in Norwich by the 1840s exposed its inherent deficiencies.

Pauperism grew rapidly in Norwich during the 1840s; by 1846 one-
sixth of the population were relieved, and by 1848 one-fifth of the
inhabitants were paupers.(20) The Norwich Incorporation published
returns of paupers relieved but their inefficient accounting means
that these provide no more than a rough overall guide to the dimensions of pauperism. Although numbers receiving relief increased,
only a very small minority of paupers were to be found in the workhouse at any one time. Most paupers received outdoor relief, and
their numbers doubled between 1838-9 (when figures of outdoor poor
were first compiled) and 1849 (Table 5). In this critical decade
the system of auditing outdoor relief broke down. When the guardians in the relief committees had ordered relief to be given, the
relieving officers were supposed to insert the amount and type of
relief(either after having visited the pauper or from prior knowledge of his circumstances) and the following week the guardians
were intended to check the relieving officers' actions. By the
early 1840s the guardians had no time for such double-checking,

TABLE 5   The size and cost of pauperism in the Norwich Incorporation, 1834-63

Year ending 25 March	Average nos of paupers in central workhouse	Average nos of outdoor poor reliev- ed each week		Total nos	Receipts from poor rates	Expendi- ture on mainten- ance of the poor
					£	£
1835	250	–		–	25,557	22,533
1836	227	–		–	19,683	16,321
1837	227	–		–	16,762	12,904
1838	239	–		–	16,595	14,975
1839	255	1,634		84,986	17,590	14,962
1840	267	1,710		88,924	18,526	16,442
1841	279	1,821		94,715	21,625	18,434
1842	328	1,934		100,617	22,298	20,468
1843	317	2,377		123,615	26,021	22,754
1844	346	2,224		115,661	26,004	24,379
1845	339	2,171		112,906	25,235	22,825
1846	307	2,108		109,617	27,829	29,120
1847	268	2,015		104,787	30,154	25,380
1848	307	2,408	604*	155,430	29,137	29,618
1849	343	2,790	599	176,274	37,853	32,388
1850	288	2,226	535	143,592	31,235	28,047
1851	233	2,062	524	134,489	25,127	25,358
1852	246	2,057	550	135,657	25,571	25,313
1853	306	1,962	561	131,243	25,994	26,320
1854	238	1,955	587**	132,239	26,805	27,039
1855	330	2,222	698	151,875	31,483	29,347
1856	272	2,215	654	149,262	32,973	32,609
1857	267	2,354	701	158,952	30,369	29,205
1858	246	3,082	869	205,499	29,031	28,590
1859	193	2,827	833	190,397	26,755	28,292
1860	257***	3,040	869	203,301	29,291	30,385
1861	425	3,268	851	214,224	32,571	35,721
1862	573	3,590	891	233,030	42,588	38,905
1863	581	–		–	37,113	36,496

*   From 1848 the outdoor poor were divided into two categories: the settled, resident poor, who formed the largest number in each year, and the non-settled, irremovable poor, who must be added to the first figure to get the average number relieved.
** From 1853-4 the figures referred not to cases but to total numbers relieved.
*** Before 1859 the figures referred only to the inmates of the St Andrew's Workhouse and after that date to those in the Heigham Workhouse.
Source: Weekly, monthly and quarterly returns in Norwich Guardians Minutes.

while by 1848 the officers were so overworked that (even after an
additional fourth relieving officer was appointed) they could not
even enter up the relief they had given in the relief books. The
guardians' Audit Committee found it impossible to check the relief
vouchers because they ran into thousands each week, so that in
practice there was no accountability for the relief granted, although the rule that no guardian might relieve applicants from his
own parish blocked the most obvious opportunity for corruption.
The guardians' discretion in relief administration was circumscribed belatedly in the 1850s by a more efficient audit, by the
relief committees doing more of their work as a board, and by the
relieving officers being more active in researching claims.(21)
    In 1847 Norwich had 35,596 people below the contemporary poverty
line who were excused payment of poor rates. Of these, 13,546 were
non-settled poor who were people living in the city but with poor
law settlements elsewhere. An official inquiry in 1848 concluded:
(22)

> Scarcely anything short of a national rate would relieve Norwich
> from the enormous pressure of the burden of the poor, who amount-
> ed last Summer to 10,000 in number, out of a population of 60,000
> .... The vast quantity of poverty existing in Norwich may be at-
> tributed in some degree to the decline of the manufactures, by
> which great numbers of the population have been thrown out of
> employ; but there can be no doubt that this burden on the city
> has been greatly augmented by the influx of poor from the agri-
> cultural parishes in the immediate neighbourhood.

In the early nineteenth century Norwich had become the 'open parish'
for east Norfolk; a city that offered employment in good times and
easily obtainable charity or poor relief in hard times. The economic interdependence of the city and its surrounding region had
first arisen because the silk and worsted manufacturers of Norwich
were dependent on domestic spinners and weavers in Norfolk villages.
Later this outwork shrank to cut-price weaving done by country weavers who came to work in Norwich but were to some extent subsidized
with poor relief from their home parishes. Norwich had grown pheno-
menally rapidly in this period, and in the second and third decades
of the century, when the textile industry was prosperous, the population had increased from 37,256 in 1811 to 61,116 in 1831, with a rise
of 34.9 per cent between 1811 and 1821 and of 21.5 per cent between
1821 and 1831. The fastest growing areas of Norwich were the hamlets
like Heigham and Lakenham outside the city walls, and here there
were few substantial ratepayers with an interest in keeping down the
poor rates who would scrutinize newcomers to prevent poor law settlements being made, and therefore stop a right to relief being established. Legal decisions in 1796 had apparently established that
each Norwich parish or hamlet was a separate unit for the purposes
of poor law settlement, so ratepayers in the wealthier city parishes
took little interest in the growing concentration of Norfolk poor in
the hamlets and parishes to the south and west of the city. In any
case Norfolk parishes generally relieved their own poor in Norwich,
and additionally the Norwich Incorporation had reciprocal relieving
arrangements with 66 parishes, so that the prospect of the non-
settled country poor becoming chargeable to the city's poor rates
seemed a remote possibility.(23) This situation was one of mutual

economic benefit to city and country. Country parishes did not have
to relieve rural surplus labourers who went to work in Norwich and
who would then need poor relief only in times of economic depression;
Norwich manufacturers benefited from an expanded labour force during
boom periods; while the Norwich poor law administrators could claim
a reimbursement for any relief paid out to the country poor from
their Norfolk parishes of settlement, and did not have to go to the
expense of removing them back to their homes. This mutually advan-
tageous arrangement was transformed abruptly both by the Poor Removal Act of 1846 and by a legal decision of 1849.

The Norwich guardians considered that the 1846 act had added a
permanent burden of £4,000 annually to the poor rates of the city.
This was because the act, which was later declared to be retrospective, conferred irremovability after five years' residence in
one parish. In simpler language, it was now illegal to remove these
non-settled poor, who therefore acquired a de facto settlement in
Norwich and could claim relief. The act would not have hit Norwich
so hard if it had not been for the case of Regina v. Forncett St
Mary in 1849, which reversed earlier legal decisions in stating that
the whole Incorporation of Norwich was one parish in deciding a person's poor law settlement.(24) Practically, this meant that the
Norwich guardians found it virtually impossible to disprove the
claim of any person to poor relief. The numbers of people relieved
with outdoor allowances rose from an average of 2,015 a week in 1847,
to 3,012 in 1848 and 3,389 in 1849, of which an average of 604 in
1847 and 599 in 1848 were non-settled poor (see Table 5). About
half of this increase in the recipients of relief was therefore
attributable to the 1846 act and the rest mainly to the structural
and cyclical unemployment in the textiles industry at this time.
However, the guardians tended to blame the 1846 act for most of
their problems.

The city's losses under the 1846 act were an indication of the
extent of its previous gains in the closely integrated economy of
eastern Norfolk, because Norwich, rather than Norfolk parishes, was
now having to relieve workers who had earlier contributed to the
prosperity of the Norwich manufacturers. The Norwich guardians
took an opposing view in seeing their economic situation as a product of the policies of Norfolk landowners:(25)

That Norwich being situated in the centre of an agricultural district is peculiarly exposed to the influx of aged labourers from
the surrounding parishes, it being the interest of the land-
holders in those parishes to pull down their cottages and compel
their labourers to obtain a residence in the boundary of Norwich
where their relatives follow them and where after they have lived
for five years they claim relief in case of sickness or want of
work by the operation of the Poor Removal Act 1846 and cannot be
removed to their place of settlement so the landowner gets the
benefit of the labourer's work but the burthen of his maintenance during sickness or want of work is thrown upon Norwich.
The guardians had found by their inquiry of 1847, that the non-
settled poor were concentrated in parishes to the west and south of
the city in the Mancroft and Conesford Wards and in the hamlet of
Lakenham, and they also believed that many of these went to work on
farms in 'close' parishes where cottages were kept in short supply.

They stated that labourers who lived in Lakenham went to work on farms in the neighbouring Norfolk parishes of Markshall, Caistor, Trowse Newton, Stoke Holy Cross and Keswick, and that those living in Eaton worked on farms in Cringleford, Intwood and Keswick.   But the Norwich guardians' accusations were inflated ones.   An analysis of the structure of land ownership, acreage and the provision of housing relative to population between 1801 and 1841 suggests that there were very few 'close' parishes within walking distance of Norwich where cottage provision was likely to be grossly inadequate for the agricultural labourers required to work the land.   These were Colney, Intwood, Markshall, Arminghall and Whitlingham to the south and west of Norwich, and Beeston and Spixworth to the north. (26)   While 'close' parishes did exist in small numbers there is no supporting evidence for the guardians' additional accusation that there had been agricultural clearances involving the destruction of cottage property.   It is clear that the numbers of labourers commuting from their homes in Norwich to work on Norfolk farms must have been very small indeed, and that this theory does not explain adequately the large numbers of non-settled poor in the city.   That the guardians should think it worthwhile repeatedly to advance this theory is an indication both of their over-reaction to the 1846 act (which also characterized rural Norfolk guardians and the official inquiry of 1848), and to their reluctance to accept some responsibility for the socioeconomic crisis in Norwich.

A slightly more convincing, if incomplete, explanation by the guardians for the presence of the non-settled poor in Norwich was that the Norfolk poor considered that 'with the casual employment, and the participation in the numerous charities of a large city, they are better off than with a larger amount of casual employment in their respective parishes, and a knowledge, that on such employment failing, their only resource is the poor law union house'.(27)   By the middle 1840s the chances of being offered the workhouse rather than outdoor relief were small in most Norfolk unions, but it is evident that suspicion and fear of the union workhouse remained among the country poor, and that it was far easier to get generous outdoor relief in the Norwich Incorporation than in a rural Norfolk union. The charitable provision in Norwich was amazingly liberal, and informed observers thought that this encouraged migration into the city.   In 1847 the Norwich guardians complained that worn-out, old labourers from rural Norfolk were lured into Norwich by the prospect of the lavish charitable assistance there.   (This argument, on the alluring quality of city parochial charities, was still being advanced in the early twentieth century.)   Yet the guardians' own statistics (reproduced in the Guardians Minutes after 1853) tended to disprove this hypothesis, because they indicated that the proportion of aged and infirm among the non-settled (or 'immigrant') poor was equivalent only to that among the resident poor in Norwich.

Dole charities in particular were held to have pauperized Norwich inhabitants.   In 1858 a Report to the Charity Commissioners had criticized the injudicious distribution of small charitable doles, and had concluded that the harm that resulted from them more than outweighed the good.   In the early 1860s £1,359 out of a total annual income of £20,036 from endowed charities was distributed as charitable doles in the form of money or kind.   The huge extent of non-

endowed charity in the mid-nineteenth century can be gauged by the
activities of three large centralized organizations in Norwich in
the 1840s. In 1844 the Sick Poor Society had helped 1,570 people
at a cost of £653. A little later, the Soup Society assisted over
3,500 people in 1845-6 and the same again in 1846-7. In this second
year it had made 215,397 quarts of soup for distribution among the
poor. The District Visiting Society had relieved nearly 8,000 people in 1846, 9,647 people in 1847 and 9,025 by 1849 through distri-
buting clothing, sheets and 6d tickets for bread or coal. In a
single month, from December 1846 to January 1847, it had handed out
£415 to 2,755 people.(28) The following year this society reported
on the extreme economic distress of the city and the necessity for
maintaining charitable assistance:(29)

> From the severe pressure of former years, the poor have parted
> with their furniture and goods to such an extent, as to leave
> them little or nothing to fall back upon in cases of emergency.
> Such cases now multiply around us, whilst, from want of employ-
> ment and other causes, the poor generally are scarcely able to
> provide their families with bread and much less able to supply
> them with fire and sufficient clothing.

In the economic crisis of the mid-nineteenth century extensive
charity was socially necessary, but its inefficient distribution,
in which Norwich charities maintained liaison neither with each other,
nor with the poor law guardians, meant that its economic benefits
were reduced.   Lack of work and low earnings were the main cause
of distress in the city. In 1842 the Soup Society had visited 1,302
families whose breadwinners were mainly weavers, wool-combers, and
shoemakers.   Their survey revealed that 226 families had had no work
at all for the previous six months and had received an average of
11d per head each week from the guardians. Another 319 families had
had 11 out of 26 weeks with employment and the rest with poor relief, which had produced an average income 1s 3d per head each week.
The remaining families had had 19 weeks in work and no poor relief
and had earned an average of 1s 8d per head each week. Evidence
to the Inquiry into the State of Large Towns in 1844 had emphasized
that poverty in Norwich arose from low and uncertain earnings and
extensive unemployment. This resulted in insufficient clothing and
food, and the deficient diet led to a rapid progress of disease and
a slow rate of recovery. An above-average mortality in the city
produced a large number of widows and orphans dependent on poor relief. This chain of poverty, ill health and recourse to poor relief had been in existence for some years in Norwich. Already by
1837 the greatest number receiving relief at the Guardian's Dispensary were weavers, because 'admission on the sick-list is a great
step towards admission on the out-door relief list, and hence, in
times of slackness of trade, there is a great increase of applications for medical relief'.(30)

III   LOCAL RELIEF POLICIES AND THE INCREASE OF PAUPERISM

The fluctuating employment and earnings of the weaver and his frequent dependence on relief suggested to Norwich ratepayers that
relief in aid of wages was being given and that the guardians were

erring on the side of humanity rather than economy in their administration.   In 1834 the guardians admitted that they were giving a
limited amount of relief to those in employment, but the rising
cost of outdoor relief in the 1840s forced a reappraisal of this
policy.   In 1844 it was decided not to give relief in aid of earnings for more than a week, and later the guardians reverted to an
earlier system of not relieving an applicant until he had been out
of work for a fortnight. Relief in aid of earnings resulted paradoxically from one of the more positive economic features of the
Norwich relief administration in its attempts to encourage the economic independence of the poor. Nearly one-third of the additional
cases of outdoor relief given by the Relief Committees between 1838
and 1848 was concerned with helping the poor to find work outside
the city, to learn a new trade such as wool-combing or shoemaking
and to resume, or set up, in an occupation through the gift of
clothes, tools or goods to sell. Where a weaver, for example, had
received some out-work from a manufacturer after a period of unemployment when he had been forced to sell or pawn his tools, the relief given by the guardians was necessary for him to set up his
loom and to survive until he was paid on the completion of his work.
Such an allowance technically constituted relief in aid of wages because the man was in employment.(31)

   The humanity of outdoor allowances in aid of wages had been called into question recently because it lengthened the handloom weavers'
struggle against the machine. While this economic argument has some
force in the North of England, where alternative employment was more
readily available to the handworker, it has little relevance to Norwich in the 1830s and 1840s because the general shortage of permanent employment there meant that relief was virtually the only alternative for the weaver. The primary responsibility of the Norwich
guardians was to relieve destitution, and this was concentrated particularly heavily among the weavers. A secondary responsibility
shouldered by the city's guardians was to lessen the dependence of
the Norwich poor on the poor rates. In the 1830s the shortage of
wool-combers in the city led the guardians to train the poor in
wool-combing. They also helped the short-lived Norwich Yarn Company,
which had been set up in 1833 to encourage the local spinning of yarn
and to employ the poor. The guardians had been active in promoting
this company, although they had found that they had no power to use
the poor rates to invest in it, as they had hoped to do.(32)   The
Norwich guardians also continued to expand an interesting scheme
for the outdoor apprenticeship of poor boys. This range and flexibility in the Norwich guardians' positive economic policies contrasted markedly with the constraints imposed on guardians in new
poor law unions, which prevented them spending even small sums of
money to help the poor to free themselves from dependence on poor
relief.

   The Norwich guardians' policy of humanity to the poor prevented
the imposition of a workhouse test until the 1860s. Before the Poor
Law Amendment Act of 1834 was passed they expressed their dislike of
its provisions, which tended(33)

   to degrade the industrious artisan to the level of the indolent,
   and dissolute, were he to be compelled, when standing in need of
   temporary assistance from the failure of employment, to sell off

   his little furniture, the produce of his early industry, and
   become with his family the inmate of a workhouse.
Until the economic crisis of the 1840s this humane policy to the
poor coincided with the economic interests of the ratepayers, who
were reluctant to spend money on an expensive new workhouse. The
guardians were conscious that whichever party on the court supported such an enterprise would be swiftly defeated at the polls.
But by 1848 this traditional policy was being questioned because
it was realized that nearly half the outdoor poor were able-bodied,
yet only 275 able-bodied persons were accommodated in the workhouse
in that year. One of the most active and intelligent guardians
stated that 'many of the able-bodied presented themselves without
any hesitation; they knew they could not be accommodated in the
workhouse, and therefore they had no fear of being sent there'.(34)
The huge distress in Norwich by 1848-9 taxed even the massive resources of the city's charities and the common fund for the relief
of the poor. The administration of poor relief was not co-ordinated
with that of charity. But many guardians were active on the major
charity for the relief of distress, the District Visiting Society,
which like the guardians' relief committees distributed to the poor
many of the products of the workhouse factories. A hardening of
attitude among influential propertied people in the society parallelled that in the Court of Guardians. In 1848 the Dean of Norwich
had congratulated the society for lessening the demands on the
guardians, but a year later J.H. Gurney talked of the 'practice of
fraudulent poverty' by the poor and looked forward to a new workhouse which would help to discriminate 'between professed and real
distress, and at the same time materially alleviate the burden of
the poor rates'.(35) In 1849 the guardians agreed to build a new
workhouse, but the ratepayers disliked the immediate expense and
the project was dropped. During the early 1850s fewer poor were
relieved but by 1855 rising numbers of paupers forced a re-opening
of the workhouse question. The relief committees advocated successfully a new workhouse, which would allow them 'the much needed opportunity of applying the workhouse test to the imposter, the idle,
and the depraved, and thereby distinguishing between that unahppily
too numerous class of paupers and the really necessitous and deserving poor'.(36)
   The opening of the new workhouse in 1859 foreshadowed the end of
the old order in the relief administration of Norwich. How successful had this been? The phenomenal rise in the numbers relieved and
the publicity over the ramshackle nature of the guardians' relief
administration had led to an accusation that the guardians themselves had increased the amount of pauperism in the city.(37) While
it is impossible with the available data to reach a definite conclusion on this question, there is some relevant evidence both on
the distribution of poor people and of certain types of poor relief
in Norwich. If the distribution of poverty and pauperism coincided,
it would suggest that there had been a responsible administration of
poor relief by the guardians. A crude index to the existence of
poverty in the parishes and hamlets of Norwich was given by a return
of the numbers of people there who inhabited houses of less than £6
annual value in 1847. The experience of the guardians in collecting
the poor rate had led to the conclusion that these occupiers were too

impoverished to pay, and this found practical expression in the
Norwich Small Tenements Act of 1847, when the owners, and not the
occupiers, of these houses were forced to pay the poor rate.

These distribution figures of people who, on a contemporary
estimate, were living below the poverty line may be compared with
those receiving poor relief. While there is no geographical breakdown of total poor relief in the city, this does exist for a minority of cases, termed 'additional relief', which were ordered by the
Relief Committees between 1838 and 1848. (There is no reason to
suppose that the distribution of the two forms of relief was markedly different.) Of 6,997 cases of additional relief minuted,
three-fifths of the recipients had a Norwich parish or hamlet
assigned as his place of settlement, which therefore provided an
indication of the geographical distribution of relief among paupers.
This was not dissimilar from the distribution of poor inhabitants
in Norwich hamlets and parishes, which suggests that the Norwich
guardians administered poor relief with some reference to the incidence of poverty in the city.(38)

The increase in pauperism and the escalating cost of relief in
the 1840s would have caused a virtual breakdown in poor law finances
(which had been experienced by other areas hit by similar crises)
had it not been for the system of common rating for the relief of
the poor which had been established in 1712. This breakdown would
have occurred because the proportion of poor people to total
inhabitants was so unequal between parishes and hamlets that
the poorer parishes could not have relieved the large number
of resident paupers without the help of the richer ones.
Unfortunately, the return of poor occupiers of 1847 was not
matched by one of total population, but when the return is
compared with the population censuses in 1841 and 1851 a broad differentiation between rich and poor parishes emerges.

A central area of the city, which is still distinguished today
by some elegant, substantial old buildings, had fewer than 20 per
cent of its inhabitants below the poverty line and who occupied
houses with an annual rental of less than £6 (see Map C). This
district stretched from All Saints in the south, included the parishes of Mancroft, Timberhill, Plea and Tombland which were near
the Castle and Cathedral, and ended with the central, riverside
parishes of Gregory, Maddermarket and Andrew. In the extreme north
and south of the city lay two poorer areas with more than 60 per
cent of their inhabitants below the poverty line. The larger
northern area formed a broad crescent shape which took in most of
the Ward Over the Water and the adjacent hamlets of Hellesdon and
Pockthorpe, the points of the crescent being formed by the parishes
of Benedict, Swithin, Margaret and Lawrence in the west of the Wymer
Ward and by Palace in the east of the same ward. The smaller impoverished area lay in the south along the trading, riverside area
of King Street and areas to the west of it, which included the
parishes of Mountergate, Julian, Thorn, Sepulchre and Southgate and
the neighbouring hamlet of Lakenham. With the exception of the
parishes of Saviour, Colegate and Coslany (which were comparatively
prosperous residential and commercial neighbourhoods linked to the
central rich area by Magdalen and Wensum Streets, Duke Street and
George Street), the principal area of Norwich poverty lay in the

Ward Over the Water. The industralized parishes of the Ward Over
the Water embodied to an extreme degree the problem of poverty
arising from unemployment. The Norwich guardians recognized this
when in 1849 they made this ward the sole responsibility of the
Monday Relief Committee while the Thursday Committee was left to
deal with the relief of the other three wards in the same amount
of time.

Confronting great social and economic problems without the assistance of the systematized relief provisions of the Poor Law Amendment Act, the Norwich guardians were pilloried for having.created
'an enormous aid to the positive propagation of pauperism'.(39)
A comparison of the Norwich Incorporation with Norfolk unions under
the New Poor Law Act of 1834 shows that this contemporary accusation was unjustified, although it apparently found some reliable
support in the conclusion of the poor law inspector in 1842. He
found that the proportion of pauperism to population was 14 per
cent in the city compared with only 10 per cent in the rest of the
county. But to achieve this favourable comment on the New Poor
Law he used a multiplier of 3½ to convert the Norwich statistics of
cases of relief (to both individuals and heads of families) to
total numbers receiving relief. This was far too high a multiplier,
because in 1853, when the guardians changed the presentation of
their figures from cases to numbers, the increase was almost negli-
gible. (In Coventry, where there was a similar change from cases
to numbers in 1854-5, the 'multiplier' was also small, and was here
about 1¾.)(40) Although the available statistics of those receiving
relief in the two areas of Norwich and rural Norfolk were therefore
not precisely comparable before 1853, it is almost certain that the
proportion of pauperism to population was lower in Norwich in 1842.
This was the exact opposite of the official view.

When a comparison is made of relief expenditures per head of
population in the census years for which exact. population figures
were available, the expenditure in the Norwich Incorporation for
1841, 1851 and 1861 was 6s 1d, 8s 2d and 10s 4s, whereas that in
the rest of Norfolk was respectively 10s 4d, 9s 6d and 9s 1d. Paradoxically, this suggests that only after the imposition of a workhouse test in Norwich in 1859 was expenditure there higher than
in the rest of Norfolk, which would hardly have pleased the supporters of the New Poor Law. While statistics of relief expenditure for only three years can provide merely a tentative guide to
the relative experience of Norwich and Norfolk, the annual series
of numbers in receipt of indoor and outdoor relief in both areas
gave a more reliable indication of the efficacy of the 1834 act in
reducing outdoor relief to the poor, and particularly to the able-
bodied. The proportion of rural Norfolk poor relieved outside the
workhouse to total paupers remained consistently high at four-
fifths or more, and the reduction to two-thirds in the 1840s in
the proportion of adult able-bodied Norfolk poor who received outdoor relief proved to be only temporary, four-fifths of this class
of pauper being relieved in their own homes in the second half of
the nineteenth century. In Norwich the proportion of all poor receiving relief outside the workhouse in any week approached nine-
tenths of the total (see Table 5). The character of the relief
administration in both areas was very similar in the mid-nineteenth

century, and this is remarkable because it showed that the local
guardians' uniformly unfavourable attitude to relief inside the
workhouse was more influential than the different poor law regulations of rural Norfolk and of Norwich.

IV   THE END OF THE NORWICH INCORPORATION

'To discountenance idleness in every way is among the duties of a
Board of Guardians, and it is only because it has not been dis-
countenanced to the extent to which it ought to have been, that the
city owes no small amount of its burdens.' So thundered the
'Norwich Mercury' on 10 May 1862, after it had seen the city
guardians fail to enforce a systematic workhouse test, even after
the erection of a new workhouse costing £29,000. The challenge
was taken up by a group of parochial delegates who met first in
August 1862, and whose researches into the recent relief administration in Norwich compared with other cities led to an indictment
of the guardians for pauperizing the poor because of their failure
to institute a workhouse test in Norwich. The guardians themselves
were weary of battling with the endemic poverty of the city and
came to an agreement with the promoters of a new bill for the poor
law administration of the city. This was introduced into Parliament in February 1863 and became law as the Norwich Poor Act in
June; the first meeting of the new board of guardians took place
on 29 October 1863. The act was acceptable to all parties because
it added to the rateable value of the new union by including the
wealthy parish of St Mary in the Marsh (the Cathedral precinct),
and rated the hamlets, with their fast-growing population, on a
higher and equal assessment with the parishes within the city
walls. It also brought the electoral areas for the guardians'
elections into line with those of the reformed municipal corporation and 16 electoral districts replaced the parishes and hamlets
of the old poor law incorporation.
    The imposition of the rules and regulations of the Poor Law Amend-
ment Act had little impact on the pauperism and poor rates of Norwich in the opening years of the Norwich Union. The reforming parochial delegates had concluded that 'The Local Act, as our present
excessive rates demonstrate, has tended *in its administration* to
PAUPERIZE the POOR of this City; whilst the Poor Law Amendment
Act has hitherto lessened or proved a check upon pauperism throughout the kingdom.'(41) The naive expectations by the reformers of
the remedial impact of the New Poor Law were to be disappointed
because Norwich poverty, and the need for poor relief, was caused
not by the supposed idleness and moral depravity which the workhouse test was designed to check, but by low wages and unemployment.
These were beyond the curative powers of the 1834 act. Also, the
policies of the Norwich guardians continued after 1863 to be determined by party politics. They perpetuated an administration of predominantly outdoor relief in which small allowances were given in
a vain attempt to save the ratepayers' money by discouraging applicants for poor relief. There was no attempt to co-operate with
charitable organizations in the city in order to produce a co-
ordinated policy for the relief of poverty.(42)

Local factors determined the character of the administration of
the Norwich Incorporation between 1834 and 1863 and forced its
dissolution.   The formation of the new poor law union in 1863 was
the culmination of a series of reforms which had been begun in 1827
and 1831 by the city ratepayers.   Between the 1830s and the 1860s
the Norwich guardians had tried during a time of unparallelled economic distress and political turbulence to balance the interest of
the ratepayer in an economical, efficient administration with the
interest of the poor in a humane and flexible system of poor relief.
The guardians had successfully resisted the imposition of the workhouse and labour tests by the central poor law authority, which had
attempted to implement the New Poor Law in the city.   In rejecting
the economic solutions of the 1834 act as inappropriate to the city
and opposing any restriction on their discretion in the administration of outdoor allowances, the guardians necessarily committed
themselves to the complex task of giving outdoor relief to several
thousand people each week.   In this they erred on the side of humanity rather than economy, and misjudged the evolving state of public
opinion in Norwich, which by the early 1860s had become conscious
that with the decline of its staple industry it could no longer
afford its traditionally liberal methods of poor relief.

The administration of the poor law in Norwich between 1834 and
1863 provided an interesting contrast with that in rural Norfolk.
The city, having continued with a policy of outdoor relief, rejected those policies in favour of the New Poor Law in 1863, whereas
the rural areas had rapidly adopted the provisions of the 1834 act,
before gradually abandoning them in favour of a resumption of outdoor relief.   The experience of Norwich had greater similarity with
that of some urban, industrial areas in the North of England, where
guardians in the new poor law era also preferred to continue with
their old poor law policies of outdoor relief, for reasons of economy and humanity.   The Norwich Incorporation had been established
in 1712 in order to relieve the poor who 'do daily multiply' to the
charge and grief of the inhabitants, but in 1863 the powers of this
incorporation were thought to be inadequate for the much greater
pauperism that had resulted from the decline of the textile industry
and the financial impact of the Poor Removal Act of 1846.   However,
the extent of pauperism in both urban and rural areas was more than
just a simple response to prevailing economic conditions, and
this can be seen if separate categories of paupers are studied in
greater detail.

CHAPTER 8
PAUPERS: I, THE ABLE-BODIED (1)

'The working people, as a rule look upon the workhouse as a prison', said George Edwards who, as a trade union leader, was in close touch with the feelings of the rural Norfolk poor in the late nineteenth century.(2) This deep-seated antagonism to indoor relief in the workhouse had begun in the eighteenth century, when local poor law incorporations had built houses of industry, and had been reinforced by the fear which the erection of the union workhouses of the New Poor Law had aroused after 1834. The labouring poor were repelled by the very idea of the workhouse, and although union workhouses had been designed mainly for the able-bodied poor, relatively few of them cared to accept poor relief if it meant entering the 'work'us'. Indoor relief was confined increasingly to the weaker members of society — to the young, the old, and the sick — who had no feasible alternative to the workhouse. 'During the last 20 years the rural workhouse has become almost exclusively an asylum for the sick, the aged, and children', wrote the poor law inspector for the eastern counties in 1892.(3) By this time the name 'workhouse' was a misnomer for what was, in fact, a combination of hospital, lunatic asylum, old people's home and school. At the turn of the century the policy of educating and maintaining pauper children in a more congenial environment than the workhouse resulted in the old, the infirm and the sick having the workhouse increasingly to themselves. Plans of Norfolk workhouses, which were made after the rule of the guardians had ended in 1929-30, make it clear that by this time these classes of inmate almost monopolized the available accommodation there.

In analysing the changes that occurred in the relief given to different types of paupers it is desirable to look beyond the abstractions both of statistics and of administrative policy. These, after all, suggested that the pauper host was anonymous; like an army, its material wants were supplied and its overall size was known, but the individuals within it had no personal identity or voice. The human implications of pauperism continue to be obscured until some attention is paid to individual case studies. The cases that were minuted in Norfolk poor law records were not necessarily typical ones. Indeed, they were often unrepresentative, since their troublesome or difficult character required a more detailed

consideration than was given to the representative, ordinary cases.
But it is salutary to remember that the difficulty was not solely
an administrative one but also concerned the intractable problems
of the individual who was seeking relief. In these two chapters
the examples chosen from the available Norfolk case studies often
feature women and children, because these were the groups most
hidden from history within the pauper host. A corrective to this
bias is supplied in Chapter 12, where men feature much more promi-
nently.

I THE ADULT

Paradoxically, although the able-bodied poor had been a prime target
for the reformers of 1834 in their policy of preventing the pauperization of the labouring class, the poor law administrators who implemented their policies never succeeded in defining who the able-
bodied actually were. Like so much else in poor law history, the
practice is more revealing than the policy and this suggests that
the able-bodied were those aged 15 years or more who could support
themselves by their own labour. Ability to earn something, rather
than physical health, tended to be the criterion for distinguishing
the able-bodied. To encourage them to earn a living wage, the central administrators of the New Poor Law declared in the Outdoor
Relief Prohibitory Order that the able-bodied were to be given
poor relief only within the deterrent conditions of the workhouse.
However, local administrators in Norfolk found it convenient largely to ignore this fundamental relief regulation. This was to have
a profound impact on the administration of the New Poor Law in Norfolk where able-bodied adults formed nearly one-quarter of those receiving relief in the early years of the New Poor Law. In the seven
winter quarters ending on 25 March between 1840 and 1846, an average
of 23.5 per cent of those paupers who were relieved were able-bodied
adults, while in the same period an average of 68.5 per cent of the
able-bodied adults relieved received outdoor rather than indoor relief. In succeeding decades the proportion of the adult able-
bodied paupers receiving outdoor relief was never lower than this
and reached a peak of 86.4 per cent in the 1870s.
    Outdoor relief to able-bodied men has been discussed previously
in Chapter 6 and attention here will be directed more to their relief inside the workhouse. Although they were more likely to receive outdoor than indoor relief, there were certain categories of
men and certain periods when workhouse relief was more likely. The
able-bodied man was more prone to see the inside of the union house
in the years 1838-43, or again after the 1870s, because the local
guardians were being then more heavily pressurized by the central
poor law administration into adopting a stringent relief policy.
Again, a farming depression like that of the early 1850s in rural
Norfolk, or the sharp decline of the textile industry in Norwich
during the 1840s brought the shadow of the workhouse nearer. During
the winter months, when there was less work to do on the farm, the
single man with no dependents or the married man with inferior
skills or an independent mind might find himself laid off by farmers as employers, and relieved in the workhouse by farmers as poor

law guardians. The farmer-guardians in rural unions were reluctant
to send married men of good character to the workhouse, both because
of the high cost of relieving them there with their families, and
because of the inconvenience which they faced as employers in re-
trieving them from it when the weather improved and ploughing or
sowing needed to be quickly put in hand. Outdoor relief to the
deferential or skilled married man was engineered therefore on the
ostensible ground of sickness in the family, which was an exception
in the order prohibiting outdoor allowances to the able-bodied man.
An alternative policy for the man with a large family was in operation until the 1850s, whereby one or more of his children was taken
into the workhouse. This practice, although technically illegal
and discouraged by the central administration in other areas, was
permitted in Norfolk unions. Permission had to be obtained from the
Poor Law Commission, or later from the Poor Law Board, but Norfolk
guardians found little difficulty in having their requests approved.
(4) Children such as these could be visited in the workhouse (as
could other inmates) by their family and by friends either daily or
on alternate days, depending on the rules made by the local guardians.

14 The Men's Yard, Wicklewood House, c. 1930

   Life within the rural Norfolk workhouse, for the relatively few
able-bodied men unlucky enough to find themselves there, was tedious
or frustrating rather than actively arduous or uncomfortable. Although work was supposed to be provided for them, it often proved
beyond the ingenuity or efficiency of the local guardians and workhouse officials to provide sufficient to fill the 10 hours per day
assigned for it in the workhouse rules. Pumping water, grinding
corn at a hand-mill, performing simple labouring jobs or doing spade
husbandry to grow wheat, oats or potatoes on the workhouse land were

common occupations. Picking oakum (that classic workhouse assignment of plucking twisted, tarred lengths of rope into fibres for
caulking boats) was the preferred task, but supplies of rope frequently ran out, leaving the inmates idle. The able-bodied man had
ample time therefore to brood on the injustices of his existence,
and perhaps if he had sufficient knowledge of past methods of
relief to contrast them with the ease experienced by his counterpart
in an incorporated house of industry in the old poor law era. Then,
there was specific accommodation for families, ample food, little
work and considerable latitude about temporary leave of absence
from the house for either business or pleasure. In the union workhouse of the New Poor Law the married man was segregated from his
family under the workhouse classification scheme and might see them
for one hour only on Sunday. This aroused such ill-feeling that
disturbances sometimes broke out. In 1846 in the St Faith's workhouse the men refused to leave their wives, and police had to be
called in to restrain them. (Later, the men were unsuccessful in
their charge, laid before a magistrate, that the police had
assaulted them.)(5)

Psychological pressures were experienced rather more than material
deprivation within the house. The workhouse uniform of stout duf-
field jacket, drabbett trousers, waistcoat, cotton shirt, neckerchief, socks and ankle shoes was probably warmer than the labouring
man's own threadbare clothing outside the workhouse, although its
worn and patched character was familiar enough. The adult male
pauper benefited to the full from the standard workhouse dietary,
and at the start of the new poor law era was given 160 ounces of
solid food a week, which compared well with the average intake of
the independent, rural labourer of only 122 ounces (see Figure 12).
Later, when local guardians eroded the standard of the Norfolk
workhouse dietaries and higher wage levels enabled the independent
labourer to eat a little better, the superiority of workhouse food
was less marked.(6) There is an illustration of the dietary in use
in the 1840s in the Aylsham Union (Figure 12) which had adopted the
second one of the six model dietaries suggested by the central
poor law authority. However, despite this material superiority the
pauper inmate must have welcomed the day when he was discharged from
the workhouse after the guardian of his parish brought the news that
there was work available in his village for him. Alternatively, the
man might discharge himself if he gave three hours notice (later,
amended to 'reasonable notice') of his intention to go, and if he
took his family with him.

One type of male pauper had a greater contact with the outside
world than the average indoor pauper. 'Trampers', or 'roadsters',
as vagrants were called locally, were becoming a more familiar
sight in Norfolk lanes by the 1860s. The professional tramps might
be well-known as individuals in the villages along their routes as
they walked their well-worn itinerary from workhouse to workhouse.
At the union, or 'spike', as they were nicknamed, the vagrant was
supposed to be given a task of work to perform in payment for his
overnight stay, but whether there was actually some digging, oakum-
picking or stone-breaking for him to do was a matter of luck. At
the workhouse they were bathed in the receiving wards before a supper of 6-8 ounces of bread with ¾ — 1½ ounces of cheese was given

AYLSHAM UNION.

WE THE POOR LAW COMMISSIONERS for England and Wales, do hereby Order and Direct, that the Paupers of the respective Classes and Sexes described in the Table hereunder written, who may be received and maintained in the Workhouse or Workhouses of the said Aylsham Union, shall, during the period of their residence therein, be fed, dieted, and maintained with the food and in the manner described and set forth in the said Table; viz.

Dietary for Able-bodied Men and Women.

		BREAKFAST.		DINNER.						SUPPER.		
		Bread.	Milk Gruel.	Meat Pudding.	Potatoes or other Vegetables.	Yeast Dumpling	Suet Pudding.	Bread.	Cheese.	Bread.	Cheese.	Butter.
		oz.	pint.	oz.	oz.	oz.	oz.	oz.	oz.	oz.	oz.	oz.
Sunday	Men	7	1	—	—	—	—	9	1	7	¾	—
	Women	5	1	—	—	—	—	8	1	5	—	½
Monday	Men	7	1	—	16	—	14	—	—	7	¾	—
	Women	5	1	—	12	—	12	—	—	5	—	½
Tuesday	Men	7	1	12	16	—	—	—	—	7	¾	—
	Women	5	1	10	12	—	—	—	—	5	—	½
Wednesday	Men	7	1	—	16	—	—	7	¾	7	¾	—
	Women	5	1	—	12	—	—	5	½	5	—	½
Thursday	Men	7	1	12	16	—	—	—	—	7	¾	—
	Women	5	1	10	12	—	—	—	—	5	—	½
Friday	Men	7	1	—	16	—	—	7	¾	7	¾	—
	Women	5	1	—	12	—	—	5	½	5	—	½
Saturday	Men	7	1	—	16	11	—	—	—	7	¾	—
	Women	5	1	—	12	11	—	—	—	5	—	½

AND We do hereby further Order and Direct, that Children under the age of nine years, resident in the said Workhouse, shall be fed, dieted, and maintained with such food and in such manner as the said Guardians shall direct; and that Children above the age of nine years, and under the age of sixteen years, shall be allowed the same quantities as are prescribed in the above Table for able-bodied Women.

And We do also Order and Direct, that the sick paupers, resident in the said Workhouse, shall be fed, dieted, and maintained in such manner as the Medical Officer for the Workhouse shall direct.

And We do hereby further Order and Direct, that the Master or Masters of the Workhouse or Workhouses of the said Union shall cause two or more copies of this our Order, legibly written, or printed in a large type, to be hung up in the most public places of such Workhouse, and to renew the same from time to time, so that it be always kept fair and legible.

Given under our Hands and Seal of Office, this Second day of October, in the year One thousand eight hundred and forty-five.

(Signed)
GEO. NICHOLLS.
G. C. LEWIS.

And We do hereby further Order and Direct, that Children under the age of nine years, resident in the said Workhouse, shall be fed, dieted, and maintained with such food and in such manner as the said Guardians shall direct; and that Children above the age of nine years, and under the age of sixteen years, shall be allowed the same quantities as are prescribed in the above Table for able-bodied Women.

And We do also Order and Direct, that the sick paupers, resident in the said Workhouse, shall be fed, dieted, and maintained in such manner as the Medical Officer for the Workhouse shall direct.

And We do hereby further Order and Direct, that the Master or Masters of the Workhouse or Workhouses of the said Union shall cause two or more copies of this our Order, legibly written, or printed in a large type, to be hung up in the most public places of such Workhouse, and to renew the same from time to time, so that it be always kept fair and legible.

Given under our Hands and Seal of Office, this Second day of October, in the year One thousand eight hundred and forty-five.

(Signed) Geo. Nicholls
G.C. Lewis

Figure 12 Aylsham Union Dietary

them. Then a night on clean straw in vagrant cells or, in the early
years, in outhouses, followed by one to two pints of gruel at breakfast and a task of work to do. Occasionally, in the winter months,
the vagrants might engineer their transference to gaol by breaking
a workhouse window, in order to benefit from the superior diet of
266 ounces of nutritive food per week, light labour and a more spa-
cious environment. The vagrant's itinerary was regular in outline
but varied in detail according to the hazards of the workhouses in
the region.(7)

The mobile poor had always posed a serious challenge to the laws
of settlement and chargeability which throughout this period provided the legal framework for the relief of the poor. Before 1834
there had been an inefficient system of passing the vagrant back to
his place of poor law settlement, in which the parish constable
superintended his transference from parish boundary to parish boundary and received in return a small payment from the county. Norfolk
was not much troubled by vagrants at this time, and payments for the
whole county averaged only £95 per annum in the years between 1827
and 1833. Vagrants could also be sentenced to a period of imprisonment with hard labour and this was usually of a fortnight's duration.
In the new poor law era, the introduction of a rural police force
and the use that vagrants made of the accommodation in union workhouses contributed to a growing awareness of a vagrancy problem in
many rural areas. The central poor law administration felt it necessary to formulate a policy for the relief of vagrants. A deterrent
strand of policy began in 1842, when vagrants were first differentiated from the rest of the pauper host and boards of guardians were
instructed to detain them for four hours' hard labour. This deterrent idea was resurrected in 1871 and reached its culmination in
1882, when it became possible to detain professional vagrants for
two nights in order to extract a punitive amount of a full day's
work from them. This policy of extreme deterrence continued into
the twentheth century. Alternating with the deterrent regime was a
discriminatory set of regulations, issued in various forms in 1848,
1868 and 1892, whereby genuine travellers in search of work were to
be differentiated from professional vagrants, and were to be excused
their workhouse task or given tickets of way for the next workhouse
on their route.

The small size of the vagrancy problem in Norfolk during the
nineteenth century made such policies largely a matter of indifference to local guardians. Vagrants were almost unknown in Norfolk unions in 1842; only half of the unions provided a task of
work in 1848, while three-quarters of them found it worth their
while to do so in 1868. Thirty years later increased numbers had
forced 17 out of the 22 unions into detaining tramps for two nights
in order to set them to hard labour for a day. At this time some
Norfolk boards of guardians set tasks of work that were virtually
impossible to achieve in order to discourage tramps. Interest in
the vagrancy problem had been aroused only when the vagrant ceased
to be an occasional and unexpected applicant at the Norfolk workhouse gates and became a more regular recipient of relief. But
Norfolk did not experience the massive impact of the Irish influx
after 1846, and except for the extreme west of the county it was
off the route of itinerant Irish harvesters before this. A county

like Norfolk, with a declining major industry (textile manufacture)
and under-employment in agriculture, was hardly an attractive des-
tination for vagrants outside the county. As a result it had fewer
even than did neighbouring rural counties. What vagrants there were
tended to be concentrated in the west of the county, in the ports of
Yarmouth and Lynn and the industrial centre of Norwich. The independence of the poor law authority in Norwich allowed them to
give an annual subscription to the Mendicity Society and to refer
vagrants to them. The society relieved an increasing number of
vagrants. In the depressed year of 1837 it assisted 97 men, 24
women and 22 children, while a decade later in 1847 (another difficult year) it helped 427 men, 37 men and 36 children.
     Numbers of casual poor increased as the century progressed, but
even in the 1890s a Norfolk workhouse might expect to relieve fewer
than half a dozen per night. In depressed years in the late 1840s
and 1860s and throughout the 1890s the unemployed travellers in
search of work formed only a minority of those in the vagrant cells
of Norfolk workhouses. (However, it is worth noting that the poor
law administration relieved only a small proportion of these
'honest wayfarers'; many labourers slept rough, while skilled
craftsmen had their own tramping system based on the branches of
their craft, and others could be assisted by their friendly society.) By 1848 some Norfolk unions had begun to employ police to
assist relieving officers in coping with the problem of the mobile
poor. Between 1867 and 1869 a few local unions adopted a ticket-
of-way scheme. This gave the traveller food and lodging in the
workhouse and required little work in return, if the man had walked
a long way; it also provided him with a relief ticket for the next
workhouse on his route.(8) Judging by the vagrancy registers in the
Aylsham Union in the north-east of the county, much of the mobility
was very restricted and involved local people seeking work within
their own region. A change had taken place in this union between
the 1870s and 1890s when more skilled workers and more family
groups including children and women were travelling the Norfolk
roads.(9)
     Women were always in the minority among the vagrant class but
they could be colourful characters, as was Mary Barns, at the end
of the eighteenth century. She was a Wighton woman who travelled
the roads of north and west Norfolk. A thief and a prostitute, as
well as a vagrant, she had been whipped publicly and put in Walsingham Bridewell for six months. Mary was a constant thorn in the
flesh to the administrators of the Wighton poor house in the Holkham,
Warham and Wighton Union, which was an area under Gilbert's Act.
Sometimes she was an involuntary inhabitant in the poor house as a
result of being passed back as a vagrant, but on three occasions
she came voluntarily to be treated for veneral disease, before
speedily absenting herself once treatment was successful. In March
1791 the Wighton poor law administrator took the unprecedented step
of writing to the Mayor of Lynn to warn him that Mary Barns was
lilely to arrive there shortly and that her residence must lead to
dire results. This letter was written as a public duty; 'She is
a most abandoned wretch... there can't be any reason for me to
wish the return of so bad a person.' Like the proverbial bad penny,
Mary Barns did keep reappearing, but she quickly left again and

absconded from the poor house on nine separate occasions. The
records closed in 1814 with the woman in the poor house 'labouring
with the evil'. Her career had apparently ended in the physical
and mental torment of syphilis.(10)

It can be seen, therefore, that women could provide some of the
more intractable problems in poor law administration. However, the
male authors of both the Royal Commission's Report of 1834 and the
ensuing Poor Law Amendment Act had remarkably little to say about
the female half of the population. The rules and regulations of
the central poor law authority had therefore to fill in the gaps
left by legal enactment, because, in practice, male guardians found
that considerable numbers of paupers were women. Whether a woman
was eligible for relief outside the union workhouse depended primarily on her marital status (whether married, a separated or deserted
wife, a widow or single woman) and secondarily on her morality (whether she was an unmarried mother or a widow with illegitimate children). Analysis of these very complex regulations suggests that
single women or those with illegitimate children were generally
offered relief inside the Norfolk workhouse. Women with dependent
legitimate children who attempted to support them by their own
efforts were, in practice, granted outdoor relief. As such, they
were an exception to the order prohibiting outdoor allowances to
the able-bodied, and poor relief to them was effectively relief
given in aid of wages. It is possible to extract from the daunting
mass of statistics reproduced in the Annual Reports of the Poor Law
Commission some interesting data about these women who, because of
either low wages or unemployment, were unable to earn enough to
support themselves and who therefore received a topping-up of income from the poor law guardians.

Between 1839 and 1846 10,620 of these female breadwinners received relief in the eight winter quarters which ended on 25 March.
They made up 4.4 per cent of outdoor paupers or 3.5 per cent of all
paupers relieved in Norfolk at this time. The breakdown of the
women into different categories is an interesting one: 4.6 per cent
belonged to a residual group which defied the categorization of poor
law officials, 9.1 per cent were deserted wives, 4.6 per cent were
wives without husbands (for example, those with husbands in a prison or asylum), 2.3 per cent were unmarried mothers and 79.4 per
cent were widows. It was the last two groups of women, the smaller
number of women with illegitimate children (who were generally relieved inside the workhouse) and the large numbers of widows (who
were almost invariably given outdoor relief), whose condition attracted most attention from the Victorians.

Widows were objects of sympathy in society, but their relief
was scrutinized carefully by poor law guardians in order that the
ratepayers money should not be wasted on inessential or over-
generous allowances. The case histories of widows in four east
Norfolk unions will illustrate the range of considerations and attitudes involved in their relief. At the beginning of the new poor
law era, three poor widows of Salhouse in the St Faith's Union
wrote to the Poor Law Commissioners in London to protest against
what they considered to be their harsh treatment by local guardians, who had refused them the traditional widow's outdoor allowance. The first, 'Widow' Jimby, had two children and was, in fact,

an unmarried woman with illegitimate children, who was on this
basis offered the workhouse (which she refused) and an allowance
of 1s 6d for her son who was a cripple. The second widow was 81-
year-old Mrs Jermany, who was refused relief because she lived with
an unmarried son whom it was thought could maintain her because he
earned 10s a work as a team man on a local farm. The third widow,
Mrs Humphreys, was able-bodied and had no dependent children. She
had been offered one stone of flour per week as a temporary allowance during illness.

These three cases suggest an unsympathetic, rather than an unjust, handling by local guardians who were attempting to reduce
the poor rates by a careful administration of relief. The next case
showed only inhumanity and harshness in the treatment of an elderly
woman. Widows were relieved quite frequently as non-resident paupers and as such could fall foul of the complicated settlement laws
which gave the right to relief in a particular parish. Seventy-
year-old Hannah Woodhouse lived in Norwich with her daughter, but
had a poor law settlement in the Aylsham Union, which was derived
from that of her dead husband. For the first 10 years of the new
poor law era the Aylsham guardians gave her a non-resident person's
allowance of 2s 6d a week. In 1846 the Poor Removal Act altered
the settlement laws to give a person a right to relief after five
years' residence in one place, and it was not clear for the next two
years whether the enactment was retrospective in operation. As a
result of this, in October 1846 the Aylsham guardians tried to
transfer Mrs Woodhouse's chargeability to the Norwich Corporation of
Guardians by unilaterally stopping her relief. The Norwich guardians relieved her (as a temporary expedient) until May 1847 and
then removed her back to Aylsham. With no accommodation there she
was forced to walk the 22 miles back to her daughter's home in Norwich. At the next meeting of the Aylsham Board of Guardians she
made a round trip of 44 miles on foot to ask for a resumption of her
non-resident pauper's allowance and was offered only the workhouse
as relief. This she refused and existed for nearly a year in a
state of great privation, being helped by charity from the Norwich
District Visiting Society. This organization took up her case with
the Aylsham guardians who eventually resumed her weekly allowance
of 2s 6d. But it was continued under punitive conditions, since
this old lady of 70 was forced to walk to and from Cawston, in the
Aylsham Union, a round trip of 23 miles, in order to receive her
allowance in person from the relieving officer there. He refused
to give it to a proxy, even though Mrs Woodhouse's sister lived in
Cawston and had arranged to send the money by carrier from Cawston
to Norwich. After 11 weeks of this arrangement the Aylsham guardians, in August 1848, stated that unless the widow came to live at
Cawston, within the boundaries of the Aylsham Union, no more relief
would be paid to her.

Considerable feeling among the rural working class had been
aroused in Norfolk by the end of the nineteenth century over the
relief of widows by poor law guardians. Widows were considered to
be respectable people who had fallen on hard times through circumstances that were not within their own control. As such, public
opinion felt that they were deserving cases who merited liberal
treatment. Two cases of widows relieved in the Erpingham Union

were cited before a Royal Commission at the end of the century, and the evidence suggests that it was the ethos of the poor law administration, as much as the monetary sums involved, that were resented at the time.(11)

The two or three relieving officers in each poor law union formed the pivotal point that provided the day-to-day contact between the poor law authority and the poor. At the beginning of the new poor law period the relieving officer had to state on a handbill or a printed notice, in each village or hamlet in his district, the day and the hour when he would visit. The relieving officer was responsible not only for administering the money and flour to the outdoor poor, in accordance with the decisions reached at previous meetings of the union board of guardians; but he also had the task of researching the background of new applicants for relief. Then, at the next weekly board meeting which the applicant had to attend, the relieving officer would be present to corroborate or undercut the applicants' tale of woe by giving a full account of their circumstances. In addition he had the responsibility (virtually impossible for a layman) of authorizing a sick person to apply to the union medical officer for medical attention. At the end of a long day he had the exacting assignment of filling in complicated sets of returns of paupers relieved, and applications received, and of cross-checking that his money and flour accounts tallied with the returns. To some extent he was helped by the Norfolk guardians' habit of fixing standard scales of allowances for each quarter. For example, the Blofield guardians decided that in the winter quarter in 1867 adults should receive an outdoor allowance of 2s 9d per week; children aged between 12 and 15 years should have 2s 3d; those aged 9-11 years old should be given 1s 9d; and children under 9 years only 1s 3d. But it is small wonder that with an arduous working day the Norfolk relieving officer tended to be brusque, and to alienate the poor by his incivility. If he were kindhearted then he was open to a reprimand by the local guardians, who took a sterner view of the duty of a poor law administrator. Mr Burrell, the relieving officer in the Freebridge Lynn Union, was reprimanded for improper conduct by the board of guardians because he had said to a pauper that he considered his case a hard one and had given the man 6d out of his own pocket.(12)

To the financial stringency shown by Norfolk boards of guardians towards widows was added a strongly punitive and moralistic attitude when unmarried mothers were applicants for relief. These moral postures also saved money for the ratepayers in a county like Norfolk with a high illegitimacy rate. A petticoat and stockings of a conspicuous colour or a distinctively striped serge dress were the public badges of shame which Norfolk guardians ordered mothers of illegitimate children to wear in Norfolk workhouses in the 1830s. The boards' strong prejudice against this class of pauper made them offer the workhouse, and not an outdoor allowance, even before the prohibitory orders of the central board made this official relief policy. Yet under the Old Poor Law illegitimacy had not been thought particularly reprehensible; relief minutes might record 'a fine boy' or 'a fine girl' having been born to unmarried mothers in the poor house. However, by the time of the Poor Law Amendment Act of 1834 Norfolk poor law administrators were becoming worried at the cost to the poor rates of a high illegitimacy rate. The Norwich guardians in 1834 were dealing with 125 cases of illegitimacy and were giving relief in 110 of them. There were three main groups of Norwich mothers involved: the brazen woman, one with as many as five bastards; the occasional idiot mother, one of whom had three children; and the unfortunate girl who was expecting her first child and who now paid a heavy price for her previous behaviour. (One father had his occupation described as 'the orator and milkman', which no doubt helped to account for his presence in these minutes of the Bastardy Committee.) A second reason for the concern of poor law guardians over illegitimacy cases was the change brought about by the 1834 act. This forced a parish seeking reimbursement from the father for the poor law allowance given to his child, to file an expensive case at Quarter Sessions, rather than as previously, to mount a cheap and expeditious action at Petty Sessions. A drop in affiliation cases was the immediate result since cases were only brought to court if proof of paternity was likely to be established. Consequently, guardians adopted a deterrent policy to the pregnant unmarried woman, or to the unmarried mother, since by offering her the workhouse as relief, they hoped to discourage applications for relief, and safeguard the public purse. Even so, nearly a third of all children in Norfolk workhouses at this time were illegitimate.(13)

'A poor man may not marry now, because there is a chance that he may not be able to provide for his wife and family — But he may beget children without a wife, and with a very small chance of being forced to provide for them at all.' The Rev. Ambrose Goode of Terrington, a sympathetic supporter of the rights of the poor, thought the 1834 act was unchristian in that it positively encouraged illegitimacy by effectively throwing the maintenance of the child upon the mother, or, in many cases, ultimately on the parish. In 1839, bastardy cases could again be heard at Petty Sessions which reduced costs for the ratepayers, but the position of the unmarried mother deteriorated because the prohibitory order, issued by the Poor Law Commission to Norfolk unions at this time, forbade outdoor relief to them. The King's Lynn guardians, who were hostile to the Poor Law Commission, expressed their sympathy for the mothers' plight in histrionic terms. The provisions of the New Poor Law were 'immoral as offering a premium for the seduction of unwary women by unprincipled men by throwing the whole burden of the maintenance of the offspring of illicit intercourse upon the deluded female'. More typically, Norfolk guardians thought that these unmarried mothers should be treated as outcasts from society. In the Swaffham Union they were excluded from the Coronation dinner on the Workhouse Green in 1838 and from the annual Christmas dinner. In the Docking Workhouse they were forced to wear a distinctive dress long after the central poor law board had banned such a uniform. Even at the end of the century unmarried mothers were punished by being put to hard labour in the workhouse laundry a few days after their confinement — a practice that any newly elected woman guardian soon stopped.(14)

The reformers of 1834 had hoped to separate poor law administration from the contentious, legal morass of proving paternity and extracting affiliation money, but they were not successful until

1844, when an act made the mother, and not the parish, responsible for seeking financial redress from the alleged father through a civil action in the courts. In practice, however, mothers came on the parish, and the poor law authorities exerted pressure on her to retrieve money from the father through either an informal approach or a legal action. However, it was not until 1868 that guardians could attach money paid to the mother in order to relieve the rates. Before this time guardians in Norfolk might make disclosure of the name of the putative father a condition of the mother getting re- lief. Between 1845 and 1859 some 3,350 affiliation orders were made in Norfolk courts or about four-fifths of the applications for orders that had been heard. The represented only the tip of the iceberg of Norfolk illegitimacy or about a quarter of illegitimate births. Norfolk in the 1840s apparently had a high and rising ille- gitimacy rate of 9-10 per cent of births compared with only 6-7 per cent for England and Wales. (These comparative returns of the Regis- trar General may be misleading, however, since in a rural area like Norfolk illegitimacy was harder to conceal than was the case in a town.) Statistics for the Docking Union suggest a rising number of illegitimate births. There were 427 illegitimate children born in the period 1836-43, 623 between 1849 and 1856 and 625 from 1861 to 1868. Of those born in the 1860s less than 10 per cent of births took place in the Docking Workhouse, with 60 births there compared with 511 outside. (This excluded the 54 who were stillborn.) (15) When public money was not involved in the relief of the mother, then general social attitudes in the Norfolk countryside towards the unmarried mother were not particularly censorious. Genteel observers thought illegitimacy an almost inevitable result of over- crowded cottages and the promiscuous mixing of men and women in field labour. Traditionally, the labouring classes regarded it rather more as a rural custom in which a girl, having proved her fertility, was rewarded at a later date by a wedding ring. The rate of illegitimacy was determined, in any case, by wider social influ- ences than the legal changes concerning bastardy and poor relief.
    Unmarried mothers in the workhouse shared the same accommodation as the childless widows, single girls unable to make a living from fieldwork during the winter months or as a domestic servant, and the married woman who had entered the union house with her husband and children. Pregnant women went to a lying-in ward when their time came, while in the larger workhouses the sufferers from venereal disease were segregated in a special or foul ward. Other- wise the old and the young, the unfortunate deserving character and the hardened 'fallen' woman, the sane and the mentally deficient were housed in the same able-bodied women's day room and bedroom. This arrangement could at best be only disagreeable or irritating, and at worst positively harmful. The Victorians themselves were particularly concerned about the 'contagious' qualities of immoral- ity which arose from this contact between the respectable and the feckless poor. In a country workhouse, where the numbers of each type of woman were often to be counted on the fingers of one hand, such an arrangement could not have been avoided. The alternative, within the relief framework of the New Poor Law, was to build much larger workhouses to serve a bigger geographical area and to provide a further sub-classification for the indoor poor. Such an arrange-

ment had its own defects in terms of expense, difficulties of administration and the isolation of paupers in a regional workhouse
far away from friends and family in the home parish.

Women were generally outnumbered by men in Norfolk workhouses
if all the categories of inmate are considered. This created difficulties for the poor law administrators, because they relied on the
able-bodied women to do the cooking, cleaning and laundry work of
the workhouse, and for the older or slightly infirm women to nurse
the sick. By the middle of the nineteenth century numbers of able-
bodied women in the workhouse had fallen so low that women from the
villages had to be employed in some workhouses to do the household
tasks. Indeed, the guardians themselves were responsible for the
short stay of single able-bodied women in the workhouse because they
took positive steps to find them work as independent domestic servants, helped them to emigrate to Australia or, in the case of the
'fallen' women, sent them to the Norfolk and Norwich Magdalen for
moral rehabilitation.(16) After 1834 the workhouse diet, with its
smaller quantities for women of bread, pudding, meat and cheese or
its substitution of butter for cheese, was extremely monotonous.
The pauper uniform was functional, rather than attractive, consisting of stays, flannel or linsey petticoat, a striped serge or
grosgrain or union chambrey gown, hessian apron, checked neckerchief, camblet jacket or shawl, slate-coloured hose, ankle shoes and
a white calico cap or cambric hat.

In spite of these conditions there were some women, like Mrs
Sexton in the Tunstead and Happing Incorporation, who became a semi-
permanent inmate of the workhouse because she entered, and then went
out, so frequently. She was one of the large pauper class of 'ins-
and-outs'. Was Elizabeth Sexton a woman more sinned against than
sinning? Was she forced repeatedly into the workhouse by adverse
circumstances, or was she one of the feckless poor and as such a
prime target for the Victorian moralist? The evidence from her
case history might support either interpretation. Between January
1839 and July 1844 she was admitted to the Smallburgh Workhouse on
nine separate occasions. On her first visit in 1839 she entered
with her husband William Sexton and five children. But by the time
of her second visit, in April 1840, her husband had deserted her,
leaving her pregnant and with five dependent children. Her child,
Louisa, was born and later died in the workhouse, and one of her
other children named Jonathan also died before she left the house
in September 1841. A week later she was readmitted; she was discharged again in March 1842, and was admitted again ten days later.
Three months later, in June, she was discharged but was readmitted
the same day. By this time she was pregnant and Richard, an illegitimate child, was born to her in the workhouse on 15 October. She
alleged later that this had been fathered on her by Mr Smith, the
master of the workhouse, during her previous winter sojourn in the
house. Her charges were never proved since it could only be her
word against his. In May 1843 the entire family emerged from the
house only to be readmitted the same day, were next discharged in
July, and were admitted again in August. Having spent the winter
of 1843-4 as indoor paupers, the woman and children re-emerged into
society in April 1844. By the following month the younger children,
under seven, entered the Smallburgh house after having been abandoned

at the workhouse gate by their grandmother. By July the mother and
older children followed them into the workhouse. Two days later
they discharged themselves, a day later sought relief there again,
and after a fortnight were discharged.(17) The later history of
Elizabeth Sexton is unknown, but one may conjecture that her five
children continued to receive much of their upbringing inside the
workhouse.

II THE YOUNG

The plight of the child incarcerated within the workhouse has been
the object of sympathy since the first appearance of 'Oliver Twist'
in 1837. How many pauper children were there in Norfolk workhouses? At the beginning of the New Poor Law era there were
slightly under 1,000 children there who were under the age of 16.
Numbers then increased to a peak in the 1850s and 1860s with nearly
1,800 children, before a gradual decline brought the number down to
less than 600 in the workhouse by 1900 and a further 200 in foster
homes or training institutions.(18)
    Children always made up a substantial proportion of the inmates
of the Norfolk workhouse; about half the indoor paupers in the
county were under 16 years of age, a much higher proportion than
the one-third that was the case nationally. A survey of 966 children in Norfolk workhouses in January 1838 revealed that 23 per
cent had been there over 12 months and a further 28 per cent between
six months and a year. This high proportion of children who were
already semi-permanent inmates so soon after the erection of the
union workhouses is explained by the circumstances of the children.
Of 896 children in the county's workhouses in the previous month,
three-quarters were illegitimate, orphaned, deserted by one or both
parents or had a father in prison. As such they were likely to stay
in the workhouse some time. The remaining children were the offspring either of widows and widowers who were workhouse inmates, or
of those chargeable because of mental or physical infirmity. In
addition there were also the children referred to earlier in this
chapter — those who were admitted as a means of relieving a low-
paid labourer with a large family.
    Children had their own quarters in the workhouse consisting of
day rooms, bedrooms, exercise yards, a schoolroom and a nursery.
Mothers were allowed access at all reasonable hours to their children until they were seven years old, when formal contact between a
child and the rest of his or her family was restricted to a short
weekly meeting. But informal contact in the dining room or chapel
might be engineered, while girls were likely to have contact with
their mothers during the performance of household tasks. Very
young children — under the age of four — slept with their mothers
at night. Babies under the age of two spent all their time with
their mother except when she was working, when they were put under
the care of an old or infirm inmate. Children in East Anglian
workhouses were considered to be mature enough to start their education at two years old and thereafter spent part of their day in
the schoolroom. The transition from dependence to independence for
the child born in the workhouse was therefore achieved gradually,

although for the older child entering the workhouse for the first
time there was the trauma of sudden separation from his parents.
On entering the workhouse the children were dressed in pauper uniforms of striped and checked gowns with aprons for the girls, and
jackets and trousers of a coarse cloth with a spotted neckerchief
for the boys. Their hair was crudely cropped. Later, when they
left the workhouse, girls going out into service were allowed to
grow their hair, since otherwise their unsightly heads signposted
their workhouse origin.(19)

During the Victorian era there was little recorded concern for
the health of the pauper child in East Anglian workhouses. Children suffered periodically from scabies, or as it was then termed
'the itch'. This was a skin disease caused by mites burrowing under
the skin and was treated by scrubbing open the burrows and washing
with soap and water. It was transmitted by close contact among the
children and particularly from the workhouse practice of more than
one child sleeping in a bed. Opthalmia was another affliction found
among Norfolk workhouse children, one causing inflammation, and
even permanent damage, to the eyes. In new-born babies the infection might be gonnorrhoeal with the baby having caught the bac-
teria in its passage through the birth canal. In older children
opthalmia either might be a form of conjunctivitis, with spots
on the lining of the eyelids, or might be associated with a tuber-
culous infection. Treatment for opthalmia was problematical for
most of this period, and in any case only the new Norwich Workhouse
had separate provision for the sick child in a children's infirmary.(20) Indeed, it was not until 1913 that the workhouse medical
officer was given the responsibility by the central administration
of keeping an individual record of each child's health and of giving
babies fortnightly check-ups. Earlier, he had the responsibility of
providing dietaries for workhouse children under nine years of age,
and several interesting examples were recorded of those in use in
Norfolk workhouses.

Most workhouse dietaries reflected contemporary ignorance about
the digestive limitations and nutritional needs of babies. Those
for older children, despite the reduced proportion of carbohydrates
and the increased amounts of protein in the form of meat or milk
when compared with the workhouse dietary for adults, were still deficient in the fruit and vegetables necessary to give the vitamins
essential for a balanced diet. This was true not only of diets in
workhouses, but of diets in other institutions, including public
schools. The children's dietary of the Flegg Incorporation gave the
nearest approximation to a well-balanced food intake among those
dietaries in use in Norfolk workhouses.(21) This had a pint of milk
and four ounces of bread for the daily breakfast of the two- to five-
year-olds. For dinner on two days a week there was eight ounces of
meat pudding and ten ounces of vegetables; there was eight ounces
of suet pudding and ten ounces of vegetables for dinner on a third
day; and on the remaining days four ounces of bread and an ounce of
cheese or half an ounce of butter. Supper consisted of four ounces
of bread, an ounce of treacle, and half a pint of milk and water.
For the five- to nine-year-olds there was the same dietetic pattern
but amounts of food were increased. In all cases, however, the workhouse diet of the child would have been superior to that of the
children of the independent, rural labourer in Norfolk.

15   The Dining Room, Wicklewood House, c. 1930

    Babies were incongruous, but common, inmates of the workhouse.
For example, in the Depwade Workhouse the number of infants fluctuated between 8 and 40 in the years from 1842 to 1844. In spite
of the number of babies in the workhouse they were apparently either
too small or too awkward to be categorized separately under the official workhouse scheme of classification. This lumped together all
children under the age of seven as one class of inmate, all of whom
were thought to require the same type of treatment. Arrangements
for babies were therefore made on a pragmatic basis. It was standard practice to assign a room as a nursery although a local inspector admitted that nurseries were 'often a neglected part of the workhouse'. The advent of women guardians had led by the 1890s to a
more sympathetic and discerning overhaul of the accommodation for
the very young. One lady guardian enlightened the male inspector
for the eastern counties on the need for nurseries to be warm,
sunny rooms.(22)
    Little significance was attached to babies dying in the workhouse,
since infant mortality in the early Victorian period was seven times
greater than it is today and a pauper baby's death merely relieved
the ratepayer's burden. Minimal contemporary concern resulted in
few records, so that historians disagree about the amount of infant
mortality in the nation's workhouses. Evidence from the Docking
Union provided some data on the deaths of illegitimate pauper babies
which suggest that infant mortality was lower inside than outside
the workhouse. Between 1861 and 1868 (and excluding stillbirths),
one-fifth of illegitimate babies died outside the workhouse compared
with only one-tenth inside it. Admittedly, the death rate of illegitimate babies may be untypical of legitimate births, and indeed the

low workhouse mortality may reveal only that women with illegitimate babies left the workhouse before the conditions there had killed their children. However, it is probable that the infant death rate in the workhouse was in fact lower because the medical attention given to the child in the workhouse by the medical officer was more skilled and continuous than that available to the poor woman in her own home. (For the same reason, maternal mortality from puerperal fever was comparatively low in the lying-in wards of the nation's workhouses.) During the mid-nineteenth century, if a death occurred in the workhouse the law did not require an inquest to be held as would have been the case if the death had occurred in a prison. In 1844, for example, Emily Howlett's eight-week-old illegitimate child had been suffocated in its mother's bed while both were inmates of the St Faith's Workhouse. The event was reported at the next meeting of the St Faith's Board of Guardians, when the guardians cursorily dismissed the matter and instructed the clerk to minute it as an accidental death.(23)

Children born in the workhouse in the mid-nineteenth century might well see very little other than its self-contained environment until they were old enough to be sent out into service. Such was the case of Sarah Linford, an illegitimate orphan who was born in the workhouse of the Freebridge Lynn Union in 1840, and who remained in this isolated community of about 150 people until 1856 with the exception of only one short break in the outside world. At 16 she was sent into service as a maid of all work at a local farmhouse. Such a restricted life became less common as more and more Norfolk boards of guardians decided to send pauper children out from the workhouse to the local village school. Children from the Freebridge Lynn Union at the turn of the century walked the one and a half miles from the union house to the school in Gayton village. They brought their lunch with them to school in a covered basket as it was too far for them to return for lunch to the workhouse. An old Norfolk craftsman who attended school with them remembers that the workhouse food, and especially the biscuits, were so good that the other pupils used to join in hungrily when they got the opportunity. An amicable child democracy apparently reigned and no invidious distinctions were made between the village and the workhouse children. Indeed, the former envied their counterparts their substantial lunches and the fact that they left school ten minutes early at the end of the afternoon to walk back to the workhouse. In other Norfolk unions the workhouse children were made to feel more of a race apart from the other children. In the Smallburgh Union the pauper children wore uniforms and were taught in a special room at the village school although all the children were allowed to play together. And in the Aylsham Union a bureaucratic desire to keep track of public property had led to an insensitive stamping of the workhouse children's clothing.(24) Even before the workhouse children were sent to the local village school in the late nineteenth century there had been a little contact between the Norfolk indoor pauper child and the outside world, either through the twice-weekly walk outside the workhouse, or the annual treat of an expedition to the seaside.

Ranking with the jaunt to the sea as one of the twin peaks of experience standing out from the tedium of the workhouse child's year was the celebration of Christmas. Although there is no account by

a pauper child of Christmas Day in a Norfolk workhouse, there is a
nostalgic recollection by a child who was the granddaughter of the
master and matron of the Erpingham Union Workhouse, and who spent
several Christmases there in the early part of the twentieth century. The naivety of a child's perception captured something which
was often omitted in adult descriptions of the workhouse — the
warmth of communal feeling within the workhouse walls:(25)

> I remember Christmas Days in the Workhouse, some of the happiest
> of my life ... it was Christmas morning and the children singing
> carols actually outside the bedroom door ... breakfast over, it
> was time to go with granny on her Christmas rounds with a present
> for everyone — sweets for the children, tobacco for the men and
> tea and a cap and apron for the old ladies. To me everyone
> seemed happy and in my grandparents special care. Across to the
> Infirmary, just separate from the House, with gifts for the bed-
> ridden and to see the decorations in the wards. Then to the big
> kitchen to watch the preparations for dinner, which was served
> in the dining hall to all the able-bodied. Families were allowed
> to sit together, a great treat for them which I was too young
> to appreciate. The great range which cooked the great rounds of
> beef, and the great cauldron in which the yellow football sized
> Christmas puddings were cooked, fascinated us, especially when
> they were hauled out of the copper on a pulley. My grandfather,
> father and the porter put on their aprons, sharpened their knives
> and carved the beef. Potatoes, greens and gravy were got ready,
> and then we were allowed to run backwards and forwards in the
> dining hall carrying loaded plates. Men and women were allowed
> a glass of stout or beer and the children lemonade.... At last
> seven o'clock and the concert began. I loved the decorated
> stage, even the 'institution' smell was exciting to me. The
> children performed, we did our duet and dialogue; the staff did
> a patriotic tableau, and everyone sang the war songs.... Many of
> the inmates had spent much of their lives at the House and had
> their one or two songs which they always sang. They needed no
> asking, and grandfather would call on them in strict rotation.
> Blind Jinny 'The Old Arm Chair'; Crutches Hardingham 'The Miners'
> Dream of Home'; Alden 'The Death of Nelson'; and so it went
> on, everyone singing the chorus.

CHAPTER 9

PAUPERS: II, THE OLD AND THE SICK

I   THE OLD

'The old might enjoy their indulgences', remarked the Royal Commission on the Poor Laws in 1834, and if the old were not precisely indulged in the new poor law era that followed, at least under central regulations they received preferential treatment in their relief. For those whose age or infirmity made them unable to earn their own livelihood it remained the norm to give them outdoor allowances, as had occurred before 1834, and not to relieve them in the union workhouses until this became necessary because of their inability to look after themselves in their own homes. However, at the local level, payments to old people were often grudgingly made and allowances were kept deliberately small so that recourse would be had to help from relatives or from charity. In Norfolk, boards of guardians maintained a careful scrutiny over relief to old people, because this made up such a substantial proportion of Norfolk pauperism and was a large burden on the county's ratepayers. In the early days of the New Poor Law, between 1839 and 1846, 35.5 per cent of outdoor paupers and 28.9 per cent of all paupers in the county were aged and infirm. At the end of the nineteenth century 31.7 per cent of those aged over 65 in the county were paupers and in this respect Norfolk had the ninth highest county total; only 5.0 per cent were indoor paupers and 26.7 received outdoor allowances in their own homes. The inadequate sums of money which were paid in the form of outdoor allowances in the country as a whole were criticized by Royal Commissions in 1895, 1899 and 1909.(1) Did the sums paid out by Norfolk guardians form an adequate amount for the elderly to live on?

A humane, local estimate in 1895 was that 4s 6d (which included 1s per week for rent) was a reasonable weekly allowance for the old to maintain themselves. Actual allowances fell far short of this. In the Aylsham and Erpingham Unions it was usual in the 1890s to pay a weekly sum of between 1s 6d and 2s 6d for a single old person, and for a married couple a sum of 1s 6d to 2s with an additional stone of flour. Similar sums were paid in the Docking, Walsingham and Guiltcross Unions of 1s or 1s 6d, and half a stone of flour per person per week, while in the Freebridge Lynn Union it was 1s and a

stone of flour. This information was given to the Royal Commission
on the Aged Poor in 1895 by men who were active in agricultural
trades unionism and who might be expected to emphasize the beggarly
allowances and the hardship of old people in the labouring class.
A different bias might be expected in the evidence of the Chairman
of the St Faith's Board of Guardians. In the St Faith's Union old
people's allowances varied from 2s to 3s 6d per week, the average
being about half a crown. But the Rev. Canon Hinds Howell was
sympathetic to the poor and as a liberal chairman did weekly battle
with the grinding instincts of the farmers who formed the majority
on the St Faith's Board of Guardians. He was asked how he expected
a poor person receiving half a crown a week to live on it. He
replied, 'I tell you it is a miracle to me, and they cannot do it
without some help or another.'

Humiliation and resentment, or gratitude and appreciation — how
did the old react to this system of outdoor relief in Norfolk?
Outdoor allowances did not make them feel that they had lost their
self-respect either in their own eyes or in those of their neighbours. Allowances were regarded as the certain outcome of a life of
low wages, although with the first stirrings of interest about old-
age pensions before the end of the century their inevitability was
beginning to be questioned. What everyone objected to was the de-
meaning and inefficient procedures that the machinery of the poor
law administration imposed upon them as a pre-condition for relief.
The long walk to the board meeting, the intensive questioning as
to their means by unsympathetic guardians, the delays in granting
relief, and the poor quality of the seconds flour allowed imparted
to the relief a penitential flavour which offset any feeling of
thankfulness in the recipient. Great bitterness was engendered
among the rural labourers in the county by the guardians' enforce-
ment of the children's legal duty to provide for their parents. The
statement of the Chairman of the St Faith's Board of Guardians suggests why this was the case, 'The St Faith's Board has never forced
an aged person to enter the workhouse except as a test, when children have been considered capable of providing a sufficient maintenance or part of the amount required.'(2)

> When one sees knots of old men gossiping by the fire or basking
> in the sun; when one find the bed-ridden old women carefully
> nursed and appropriately fed, it is difficult to help contrast-
> ing their condition with that of some of the out-door poor who,
> when failing under the weight of years and infirmity, pass al-
> most solitary lives in miserable dwellings and are half-starved
> on the pittance which they obtain from their scanty earnings
> or from private charity, even supplemented by such doles of
> 1s 6d and 2s a week, with perhaps half a stone of flour, as are
> ordinarily granted from the rates. It is common to hear an old
> inmate say that he could not bear the notion of entering 'the
> house' but that if he had known it was so comfortable he would
> have come there long ago.

This account of a typical scene in an eastern counties workhouse(3)
was given by the poor law inspector, Mr H. Preston-Thomas, and is
interesting for the insight it gives into the social significance
of the union workhouse. It was remote from the direct experience
of many poor people and its isolation had produced a folklore of

fear and even horror which had small resemblance to the reality of
conditions in the workhouse.

Although old people's preference for their own homes with familiar surroundings and free access to their relatives and friends is
understandable in psychological terms, yet in material terms their
choice of outdoor rather than indoor relief was probably a bad one.
Guardians in Norfolk, as in many other areas, gave outdoor allowances to old people which were only pittances and must have resulted in semi-starvation when they were not supplemented by other
sources of income. In contrast, relief inside the workhouse continued to partake of the tradition of the pauper palaces with their
liberal treatment of the aged.

Why did Norfolk poor law administrators operate these two di-
verse policies for old people? The small outdoor allowances given
reflected the guardians' concern for the ratepayers' pockets because of the large numbers of old people being relieved in this way.
It may also have been finely judged, and reliance placed on the
allowance being supplemented by help from relatives or charity,
which would bring the total income up to subsistence level. For
those who stubbornly and 'misguidedly' chose their own homes rather
than the pauper palace that had been generously provided for them,
discriminatory relief may well have been thought justifiable, and
the humane local tradition in the relief of old people was then
channelled narrowly towards those who accepted the preferred solution of indoor relief.

Inside the workhouse the detailed arrangements for old people
varied quite widely even within Norfolk although they were characterized generally by a humane consideration for old people's
needs. The central poor law board's workhouse classification scheme
grouped together the aged and the infirm. In consequence, in some
workhouses old people were dealt with according to their age and
those over 60 years of age had their own day rooms, bedrooms and
exercise yards. In others, the old were categorized according to
the state of their health, with the frail in the infirmary and the
vigorous in the accommodation for the able-bodied. A difference
can be seen, for example, between the plans of the Henstead and
Depwade Union Workhouses which segregated according to age (Figures
3 and 4, pp. 63 and 64) and the Downham Market Workhouse (Figure 5,
p. 67), which segregated according to the infirmity of the inmate.
Some married couples had their own rooms in the union workhouse
since after 1842 poor law guardians were permitted, and after 1847
enjoined, to provide married accommodation for couples over 60 who
did not want to be separated from one another. But in 1863 only 15
out of the 22 Norfolk workhouses were known to have made such rooms
available for their Darbys and Joans. Poor law administrators tended to justify the small number of rooms available with the argument that not all couples in fact wanted to be together. This may
well have been true if one partner wanted the nursing care that
was available only in the infirmary, but it is possible that the
numbers of these cases were equalled by those of old people who
after half a lifetime together found themselves involuntarily separated one from another. This had not always been the case under
the Old Poor Law. The plans of the Smallburgh House of Industry
(Figures 1 and 2, pp. 42 and 43) showed six cottages for the aged

as having been provided in this old poor law incorporation.(4)

Once inside the union workhouse of the New Poor Law, the old were liable to become permanent inmates. In the mid-nineteenth century one-fifth of the workhouse inmates were aged over 60. Nearly two-thirds of the 234 inmates in Norfolk workhouses in 1861 who had been inmates for a continuous period of five years or more were the aged and infirm. Among them the men outnumbered the women by three to two. The longevity of Norfolk people was remarkable; in 1861, for example, there were 19 nonagenarians and one centenarian in the county's work-houses. When the mortal coil was finally shrugged off, a pauper in the Henstead, Aylsham or Loddon and Clavering Unions might expect only an unmarked grave in the burial ground within the work-house grounds, whereas one in the Norwich Incorporation had a decent funeral in which his coffin was borne in a hearse to his parish church where there was a brief service and the bell tolled his pas-sing years. Perhaps the humane treatment received by old people in Norfolk workhouses helped prolong their lives, since, although the national poor law policy towards the aged was not liberalized until the 1890s, Norfolk boards of guardians had always tried to give sym-pathetic consideration to their needs. The traditions of the old poor law pauper palaces were imitated in the workhouses of the New Poor Law. Even in the Aylsham Union (which overall was one of the most stringent unions in the county), there was a warm concern for the wellbeing of the elderly. 'The Aylsham Workhouse Visiting Com-mittee having reported that the aged men in the house complained of the cold in consequence of their waistcoats not being of suffi-cient length, it was ordered that the Master do cause the same to be altered accordingly.'(5)

16   Inmates of Freebridge Lynn, c.1930

The official workhouse regulations issued by the central administration permitted the aged to be given an ounce of tea per week
and milk and sugar. There was also a more generous dietary with
bread, butter, tea and sugar instead of gruel at breakfast, and an
additional day when meat pudding was served instead of bread and
cheese at dinner. Norfolk guardians were also broadminded in
sanctioning the medical officer's orders of porter and beer, and
tobacco or snuff, to the aged and infirm in the workhouse. The old
men cultivated the garden of a Norfolk workhouse and elderly men
and women had fairly free access to it. In the St Faith's Union,
for example, they were allowed to take walks there in the summer
months between the hours of 10 am and 12 noon, and from 3 to 5 in
the afternoon. Old people were allowed to get up an hour later
than other inmates, rising at 7 am instead of 5.45 am in summer and
at 8 am rather than 6.45 am in winter. Sunday attendance at the
workhouse chapel, where they had special forms with backs fitted
on them, might be replaced by a visit to another chapel or church
so long as a certificate of attendance was produced. In some
unions old people were allowed out on Sundays, and most unions permitted a visit of a week or month to friends or relatives at some
point during the year. Later in the century the Brabazon Scheme
was initiated, and visiting ladies taught older inmates handicrafts,
as a means both of filling in the hours, and in order that sales of
work might provide funds for old people's treats.

Some old people exploited their privileged position. In the
Forehoe Incorporation old men were threatened with a withdrawal of
their tea and sugar if on entry they refused to have a bath. And
on another occasion they were kept from the workhouse garden because their gardening prowess had produced a more luxurious diet
which was not sanctioned by the official workhouse dietary.(6)   In
general, however, the Norfolk guardians maintained a benign administration of indoor relief to old people, and one that mitigated as
much as possible the conditions in a union workhouse that had been
designed for the able-bodied, as well as the elderly, pauper. The
house of industry or workhouse therefore inevitably provided standards of care that were less liberal than an almshouse designed
purely for the impotent poor. Humanity was diluted because of the
necessity of providing in the same building a more abrasive environment for the able-bodied.

St Augustine's Infirmary in Norwich had been designed solely for
the comfort of old people, and paupers there experienced the relaxed
atmosphere and solid standards of comfort that were more characteristic of a charitable hospital than a workhouse. Admission was by
guardian's nomination and was for a select few only. It was confined to those over 65 years of age who were of a good character,
and who had been receiving poor relief for the previous six months.
Inside the infirmary the inmates wore a uniform. For women this included a blue and brown check camlet gown, hessian apron, shawls,
and straw bonnets, while men wore jackets and trousers of blue pilot
cloth, flannel waistcoats, shirts, check handkerchief and worsted
stockings. They could wear their own clothes when they went outside the infirmary as they did quite freely in order to do odd jobs
of work or visit friends or relatives in the city. Meals were enlivened by an annual treat of beans and bacon in July and by a

supplement of pork and pea soup at dinner during the winter. Additional indulgences might include tobacco, porter or wine. Hours were whiled away in the garden, in reading books or periodicals, or in playing nine-pins, cards, dominoes, draughts or bagatelle. Musical entertainments were provided regularly. Their sleeping conditions were comfortable and consisted of hair or flock mattresses (instead of the usual straw ones) and coloured rugs and counterpanes. It was a sad day for the inmates when the Infirmary was closed in 1859 and the old people transferred to the new workhouse at Heigham as part of an economy campaign by the guardians. However, there was some attempt to categorize old people according to their character even at the Heigham workhouse. Deserving old people inhabited a row of cottages set apart from the workhouse while certain others had privileged treatment and had more comfortable day rooms furnished with armchairs.(7)

II THE SICK

Nearly three-quarters of the cases of pauperism in England and Wales involved sickness in the mid-nineteenth century yet the reformers of 1834 had not planned a medical service within the New Poor Law. The system of medical relief grew up therefore in a piecemeal and pragmatic fashion before receiving a coherent administrative framework in the General Consolidated Order of 1847. There was national concern in the early days over the way the medical service was developing — medical officers were often paid insufficient salaries and might even have to tender for their post; their districts were frequently (and particularly in rural areas) too large for them to do the job efficiently; and the divided responsibility for pauper patients between relief administrators and poor law doctors raised questions both about professional medical autonomy and about the purpose of relief to the sick poor. Norfolk avoided the worst of these problems since guardians were advised by Dr Kay who, before becoming a poor law inspector, had been a medical practitioner. Medical officers were appointed by the guardians and in Norfolk it was customary to invite all resident doctors who had surgical qualifications to apply for the post of medical officer. Tender was never resorted to. Salaries were fixed annual payments although the Wayland and Swaffham Unions and the Flegg Incorporation later tried an improved system, which fixed the basic salary according to the size of the permanent pauper list, and with an additional case load payment of 7s 6d which fluctuated according to the numbers of the occasionally sick poor. Several doctors were appointed in each union and their districts varied in size from as little as 1,000 to 3,000 square acres in the Blofield or Mitford and Launditch Unions, to those of as much as 25,000 or 33,000 square acres in the Docking and Thetford Unions. With a case load of 275 cases per year, a salary of £65, and a district of 22 square miles, the typical Norfolk medical officer differed little in 1837 from the national norm for a poor law doctor. Conditions had improved by mid-century, with increased numbers of poor law doctors being employed in Norfolk; 108 in 1844, 117 in 1852 and 122 in 1861. The salary bill rose, in the same period, from £5,000 to £6,000, which gave doctors smaller districts but an equivalent salary.(8)   Informed observers in Norfolk concluded that the general standard of medical care given to paupers had improved in the county after 1834.(9) The medical service that was established in Norfolk in these early years should therefore have provided sick paupers within the county with a standard of medical care that compared quite well with that in other rural areas.

The sick poor were generally treated in their own homes in the new poor law era (as they had been before 1834), since the Prohibitory Order which forbade outdoor relief to many categories of poor exempted the sick from its provisions.   In 1870 two-thirds of the sick poor in England and Wales were treated in their homes, although by this time, because of the improvement in medical facilities inside the workhouse, the sick were encouraged to take advantage of these by becoming indoor patients.   The medical officer was responsible for making periodic visits to the homes of chronic sick on the permanent pauper list in his district and for attending other cases when required to do so by the poor law relieving officer.   Cases might include those of fever, consumption or puerperal fever (in maternity cases), and frequently — in the marshy areas — cases of rheumatism and ague.   The poor law medical officer was hard working and underpaid;   from a small salary he had to provide the cost of most drugs and medicines from his own pocket.   After 1842 guardians could insist, and after 1858 were compelled to insist, that the poor law doctor was qualified in both medicine and surgery in order to be allowed to treat pauper patients.   As a result, paupers were looked after by a better qualified doctor than the typical rural practitioner who treated the independent poor.   Again, while every pauper patient was treated in his own home, the ordinary labourer might often have to attend the dispensary at the doctor's house.(10)

Why then, in spite of all these advantages, were there so many allegations of negligence or neglect made by the Norfolk poor against their union medical officers?   Nearly all allegations were found, after investigation, to be groundless as far as professional negligence was concerned.   Complaints by paupers were not always well-founded, as a Briston guardian found when he charged an Erpingham medical officer with neglect, only to find that the patient had forgotten about a visit which the doctor had made to him.(11)   Where neglect had occurred in this context, it was generally a result of the administrative system and particularly the large size of the medical district, or the divided responsibility for medical relief.   Both of these caused delays which sometimes proved to have fatal results.   The central poor law authority had created a cumbrous system by which a poor man when taken ill had to apply to the union relieving officer (or in emergency to the parish overseer or local magistrate) for a note authorizing medical relief, which he would then present to the medical officer.   Until he received this authorization the doctor was not supposed to attend the sick man.   This created delays, because perhaps three or four miles had to be walked to the village where the relieving officer was, a note obtained, a further walk to the doctor's house, an additional wait if the doctor was visiting a patient elsewhere, before the doctor got to the sick pauper after many hours had elapsed.

The relieving officer judged the applications that came before him not on the grounds of the seriousness of the illness but on the income of the patient. The Forehoe Board of Guardians, for example, approved the action of their relieving officer who in 1841 refused to authorize medical treatment to a child, who died for the lack of it. The reason for refusing relief was that the Havers family, with only three children and a weekly income of 13s were thought to be able to afford to pay for their own medical treatment through a sick club.(12)

The shortage of medical practitioners in one area of rural Norfolk did produce instances of medical neglect by a poor law doctor. Negligence occurred because he held appointments in more than one poor law union, and did not make arrangements for a deputy to act in his absence. Mr R.J. Tunaley began his poor law career in the Depwade Union and complaints of his neglect of pauper patients in 1839 occurred shortly after his appointment. Probably as a result of these allegations he switched to the Henstead Union, where he held an appointment as a poor law medical officer until his resignation in 1855. His career there was marked by continuous complaints. For example, in May 1843 he received an order for immediate attendance on a sick woman. He did not visit her and the woman died. Henstead guardians said that they had every confidence in Tunaley, and so the Poor Law Commission did not dismiss him, as they wished to do. While holding the Henstead appointment, Tunaley also obtained a medical district in the Forehoe Incorporation. In 1846, a Wymondham citizen wrote to the Poor Law Commission alleging that Tunaley did not visit pauper patients in spite of their possession of medical orders from the relieving officer. As a result, three people had died and one had gone blind. The Forehoe guardians cleared Tunaley but the Poor Law Commission maintained that the evidence suggested that he had been guilty of gross neglect. The Poor Law Commission deferred to the wishes of the local guardians and did not dismiss Tunaley, although it required him to appoint a substitute to act in his absence. Further cases of negligence occurred in 1848-9, in which a child died and needless suffering was caused to other outdoor paupers. This time it was the Forehoe guardians who demanded that he appoint an assistant (the previous arrangement for a substitute having apparently lapsed), and they also objected to Tunaley's practice of making his pauper patients visit him in his surgery. Tunaley managed to get away with medical negligence because, on the one hand, he was one of the few surgeons available in the Wymondham area whom the Forehoe and Henstead guardians could have employed, and on the other hand he was an influential man who was also the surgeon to the local Bridewell, and registrar for the Wymondham District. Tunaley did not confine his neglect only to pauper patients; he had had an action brought against him at Norfolk Assizes in 1844 in which it was alleged that gross neglect of one of his ordinary patients had led to a boy's foot having to be amputated. The case went against Tunaley but the judge's favourable summing up led to damages of only a farthing against the doctor.(13)

The rudimentary arrangements made for the sick paupers inside the union workhouses of Norfolk compared unfavourably with those that had been made for the medical relief on the outdoor poor. In

planning the workhouses of the New Poor Law there seems to have been
little appreciation that provision needed to be made for the sick.
Since the attention of national reformers was concentrated on the
relief of the able-bodied, this omission on the part of the Poor Law
Commission is perhaps not surprising. But at the local level, the
Norfolk guardians after 1834 had the old poor law precedent of the
East Anglian house of industry to guide them, and it is puzzling
that greater attention was not paid to this. Frequently, the pauper
palace had had sick or hospital wards for the ordinary patients,
a pest house in the grounds for infectious cases, a dispensary or
surgery for the provision of drugs and the services of a midwife
and a surgeon. Serious cases involving surgery would be sent to
voluntary hospitals to which a subscription was paid. This utiliza-
tion of local hospitals was imitated by the Norfolk boards of guardians under the New Poor Law, in spite of discouragement by the
central poor law administration. Unions in east Norfolk made use
of the Norfolk and Norwich Hospital in Norwich, and those in the
west of the county used the West Norfolk and Lynn Hospital in
King's Lynn. The Poor Law Board sanctioned this practice belatedly
in 1851. But it was not until the 1860s that Norfolk rural unions
began to provide separate infirmary buildings or infectious wards
along the lines of the old poor law incorporations. This came after
adverse publicity on national arrangements for the sick poor in
workhouses in the 'Lancet', and pressure from the Poor Law Medical
Officers' Association, and the Association for the Provision of
Workhouse Infirmaries, for improved facilities for the sick indoor
pauper. After the 1860s more rapid progress in the improvement
of medical facilities was made in urban than in rural unions. In
spite of the activity of Norfolk poor law, medical officers in
medical pressure groups and the suggestions of the local poor law
inspectors (particularly Sir John Walsham and Mr Harry Farnall),
progress in Norfolk was slow. As late as 1896 only eight Norfolk
unions had separate infirmaries or infectious wards and these were
administered as part of the workhouse rather than, as was beginning
to be the case in some urban areas, as a state hospital which provided free medicine. In rural areas such as Norfolk, the decline
in the number of indoor able-bodied paupers by the late nineteenth
century resulted in a surplus of accommodation in the workhouse
which could be converted into sick wards for the aged or infirm.
The proportions of these rooms were seldom ideal for their new use,
while the parsimony of the local boards of guardians produced relatively little in the way of medical appliances, equipment or furniture. The poor law inspector H. Preston-Thomas noted in the 1890s
that the accommodation for the sick in the workhouses of the eastern counties was inferior to that in general hospitals.(14)
    The chief impediments to medical progress in rural unions were
the prejudices, parsimony and ignorance of the boards of guardians.
Not every board, of course, could provide a chairman with such
eccentric views as the Forehoe Incorporation. Here, the Earl of
Kimberley successfully opposed the installation of baths and other
sanitary improvements at the Wicklewood house in the 1890s on the
grounds that bathing was dangerous to health.(15) Most Norfolk
guardians were indifferent about the medical arrangements in the
workhouse although they had the responsibility for determining the

KING'S LYNN UNION.

SICK DIETARY.

FULL SICK DIET. No. 2.

DAILY.

Bread	⅜ lb.
Tea	2 pints.
Sugar	1 oz.
Butter	1 oz.
Dumpling	5 oz.
Meat	6 oz.
* Vegetables.	

HALF SICK DIET, No. 3.

DAILY.

Bread	¾ lb.
Tea	2 pints.
Sugar	½ oz.
Butter	½ oz.
Dumpling	5 oz.
Meat	3 oz.
* Vegetables.	

FEVER DIET, No. 4.

DAILY.

Bread	⅜ lb.
Gruel, Milk, or sweetened Tea	4½ pints.

LOW SICK DIET, No. 5.

DAILY.

Gruel	1½ pint.
Bread	12 oz.
Dumpling	10 oz.

WOMEN DURING CONFINEMENTS.

First 4 Days.

FEVER DIET.

Next 3 Days.

DAILY.

Bread	¾ lb.
Dumpling and Gravy	10 oz.

Next 14 Days.

SICK DIET No. 3.

WOMEN SUCKLING CHILDREN.

DAILY.
House Diet,

Bread extra	2 oz.
Sugar	½ oz.

INFANTS at 9 months after weaning.

DAILY.

Bread	1 pound.
Milk	1 pint.

After 2 years.

Children's house diet.

NURSES' DIET.

DAILY.

Bread	18 oz.
Meat	8 oz.
Dumpling or Pudding	5 oz.
Potatoes	6 oz.
Butter or Cheese	1½ oz.
Sugar	1 oz.
Porter	1 pint.
Tea, weekly	2 oz.

* Monday, Wednesday, Thursday and Saturday, Vegetables in lieu of Bread, for Dinner.

Saint James's Workhouse,
Lynn, June, 21st. 1848.

W. S. Plowright, Printer, Lynn.

Figure 13   King's Lynn Union Sick Dietary

quantity and quality of the accommodation for the sick.   They also
approved the medical officers' recommendations on the diet for the
sick, and the Sick Dietary in use in the King's Lynn Union in 1848
is illustrated in Figure 13.   The medical officer who was assigned
the workhouse as part of his duties found himself hamstrung by the
possession of inadequate powers.   He could, under the 1847 General
Order, make no more than recommendations to the local guardians
and the central poor law board on the dietaries, hygiene, ventilation and numbers in the workhouse, although he himself bore the
overall responsibility for the general health of the workhouse inmates.   The reports of the medical officer in the St Faith's Union
give an interesting insight into workhouse conditions and the stone
wall of indifference with which the guardians greeted his observations in the 1840s.   In his reports to the guardians, the hygiene
of the inmates was criticized and suggestions made for the provision of piped water to the bedrooms and of clean towels;   the
practice of bathing entrants to the house in the same water was
condemned for spreading vermin and disease;   and the bad ventilation and overcrowding in the wards were alleged to be affecting the
health of the paupers.   The professional frustration and personal
resentment which this type of situation created for Norfolk poor
law doctors can be inferred from the recollections of the London
medical officer, Dr Joseph Rogers, in his account of his battle to
improve facilities in the Strand and Westminster Unions.(16)   However, not every medical officer was an ardent reformer nor every
board of guardians unsympathetic to the needs of sick paupers.   In
some areas there were attempts by guardians to get doctors to visit
their patients in the workhouse daily, rather than the twice or
thrice weekly visit, that was the norm in the country areas.(17)

  The nursing was the weakest point.   Not infrequently a single
  paid nurse was in charge of thirty or forty patients, and this
  meant that almost everything for the sick had to be done by
  pauper inmates.   They had nothing to gain if they did the duty
  assigned to them well, nothing to lose if they did it badly;
  the fact that being able-bodied women, they were workhouse
  inmates proved, *prima facie*, that they were not of high character;   so most of them were not disposed to take much trouble in
  attending to helpless old folk requiring assistance in various
  respects by night and by day.   But things were steadily mending.
  Guardians were beginning to recognize the fact that nursing is
  a skilled business, and that it is worth while to pay for its
  being done properly.

This revealing description of the medical care of the sick in the
workhouses of East Anglia in the 1890s was written by the local poor
law inspector.   He was correct in thinking that it was only at this
time, in the 1890s, that an adequate supply of nurses was beginning
to be employed in workhouse sick wards in Norfolk.   Under pressure
from the Local Government Board in London, Norfolk boards of guardians increased the numbers of nurses they employed from 41 in 1891
to 145 in 1896.   Of these, half in 1891 and two-thirds in 1896 had
had prior training.   The ratio of nurses continued to improve from
a ratio of 1 nurse to 24 patients in 1898, to 1 nurse to 17 patients
in 1900.   While standards of nursing care in local workhouses did
not plumb the depths of a Sarah Gamp or Betsey Prig, neither did it

reach Florence Nightingale's ideal of one nurse to every dozen
patients. But although pauper inmates continued to be used unoffi-
cially as sick attendants (despite the prohibition of the practice
by the central board in 1897), substantial progress had been made
in nursing sick paupers since the time in 1844-5 when the 22
Norfolk unions could boast of only four nurses between them. Indeed,
since training for nurses got under way only in the 1850s and 1860s,
and it was not until 1879 that a national pressure group was set up
in the form of the Association for Promoting Trained Nurses in Workhouse Infirmaries and Sick Asylums, it is hardly surprising that
the indoor paupers in Norfolk workhouses had to wait so long for
reasonable nursing care. Increasingly, nurses in workhouses found
themselves dealing with the tedium of geriatric cases rather than
with more varied cases of fever, bronchitis, pneumonia, consumption,
syphilis, rheumatism or eye diseases which had previously occupied
them. Boring work, social isolation and poor facilities continued
to make it difficult for rural boards of guardians to recruit or
retain good nurses.(18) But if it had been an uphill struggle to
make improvements in the case of the physically sick in Norfolk
workhouses in the late nineteenth century, the going was still
harder where the mentally sick were concerned.

The central poor law authority after 1834 did its best to ignore
the presence of mentally sick paupers; they were not recognized
as a separate group under the workhouse classification scheme and
had no specialist accommodation assigned to them. Each rural workhouse, in these early days, might therefore contain one or two
paupers of unsound mind in the day rooms or bedrooms of the able-
bodied or aged inmates, who would be a constant irritant to the
other inmates. Harmless idiots could be retained in the workhouse
under a certificate obtained from a local magistrate. Overcrowding
in lunatic asylums resulted in the provision of 1862 which allowed
chronic lunatics to remain in the workhouse. In 1863 only four
workhouses in Norfolk had separate lunatic wards, and a further
five segregated the mentally deficient from the other paupers,
while the remaining thirteen unions followed the usual national
practice of mixing those of unsound mind with sane paupers. The
workhouse medical officer had the responsibility of reporting to
the guardians the name of any pauper of unsound mind in the workhouse and of stating whether he thought them dangerous and suitable
for dispatch to the lunatic asylum. Boards of guardians were reluctant to send any but violent lunatics to the asylum because of the
much greater expense to the poor rate of the lunatic's parish. In
the 1840s it cost 6s a week to keep a pauper lunatic in the Norfolk
County Asylum at Thorpe, or more than double the cost of maintaining him in the workhouse. Some pauper lunatics might be sufficiently fortunate to be sent to the Bethel, an excellent small
licensed house in Norwich, which had been founded in 1713 as one
of the first private institutions for the care of the mentally sick.
Some harmless lunatics were given outdoor relief and lived in the
homes of friends or relatives, or at a later date were boarded out.
Increasing sensitivity to the problem, together with a more accurate
identification of mental illness, contributed to the growing number
of people of unsound mind stated to be receiving poor relief in
Norfolk. In 1842 there were 401 of these cases, of whom 91 were

relieved in the workhouse, 6 in licensed houses and 164 in the
county asylum, while 140 were residing with friends or elsewhere.
Thirty years later there were 1,138 people of unsound mind being
relieved by Norfolk guardians of whom 265 were in the workhouse,
7 in licensed houses, 599 in the county asylum and 266 with friends
or elsewhere. Those with weak minds who were relieved in the Norfolk workhouse tended to become permanent inmates there. In 1861
one-third of the adult inmates who had been there continuously
for over five years were mentally handicapped. One of these inmates was Rachael Dixon, 'an idiot' of King's Lynn, who had been in
a Norfolk workhouse for the longest period of all, having entered
sixty-six years before, in the previous century.

The insane paupers who remained in Norfolk workhouses were
treated humanely and well. This was in part the result of pressure
from the Lunacy Commissioners who after 1845 had authority over all
lunatics and whose periodic visitations to workhouses ensured that
insane paupers had a better material standard of living than that
administered to sane paupers by the central poor law board. For
example, the Visiting Commissioners praised the tranquil state and
excellent care given to two paupers of unsound mind in the St
Faith's workhouse in 1838 and the liberal diet of the four chronic,
harmless lunatics in the Blofield workhouse in 1869.(19)

The Lunacy Commissioners were less than enthusiastic about the
pauper lunatic asylum run by the Norwich guardians. About sixty
lunatics were maintained in this infirmary asylum during the mid-
nineteenth century; an arrangement which the poor law inspector
in 1843 found to be well-managed, useful and satisfactory. Not so
the Visiting Commissioners in Lunacy, who thought its accommodation
and equipment deficient and its personnel untrained. As a result,
relations between the Norwich Guardians, the City Licensing Magistrates and the Lunacy Commissioners became so bad that in May 1860
it was reported (though without any factual foundation) that the
guardians would throw in their hand, unlock the asylum gates, and
turn the lunatics out on the town. Little was done to resolve this
contentious issue because of the lack of alternative accommodation
in lunatic asylums in the eastern counties. Although the Borough
of Norwich had bought a site for a lunatic asylum in 1866 it delayed building there.(20)

While the medical services of the poor law guardians concerned
only the poorer section of the population, their growing duties
in the field of public health affected not just paupers but the
community as a whole. In rural areas the underdeveloped state of
local government, before the closing years of the nineteenth century, gave boards of guardians and their medical officers a responsibility for public health. This positive practice of social
medicine grew slowly within the negative framework of a deterrent
destitution authority. Rural guardians were slow to realize that
their preventive functions in public health of forestalling destitution by an early discovery of cases of infectious disease, and of
eliminating sanitary nuisances which spread disease within the community, were in fact complementary to the curative function of poor
law medicine. However, Norfolk poor law administrators tended to
view any expenditure of money in preventing disease and destitution as unnecessary and were less than enthusiastic about performing

CHOLERA.

KING'S LYNN UNION.

Two Cases having appeared in this Union, the Public are respectfully requested to seek immediate medical assistance in any case of Diarrhœa or looseness of the Bowels.

Application may be made to the Union District Medical Officers, viz.

Mr. SMYTHE, Chapel Street.

Dr. HUNTER, White Lion Court.

The Guardians will be happy to receive information of any existing nuisance.

BY ORDER,

JNO. JAS. COULTON,

Lynn, August 11th, 1854.   CLERK.

AIKIN, PRINTER, LYNN.

Figure 14   Cholera in the King's Lynn Union

their additional duties. In 1848-9, 1853-4 or 1866 outbreaks of
cholera forcibly alerted them to the importance of their role. But
even during the cholera outbreaks of 1854 the King's Lynn guardians
took a parsimonious attitude to public health. The poster in
Figure 14 shows that they respectfully advised the Lynn citizens on
11 August that they should seek medical assistance if they suffered
from diarrhoea — an early warning of the onset of the disease. But
the board of guardians were appalled to find an increase in requests
for free medical assistance from the poor to the poor law medical
officers. So they sternly warned people in a second poster of 18
August that they were not to apply for medical relief unless they
were destitute and could not afford to pay for their own doctor.
Even in a time of social crisis they were convinced that the line
between pauperdom and independence must not be breached unnecessarily.(21)

In the early 1870s came one last attempt to invigorate and
rationalize the involvement of the poor law authorities in rural
public health which had resulted from ineffectual legislation in
1846, and 1860. The Public Health Act of 1872 constituted the
poor law union as the rural sanitary district and the boards of
guardians as the rural sanitary authority. The guardians had to
appoint an inspector of nuisances and a medical officer of health
but were left free to appoint either a full-time new official or to
give their hard-pressed poor law doctors an additional part-time
responsibility. Local indifference to issues of public health
persisted, and there was some consternation when in 1862 the Prince
of Wales bought the Sandringham Estate in west Norfolk, because the
local santiary area of Freebridge Lynn was in as bad a state as
any in the entire country. Here 'infectious disease was allowed
to spread unchecked, while nuisances flourished without interference'. The local guardians had given their medical officer the
impression that he was never to act on his own initiative and was
to wait for local requests for his intervention, which rarely came.
Discreet pressure during the 1870s from the Medical Department in
the Local Government Board eventually improved matters, according
to H. Preston-Thomas, who was at this early stage of his career the
senior clerk to Sir John Simon. Simon, the medical officer of the
Privy Council and head of the Local Government Board's Medical
Department, retired in 1876, and with his departure the financial
pressures of the poor law as destitution authority eclipsed the
policies of social medicine, which Simon had done so much to
develop.(22)

Pauperization through sickness and recourse to poor law medical
assistance had worried poor law administrators in the first years
of the New Poor Law. A notable but short-lived result of this preoccupation by Dr Kay, the local poor law inspector, were the medical
clubs for the poor which had been set up by guardians and medical
officers in about half the Norfolk poor law unions in the 1830s.
This was a vain attempt to get the rural labourers to insure themselves against sickness and to prevent a later recourse to poor
relief. The medical club begun in the Loddon and Clavering Union
in 1836 was not untypical. It was open to all members of the labouring classes, to servants in farmhouses and to tradesmen's families,
provided that the weekly income did not exceed 18s. Contributions

were on a scale that ranged from 1d per week for a single adult to 2½d for a large family. In return, the poor got free medical treatment during illness, free vaccination, and attendance for confinements at half the usual medical fees. Drunkards, profligates and those who were already sick were not eligible for membership.(23)

These poor law-inspired medical clubs were not a success, because they were intended to be self-supporting, and the subscriptions were too high for the labourers to afford. In contrast, the 'independent' sick clubs patronized by local gentry received a major part of their funds from donations and were consequently more successful. In areas without one of these subsidized sick benefit societies, the low-paid Norfolk agricultural labourer was forced by his poverty to rely on the services of the poor law medical officer in the first half of the nineteenth century. Later the spread of the affiliated friendly society, the Ancient Order of Foresters, brought medical assistance within the financial capability of the rural labourer in the county.

Medical relief conferred pauper status and before 1885 it disqualified the recipient from the vote. Exceptionally, vaccination, which was provided freely by the nation's poor law medical officers after 1840, did not confer pauper status on the patient. In spite of this few availed themselves of the service, so in 1853 vaccination was made compulsory for children shortly after birth. Immediately before the act there had been 15,000 vaccinations each year in Norfolk but the act led to 27,000 vaccinations being performed in 1853-4. These numbers soon slumped back to former levels despite the efforts of the poor law guardians to publicize their free service. This was because prejudice against vaccination was very strong in rural areas. Indeed, some years earlier, in 1847, villagers in the Henstead Union had believed that the state's encouragement of vaccination formed a plot to kill children under five, and that Queen Victoria was a modern Herod.(24)

Patients of medical officers in Norfolk were frequently as much in need of nutrition as medicine. Medical 'extras' in the form of beef, mutton, wine and porter figured largely in local doctor's expenditure on his outdoor pauper patients. Two out of every five of the non-chronic sick on the outdoor relief list of medical officers in the eastern counties were receiving medical extras in 1870. Norfolk guardians were profoundly suspicious of these extras, which they felt were more in 'aid of relief' than in 'aid of sickness'. As such they were a trespass by the medical officer into the territory of the relieving officer or poor law guardian. The doctor was conscious that low wages had produced physical debility and that without some supplementation of diet illness would continue to flourish. There was a basic conflict of interest between the medical officer who practised curative and preventive medicine, and who discerned clearly the connection of illness with local poverty, and the guardians, who were concerned primarily with the relief of destitution, and whose humanity to the poor had to be counterbalanced by their duty to the ratepayer. In spite of this, the doctor's accounts (which included the medical extras) were always sanctioned by Norfolk guardians, which suggests that medical officers and guardians rubbed shoulders amicably enough in practice, and that differences of interest did not flare into open conflict.(25)

After reviewing the available evidence, it would appear that the Norfolk poor law administrators' treatment of the poor was far more humane than the stereotyped view of the 'grinders of the poor' might have led one to suppose, and that this humanity was most marked in relation to indoor paupers. Popular conceptions of the workhouse, from the Victorian period to the present day, have too often been based on over-generalizations arising from a relatively small number of cruel incidents — the Andover Scandal of 1846 is the most notable example — from which a blanket condemnation of poor law administration is made. When harshness in poor law administration did not exist in reality, then contemporary opponents of the 1834 act had to suggest that it did. This was most evident in G.R.W. Baxter's 'The Book of the Bastilles' of 1841, a compilation of alleged incidents of cruelty and abuse that had occurred in the nation's workhouses. A comparable, if isolated example, from Norfolk was the case of Jemima Livock. She was an epileptic pauper who had been found dead in the Depwade Union Workhouse in 1839 after spending a night shut up in solitary confinement in the Receiving Ward. Although an inquiry exonerated poor law officials from blame, the incident produced adverse local publicity about the workhouse system, as the illustration of a contemporary pamphlet in Figure 15 indicates.(26) This suggests that many well-to-do Victorians were ambivalent about the workhouse. On the one hand they had a day-to-day indifference about the fate of those inside its walls, and a continued reluctance, in their capacity as ratepayers, to finance a liberal system of poor relief. On the other hand, they had a hidden guilt which found expression in the exposure of workhouse 'scandals'.

In formulating their relief policies poor law administrators in the county had always to balance their financial accountability to the ratepayers against their social responsibilities to the poor. They had to recognize that, even where there was public sympathy for deserving categories of poor, such as old people or widows, that this was not necessarily matched by the readiness of local ratepayers to finance adequate relief. Administrators therefore compromised and gave meagre sums to these categories of poor in outdoor relief, while continuing the liberal traditions of the East Anglian pauper palaces for those accepting indoor relief. Where public attitudes were informed by moral disapproval, as in the case of vagrants or unmarried mothers, the relief administrators' task was a simpler one, since illiberal treatment sanctioned by morality saved the public purse. The criteria for the relief of the adult able-bodied poor were more complex and the key determinants of policy were the state of the local labour market and the balancing of the employers' interests against those of the ratepayers. This dictated a system of predominantly outdoor relief of small allowances made in aid of wages. The humanity of outdoor relief to people in their own homes, as against that of indoor relief in the workhouse, turns on a subjective judgment about the relative value of freedom against material wellbeing. There is no doubt that the material standard of living of the inmate of a rural Norfolk workhouse was superior to that of the labouring poor in the surrounding countryside. Similarly, the achievement of the poor law medical service must be set against the relatively low standards of

THE

PARTICULARS OF THE DEATH

OF

JEMIMA LIVOCK

OF TASBURGH, NORFOLK;

WHEREIN IT IS SHOWN THAT SHE, BEING SUBJECT TO FITS,
WAS LOCKED UP ALONE IN THE RECEIVING WARD OF THE

DEPWADE UNION WORKHOUSE

On the Night of Sunday, June 16th

And was found a Corpse the following Morning.

WITH THE WAY IN WHICH
THE WHOLE HAS BEEN BROUGHT TO LIGHT, AND EXPOSED
BY THE EXERTIONS OF

MR. J. RICHES. OF NORWICH.

PUBLISHED AND SOLD BY
J. RICHES. ST. GEORGE'S COLEGATE, NORWICH.
AND MAY BE HAD OF ALL BOOKSELLERS.

PRICE THREE PENCE

Figure 15   The Death of Jemima Livock

contemporary medical care.   The generally high standards of social
welfare that were achieved by Norfolk administrators of the poor law
were determined mainly by local tradition, which was tempered by the
social and economic circumstances of nineteenth-century Norfolk.
However in some areas of social policy initiatives by the central
poor law administration were important;   the most notable example
of this was in the field of pauper education.

CHAPTER 10

PAUPER EDUCATION

'Parents think very little of schooling in these parts. The best
chance the children have is the workhouse.'(1) This informed
comment by a Norfolk relieving officer in 1843 referred to the poor
attendance of the village child at the elementary school which resulted from the dependence of the low-paid, rural labourer on the
earnings of his family in fieldwork on local farms. It also indicated that in the early days of the New Poor Law schooling inside
Norfolk workhouses provided an unusually good system of pauper
education. To a considerable extent this was the product of the
work of Dr J.P. Kay (later known as Sir James Kay-Shuttleworth),
who was the poor law inspector for East Anglian from 1835 to 1838.
His policies on the training of pauper children were approved by
the central administration, the Poor Law Commission, which publicized them by printing his report on the subject in their fourth
report. Indeed, Kay-Shuttleworth's ideas on the education of poor
children were to affect not only the development of pauper education but that of elementary education as well, through his work
from 1839 to 1849 as the secretary to the new central administrative body for education, the Committee of Council on Education. It
is interesting that these ideas on the model school, pupil teaching, the role of the education inspectorate, and the nature of the
curriculum were first put into practice in the workhouse schools of
East Anglia. Yet Kay-Shuttleworth could not have been so successful in developing pauper education in Norfolk if local owners and
occupiers of property had not found his opinions congenial.

That the education of poor children was essential in order to
achieve social stability was widely believed in the 1830s. Kay-
Shuttleworth applied this idea to workhouse education and argued
that it would lead to 'the rearing of hardy and intelligent working men, whose character and habits shall afford the largest amount
of security to the property and order of the community'. Local
property-owners were receptive to this observation because they saw
the New Poor Law as a means of imposing social discipline in the
disturbed Norfolk countryside, while workhouse education offered a
way to convert the children of feckless pauper parents into dutiful
and hard-working adults. Kay-Shuttleworth also contended that workhouse education would be 'one of the most important means of

eradicating the germs of pauperism from the rising generation' and
would be 'the means of avoiding the ultimate dependence upon the
ratepayers of the children'.(2)   Arguments that workhouse schooling
would snap the chain of hereditary pauperism and reduce the poor
rates by enabling children to earn an independent livelihood as
adults proved attractive to Norfolk occupiers who were the local
ratepayers. There was therefore support in Norfolk after 1834 for
the development of a system of pauper schooling from the minimal
educational arrangements that had existed under the Old Poor Law.

17   Downham Market Union House, Court House and National School, c.1860

I   THE ORGANIZATION OF WORKHOUSE SCHOOLS

Before 1834 educational provision in Norfolk was non-existent in
parish poor houses but was provided in borough workhouses and rural
houses of industry. As in the schooling given to the children of
the independent poor, either in charity schools or the schools of
the National or British Societies in the early nineteenth century,
the education given to the pauper child was designed primarily to
give a moral training. For this purpose a narrow curriculum was
all that was required. In the St James Workhouse in King's Lynn
the child was taught to read the Bible and learn the Catechism so
that a basic Christian morality of service and hard work was incul-
cated. The pauper child was not taught to write at the St James
Workhouse, as this might have led to aspirations beyond his humble
station in life. In the rural incorporations a more enlightened
view was sometimes taken, and a child in the house of industry in
the Tunstead and Happing or Loddon and Clavering Incorporations was
taught the four Rs — reading, writing, arithmetic and religion.(3)
In the early nineteenth century schooling for the poor child needed
to be cheap, and so limited instruction was transmitted by lowly
paid, largely untrained teachers. Workhouse schools were no exception to this, and the Norfolk pauper child was instructed by a

teacher drawn from among the adult inmates of the workhouse.

By modern standards discipline was harsh for the workhouse child. The most notorious example in Norfolk was the punishment of William Rayner, a 12-year-old boy who had attempted to run away from Norwich Workhouse in 1804. For this offence he was padlocked to an iron collar attached to a yoke which stuck out 15 inches on each side, while fettered to one leg was a long chain with a wooden weight two feet long at the end of it. This retribution was exceptional in lasting for three weeks, but the type of punishment was not unusual at the beginning of the nineteenth century. Joseph Lancaster of the British Society was at this time advocating the attachment of a wooden log to the neck, or shackling pieces of wood to the legs of children, who persistently talked or who were idle.(4) Discipline was thought to be an essential ingredient in the training of poor children for the life of labour that was to be their lot. In the rural incorporations of Norfolk intellectual preoccupations in the education of the pauper child soon gave way to employment in a pauper manufactory. As in the contemporary schools of industry, the aim in these workhouse factories was to inculcate habits of industry, give training in a manufacturing skill, and defray costs from the profits made by productive enterprise.(5) This stress on a training in industrious habits was also obvious in the East Anglian incorporations in the case of child apprentices. Children of the independent poor could be sent at the age of 12 or 13 years to the local house of industry, where they were taught industrious habits and social discipline through their employment in pauper manufactories, before being apprenticed by the incorporation to local occupiers.

The East Anglian incorporations were authorized under their local acts to apprentice poor children from parishes in the constituent hundreds to substantial occupiers who were selected in rotation. The system had become unpopular by the end of the old poor law era because it was difficult to operate fairly and many apprentices did little good either to their masters or themselves. In the Norfolk incorporations the system was restricted in scope and was increasingly well regulated by the 1820s and 1830s as a result of local criticism. While the system of compulsory apprenticeships in East Anglia could involve economic hardship to ratepayers and human misery for the apprentice, yet the abuses in the system were exaggerated by Kay-Shuttleworth in his reports in 1836.(6) He did this in order to highlight the advantages to be expected from his plans for workhouse education under the New Poor Law.

The Poor Law Commissioners' basic scheme of three hours' schooling a day for the boys and girls in the workhouse after 1834 was developed by Kay-Shuttleworth into a tripartite form of pauper education made up of industrial, moral and intellectual training. Industrial training was designed to give the pauper child skills that would prevent future dependence on poor relief, moral training which would underpin this in giving the child habits of industry and self-reliance, and intellectual training, which was to include a wide variety of subjects in order to counteract the restrictive institutionalism of the workhouse environment. He argued persuasively that the State represented by the board of guardians, was in loco parentis for the pauper child. Since 'the child is dependent

on the boards of guardians for more than maintenance: it must be
trained in industry, in correct moral habits, and in religion; and
must be fitted to discharge the duties of its station in life.'(7)

The farmers, who formed the majority of the elected guardians in
Norfolk unions, regarded the New Poor Law as a means of reducing
the poor rates, and were prepared to implement items in Kay-
Shuttleworth's programme of pauper education if they would produce
economy for the ratepayer. As a result they were more sympathetic
to industrial and moral training than to giving a pauper child an
intellectual education which they thought might induce undesirable
social mobility among the labourers. As in other contemporary
schemes to educate poor children there was some local resistance to
teaching pauper children to write, since this might educate them
above their station. There was also some hostility to having maps
in the workhouse schoolroom, since geographical knowledge might
lead later to migration and a diminution of the reserve of labour
which was useful to the farmers during harvest. Moreover, an academic education for the pauper child could conflict with the idea of
the New Poor Law as a means of social discipline for the poor.
According to Kay-Shuttleworth, some East Anglian guardians regarded
it as 'putting the torch of knowledge into the hands of rickburners',
since the ability to read radical publications might lead to further
disturbances in an unsettled countryside.(8) Also, it was difficult
for the assistant commissioners to convince farmer-guardians that
immediate expenditure on implementing the provisions of the New Poor
Law would lead to an eventual saving of money. In the context of
workhouse education this led in the early years to unsuccessful
attempts by Norfolk boards of guardians to continue with the old
poor law practice of employing a pauper at a notional 'salary' to
act as the workhouse schoolteacher.(9)

Yet the organization of workhouse education was an urgent necessity for both humanitarian and economic reasons. Already by
January 1838 there were nearly 1,000 children in Norfolk workhouses.
There was a higher proportion of children to adults than in other
areas, and most were likely to become long-stay inmates. About
two-thirds of the children in East Anglian workhouses at this time
had some ability in reading and about one-third in writing. This
gives only a very approximate idea of the educational needs of
pauper children since the criteria used in testing their literacy
was not specified.(10) But faced with a situation of numbers of
semi-literate pauper children, each of the boards of guardians in
the 22 Norfolk poor law unions and incorporations was prepared to
provide a workhouse school after 1834 in order to meet their educational needs. In the 1850s and 1860s, when the Poor Law Board
published statistics on the number of children in workhouse schools,
Norfolk had between 1,100 and 1,500 pauper schoolchildren out of a
total of 30,000—41,000 in all the workhouse schools in England
and Wales. At this time the number of children in individual workhouse schools in the county ranged from an average roll of 22 in the
Flegg Incorporation to 113 in the Mitford and Launditch Union and
167 in Norwich. Twelve schools had under 50 pupils, eight had between 50 and 100 and only two had a school roll of over 100 children. The fundamental problem, therefore, in developing pauper education in Norfolk was the involvement in the organization of rela-

tively small schools of many guardians who had little experience or appreciation of education.

Kay-Shuttleworth used a policy of conciliation, help and persuasion to overcome this problem. As in other aspects of poor law administration, he obtained the backing of the more 'progressive' boards of guardians for his ideas and hoped that innovation would spread through imitation and his own encouragement. Recognizing that the clergymen among the ex officio guardians were most likely to be sympathetic to the educational needs of the pauper child, Kay-Shuttleworth developed the function of the chaplain in the workhouse rules, which was to 'examine and catechise the children, at least once every month', into a more active supervisory and advisory role. In the Walsingham Union the work of the chaplain was supplemented by an education committee, composed of four interested clergymen. After 1837 the new Bishop of Norwich, Dr Edward Stanley, gave a lead to the clergy of the diocese and visited workhouse schools on several occasions. In urban unions a genteel interest in pauper education was developed by ladies committees, who made periodic visits and who helped in the placing of pauper girls into domestic service.

But the driving force behind the creation of workhouse schools in East Anglia in the first years of the New Poor Law was Kay-Shuttleworth himself. The importance he attached to education was demonstrated to the guardians in practical terms. In the Loddon and Clavering Union he brought the workhouse children into the guardians' board room, asked them to read a passage from St Matthew's Gospel, and then examined the children's comprehension of the passage. More commonly, he acted as a catalyst in opening Norfolk guardians' minds to the widening range of educational methods that could be adopted in the workhouse school. He left varied selections of books for the schoolroom so that the guardians, chaplains and teachers could choose from the best that were available. In addition, he persuaded the more enthusiastic boards of guardians to buy books which gave descriptions of the most advanced educational methods and ideas being practised elsewhere — class teaching, moral training and industrial schooling.(11) Since few boards of guardians were sufficiently progressive to try out the newest methods, there was an uneven development of pauper education amongst the poor law unions of Norfolk.

Most workhouse schools in Norfolk during the first decade of their existence were organized on the monitorial system which was still the most commonly practised method in the nation's elementary schools. In this system, older children, called monitors, were instructed by the teacher and then passed on the information to smaller groups of children. This was how the King's Lynn Workhouse School used it in 1838:(12)

While the first class read a portion of Scripture to a master, second and third read on cards to monitors, then Arithmetic, and write on slates, fourth read and spell small words and count figures. Afternoon while first class read instructor of exercises on familiar subjects to a master, second and third read to monitors on cards, then writing in books, and on slates, fourth as in morning. After reading they are examined by questions relating to what they have read, the principal words spelled and explained by Grammar.

A few Norfolk boards of guardians were sufficiently aware of new educational methods for the school to be organized for simultaneous or class teaching. Common instruction was given by the teacher to a whole class who might be seated in a raised gallery at the rear of the long schoolroom. Afterwards the class split up into smaller groups which were taken by assistants.

Class teaching was used in the excellent school in the Guiltcross Union. Here four hours a day were devoted to the children's instruction, instead of the three hours enjoined by the Poor Law Commission's rules. Between the hours of 10 am and 12 noon and 2 pm and 4 pm the guardians sternly forbade the master or matron the services of the children in the household tasks, which were a common cause of disrupted schooling for the pauper child in the workhouse. A generous variety of books was provided by the guardians; not only the catechisms, biblical abridgements, books of miracles and parables which were common in elementary schools of the day, but also Irish National Lesson books, which were among the best schoolbooks available in the mid-nineteenth century. Maps were provided for the schoolroom, and swings and gymnastic equipment for the school yard. The breadth of the curriculum can only be inferred from the resources provided in the 1830s, which suggested that it was already as liberal as in the 1850s, when English history, geography and grammar were taught as well as the customary reading, writing, arithmetic and scripture.(13)

Pauper children in East Anglian workhouses began their schooling at the age of two. Commonly boys and girls were taught in their early years by the schoolmistress before the boys graduated to the more advanced instruction given by the schoolmaster. In a few unions co-education was found throughout the school with the mistress taking the young children and the master the older pupils. This was partly the result of the recruitment by Kay-Shuttleworth of teachers trained in Scotland, where co-education was usual in the parochial schools. The Walsingham Board of guardians adopted co-education in their workhouse school after having been convinced by the arguments of the Scottish teachers. Among the reasons adduced by Mr Archibald Dunlop, the Scottish teacher in the Downham Market Union for favouring co-education were these:

If the boys and girls were to be educated separately it would be injurious to both because it would deprive the girls of the concentrated answers produced by the stronger minds of the boys; and it would deprive the boys of the quick perception, and sometimes strong feeling evinced even by very little girls.... The boys require to be educated with girls in order to soften the boisterous manners consequent on their exuberant animal spirits; and the girls require to be educated with boys in order that they may set more value on intellectual and moral qualifications and less on show....

A colleague, Mr Ben Horne of the Thingoe Union in Suffolk, argued persuasively that it was important to keep brothers and sisters together in the school since for orphaned and deserted children in the workhouse such contact made them feel they were still members of a family.(14)

The workhouse teacher's influence over the pauper child was greater than that of the ordinary schoolteacher over his pupils in

the elementary school.(15)   Many children in the workhouse had no
parents, and even for the few who had parents in the building contact was infrequent, so that the teacher and the guardians were in
practice in loco parentis for the pauper child.   The teacher was
responsible not only for the children's instruction, but also for
keeping the children clean and well-mannered.   Most teachers were
actively concerned to promote the overall welfare of their charges
in addition to their specifically educational responsibility.   But
a few were neglectful of the children's hygiene, and heads became
ridden with lice.   There was occasional violence, as when the St
Faith's schoolmaster made a violent attack on a small girl in 1843
and was dismissed by the guardians.   More rarely there was sexual
irregularity, as in the Henstead Union in 1853 when the schoolmaster was dismissed because of pederasty.   The guardians were
therefore the child's ultimate defence against the inadequate personality of a teacher.   In theory, a refractory child was punished
by a temporary diet of bread and water which was prescribed in the
regulations of the central poor law administration.   In practice,
corporal punishment was resorted to on rare occasions for the boys,
as when in 1842 the Blofield guardians authorized eight strokes of
the lash for each of the boys who had broken workhouse windows.(16)

Children began their schooling in the workhouse at an earlier
age than their counterparts outside.   Their attendance was necessarily more regular (unless they were one of the 'ins and outs',
whose sojourn in the workhouse was only a fleeting one).   So the
indoor pauper child became proficient at rote learning, although
the sterile surroundings of the workhouse stunted his vocabulary,
imagination and understanding.   The workhouse child obtained academic instruction that was efficient when judged by the factual
criteria of a Gradgrind, but was nevertheless deficient in terms of
an education for life.   Deprived of parental affection, the enrich-
ing influence of a home and a varied environment, the workhouse
child could not attain the same educational standards as the ordinary child.   Judged even by the narrow examination standards of
the Revised Codes of 1862 and subsequent years, which regulated the
nation's elementary schools, the pauper child was at a disadvantage.
This was apparent by 1878, the first year in which pauper children
were examined by the same code as elementary school children, when
the workhouse child scored well only on mechanical learning.(17)

The calibre of the workhouse teacher was of fundamental importance in the development of any system of pauper education, and in
the first years of workhouse education in East Anglia, Kay-Shuttleworth used a number of methods to try to improve the standard of
teaching.   Untrained teachers visited the excellent schools at
Gressenhall Workhouse in Norfolk and Barham Workhouse in Suffolk,
where they learned how to teach by watching competent teachers at
work.   Later, when Kay-Shuttleworth had recruited several good
Scottish teachers (who had been trained by two of the foremost ex-
ponents of teacher education, David Stow in Glasgow and John Wood
in Edinburgh), inexperienced teachers were able to visit neighbouring unions where they were teaching.(18)   The device of the organizing master was copied from the National Society as a means of raising standards of teaching.   The best of the Scottish teachers were
used as mobile organizing masters who visited workhouse schools in

East Anglia to improve teaching methods.(19)

Central to the later organization of teacher training in England was the system of pupil-teachers. This had begun obscurely in a Norfolk workhouse, when in 1838 a 13-year-old boy called William Rush had on his own initiative taken over the organization of the Gressenhall school in the Mitford and Launditch Union, when the teacher fell ill. The chairman of the board of guardians, F.W. Keppel, was amazed to find that a pauper child was acting as an efficient teacher and that lessons were continuing as usual. He sanctioned the position and Rush controlled the schoolroom until the teacher returned. Kay-Shuttleworth was very impressed with this spontaneous event and described how a number of similar incidents grew into a system — that of the pupil-teacher.(20)   These scattered experiments in East Anglian workhouse schools, informed by a visit to Holland in 1838 where a system of pupil-teachers was in operation and developed practically at Norwood and elsewhere, led Kay-Shuttleworth to instigate a pupil-teacher scheme in 1846 that was to revolutionize English teacher training. In this scheme (which was initiated by the Committee of Council on Education, of which Kay-Shuttleworth was secretary), there were grants by the state to pupil-teachers serving a five-year apprenticeship under an experienced teacher. This was followed by the opportunity to compete for a Queen's Scholarship to a training college. Few workhouse schools had either the facilities for a pupil-teacher or a suitably qualified teacher with a certificate of competency or efficiency to supervise him. But at Gressenhall several pupil-teachers served their apprenticeship and then became workhouse teachers at other schools in Norfolk. The first local pupil-teacher, William Rush, was sent by the guardians to the model pauper school at Norwood, and then to the Battersea Training School where he became a fully trained teacher. By 1849 he was teaching at the workhouse school in the Walsingham Union, and was paid £60, which was the highest salary of any Norfolk workhouse teacher. Probably because of failing health he left the taxing conditions of workhouse service and went to teach at the National School in Broadstairs, Kent, where he died shortly afterwards from tuberculosis.(21)

The inadequate supply of well qualified teachers to workhouse schools and the virtual impossibility of retaining them in an educationally unattractive sector was the fundamental problem in establishing a good system of pauper education in the first years of the New Poor Law. During their first decade, union schools in Norfolk averaged a change of teacher every 18 months. This rapid turnover resulted from the low salaries offered by many guardians, the unappealing conditions of service in a workhouse and the lack of prior training of many workhouse teachers which made them unequal to the demands made upon them. Annual salaries varied from £15 to £35 for a schoolmaster and £10 to £20 for a schoolmistress. Board and lodging were also provided. (The salaries of elementary teachers in the county at this time varied from £8 to £60 pounds with an average of about £28.) The former occupations of Norfolk workhouse teachers in 1847 included that of hairdresser, tailor, saddler, parish clerk and workhouse porter, while those of schoolmistresses included that of dressmaker, housekeeper and lady's maid. Recruitment of such unqualified staff produced frequent resignations and unstable

educational standards in the schools. Friction between the master
and matron of the workhouse and the teachers was endemic. The
teachers resented the fact that they were subject to the orders
of the workhouse master, whom they regarded as less well educated
than themselves. They opposed the demands of the matron for the
services of the children in household tasks during lesson time.
The isolated position of the teachers within a dreary and monotonous environment occasionally stimulated romance, but the guardians
were swift to crush such 'improper relationships'. In the Downham
Market Union in 1838 the schoolmistress was dismissed her post for
her affaire with the schoolmaster. The guardians at first applied
the usual Victorian moral standard and merely suspended the schoolmaster, but had second thoughts and later sacked him.(22)

The difficulty of establishing a system of pauper education that
would result in the social control of the poor and an economic saving
to the ratepayer goes far to explain the fact that the state's
incursion into education was most fully developed in workhouse
schooling in the mid-nineteenth century. The Committee of Council
on Education established an inspectorate for workhouse schools in
1846, financed Kneller Hall, which was a training college for workhouse teachers which opened in 1850, and made grants for the salaries
of workhouse teachers in 1846. The role of the inspector of workhouse schools was influenced by Kay-Shuttleworth's own experience as
an assistant poor law commissioner, and the instructions given to
the inspectors in 1847 differed little from the views he had put
forward a decade earlier. His earlier efforts to persuade the
guardians that education was a worthwhile long-term investment, when
their dominant concern was a desire to economize on the poor rates
in the short term, resulted in greater powers being given to the
inspector of workhouse schools than to elementary school inspectors
in the 1840s. The grant of state money for the whole of the teacher's salary was dependent both on the inspector's estimate of the
teacher's ability and his approval of the educational facilities
provided in the workhouse by the guardians. The guardians had to
provide the books and apparatus recommended by the workhouse school
inspector and also give the workhouse schoolteacher good accommodation and free him from the task of supervising the children out of
school hours. It was Kay-Shuttleworth who succeeded in placing the
inspectors of workhouse schools under the Committee of Council on
Education and not under the miserly poor law administration. This
arrangement was reversed in 1863, and it was not until 1904 that
pauper education was recognized to be the rightful responsibility of
the Board of Education.

Teacher supply remained the Achilles heel of pauper education in
spite of reforms by the State. The system of graded certificates of
ability for workhouse teachers with payment at the appropriate rate
from parliamentary grant, which was introduced in 1846, did not
always work as it had been intended to do, as a ladder of progress
for the teacher. In practice, the lowest certificates of permission and probation were not transitional achievements that led to
certificates of competency and efficiency, but often stationary
qualifications which the limited ability of workhouse teachers,
depressed by poor conditions of service, could do little to improve.
Only six of the first batch of certificates given to Norfolk work-

house teachers were of competency or efficiency, although the
general standard improved during the 1850s. But difficulties remained. A poor law board circular of 1850, which made a teacher's
salary dependent on attendances, led to an exodus of teachers which
was only partly stemmed by higher capitation allowances in 1853.(23)
Kneller Hall, the training college for workhouse teachers, made
little impact during its brief five-year existence. When it closed
in 1855 only 64 of its 83 graduates were still teaching; 46 were
in workhouse schools, of which only one was teaching in Norfolk. A
major reason for the college's closure was the failure to replace
workhouse schools by district schools except for a few which were
situated in London and the North of England, and the consequent
lack of a career structure for the teacher in poor law service.(24)

II   PAUPER EDUCATION AND SOCIETY

Edward Twisleton, the poor law inspector for the eastern region,
provided in 1840 a perceptive summary of local attitudes to education:(25)

> Small farmers, and many of the gentry, have a decided repugnance
> to educating the poor.... No statement of moral or distant ad-
> vantages will have much effect, unless a good argument to the
> pocket can be maintained. The *expense* is the point on which
> everything will turn.

This parsimoniousness led to the arguments put forward for educating
the pauper child being geared to the expected economy that would
result; industrial training would make the pauper child an independent adult, and district schools for several poor law unions
would cost no more than the old poor law expenditure on apprenticeships premiums for children. Kay-Shuttleworth envisaged two district schools for Norfolk with 400 or 500 children in each. This
would overcome some of the difficulties that beset the small school
in a single workhouse by offering improved educational facilities,
and by attracting and retaining well qualified teachers. Even
closer to the hearts of the workhouse inspectorate was the fact that
in district schools the children would be freed from the 'moral
contamination' of their parents and of other adult paupers in the
workhouse.(26)

The small numbers of children in the majority of Norfolk workhouse
schools gave an economic justification for district schools. Norfolk
guardians expressed some interest in them after they were permitted
in legislation of 1844 and 1848 to set up this type of school. But
nothing came of it in the 1840s, or again at the end of the century,
when the Workhouse Amalgamation Movement had encouraged guardians
to think of sharing their resources and economizing on administrative
overheads. Having spent ratepayers' money on the workhouse school,
Norfolk guardians were reluctant to contribute money for a district
school which would be remote from their control. They found it more
convenient to have all the paupers under one roof and were reluctant
to embark on the practical problems of shuttling the children of
short-stay inmates between school and workhouse. They did not even
embark on the modified experiment of running a separate school that
was detached from the workhouse but served only one or two unions,

as did a few boards of guardians in the neighbouring county of
Suffolk.

Pauper children therefore remained within the imperfectly classified Norfolk workhouse. To counteract the debasing effect of
other paupers, the poor law inspectors argued that industrial
training was essential for the children. It would also serve as
an alternative to apprenticeship; a good training would fit the
child for independent employment and the consequent savings on
apprenticeship premiums would help pay for the schooling. Under
the New Poor Law apprenticeship in Norfolk was reserved for the few
physically handicapped children who would not otherwise find employment. Normal children would get an industrial training, which in
Kay-Shuttleworth's view would give them a training as much in the
habit of industry as in the skills of industry. Industrial training was central to his perception of the relationship between education, pauperism and the social order, since through inculcating
industrious habits an upright, hard-working member of the community
would be created from the offspring of feckless parents. This educational philosophy proved congenial to the propertied classes in
Norfolk, and hence to the ex officio members of boards of guardians,
whose view of the New Poor Law was essentially that of a means to
impose social discipline on the poor. While Kay-Shuttleworth's
theoretical views on industrial training were influenced by the
fully developed systems of De Fellenberg and Wehrli at Hofwyl in
Switzerland, the constraints of the rural workhouse system dictated
a simpler form of industrial training in practice. However, the
Walsingham Board of Guardians were sufficiently interested in the
ideas of agricultural training to send their workhouse teacher to
Ealing Grove to study the advanced ideas practised there in the
school opened in 1834 by Lady Noel Byron. They also bought for each
member of the board a copy of B.F. Duppa's 'Industrial Schools for
the Peasantry', which gave an account of the training at Ealing
Grove.(27)

In most Norfolk workhouses the schoolchildren's day was divided
into two parts, with academic lessons in the morning and industrial
training in the afternoon. In the Downham Market Union the guardians ordered the schoolmistress somewhat breathlessly to instruct
the girls in: needlework; knitting; scouring and cleaning floors;
cleaning grates and fenders; washing pots, pans, plates and dishes;
rubbing furniture; washing and ironing clothes; getting up linen;
waiting at table; making beds and lighting fires. In the Loddon
and Clavering Union a guardians' committee gave anxious thought to
the subject and reported that the boys could garden on the workhouse land and grow vegetables for the kitchens and that the girls
could learn to cook in the kitchens under the matron's surveillance.
Boys who intended to be indoor servants could be employed in cleaning boots and shoes, and in cleaning and harnessing the guardians'
horses when a board meeting was held. Others who might become
tailors and shoemakers could mend the shoes and clothes of the workhouse inmates. Other unions gave a training in rural crafts such
as making baskets and nets, and in plaiting straw hats.(28)

A basic weakness in this type of industrial training was that,
understandably enough, it was difficult for many of the guardians
to realize that, although children were assisting in the household

economy of the workhouse, the aim of such activity was a long-term
social and educational one. Between Kay-Shuttleworth's initial
impetus of 1836-8 and the second educational initiative of the
workhouse school inspector, H.M. Bowyer, and the poor law inspector,
Sir John Walsham, after 1847, industrial training in Norfolk workhouses had become haphazard and intermittent. As Bowyer commented
dryly, 'the acres are not devoted to the boys, but the boys to the
acres'.(29) Bowyer and Walsham worked harmoniously together and
their joint efforts gradually remedied this situation. One of
their successes was the workhouse farm in the Guiltcross Union,
which imitated the earlier experiment at Quatt in Shropshire. Here
a farm of four acres provided a training for boys in agricultural
work and for girls as dairy maids. It also made a profit. Although
the girls readily found jobs as dairy maids, the local farmers opposed the scheme. They apparently had a blind prejudice against
a workhouse having cows and also resented the farm's commercial competition. This hostility deterred other farmer-guardians from similar initiatives. Some unions built separate laundries and wash-
houses to train the girls. Few unions had sufficient children to
make it worthwhile to employ specialists for industrial training,
so that the abilities of the teachers and other workhouse officers
circumscribed the training programme. By the 1860s Bowyer reluc-
tantly admitted that the industrial training had reached the fullest
development that was possible within the constraints of the workhouse system.(30)
    Different circumstances in the Incorporation of Norwich made
possible a more ambitious experiment in industrial training in the
children's homes. The Norwich guardians had continued with their
apprenticeship policies after the 1834 act, and gave premiums to
traders to train poor boys in a craft. Between 1834 and the dissolution of the incorporation in 1863, 130 boys had been apprenticed
into 20 trades, but with 80 per cent of the boys going into shoemaking. These were outdoor apprenticeships because the boys continued to live with their parents. In 1847 the guardians opened
a boys' house for the outdoor apprentices who had no home. Selected
boys after the age of seven (or in 1863 after the age of nine) were
taken from the workhouse school into the boys' home where they had
an interim period of schooling before being found a job in the city.
They went out to work from the home for a period of about two years.
They gave up their wages in return for their maintenance and were
given 2d or 3d a week as pocket money. The boys had to accept the
rules of the home and to continue to work well for their employer,
or they were sent back to the workhouse school. Eventually, when
they were capable of earning enough to support themselves or when
they held situations as indoor servants or apprentices, they left
the home. The success of the boys' home led to the institution of
the girls' home in 1850. Here, pauper girls completed their education by a systematic training as domestic servants within the
home. The matron instructed them in cookery, washing, ironing and
household work while the schoolmistress taught them needlework and
some academic subjects. Both homes were quite separate from the
workhouse and the girls' home was described as having a 'cheerful
and airy' situation out of the town, with an atmosphere of 'homely
comfort'. Later, the Yarmouth guardians adopted the idea and opened
a girls' home too.(31)

This Norfolk experiment was the product of local initiative and was viewed with hostility by the central poor law administration. The extra expenditure incurred by the Norwich guardians in running a parallel set of educational institutions (with both a school in the workhouse and homes outside it) was the main object of unsuccessful attacks by the Poor Law Board. It first challenged the expenditure on the homes as illegal in 1853-4 and then resumed hostilities when the incorporation later planned a new and larger workhouse. The local inspector, Sir John Walsham, and the inspector of workhouse schools, H.G. Bowyer, supported the continuance of the valuable educational work of the homes and approved the separation of the children from other workhouse inmates, although they nervously safeguarded their professional position by making ritual criticisms about the high level of expenditure. Their favourable opinion was echoed by Louisa Twining, a witness to the Royal Commission on Popular Education in 1861, who drew a critical picture of workhouse education but specifically mentioned the Norwich homes as a shining exception.(32) The Norwich children's homes continued until the twentieth century, and were the nearest approximation to be found in Norfolk of the later national experiments in establishing cottage, and scattered, homes for pauper children.

To what extent was the Norfolk workhouse school successful according to Kay-Shuttleworth's earlier criterion of 'the rearing of hardy and intelligent working men, whose character and habits shall afford the largest amount of security to the property and order of the community'? In 1838, 142 children had gone out from Norfolk workhouses into service or other situations, of whom 112 were doing well a short time later and only 2 had returned to the workhouse. A later inquiry by Sir John Walsham revealed that between 1850 and 1860 14 per cent of 989 children sent into situations from Norfolk workhouses had returned there, of whom only half had returned through some fault of their own. This compared well with the national proportion of 20 per cent who had returned and 9 per cent who had come back because of their own misconduct.(33) H.G. Bowyer produced additional statistics in 1871-2 to support his conclusion that, in the eastern counties, 'the children educated in workhouse schools very rarely relapse into pauperism, and that a large proportion of them are enabled, by the care bestowed upon them during their infancy, to rise to a higher class of society than that in which they were born'.(34) Only one quarter of the children he enumerated had returned to Norfolk workhouses, of whom one-third had returned because of ill health or through no fault of their own. A general statistical investigation into workhouse education in 1880 reached the conclusion that it was 'gradually stopping the supply of criminals' and that nationally a majority of the children did well and were dis-pauperized.(35) Of course such fragmentary evidence is not conclusive, but it does suggest that pauper education made some small contribution to the creation of a more stable society.

The schooling in some Norfolk workhouses was unusually good when compared with the national history of workhouse education. Certain unions excelled in giving pauper children a good start in life. Of 67 boys sent out from the Norwich boys' home between 1847 and 1854, 56 did well and only 8 failed to earn a living. Most became

apprentices, errand boys or indoor servants, but several became
soldiers or sailors and one became a schoolmaster. The Mitford
and Launditch Union School had an impressive record. By 1842 60
children had gone into service and only 2 had returned to the workhouse. Between 1842 and 1846 another 80 children had been found
situations. A later return of 1871 listed the variety of trades
and occupations of the boys educated in this Gressenhall School
which included 3 schoolmasters, 2 solicitor's clerks, 1 workhouse
master and 2 accountants.(36) The girls in the Norfolk workhouses
found no difficulty in finding situations as domestic servants
and were particularly sought after when they had been trained in
the Norwich girls' home. In practical terms, the industrial
training for girls, and the academic education rather than industrial training for boys, was successful in getting them situations.
The industrial training for boys concentrated on agricultural training, which did not stop the boys being at a disadvantage when they
became farm labourers, while the training in shoemaking or tailor-
ing merely increased the existing over-supply of workers in these
trades.

Pauper education in Norfolk compared well not only with workhouse education in many other areas but on occasions also with
the elementary education that was available to the independent
labourer's child in the county. This was evident in the early
years of the New Poor Law, when workhouse education in East Anglia
had benefited from the exertions of Kay-Shuttleworth but village
schools had scarcely been improved by the State's growing incursion
into elementary education. Indeed, this superiority of pauper over
elementary education needed some defence since the union workhouse
of the New Poor Law involved the concept of 'less eligibility' in
which the lives of the pauper were to be less attractive than those
of the independent poor. Kay-Shuttleworth argued that contemporary
neglect of popular education was no justification for ignoring the
needs of the pauper child. As an enthusiastic reformer, he over-
estimated the importance of the East Anglian workhouse school and
its impact on the village school in an analysis made in 1838, although his argument is acceptable if restricted to the best workhouse schools in the area.(37) However, the standard of workhouse
schools in the county varied a great deal, and many were no better
than the neighbouring village schools at this time. In 1847 less
than a quarter of the Norfolk workhouse schools had adequate general
instruction and many still had inadequate supplies of secular books
and of maps.(38) Some improvement was made in the general standard
of Norfolk workhouse schools after this date because of the appointment of a workhouse schools inspector in 1847. He possessed both
stick and carrot in persuading Norfolk boards of guardians to improve their schools, since without the inspector's approval of the
educational facilities in the workhouse and a satisfactory result
of his examination of the workhouse teacher, no state grants towards the teacher's salary would be forthcoming. As a result there
was a general levelling-up of standards among workhouse schools.
Nationally and locally workhouse schools reached a high water-mark
in the 1850s and 1860s and the education given to the pauper child
compared well with that of the independent child. The pupil in
a workhouse school in Norfolk had an academic curriculum that was

at least as varied as that in local village schools and in addition
benefited from an industrial training. But after 1870 the development of rate-aided elementary education in areas that set up school
boards ended the superiority of the pauper educational sector,
while there was a parallel run-down of workhouse schools.

Only indoor pauper children attended the Norfolk workhouse school
and in the early days of the New Poor Law the outdoor pauper child
had little prospect of receiving much education. Since there were
about four times as many outdoor as indoor pauper children, this
was a singular omission. Norfolk boards of guardians insisted that
parents should send their children out to work before they fell back
on poor relief. The first question asked of an applicant for relief
by the Walsingham Board was '"What is the age of your children?" —
If they are nine or ten they are held capable of earning something.'
(39) Later some Norfolk boards of guardians made financial provision for the children of parents receiving outdoor allowances to
have some schooling. This was before the act of 1855, which legalized the practice by permitting guardians who wished to pay the
school pence of the outdoor pauper child to do so. By 1869 19 per
cent of the outdoor pauper children who were at school in Norfolk,
or nearly twice the national average, were being paid for by the
guardians.(40) However, it was not until seven years later that
legislation required guardians to pay these school fees. Local
opinion in the mid-nineteenth century was divided on the desirability of poor law guardians using the poor rates in such a way and
also over the advisability of pressurizing the parents into sending
their children to school. In 1850 the Downham Market Guardians
were attacked bitterly for reducing a widow's allowance after she
had failed to send her children to school. But three years later
the Rector of Burnham was asking the Poor Law Board to authorize
the Docking Guardians to pay school fees to enable the young children of a widow on poor relief to attend school.(41)

Failure to attend school was a fundamental problem in the attempt
to educate both the child of the outdoor pauper and the child of the
independent labourer. Local people blamed the New Poor Law, with
its reduction in outdoor allowances, for curtailing children's
schooling because this made the family poorer and more dependent on
the children's earnings. School attendances at Norfolk elementary
schools were notoriously low, and from the 1840s to the 1860s Her
Majesty's Inspectors complained of the widespread employment of
young children in field work (and especially in gangs) and the closure of the village schools from the beginning of August to the end
of November. The labourer's child, like that of the outdoor pauper's
child, commonly ended his schooling at the age of nine because of the
poverty of the family and the liking of the Norfolk farmer for cheap,
young labourers. In 1853 25 per cent of outdoor pauper children
under the age of 15 were at work in Norfolk, although by 1869 this
had declined to 21 per cent of the total. This was higher than the
average for England and Wales, where the comparable figures were 18
per cent in 1853 and 14 per cent in 1869. However, an increasing
proportion of outdoor pauper children went to school. In Norfolk
this rose from 44 per cent in 1853 to 58 per cent by 1869, by which
time attendance was only slightly below the national average of 62
per cent.(42) In 1873 legislation made school attendance compulsory

for the outdoor pauper child. Sandon's Act of 1876 and Mundella's
Act of 1880 were intended to achieve compulsory school attendance
for all independent children aged between 5 and 10 years, while
schooling continued for those aged 10 to 13 who had not yet achieved
a satisfactory standard of attendances or of educational proficiency.

In many areas in rural Norfolk where no school boards had been
set up by 1876, the job of enforcing the legislation on school attendances fell to school attendance committees, which were made up of
poor law guardians. It is interesting that their involvement in
the attendance problem was broadly similar to the guardians' earlier
degree of concern for the education of the pauper child in the workhouse. In the Loddon and Clavering Union the 1876 act was implemented rapidly and efficiently. The relieving officers were appointed as school attendance officers, and they compiled a register of all
the children under 14 in their districts with details of school
attendances and educational qualifications to determine whether the
child should still be at school. The school attendance committees
in the Henstead and Walsingham Unions also appeared to have been
fairly active in warning local employers against employing children
illegally and also prosecuted parents if they did not send their
children to school. But in the Swaffham Union the infrequent visits
of the school attendance officer led Her Majesty's Inspector of
Schools to complain in November 1882 that the education acts were
'almost a dead letter' in Swaffham. The Docking Guardians revealed
their own underlying hostility to popular education when they supported a request by local ratepayers to the Education Department
to lower the educational qualifications needed for a child to leave
school from the fourth to the first standard because this was 'sufficiently advanced for a district entirely agricultural'.(43) This
highlighted the main weakness of the school attendance committees.
In all rural areas the main employers of child labour were farmers,
and the guardians who were expected to enforce the laws against employing young children were drawn from the same class.

After 1870 the elementary and pauper sectors of education moved
more closely together as a result both of the guardians' involvement
with elementary education through school attendance committees and
of changes in the education of the indoor pauper child. As numbers
of children in Norfolk workhouses declined to a point where it was
uneconomic to provide a school for them, they were sent out to the
village school. This policy had begun in the 1850s in two Norfolk
unions, in spite of the hostility of the central Poor Law Board,
and had become almost universal by 1900 when there were fewer than
600 indoor pauper children in the county. After 1870 this practice
was favoured by the central poor law administration, because of the
increasing difficulty of recruiting competent workhouse teachers,
and because of a growing appreciation of the dangers of institu-
tionalizing children. Workhouse children might also be allowed by
the end of the century to play with their school friends during the
school holidays. Efforts were made in other ways to involve the
indoor children in the life of the community. One example of this
was that the children from the Walsingham Union Workhouse went to
help at hay-cock time on the Cranmer Hall estate of Sir L.J. Jones,
who was an active ex officio guardian of this union after 1885.
Beginning in 1869 had come a national experiment in boarding out

orphaned children in the workhouse with foster parents in their own
locality. By the 1890s there were nearly 200 of these children in
Norfolk whose care was overlooked by two Norfolk boarding committees.
Another innovation was the practice in the 1870s of sending pauper
girls from Norfolk workhouses to the Fakenham Girls' Industrial
School where they were trained as domestic servants.(44) Whereas in
the 1830s a separate and preparatory education had been thought necessary in order to condition pauper children for their place in society, by 1900 a common education for both pauper and independent
children was seen as a desirable means to increase the integration
of the workhouse children into the community. These evolving attitudes to the education of poor children were a reflection of much
wider changes in Norfolk society, and these developments are analysed in the final two chapters of this book.

CHAPTER 11

THE PROPERTIED AND THE POOR

Norfolk's geographical position has meant that events within the county have been rather isolated from national developments. Local self-confidence brought about by the wealth of the Norfolk economy during the eighteenth century reinforced this sense of detachment and gave a cohesive, inward-looking, yet not wholly separatist, character to local attitudes and actions. Nowhere was this more evident than in the independence and individuality of policies developed by the propertied towards the relief of the poor at this time. But the erosion of the industrial, commercial and (to a lesser extent) agricultural wealth of the county by the mid-nineteenth century and the accompanying changes in Norfolk's social structure were to produce significant differences in the administration of poor relief. A convenient mechanism for resolving this changed balance of power within local society as far as the administration of the Poor Law was concerned was provided quite fortuitously by a national reform in 1834. The impact of the Poor Law Amendment Act in Norfolk after 1834 should be seen not in the stereotyped terms of the victory by a centralist administration in London over local guardians. In Norfolk, the New Poor Law was the trojan horse by which one social group within the propertied classes gained an ascendancy over poor law administration and so transformed local relief policies to the poor. These quite distinctive changes in Norfolk society in the late eighteenth and early nineteenth centuries give an exceptional interest to the history of the Old and New Poor Laws in the county.

I NORFOLK SOCIETY AND THE POOR

Norfolk society included relatively few aristocrats at the close of the eighteenth and the opening of the nineteenth century. Their insignificant role in public affairs allowed the 200 or so landed gentlemen in Norfolk a considerable amount of social initiative, while the gentry's economic independence was sustained by their ownership of an unusually high proportion of the land in the county. Often indistinguishable from the gentry in local matters were the Norfolk clergy. Their vigorous sense of public responsibility was recognized in the fact that two out of five Norfolk clergymen served in the Norfolk Commission of the Peace compared with a national average of only one clergyman in four who acted as a magistrate.   Intermediate in society between the landed gentleman (who had at least 1,000 acres of land to sustain his position) and the labourer (with little but his daily earnings between his family and the workhouse door) was an increasingly influential body of far- mers.   The rising social expectations and economic substance of the Norfolk farmer in this period strikingly narrowed the gulf between gentlemen and yeomen and widened the distance between farmers and the labouring poor.(1)

The attitude of members of Norfolk landed society towards the poor can be illustrated by the provision of labourers' cottages on their estates.   Before the mid-nineteenth century these cottages could only be regarded as a function of the social responsibility that the propertied owed to the poor because the small rents that could be charged a low paid agricultural labourer for a new or im- proved cottage provided an uneconomic return on the landlord's capital expenditure.   The general state of English cottages had been condemned in 1775 by Nathaniel Kent, an experienced land agent and commentator on agricultural development, when he described the 'shattered hovels which half the poor of this kingdom are obliged to put up with'.   He felt it necessary to remind landowners that 'we are apt to look upon cottages as incumbrances, and clogs to our property; when, in fact, those who occupy them are the very nerves and sinews of agriculture'.   This prompting was certainly appropriate for the smaller Norfolk landowner, since a survey in the 'Norfolk News' as late as 1863 revealed that on several estates cottages were in an appalling state of repair and that there were also inadequate numbers of cottages to house the resident labour- ers.(2) On the large Norfolk estates cottage provision was better because it was regarded as part of a traditional paternalistic res- ponsibility for the labourer.   However, the inadequacies of cot- tages even on the largest Norfolk landed estates suggests that the feeling of social responsibility towards the dependent labourer was a circumscribed one.   The small value set on dependency by the landed gentry is illustrated in Chapters 5 and 12, where the crea- tion of open and close parishes and the progress of enclosure sug- gests the emergence during this period of a more restricted view of the duties of the landed classes towards the poor.

On the Holkham estate a survey made by the agent, H.W. Keary, in 1851 indicated the practical limitations of social paternalism in the provision of cottages.   Cottages were in a far from satisfactory state, with half in poor repair (often with leaking roofs and in- sanitary conditions), although the estate acknowledged cottage repairs as one of its responsibilities.   Yet some of the cottages on this 43,000 acre estate were excellent and were fully up to the contemporary standard for model cottages.   T.W. Coke, later created the first Earl of Leicester, had built over 50 cottages between 1790 and the year of his death in 1842.   With the publicist's eye for maximizing impact he had concentrated his efforts to improve cot- tages on the show village at the gates of Holkham Hall and on farms in the immediate neighbourhood.(3)   An observer described them as 'perhaps the most substantial and comfortable which are to be seen

in any part of England, and if all the English peasantry could be
lodged in similar ones it would be the realization of a Utopia'.(4)
Unfortunately, these cottages were not typical of the overall standard in Norfolk. As model cottages they were part of a conspicuous
display of agricultural improvements made by Coke, which helped to
make the estate famous for its lack of cost-consciousness.

Yet a certain lack of cost-consciousness was characteristic of
expenditure by landowners during much of the nineteenth century,
since the return on agricultural capital was about half the usual
rate on investments in commerce or industry. Increasingly during
the early nineteenth century the landlord was shouldering the burden of providing fixed capital on the estate, including cottage-
building and repairs. He was doing it as a social investment
which was designed to retain a good class of tenant farmer on the
estate, and hence to conserve the rental and maintain his own income. Rather than conceding rent rebates or reductions in the years
of agrarian crisis like those of 1814-15, 1821-3, 1833-6 or 1850-2,
many landowners preferred to cushion their tenant farmer against
adverse economic circumstances by increasing expenditure on the
estate through improving farm buildings or providing better cottages. It is interesting that on the Holkham estate nearly all
the cottages had been improved or new ones built by 1900. During
the period 1850-80, the second Earl of Leicester spent 0.7 per cent
of the Holkham rental, amounting to £10,000, on 100 new cottages,
while in the more economically depressed years of the 1880s and
1890s proportionately fewer cottages were built, with 0.3 per cent
of the rental assigned for this purpose. These later cottages were
superior to those built in the time of the first Earl and nearly
all were built in pairs, rather than in rows, had two storeys, and
contained three bedrooms. By the second half of the century cottages were no longer considered to be a desirable form of social
paternalism to the labourer but rather a business proposition designed to recruit and retain good tenant farmers on an estate.(5)

Although the deferential framework of the landed estate was not
shattered finally until the agrarian depression at the end of the
nineteenth century, the increased independence of the Norfolk
tenant farmer is noticeable much earlier on. Even before 1815 the
growth in the granting of farms on long leases had contributed to
the farmers' growing independence in relation to the landowner,
while the high profits of wartime agriculture had reinforced the
tenants' self-confidence. This resulted in increased expectations
by the farmer. Socially, these were recognized to a considerable
extent as was shown by the elegant farm houses built by the Cokes
for their Holkham tenants. With their classical style, these farmhouses looked like the residences of gentlemen. But the economic
expectations of the farmers received a rude shock in the more difficult farming years that followed the war, when wheat prices in
the 1820s and 1830s were only two-thirds as great as those in the
period between 1800 and 1815. The landlords failed to alleviate
sufficiently their tenants' economic distress through rent reductions (as Chapter 5 has shown), and this politicized the Norfolk
farmer, who thought that the landlord was setting too low a valuation on his social dependency. In 1822-3 farmers asserted their
political independence from the landlord by summoning their own

county meeting, and in the 1830 election they went even further and
sponsored their own reform candidate.(6)   The rural disturbances of
1830 exposed the full resentment of the farmer towards the landlord.
The landowner's exaction of high rents was held to be responsible
for the low wages paid to the agricultural labourer, and this was
an important cause of the rioting. A continuation of this economic
situation made farmers seize the wider opportunity which the 1834
act gave them to serve as poor law guardians. In that capacity
they carried out a local relief policy which made the New Poor Law
into an instrument to further the economic interests of their class
by utilizing poor relief to economize on the farm labour bill.

The social distance between farmer and labourer widened with
the decline of the living in system in Norfolk at the end of the
eighteenth century. The labouring poor no longer lived on the farm
and ate at the farmer's table. By the nineteenth century the
labourers were recognized as a distinct group within a strict social
hierarchy which was maintained at all times. This can be seen, for
example, in the seating arrangements of Hunstanton Church in the mid-
nineteenth century where the labourers sat in open pews in the
centre while the farmers acted like gentlemen and sat round the
sides of the building in high boxed pews with doors which were
closed firmly against the common people. This social chasm reflected a growing economic disparity between the farmer and the labourer and one in which the former's gains were all too often based on
the latter's losses. An increase in profits for the farmer did
not lead to an increase in wages for the labourer, whose wages for
much of the first half of the nineteenth century declined in real
terms whenever wheat prices rose. The doles and perquisites with
which the labourer was compensated by the farmer for his inadequate
wages were made to appear as charity and served to underline his
inferiority. As parsimonious poor law guardians, negligent charity
trustees and opponents of adequate-sized allotments, farmers effectively controlled in many parishes the alternative means by which a
labourer could supplement his meagre family budget and lessen his
dependence on the farmer. Norfolk farmers wished to prolong the
labourers' subjection as was shown by their continued hostility
to the education of the labourer's child because this might aid his
social mobility, and also by their opposition to the unionization
of the labourer which was grounded in the fear that this would help
his bargaining power and increase his independence. Only among the
wealthier farmers did individuals acknowledge the traditional social
responsibility of the better off to the poor by providing more regular employment and better earnings on the farm, and by helping to
support schools and benefit societies in the neighbourhood. The
social philosophy that lay behind their patronage of the labourer
was generally of an old fashioned kind.(7) This is neatly encapsulated in the title of one of the earliest Norfolk agricultural
societies established in 1831, 'The Launditch Society, for the purpose of encouraging and rewarding good conduct in Agricultural
Labourers and Servants'.

In the early nineteenth century it was the gentry and the clergy
who were most concerned to fulfil a paternalistic duty towards the
poor. As magistrates, they were actively involved in the social
administration of Petty Sessions, and as poor law guardians and

directors in the local unions and incorporations they took responsibility for the institutional relief of the poor. In their private
as well as their public lives, the landed gentry fulfilled their
traditional social responsibility to the poor by making a liberal
charitable provision. By 1843 past benevolence in the charities
established by the propertied classes in Norfolk amounted to an
annual income of nearly £37,000, most of which was distributed
through doles of bread, coal or blankets. Charitable works were
still regarded as an essential duty by the landed gentry as the
activities of the Howard and Le Strange families indicated. The
Howards of Castle Rising were a subsidiary branch of the family of
the Duke of Norfolk. They owned 4,000 acres in Norfolk but seldom
visited their Norfolk estates. However, in the late eighteenth and
early nineteenth centuries they regularly instructed their agents
to distribute clothes, blankets and rugs to the poor in the locality, and during times of high bread prices had soup and meat given
out to the labourers' families. There was a mutual expectation by
gentry and labourer of assistance on the one hand and loyalty on
the other. The provision of a poor house and of a new school in
Castle Rising in 1813-15 was seen by the Howards as a means of
social control of the poor. It was hoped that the school's 'good
effects will in time be visible in the morals of the rising generation'. This was a heartfelt hope on an estate that lay in an area
renowned both for its strict game preservation and for the daring
of its poachers.(8)

   During the mid-nineteenth century the Le Strange family were
clearly participating in the same tradition of social paternalism.
The impact of this gentry family on their neighbourhood and the
relationship that they established with the poor is unusually
obvious because their seat at Hunstanton Hall had been unoccupied
since 1768. Henry Styleman Le Strange came of age in 1836, took
over the estate of 8,000 acres, and married Jamesina Stewart, a
lady of strong social conscience, in 1839. Together they initiated
a social transformation. He established and re-endowed schools,
including a Clothed School, where the children wore uniforms in the
Le Strange colours of red and white. She made herself responsible
for improving the accommodation in cottages and raising the tone of
their inmates by simple lessons in cookery and child-rearing. The
Hunstanton Hall account book of charities to the sick and poor records the presents that were made of broth, tea, sago pudding,
bottles of porter, mutton, sugar and candles on personal visits to
the poor in their own homes. The family congratulated themselves
that they had 'raised the tone of our people', but by the 1860s
they were discontinuing some of their social patronage because its
naked paternalism was at odds with the growing independence of the
labourer.(9)

   Changing social attitudes by the mid-nineteenth century also
curtailed the role of the Anglican clergy in the Norfolk village
community. Like the landed gentry, Norfolk clergymen had been
actively involved with the affairs of the poor in the late eighteenth centuries, whether as justices, poor law directors and guardians or as the authors of numerous pamphlets on poor relief. Many
gave years of unrecorded service within their own parish, were
active as charity trustees, and gave generously of their time and

money to village schools. On the other hand, absentee clergy in
the west of the county were guilty of neglecting the interests of
the labouring poor who had such a strong claim to their interest
and concern. By 1830 some sections of the local community blamed
the degraded condition of the low paid rural labourer on the Norfolk
clergy's selfish exaction of high tithe payments, and in the south-
east of the county this led to wage—tithe riots. The growth of
Dissent and particularly of Primitive Methodism after 1830 decimated
the number of labourers who attended the parish church. The authority of the incumbent of the parish was also undercut by the reforms
of the Poor Law, and of the Rural Police in the 1830s, which decreased the role of the parish vestry in which the vicar or rector
had always been prominent. Later, in the 1860s, the work of the
Charity Commissioners exposed mal-administration by certain trustees
in Norfolk charities and led to suspicious murmurings by villagers
against their parson's integrity and efficiency in his administration of the charitable provision for the poor. The erosion of good
feeling between the clergyman and his parishoners was carried a
stage further with the conflicts that occurred in the 1870s over the
right of Dissenters to be buried in the churchyard of the parish
church and the dissatisfaction over the sectarian nature of the
education in the village school. (10) The unstrained relationship
between parson and poor, with a habit of service on the one hand
and respect and affection on the other, that had been typified by
a Parson Woodforde at the turn of the century was no longer easy
in Norfolk by the mid-nineteenth century.

'The broken links of the chain of social dependence' was the
comment in 1834 of an informed observer on Norfolk society at the
time when it was poised between the Old and New Poor Laws. The
propertied classes were accused of abdicating from their traditional
social responsibility to the poor by spending too much time and
money away from their Norfolk estates, and the poor were said to
have responded to this with idleness and incendiarism. (11) The
traditional Norfolk society, in which the gentry and clergy had
given paternalistic protection to the poor who had responded
with dependent loyalty, had received a fatal blow in the rural disturbances of 1816, 1822 and 1830. The lesson which the propertied
classes gradually learned from these riots was that the older
methods of social control had failed. The vertical lines of connection, of mutual interest and social harmony, which they had
cemented with an active and liberal administration of the Old Poor
Law, had not elicited loyalty from the poor. Many therefore welcomed the more stringent provisions of the New Poor Law, which they
hoped might impose social discipline on the labourer. The transitional state of Norfolk society in the 1830s means that the nobility,
the gentry and the clergy still recognized their traditional duty
to uphold law and order and so acted as the midwives of change in
imposing the new system of poor relief; but their emerging sectional interests led them increasingly to confine their attention
only to the poor on their own estates. This left the management
of the New Poor Law to the farmers whose thrusting self-confidence
led to a vigorous pursuit of their own class's economic interest
in the administration of poor relief. The Norfolk farmer acted as
a catalyst in the slow transformation of this traditional society
into one that was based on class.

II   IDEAS ON POOR RELIEF BEFORE 1834

The richness of the pamphlet literature on the Old Poor Law produced by Norfolk writers suggests the strong social responsibility
that the propertied groups felt for the labouring poor. It also
indicated their political freedom to innovate in the administration
of poor relief. Ideas that were put forward in local books and
pamphlets shaped a continuing debate on poverty and pauperism and
one that activated the changes in the Norfolk administration of the
Old Poor Law which have been discussed earlier. These Norfolk
opinions were related to the contemporary national discussion, but
their timing and emphases often differed from those in the broader
debate. In the second half of the eighteenth century the establishment of the East Anglian Incorporations under Local Act provided a local focus for the discussion on pauperism, and this debate therefore had an unusual coherence, and also anticipated the
trend in general opinion against workhouses.
     The projected incorporation of the hundreds of Mitford and
Launditch in 1774-5 provoked a sharp dialogue among resident gentlemen there which raised themes that were to reverberate through local
poor law literature for the next 60 years. These included: the
relative humanity or economy of relieving the poor within institutions and the effect this had on their health, morals and industry;
the comparative merits of different social groups in administering
these institutions; and the wider social, economic and political
implications of different methods of relieving the poor. The debate
was initiated by the Rev. R. Potter of Scarning, who found in the
East Anglian houses of industry 'scenes of health, cleanliness,
comfort, cheerfulness, industry, good order and good morals', and
these qualities he considered made it inappropriate to label them
as workhouses. Careful supervision by local gentlemen who moderated
a desire for economy with humanity would prevent the niggardly economies that were frequently made by magistrates and overseers in
parish poor houses, and would maintain that industrious and well
ordered poor upon whom depended national strength and riches. A
less idealized view was given in a reply by Thomas Mendham of
Briston, who asserted that the magistrates were the 'best friends
the poor ever had', and who firmly described the houses of industry
as workhouses. These would oppress the poor, cause unnecessary expense to ratepayers, and depopulate the countryside. Mendham concluded that the poor needed their interests defending against this
projected reform.(12)
     The correspondence columns of the 'Norfolk Chronicle' showed
that the poor had supporters who defended their cause by powerful,
emotive references to the house of industry as prisons for the peasantry. A correspondent hoped that John Howard, the penal reformer,
would inspect houses of industry because these were 'lock-up houses'
and 'nurseries of pestilential disorder'.(13) This theme of houses
of industry as prisons became increasingly insistent in local writing and showed the influence of a more sympathetic and humane attitude to the poor which was developing in society as a whole as the
eighteenth century progressed.(14) An anonymous Yarmouth writer of
1785 predicted national ruin from these 'vast compilations of buildings for the reception and imprisonment of the poor' which crowned

every eminence. He asked rhetorically whether the temporary reduction in expenditure which they had achieved could justify sacrifices
by which 'the true national strength and security ought to be bar-
tered; for which the health, population, morals and happiness of
the lower orders of our people ought to be sacrificed?'(15)

By this time such expectations of economy were unusual, since
by the 1780s earlier hopes that putting the poor to work in East
Anglian institutions would be profitable had been disappointed. In
Norwich the leader of the campaign against expensive indoor relief
in the 1780s was Dr Rigby. He later summarized his opposition, on
the occasion of the proposed erection of a new Norwich workhouse in
1802, by the arguments that workhouses were 'injurious to the manners of the poor; that they generate disease, and that they are much
more expensive than relieving the poor by out-door allowances'. His
ideas were taken up by J. Grisenthwaite of King's Lynn, who supported
his reforming ideas by stating that in the last 40 years expenditure
in the workhouse in Lynn had increased seven-fold, whereas the numbers of paupers had only increased four-fold. Local opinion in
rural areas was less uniformly hostile to indoor relief than was
that in the towns, although Sir F.M. Eden showed that there was
disillusionment with the rural houses of industry in East Anglia
at the end of the eighteenth century. In contrast, a sustained
defence of the houses of industry in Suffolk was provided by Thomas
Ruggles, who found them economical, healthy and well ordered institutions. In Norfolk, a former director of the Mitford and Launditch
Incorporation, Edward Parry, provided a more cautious and qualified
vindication of the rural house of industry in 1797. The Gressenhall
house of industry had 'the merit of being managed with great attention to the health, comfort, and in some degree, to the morals of
the poor'. Its great defect was in its failure to house industry;
children were brought up there to be too delicate for service, and
labourers were maintained there in idleness.(16)

Economic dissatisfaction with poor law institutions was reinforced
during the bread crises at the end of the eighteenth century by a
humanitarian sympathy for the labourer in his economic distress. The
Rev. J. Howlett of Great Dunmow in Essex voiced this humanitarian
concern after his tour of the houses of industry in Norfolk and Suffolk in 1789. He thought that the most notable feature of these
institutions was that 'the general aversion of the poor from entering these houses, as it were, compels them to do their utmost, and
even to submit to great hardships, rather than apply for parochial
relief'. Arthur Young, the famous agricultural commentator who
lived at Bradfield in Suffolk, put into words in 1800 a sentiment
that was common at that time. That the Suffolk poor endured hunger
was proof of 'what workhouses are, that the poor should submit to
such a horrible state rather than go into them'.(17) Public opinion
in Norfolk grew increasingly hostile to the rural houses of industry
and this had forced a reversion to parochial relief in three of the
five rural incorporations before 1834.

By the 1820s humanitarian and practical reasons had led to a widespread use of outdoor allowances to relieve the able-bodied poor in
Norfolk parishes. An idiosyncratic crusade was mounted against this
allowance system during the 1820s by the Rector of Little Massingham.
In a series of aggressive publications, C.D. Brereton blamed

allowances for demoralizing the peasantry by increasing prodigality, bastardy and crime, and decreasing thrift and industry. This 'law of maintenance' had replaced wages by poor relief, and the consequent distortion of the labour market had led to discrimination in employment against the single labourer and a worsening of social relationships between master and man. The magistrates were blamed for the growth of the allowance system. Their mischievous and unconstitutional interference with the parish overseer and their disregard of the parish vestry were blamed by Brereton for the destruction of his beloved parochial system with its older tradition of pensions for the impotent poor. The Petty Sessions, where the justices heard poor law cases, was described as the 'focus of evil passions and evil counsels' which had converted the industrious Norfolk labourer first into a pauper and then into a criminal. Brereton felt more than just an abstract hostility to the justices and their allowance system because his own earlier attempts to end allowances in Little Massingham had been frustrated by the justices and local farmers. In a letter to the Chairman of Swaffham Petty Sessions in 1826 he forecast that within 10 years the feeling against the present system of poor relief would be as strong as that against slavery, and that 'unless the magistrates return from the present mode of proceeding they will become as unpopular as the colonial planters'.(18)

These opinions verged on abolitionism, and the extremity of Brereton's arguments provoked a counter-reaction by two other writers. Brereton's abolition of allowances to the able-bodied poor would deprive them 'of their only security against starvation', wrote W. Copland of Sharrington in 1824. He thought that the magistracy were acting expediently rather than arbitrarily in helping the labourer at a time when heavily taxed farmers were unable to employ the poor. His argument was supported the following year by The Rev. P.S. Wood, vicar of Middleton, who dismissed Brereton's ideas as 'starvation principles'. He defended the role of the magistracy who, he said, interfered with the income of the labourer only when agricultural wages were so low that they did not give adequate subsistence.(19)

By 1830 the allowance system was as unpopular in Norfolk as it was elsewhere, and the Norfolk magistracy blamed themselves for its prevalence:(20)

> If blame there be that can fairly attach to any class of persons,
> it belongs rather to the magistrates, of which class I am one
> myself.... Our bad practice has not been the growth of a day,
> we have gradually and imperceptibly to ourselves been led into
> it, some justices perhaps much by a false feeling of humanity,
> or by the irresistible impulse to relieve extreme and unmerited
> distress.

This speech to the Grand Jury of Norfolk was made by Lord Suffield in his role as a chairman of Norfolk Quarter Sessions. The Norfolk magistracy used these addresses to the Grand Jury as a means of educating opinion within the county on contemporary matters of social or economic importance. Those in 1829 and 1830 showed that local ideas faithfully reflected trends of national opinion in rejecting the allowance system and advocating schemes for employing rather than relieving the poor.

In the early 1830s the Norfolk debate reached the most vigorous and defined stage in its continuing discussion on poverty and pauperism. The small range of reforms that were proposed indicated a narrowing area of controversy. The number of pamphlets, which often went through several editions, showed clearly the increased concern about the labourer's condition which had resulted from the disturbances of 1830. It was widely recognized among the propertied classes in Norfolk that justice was on the side of the labourer in his desperate protests about his low wages and inadequate poor relief. Indeed, the unusual degree of humanitarian leniency shown in the statements by the Norfolk magistracy incurred hostile criticism from the Prime Minister.(21) The riots created a more positive and radical climate of opinion about remedies for pauperism. All local writers were by now to some extent Malthusians in recognizing that surplus labour existed in Norfolk. Disagreement came only over whether this was a localized or general problem, a permanent product of the Malthusian law which postulated that the growth of population would outstrip that of subsistence, or merely a temporary product of an agriculture depressed by high taxation. Differing explanations of surplus labour resulted in varied prescriptions to cure it, including employment schemes, emigration and a modification of the settlement laws which were alleged to impede labour mobility.

One of the earliest and most influential writers was the Heydon land agent, J. Richardson. He argued that surplus labour was a local and temporary problem which arose from a lack of capital by the propertied classes and the impediments which the law of settlement placed on the labourers' mobility. He criticized the existing poor law administration as leading to 'a restraint upon the free circulation and price of labour, an unlimited provision for poverty, an indiscriminate application of that provision to imprudence, to misfortune, to idleness, and to vice'. He advocated that the county should hire district farms to provide work for the unemployed and that the county rather than the parish should be the unit of settlement. Richardson's work interested John Weyland, M.P. for Wiltshire and a chairman of Norfolk Quarter Sessions, who commended it to Norfolk gentlemen. Weyland also put forward his own analysis, which was a reversal of his earlier anti-Malthusian stance in his belated recognition that a surplus labour problem existed. This was only a temporary phenomenon caused by a lack of capital, and Weyland urged proprietors to employ the poor on improving their estates and advised occupiers to implement a labour rate. Weyland's arguments were challenged by R.M. Bacon, the editor of the 'Norwich Mercury' and a keen correspondent and adviser to Lord Suffield on the question of the poor. After a careful argument, Bacon concluded that a permanent surplus of labour existed and that this required a programme of home colonization of wasteland in order to increase employment.(22)

The debate was widened by writers who put forward more radical proposals to deal with the unemployed Norfolk poor. T. Drummond stated that surplus labour was caused by a lack of small tenancies. Since population and agriculture were the bases of national strength and prosperity, British vigour would be restored only if small farms were created to employ the poor. In contrast, R. Calver argued that mechanization had created unemployment and proposed as a remedy the creation of a board of national improvements to increase demand for manual labour. Less individual in their theses were T. Watts and S. Adams, who both advocated a labour rate. Watts wanted this in order to compel occupiers to employ their fair share of labour, any surplus labourers being set to work on wasteland. Adams wanted a labour rate established on a county basis by a local act of Parliament but recognized that certain parishes had such a large labour surplus that this measure would have to be supplemented by emigration. Neither were unduly worried by the element of compulsion in establishing a labour rate that would force occupiers to employ their quota of labourers. The widespread adoption of the labour rate by Norfolk parishes at this time suggests that local opinion had shifted towards favouring the more radical solution to the problem of the unemployed poor. There were still some who argued that a labour rate should not be imposed in a free country, but their outrage was less than those of earlier writers. In 1817 George Glover, the vicar of Cromer, had thought that any national measure to employ the poor compulsorily involved 'at once bursting through every barrier of civil liberty, and subjecting the private concerns of every private individual to the management and control of a state steward'.(23)

Before 1834 most of the local debate had been in reformist terms, with one generation criticizing the innovations of their predecessors for failing to stem the growth of pauperism. There were a few who gave qualified support after 1815 to those who wished for the abolition of the poor law. H. Bathurst, a clerical magistrate, suggested in 1825 that friendly societies should replace the poor law and that both labourers and local ratepayers could finance them. Five years later W.H. Meteyard put forward an abolitionist programme which would have swept away Poor Laws, Game Laws and Corn Laws, but it is problematical whether in the existing context of Norfolk debate he expected to have his radical proposals taken too seriously. In spite of continuous criticisms by Norfolk writers about the oppressive and unfair operation of the laws of settlement and removal, only H. Barrett in 1829 had been prepared to grasp the nettle firmly by proposing their abolition, even if this necessarily meant the creation of a national poor rate.(24)

III   ATTITUDES TO THE NEW POOR LAW

The proposals of the Royal Commission on the Poor Laws of 1832-4, which were embodied in the Poor Law Amendment Act of 1834, cut through the prevailing intellectual confusion in the national debate on poor relief and pauperism. It rejected some of the favourite panaceas of the day like the labour rate, while it faithfully reflected the strong contemporary hostility towards allowances and included the ideas of local reformers from Nottinghamshire on the role of the workhouse in depauperizing the poor. This national measure apparently closed the option of local initiative and reform in dealing with pauperism.(25)

How did this New Poor Law relate to the preceding local discussion about pauperism, and what reception did its ideas receive from Norfolk society?

The specific proposals in the 1834 act were very different
from existing poor law practice in Norfolk, but its underlying
social philosophy was in sympathy with attitudes that were emerging, but were not yet fully articulated, in Norfolk society. The
lynchpin in the practical operation of the New Poor Law was the
workhouse, which had already been tried and found wanting in
Norfolk. The proposal in 1828 of the Norfolk clergyman, P.S.
Wood, for central workhouse establishments had found no support in
Norfolk, although the anti-pauper system of the Rev. T. Becher,
which had inspired his proposals, was to be embodied in the 1834
reforms. While the Royal Commission's attack on outdoor allowances
reflected local hostility to this form of poor relief, Norfolk
opinion preferred employment schemes rather than indoor relief in
the workhouse as the alternative method for relieving the poor.
Local opinion did, however, favour the economical aim of the New
Poor Law because previous local-based reforms of the Poor Law had
failed to reduce poor law expenditure or to alleviate the burdens
of the Norfolk ratepayer. There had been an interesting change in
the weight of emphasis given in the Norfolk literature on pauperism
during the previous 60 years from an early humanitarian concern for
the poor to a later economic anxiety about the plight of the ratepayers. As a variety of local initiatives had failed to eliminate
surplus labour, there was a growing tendency to see the unemployed
poor in moral rather than economic terms. The Rev. William Gunn
of Smallburgh wrote in 1834 that, while poverty was indispensable
and a source of wealth and national prosperity, destitution was
an evil. He thought that a distinction should be made in the treatment of the destitute between those who were innocently destitute
and those who were culpable.(26)
   Implicit in the philosophy of the New Poor Law was this division
of the labourers into the good poor, whose hard work would keep them
from the workhouse (except when misfortunes occurred when they would
be aided by charity), and the bad poor, who would be assisted only
in a workhouse run along punitive lines. The desirability of social
discipline for the bad poor struck a sympathetic chord in the minds
of the propertied classes in Norfolk, who had been alarmed by the
labourers' actions during the disturbances of 1830. The correspondence of local justices and gentlemen with the Home Office at that
time had vividly suggested the vulnerability and insecurity which
they felt for their persons and property. They had comforted themselves with a conspiratorial theory of revolt; the rioting was
blamed on the disloyal, faceless poor from villages other than one's
own. 'Our village rather *shines* in the gallant feeling and disposi-
tion it shows', wrote Lady Catherine Boileau, the wife of J.P.
Boileau, who was a deputy lieutenant of Norfolk, at the height of
these disturbances.(27) The distinction that was drawn at this
time between the good and bad poor was of course inherent in the
'close' and 'open' parish system which the propertied classes had
so carefully constructed in Norfolk. In 'close' parishes there was
a conscious policy by the small number of landowners there to restrict residence only to the good poor and to inspire loyalty from
them by benevolent treatment. In Great Melton, for example, the
poor law guardian stated that '(as almost all the cottages belong
to one large owner within the parish and are let at very low rents

to only industrious and deserving tenants) there is every induce-
ment to the poor man to be steady and industrious'. The same
philosophy prevailed in Shernbourne on the other side of Norfolk,
where 'it is hoped the poor are too well taken care of in the
parish to be dishonest'.(28)

After the popular disorders of 1816, 1822 and 1830, Norfolk
property-owners feared a spirit of insubordination among the poor
as a whole, and they therefore welcomed the New Poor Law as an
instrument of social discipline for the labourer. 'What they
expect, is, that the building of the workhouses will be the signal
for tumult among the lower orders', wrote the assistant poor law
commissioner, Sir Edward Parry, after his discussions with Norfolk
justices in 1835. The chairman of Norfolk Quarter Sessions wrote to
Lord John Russell to ask for the appointment of a special constabulary force for the county because once the labouring classes had
begun to riot it would be too late to swear in special constables.
The magistrates complained that 'the farmers though unanimous in
favour of the Poor Law Amendment Act are intimidated by the
labourers, and from a fear of damage to their property by incendiarism and otherwise, are deterred from taking an active part'.(29)

In spite of rioting at Bircham and other places in the county
the new poor law administration soon got under way. Resolutions
by Norfolk boards of guardians give an insight into their satisfaction at the impact which the New Poor Law had already had on the
labourer. His condition had changed 'from idleness and improvi-
dence to industry and forethought', he had learned 'habits of order';
and 'the voice of murmuring and complaint had been changed for
silent and contented industry', so that their employers were 'beyond measure more comfortable in the superintendence of those employed'.(30) Norfolk guardians underlined the disciplinary nature
of the reformed system of relief by making it into an instrument
of social control in which poor relief was refused to those who
frequented public houses or kept a gun and a dog.(31)

Many of the landed gentry supported the New Poor Law but saw
their role in relation to it as being mainly a short-term and strategic, rather than a long-term and routine, one. This expectation
was confirmed by the policies that the assistant poor law commissioners adopted in Norfolk. The first assistant commissioner, Sir
Edward Parry, wrote an interesting letter to Sr W.H.J.B. Folkes,
an owner of estates of about 8,000 acres at Hillington, who was
also M.P. for west Norfolk from 1830-7. Parry persuaded Folkes to
act as the first chairman of the Freebridge Lynn Union, and assured
him that he need serve for only one year because *in the mean time,
the machinery would be fairly set a-going, which is of course, a
great thing in the commencement of a totally new system'. Folkes
agreed and (by virtue of his office as magistrate, which gave him
ex officio membership of a board of guardians) served as chairman
of the board. Parry's successor, Dr Kay, also appreciated the help
that the gentry could give the reformed poor relief system, and he
spent four nights in every week at the seats of country gentlemen
planning how to implement the New Poor Law without provoking resistance by its opponents. He visited T.W. Coke at Holkham Hall and
the Earl of Albemarle at Quiddenham Hall in a successful attempt to
get these two leaders of Norfolk society to use their influence to

support the introduction of the 1834 act in their localities. Albemarle used his power indirectly through the presence of his bailiff, steward and tenants on local boards of guardians in the south of Norfolk; while Coke, the 'great commoner', characteristically gave more open support. He accompanied Kay to the meeting of owners and occupiers that agreed to form poor law unions in the north of the county, and also agreed to serve as the first chairman of the Walsingham Board of Guardians. Coke saw this chairmanship as a symbol of his support for the 1834 act rather than a working office, and attended only three times during his period of tenure from 1836 to 1839.(32)   Gentlemen whose social standing was shown by their office of magistrate and deputy lieutenant put in good active service as the first chairmen of Norfolk unions. Sir Thomas Beevor of Hargham Hall, the Hon. F.W. Irby Esq. of Boyland Hall and Sir William Beauchamp Proctor of Langley Park provided quite vigorous leadership in the Wayland, Depwade and Loddon and Clavering Unions respectively.

18   Aylsham Union Workhouse.   Ink and wash by W. Mileham, 1855

19   Aylsham Union Workhouse.   Pencil drawing by W.J. Martins, 1877

The differences in opinion within Norfolk society about the
desirability of varied poor law policies did not end in 1834, and
both clergy and magistracy were deeply divided over the provisions
of the Poor Law Amendment Act. The Rev. J. Fellowes of Shotesham,
a clerical magistrate, was a convinced supporter of the 1834 act
and wrote a clear pamphlet in simple language to explain its operation to local inhabitants. He aimed to remove 'all unnecessary
uneasiness and alarm' because 'I have reason to believe that much
misapprehension still exists amongst many of you with respect to
the provisions of the New Poor Law.' In the neighbouring parish
of Kirstead the Rev. S. Hobson wrote several pamphlets in 1836-7
under the pseudonym 'a Norfolk Clergyman'. These aimed at a reader-
ship among the labouring poor but went wide of their target with
their prolix paternalism. His theme was that the poor were part of
one national family and that the clergy, magistracy and gentry were
also members of the family who wished to help the labourer. They
could only do so if the poor obeyed the laws of God and man and if
they helped themselves by involvement in socially desirable projects of self-help such as medical clubs, friendly societies and
savings banks:(33)

> When it is seen, that you are anxious to avoid having recourse
> to parish relief, and desirous of maintaining yourselves
> *independently,* as you have a right to do, by the labour of your
> hands, there is little doubt, but the higher classes of society
> will zealously exert themselves in your favour.

Clerical supporters of the New Poor Law stressed that it was the
law of the land and that its provisions were not intended to punish
the poor, while clerical opponents of the 1834 act emphasized that
it was against the law of God and oppressed the poor. 'I consider
the Poor Law Amendment Act to be harsh and unjust in its operation,
impolitic in its consequence, immoral in its tendency, and unchristian in its principles', wrote a persistent clerical critic in 1836.
He was T.B. Morris, the Rector of Shelfanger, who translated his
views into action during 1836-7 by complaints to the Guiltcross
guardians about their inhumane administration, and by sermons from
his pulpit against the New Poor Law. Coming as these did from
Shelfanger, which lay in an area disturbed by machine-breaking,
incendiarism and riots in 1816, 1822 and 1830 and by popular protests against the Guiltcross guardians in 1836, the central Poor
Law Board was justifiably alarmed by Morris's actions. The flat-
tering attention given by the Poor Law Commissioners and by Dr Kay
to some of the Morris's favourite projects for helping the poor
apparently ended his opposition to the New Poor Law and prevented
him from giving his projected evidence to the Select Committee which
was to conduct an inquiry into the working of the Poor Law Amendment
Act.(34) Less amenable to pressure from his betters was the Rev.
F.H. Maberley, whose continued crusade against the New Poor Law in
the eastern counties alarmed local poor law administrators. Maberley
was blamed for the violence in south-west Norfolk which had followed
one of his large labourers' meetings at which he had denounced the
1834 act. He regarded the New Poor Law as 'tyrannical, unconstitutional, anti-scriptural, anti-christian, illegal, unnatural, cruel,
and impolitic in the extreme. Also that it is a system of robbery
and degradation towards the poor.' However, Maberley lived at Bourn

in Cambridgeshire, and was the absentee incumbent of a Suffolk
living, so that nearly all his activities took place well to the
south and west of Norfolk.(35)

A humanitarian defence of the rights of the poor poised the
clergy on the horns of a dilemma, because in condemning the New
Poor Law as contrary to the laws of God they might be understood to
be inciting the poor to disobey the laws of man. Morris had ration-
alized his actions by stating that as a clergyman he advocated sub-
mission to the New Poor Law, but that as a private individual he
denounced 'the atrocities which render it a disgrace to the legis-
lature'. A less subtle stance was taken by the Rev. Ambrose Goode
of Terrington, who in November 1835 published the first edition of
a handbill attacking the New Poor Law:

> In this situation of dependent misery [for the labourer] what
> says the wisdom of our present legislators? Why this, take
> away weekly relief! Make the work-house ten times larger. Let
> that *alone* be the last resort for honest industry in distress....
> Is this the boasted liberty of an Englishman?... But if this Whig
> act infringes upon the rights of the poor, it is no less a de-
> fiance of the law of God — The great Protector of all has said,
> 'Increase and multiply,' .... But if the principle of the law is
> bad, its execution is worse. — Indeed there is no fixed prin-
> ciple, its execution depends upon the variable breath of com-
> missioners ... and thus has all the attributes of tyranny with-
> out the responsibility of law.... Look to yourselves — Men must
> live.... The voice of the people is sometimes an angry surge.
> — Unheeded, it becomes a record of blood.

Ambrose Goode played an active part in the affairs of Freebridge
Marshland and was well thought of in the neighbourhood so that the
two editions of his handbill during 1835-6 caused a local uproar.
The poor of King's Lynn were excited by it, and the guardians there
were so incensed by Goode's populist stance that they refused to
add Terrington to the poor law union of King's Lynn because of his
'baleful' influence. Social pressure was put on Goode and on his
printer, while a tame pamphleteer was recruited in November 1835
by the Poor Law Commission to reply to the arguments in Goode's
broadsheets.(36)

John Godfrey responded to the poor law authority's request because he was a fervent supporter of the New Poor Law and one who
saw it as a means of disciplining the poor. He was related to the
farmers of Great Bircham, who six weeks earlier had narrowly escaped
with their lives during a serious riot by the labourers. As such,
his viewpoint may perhaps be seen as a rare written expression of
the Norfolk farmers' attitudes to the poor and the New Poor Law.
Godfrey wrote 'A Poor Man's Answer' in reply to Goode's handbill,
in which he accused Goode of violating his duty in reviving a spirit
of revenge instead of preaching a peaceful obedience to the law.
Earlier, and apparently before the rioting in August 1835, Godfrey
had written a handbill 'A few words on the New Poor Law Bill',
under the pseudonym 'a Poor Man of Snettisham'. In this he argued
that the Old Poor Law had produced midnight crimes and guilty consciences among the poor, but that the New Poor Law would encourage
the industrious and make the poor into more useful members of
society. 'Should you or I go to the workhouse, we must not expect

to find the comforts of our cottage there, we shall be under strict
management, we shall have no money, but we shall have wholesome
food, and for which we ought to be thankful.' After the events at
Bircham he wrote 'The Poor Man's Friend', in which he denounced the
rioting and pleaded for better social relationships. Godfrey's
ready pen proved a considerable asset to the poor law authorities
in west Norfolk. He was also asked to write a reply to Thomas
Marster's hard hitting pamphlet, 'Reform and Workhouses'. This was
published in Lynn in 1835, and accused the New Poor Law of being 'a
heartless cold-blooded tissue of indiscriminate cruelty' which would
promote starvation and depopulation.(37)

Similar sentiments were being expressed at the other side of the
county by an influential section of the Norfolk magistracy who
opposed the 1834 act on both humanitarian and political grounds.
A Blofield justice expressed a common magisterial sentiment when he
said that the Poor Law Commission offered the poor 'the alternative
of starvation or a gaol'.(38) Before 1834 the Norfolk justices had
been active and liberal administrators of poor relief and they
resented the diminution in their power made by the New Poor Law.
Now they could only act as ex officio guardians, whose discretionary
action was narrowly circumscribed under relief regulations of the
central Poor Law Board which were enforced by the stringent accounting procedures of the district auditors. Opposition by Norfolk
justices to the implementation of the New Poor Law was particularly
marked in east Norfolk because the magistracy had earlier been
especially active there in the Old Poor Law incorporations under
local act. As Chapters 4 and 5 have shown, magisterial hostility
to the 1834 act was shown in poor rate excusal cases coming up
before petty sessions in the Blofield, Henstead and Guiltcross
Unions, and by the obstructionist attitudes of ex officio guardians
in all these unions and in the Mitford and Launditch and Loddon
and Clavering Unions. The partisan political loyalty of Tory
magistrates was also a powerful factor in their opposition to the
1834 act as a Whig measure.

Activities in the Blofield Union showed clearly the magisterial
stance against the New Poor Law. The Blofield justices had been
proud of the low levels of pauperism achieved with a humane distribution of relief in their poor law administration before 1834. They
had been keen to start a New Poor Law union and had nominated their
protégés as union officials, but their enthusiasm was later quenched
by the central Poor Law Board's drive to restrict their discretionary
authority as relief guardians. In a parliamentary debate of 1839,
their first chairman, H.N. Burroughes (who had become the Tory M.P.
for east Norfolk), opposed the continuation of the powers of the
Poor Law Commission. Two months later the Blofield guardians took
their defence of local discretionary power a stage further by an
outright rejection of the Poor Law Commissioners' order prohibiting
outdoor relief to the able-bodied. The central board ignored their
action and the auditor disallowed expenditure on this type of allowance. The jealousy of central power continued on the Blofield Board
of Guardians, which in 1842 unsuccessfully asked for the withdrawal
of the prohibitory order because it caused hardship to the poor. By
this time a certain tension was evident among the Blofield guardians,
between the justices as ex officio guardians and the farmers as

elected guardians. Both were united against the central power's
restriction of local discretion over relief but for opposite reasons,
since the justices wanted a liberal, and the farmers a frugal, administration of poor law allowances.(39) While the magisterial
position of outright opposition to the central board in the early
years of the New Poor Law suffered defeat, the later, cautious mani-
pulation by the farmer-guardians of the central board's own regulations was to be successful. The justices had at first dominated
the farmers on the board of guardians by virtue of their superior
status and education, but power gradually shifted to the farmers
because they attended board meetings with much greater regularity.

Resistance to the centralization of the 1834 act was also strong
in the highly politicized towns of Norwich, Lynn and Yarmouth. The
Conservative M.P. for Norwich, Sir James Scarlett, had been prominent in reducing the central poor law authority's powers at the
parliamentary committee stage of the Poor Law Amendment Act.   In
King's Lynn the guardians regretted the renewal of the powers of the
Poor Law Commission in 1841, which they regarded as oppressive,
unconstitutional and 'superfluous now that the machinery has been
long put into motion and the working of it well understood'. The
Yarmouth Board of Guardians was described in 1838 as 'carrying out
the [1834] act as though it conceived itself to be entirely independent'.(40)

The greatest hostility to the New Poor Law in Norfolk came from
within social groups such as the clergy and magistracy who had been
most active in the administration of poor relief before 1834, and
also from areas in the east of the county which had initiated a
reformed system of old poor law administration. Resistance to what
was regarded as a superfluous reform could result in uncompromising
attitudes. The Yarmouth guardians resolved in 1838 that 'If the
guardians are not to use their discretion in affording the relief
to the poor ... the guardians will not attend to the business of
the parish but the Poor Law Commission, must do the business themselves'.(41) In this defence of local power over poor law administration in the first years of the New Poor Law, there were underlying similarities to the struggles between local administrators in
the North of England and the central poor law administration. But
after the first years of the New Poor Law the erstwhile influential
sections of Noroflk society virtually abdicated from their wider
social responsibilities to the poor. They did not relish their
designated role as relief guardians who were merely mechanical ad-
juncts to the central administrative engine of the Poor Law Commission. Nor, after the riots of 1830, did they wish to concern themselves with the bad poor, whose fecklessness would lead them to the
workhouse. Instead, Norfolk gentlemen undertook a paternalistic
responsibility for the good poor by the provision of model cottages
and charities on their estates, and the labourers were expected to
show gratitude and loyalty in return. The gentry's withdrawal left
a vacuum in poor law administration which was filled by a rising
class of tenant farmers. They welcomed the opportunity to act as
poor law guardians because this enhanced their social status, while
their opportunistic administration of relief benefited their own
economic position.

CHAPTER 12

REVOLT BY THE POOR

The slow transition from a hierarchical to a class society resulted
in an uneasy ambivalence in the Norfolk labourers' attitude to poor
relief. In this intermediate society the labouring poor appealed
first to the security of the values of the traditional community
and then to the freedom of a newly emergent and independent way of
life. The poor were responding to developments in the local economy
and to the changing attitudes by the propertied towards the poor in
Norfolk society which had led to alterations in the use of poor relief. Their real objection was to these changed attitudes and
values, although their protests were directed apparently against
reform in the Poor Law, which was the outcome of this different
ideology. Poor relief as a means of succouring the sick or aged
became less significant than its use as a semi-permanent means of
alleviating the deteriorating economic condition of the labourer.
It had been customary to use poor law allowances as shock absorbers
in years of harvest failure or high bread price when the gentry,
clergy and farmers in Norfolk showed their paternalistic responsibility for the lower orders in their distress. But by the early
nineteenth century these allowances were being used as a regular
supplement to below-subsistence incomes and this suggested to the
labourer that the propertied groups were abdicating from their
traditional social duty towards him. Initially, the labourer revealed an unthinking trust in his betters and his early protests
were essentially reminders to them to restore the status quo and
to give back to him his social right to a living wage and an independent livelihood. Then came a belated recognition that his
rights were no longer being adequately protected by paternalistic
patronage and his protests became more violent. To the Norfolk
gentry these riots and disturbances seemed to show the labourer's
disloyalty and ingratitude, and in consequence the New Poor Law was
welcomed as a form of social discipline and control. The deepening
mutual alienation of the propertied and the poor, in which each
group blamed the other for a deterioration in social relationships,
resulted in a sequence of events that had the inevitability of a
Greek tragedy. Mutual interest and connection became progressively
eroded in Norfolk society. Nowhere was this more evident than in
the comparison between the protests by the poor against a reformed

system of poor relief in the old poor law incorporations of East
Anglia and the more violent disturbances that the imposition of the
New Poor Law provoked in the 1830s. The harsh deterrence of the New
Poor Law alienated the labourer from his state of dependency and
his growing independence eroded his social conservatism. Ultimately,
the Norfolk labourer found the self-confidence to make economic demands based on class interest, and these were expressed through the
agricultural trade union movement of the late nineteenth century.

I   THE WORKHOUSE AS PRISON

In 1775 the labouring poor and small occupiers of the hundreds of
Mitford and Launditch petitioned Sir E. Astley and W. Coke Esq.,
the two M.P.s for Norfolk, to oppose the projected parliamentary
bill to incorporate the parishes in their area for a reformed relief
of the poor:(1)

> In this struggle it is easy to foresee who must submit; for you
> know, and we know, the weakest must go by the walls. But we
> do implore you to speak for us in Parliament, where we cannot
> speak for ourselves, and to stop as you easily can, that impri-
> sonment of our persons, that separation from our children, that
> destruction of our race, that loss to the kingdom, and that curse
> from the Almighty which must attend establishing a poor house
> upon the specious fallacy of providing for our comfort, by the
> breaking of our hearts.

In appealing from their state of helplessness to the defence of
their interests by their betters they must have been hopeful of
success, both because of the traditional protection which the propertied had given to the poor, and because eleven years had passed
since the formation of the first poor law incorporation in Norfolk.
The county's gentlemen had been deterred from further experimenta-
tion in the administration of the Poor Law by the protests in 1765
of the Suffolk poor, who had agitated against three newly formed
poor law incorporations in Suffolk.(2)

That a free-born Englishman had the right to be relieved in his
own home and should not be relieved by being imprisoned in a workhouse was to be a recurrent theme in East Anglian popular protest.
A memorial from an inhabitant of the hundreds of Tunstead and
Happing asked his Member of Parliament in 1785 to oppose the private
act of Parliament in which it was planned to incorporate the area
for the reformed relief of the poor. This is interesting in being
an early example of the poor law 'Bastille' literature which is more
usually associated with the later union workhouses of the New Poor
Law. The memorial argued that the houses of industry within the
East Anglian poor law incorporations threatened 'our liberty and
laws [since] if persons are starved, beaten, or even murdered no
appeal can be heard by any but the committee of the house [and] this
makes a poor man's case worse than a criminals for they have a fair
and publick trial by the laws of their country'. Although the petition closed with the threat that, if the bill became law, 'we are
determined to defend our laws and libertys or to loose our lives',
the poor of this area did not rise in revolt when the revised system of poor relief was introduced. Indeed, the Norfolk poor confined

their protests about the changes in the relief system of the Old
Poor Law largely to words so that there were no riots comparable
with those in Suffolk in 1765. This is probably because the five
Norfolk poor law incorporations were geographically scattered and
were set up gradually over a 20-year period between 1764 and 1785,
so that there was less opportunity for a concerted opposition to
them than in Suffolk, where reform was faster and where most of the
east of the county was affected. There were isolated acts of violence in Norfolk which indicated the hostility of the poor to the
reform of poor relief, as for example in the Flegg Incorporation
in 1775, when there was damage done to the property of the gentleman who had sold the land on which the house of industry was to be
erected.(3)

These eighteenth-century protests by the East Anglian poor had
some effect either in delaying reform or in discouraging it alto-
gether. Property-owners in south and west Norfolk who had been
considering a revised system of relieving the poor in 1764 and 1770
abandoned their plans after the disturbances by the Suffolk poor.
This suggests that the labouring poor's appeal to the local gentry
to defend their interests had found a response in the latter's belated recognition of the legitimate values of the traditional social
order. Functional protest, either through direct action or through
peaceful memorials, was customary within a paternalistic society
and was frequently successful.(4) After 1814 the confusion of independent wages and poor relief necessarily brought poor law administrators into the eye of the storm during the disturbances of 1816
and 1830, when the Norfolk labourer was protesting against the
deterioration in his real income.

The riots of 1816 were more serious than earlier bread riots in
that they affected a much wider area so that south-west Norfolk,
north Cambridgeshire and west Suffolk were in turmoil. The rioters
showed a selective hostility to the millers and bakers who supplied
bread and flour at high prices, to the farmers who paid low wages
and provided inadequate employment, and to the parish overseers and
magistrates who controlled the poor relief which was a necessary
supplement to the labourers' low earnings. Their characteristic
demands were for cheap bread, subsidized from the poor rates, and
for higher wages. In the major disturbances of 1816 the Suffolk
and Norfolk rioters wanted cheap bread. They demanded work, wages
at 2s a day and subsidized flour. They were promised the wage they
had asked for, and also flour at 2s 6d a stone, which was subsidized
by money from the poor rates.(5) The labourer's claims revealed
his state of social dependency in asking for a continued supplementation of wages by poor relief rather than a sufficiently high wage to
secure his economic independence. However, there was a new threatening tone and a bitterness in these riots which suggested the labourers' growing estrangement from a traditional society. 'Bread or
Blood!' the rioters cried in 1816, and this was to become the rally-
ing cry for the East Anglian poor in the riots of 1830 and 1835-7.
A deeply felt grievance in 1830, and virtually the only cause of
dissatisfaction in 1835-7, was the administration of the Poor Law.

Three months after the rural labourers' revolt had begun in the
south of England, the Swing riots began in Norfolk during November
1830. Whereas the bread riots of 1816 had been confined mainly to

the south-west of Norfolk and the machine-breaking in 1822 had
affected the south of the county, virtually the whole of Norfolk was
in turmoil in the winter of 1830-1. Made desperate by low wages and
lack of work, many more Norfolk labourers were drawn into the disturbances of 1830 than had been the case in 1816. Now, their demands
were more clearly economic in nature; they wanted higher wages and
more continuous employment. This contrasted with the demands of
1816, when the labourers had been indifferent as to whether their
increased income came from wages or from poor relief. The rioters'
growing independence from a paternalistic, local society is indicated by their growing hostility to the Poor Law. Their earlier
acceptance of poor relief as a safety net to be used in difficult
times had given way to resentment that poor relief had become a
permanent supplement to low wages. Obvious targets in their hostility to poor law administration in 1830 were the Norfolk workhouses, which appeared as symbols of this oppression of the poor.
At Attleborough rioters took food from the workhouse,
at Forncett they tried to pull the workhouse down, while rioters
had to be stopped by dragoons on their march to destroy the Smallburgh House of Industry.(6)

Social conservatism appears to have fought with a newly emergent desire for economic independence in the labourer's mind, while
there was a corresponding tension in the attitudes of local property-
owners, where growing sectional economic interests strained against
a tradition of social responsibility. Social paternalism produced
in the short term a remedial response to disturbances by the propertied classes in Norfolk. After the 1816 riots, flour subsidized
from the poor rates and higher wages were conceded, while the use of
threshing machines decreased after the disturbances in 1822 and
1830. The riots of 1830 produced higher wages and increased poor
law allowances and poor law employment schemes, which most frequently involved the use of a labour rate. In the long term, however, self-interest led to a hardening of attitude by gentry, clergy
and farmers, since these expensive concessions had not succeeded in
buying the labourer's loyalty. Political economy replaced moral
economy in the countryside. The New Poor Law was welcomed by the
owners and occupiers of land in the county precisely because Norfolk
had been the scene of so many disturbances that it was thought that
a harsher system of poor relief would discipline the labouring poor.
Norfolk gentlemen expected that the new system would provoke resistance from the poor, but were still prepared to impose it. They
asked the Secretary of State for Home Affairs if they could be
allowed to form a special constabulary force as a preventive measure
before the Poor Law Amendment Act of 1834 had been implemented in
the county.(7)

There are interesting similarities, as well as contrasts, between
the disturbances of the East Anglian labourers that were directed
against the new poor law unions in the 1830s, and the resistance by
the poor to the old poor law incorporations seventy years before. In
each period the poor objected to the infringement of their traditional rights and appealed for the restoration of social justice.
Protest against the New Poor Law in East Anglia began in Suffolk,
and the resistance by the Suffolk poor to the imposition of the New
Poor Law was às fierce as that encountered by the Poor Law Commission

anywhere in the south of England. It was concentrated in the Hoxne, Plomesgate, Cosford and Ipswich Unions in east Suffolk — the area that had been heavily incorporated under the Old Poor Law — and mainly took the form of assaults on relieving officers and a work-house master, and of threats to poor law guardians.(8)

In the Plomesgate Union the labourers found an articulate, middle-class champion in Mr W. Lewin, who drafted a petition against the New Poor Law for the labourers in the Wickham Market area to sign, before presentation to Parliament. The petition is imbued both with Cobbetite thinking on the permanent obligations that the pro-pertied owed to the poor, and with the sentiments of the unstamped press, which had a considerable circulation in East Anglia. The earliest draft of the petition spoke of the poor being 'half-famished and half-starved in the midst of plenty', of the New Poor Law 'grinding them down to the dust', and of the new union work-houses resembling 'prisons' which broke up the family unit. The final petition, which attracted many signatures, stated that the poor 'had an important right of fair work at fair wages — or a fair maintenance within a workhouse — or a generous and just allowance without — until they could find employment — but this miscalled "amended" poor law has deprived them of that right'.(9) It is significant that in the 1830s some East Anglian labourers included within their 'traditional' rights that of a 'fair main-tenance within a workhouse', which suggests that they had accepted the incorporated houses of industry, with their liberal and humane regime, as part of the status quo. What they now objected to were the changes in indoor relief which the New Poor Law had brought, rather than the actual introduction of indoor relief, as they had done in the eighteenth century. They were hostile to the recent introduction of a harsh and deterrent regime in the union workhouses of the New Poor Law. These attitudes were confined to east Suffolk, where the old poor law incorporations were to be found.

The explosive quality of the Suffolk poor law riots was not re-peated in Norfolk, where the new administration of relief was intro-duced more gradually between 1835 and 1837. In Norfolk, the disturb-ances were more widespread and covered not only the area of the earlier incorporations but the west of the county as well. The con-servatism of the Norfolk poor is clearly shown by the interesting difference in the form of the protest between areas in the east of the county, where there had been old poor law incorporations with indoor relief in houses of industry, and those areas in west Norfolk, which had no tradition of indoor relief. In the former the poor pro-tested not against indoor relief but against the harsher environment in which it was administered after 1834, whereas in the latter the poor objected to the replacement of outdoor allowances by indoor relief.

In May 1836 the incorporation of Loddon and Clavering, which had been established in 1764, was transformed into a new poor law union. Trouble had been expected from the paupers at the Heckingham House because they were notoriously turbulent and had even assaulted the first assistant poor law commissioner, Sir Edward Parry, on an earlier visit there. In this incorporated area of east Norfolk, the paupers had by the early 1830s been able to enjoy a comfortable and free life, which had included a lavish dietary and freedom to do

much as they pleased either inside or outside the house of industry.
It was feared that the paupers would resent the introduction of classification in the workhouse, and the break-up of family life that
this would entail, so police had been sent for from London to re-
inforce the authority of guardians and workhouse officials. But before the police arrived the workhouse was set on fire on 23 April
1836 and very substantial damage was done to the fabric of the
building. An unusually large reward of £500 was offered by the
guardians, the Norwich Union Fire Office and the Government for the
apprehension of the incendiarist. This was thought to be James
Barrett, who had been an inmate of the workhouse. He was described
as 'Brickmaker and Woodman. Aged about 30 years — height about
five feet nine inches — whiskers to the cheek and inclined to be
sandy — dark eyes — dark brown hair — had on a dark velveteen
jacket like a gamekeeper's — a small rush flail basket over his
shoulder on a stick. Trowsers lightish — hat black — stockings
grey worsted.' This excellent description led to the apprehension
of Barrett, who was sent for trial at the assizes, where the bill
against him was ignored, presumably because of inadequate evidence.
Nearly a year later on 22 March 1837 married men in the Rollesby
house of industry, in the neighbouring Flegg Incorporation, destroyed half the house of industry when they set the building on fire
to prevent being separated from their wives under the new poor law
classification scheme which was to be implemented on that day. Local
magistrates were either unable or unwilling to fix the crime on any
individuals.(10)

    In other areas of Norfolk where outdoor relief had been the norm,
and relief of the able-bodied poor inside a workhouse was virtually
unknown, the poor did not protest about changes in the form of indoor relief. Rather, they were incensed at the introduction of workhouse relief at all. John Collison, who lived in Grimston in west
Norfolk, objected to being given relief 'in a house but little better
than a comon prison'. As one of the respectable poor he was angry
at being brought by the 1834 act on a level 'with lawless, drinking
and worthless part of the comunity [sic]'. He felt that his 'birth-
right' had been stolen from him, and protested about the changes
brought about the New Poor Law in a letter to his M.P., Sir William
Folkes, the member for west Norfolk.(11) Elsewhere, the less liter-
ate showed their hostility to the new law by direct action. The
Norfolk boards of guardians found that they had to appoint watchmen
to guard the fabric of the workhouses as they were being built.
Otherwise the poor demolished them stealthily by night as fast as
they were built up during the day. At the Depwade Union Workhouse
at Pulham St Mary these guerilla attacks by the labouring poor became so effective that strong defensive action had to be taken.
Round the workhouse high surrounding walls with corner sentry posts
were built which had loopholes in them so that armed watchmen could
be deployed (see Figure 4)..   These were extreme but necessary
precautions for the guardians to take, since they were aware of the
disturbed history of this area in south Norfolk where there had
been incendiarism in 1816, machine-breaking in 1822 and wage and
tithe riots in 1830. Also, only five miles to the north at Forncett,
the poor had attempted to pull down the workhouse during the riots
of 1830.

'Can a man live on half a stone and 15 pence? We are bound in
a bond of blood and blood will be spilt before this is finished.'
This cry, from a rioter at Great Bircham in the Docking Union, in
the north-west of the county, is a good indication of the white-hot
anger of the labourers when changes brought about by the 1834 act
first affected their lives. This occurred when a money allowance
was replaced by flour or bread in their outdoor relief. Accounts
of these riots differ in detail, and the following description is
taken from the more reliable observers. The Great Bircham riot
occurred at the end of June 1835 when the parish overseers, Mr
Kitton and Mr Hegbin, paid the parish men working on the roads an
allowance that was half in money and half in kind (i.e. in flour or
bread). There was already smouldering hostility in the village
because the local farmers, Kitton and Hegbin among them, had offered only ls 3d as the standard payment for mowing an acre of hay.
The resident labourers had struck work as a result and the farmers
had replaced them with blackleg labour from neighbouring villages.
The labourers employed by Mr Denny on his farm were forcibly removed
from the fields by irate groups of strikers. The scene had been well
primed for a confrontation between the labourers on the one hand and
on the other the farmers in their dual capacity as employers and poor
law administrators. During Monday, 29 June, several hundred poor
people from neighbouring villages assembled in Great Bircham and as
the day wore on angry groups stormed the farm houses of the two
parish overseers, Mr Kitton and Mr Hegbin, as well as that of another
unpopular farmer, Mr Howlett. When darkness came the occupants fled
into their fields and cowered there all night while the rioters
turned cattle into the standing corn, destroyed furniture and tried
unsuccessfully to set buildings on fire. The village quietened down
eventually although a small disturbance developed over the arrest of
the rioters. But order was gradually restored by a small detachment
of coastguards who arrived the following day, and by a troop of dragoons from Norwich who had appeared by Wednesday, 1 July. However,
the antagonism of the poor to the New Poor Law and to those who administered it had been made plain. Local property-owners were extremely reluctant to enrol in a special constabulary force so that
the Docking Union Board of Guardians had to resort to appointing
two police officers from the Metropolitan Force. Local farmer-
guardians were sufficiently intimidated by the incipient unrest that
an unusual number resigned during their year of office in this first
turbulent year of the Docking Union's existence. Until the union
workhouse was built, and a means of disciplining the labourer existed, local farmers were careful not to provoke the poor into
direct action by lowering their wages, which they wished to do because of the declining price of wheat. The local property-owners'
concern about the turbulent state of the poor was indicated by the
unusually large number of local magistrates who attended at the
Walsingham Sessions when the Bircham rioters were tried. By the
standards of the day the sentences were light, even conciliatory;
ten men were sentenced to imprisonment with hard labour for periods
that ranged from one month to two years.(12)
'I am quite convinced that the present occasion is the turning
point of all our operations in this county,' wrote the Assistant
Poor Law Commissioner Sir Edward Parry in an anxious frame of mind

after the Bircham riot. Was this first clap of tunder the local
prelude to a county-wide storm? In fact, the next riot did not
erupt for another six months, although when it did occur it broke
out in the adjacent area of the Freebridge Lynn Union. On 5 February 1836 a crowd from Little Massingham assembled at Grimston
where they stopped the meeting of the local board of guardians.
They threatened that if the policy of relieving the poor with bread
or flour was to be continued there would be violence at the next
board. Firm action quelled the disturbance and the crowd dispersed after the three popular leaders were arrested. John Neave,
William Barnes and John Langley were tried and sentenced for periods of up to six months' imprisonment. Local ratepayers and landowners continued to be sufficiently apprehensive about potential
unrest that they employed two policeman from the metropolitan force
to deter trouble-makers in the Freebridge Lynn Union.(13)

This policy was successful, and the focus of popular disturbance
now moved south-east to the Guiltcross Union, an area that had a
tradition of rioting and unrest. On 16 February 1836 a crowd of
several hundred people assembled at Kenninghall where the board
of guardians was meeting. 'We came here for bread, and bread or
blood we will have', they cried. Five self-appointed leaders,
William Carman, William Mayor, John Rush, William Fortis and
Ephraim Doe, forced themselves into the meeting to present their
point of view to the guardians. They found themselves apprehended
and the door barricaded against reinforcements. Others led by
Robert Cook made determined assaults on the door and windows with
sticks and stones before the Rev. John Surtees arrived and read the
Riot Act. The crowd dispersed and the six leaders were arrested,
committed for trial and eventually sentenced to periods of imprisonment varying from three to twelve months. At their trial it
was revealed that not all were paupers and that one man, John Rush,
was a man of excellent character who had worked for one employer for
25 years. The previous good character of several of the Bircham
rioters had also been remarked upon at their trial.(14) This suggests that popular resistance to the New Poor Law included members
of the respectable poor whose economic plight had made them desperate about the New Poor Law's effect on their deteriorating
standard of living. However, the social composition of the crowds
who protested against the 1834 act cannot be determined with any
accuracy; it is not even clear whether women participated as they
had certainly done in the eighteenth-century Suffolk riots, and in
the Norfolk disturbances in 1816, 1822 and 1830.

Before the poor law disturbances of 1835-7, Norfolk disturbances
had been remarkably free from personal violence, and the labouring
poor had expressed their feelings in attacks on property rather
than people. But the impotent hatred that the labourer felt for
the New Poor Law led to vicious attacks not only on the property,
but also the persons, of those whose job it was to administer the
new system of relief. At first it was the parish overseers whose
lives were tormented by the glowering antagonism of the poor. The
attacks on the Bircham overseers were the most notorious examples
of this, but they were not isolated incidents. In the parish of
Great Massingham, in the Freebridge Lynn Union, one of the parish
overseers found that his pony had had its throat cut while the other

overseer found two of his horses had been stabbed. The appointment
of union relieving officers to administer relief made them the new
target for the poor's hostility. The first expression of this was
in October 1835 when a Swaffham Union relieving officer was stabbed
by Henry Riches, a horse-dealer by trade. Later, on 24 May 1836,
Timothy Murrell, an Erpingham Union relieving officer, was assaulted
after attending a board of guardians meeting at Cromer. He was
accused of trying to starve the poor and was then set upon by three
men. They were sent for trial and sentenced to three months' imprisonment for common assault. A crescendo of violence was reached
on 10 June 1836 when John Cunningham, a relieving officer in the
Henstead Union, was left for dead having had his throat cut and
his head battered in a cowardly attack in a country lane. His
assailant was William Buck, who took his revenge, for having been
refused relief earlier in the day, by this assault and by robbing
Cunningham of £13. Cunningham lived and supplied evidence against
his attacker. In spite of a reward of £100 offered by the Government and the Henstead Union, Buck was not brought to justice. Everywhere in the Norfolk countryside guerilla warfare was waged against
the New Poor Law by poor people who plundered the bread and flour
from the carts of the relieving officers.(15)

   Between July 1835 and March 1837 there were major popular protests
against the New Poor Law in eight Norfolk unions and incorporations
and minor unrest in most of the remainder. The intrinsic lack of
organization and leadership among the Norfolk labourers meant that
these scattered, spontaneous disturbances were ineffectual. The
policy of the assistant poor law commissioners in implementing the
revised relief regulations in a piecemeal fashion, union by union,
and within each union, parish by parish, was successful in preventing a unified resistance from arising among the labouring poor. The
Norfolk gentry, clergy and farmers who were members of boards of
guardians were experienced in dealing with riots after the upheavals
of 1816, 1822 and 1830. They kept a cool head and successfully
brought to trial many of those who violently opposed the social
injustices of the New Poor Law. In deciding on the punishment of
the opponents of the new relief system, the Norfolk magistracy (who
it must be remembered were also ex officio poor law guardians) seemed
to be concerned not to create popular heroes by harsh sentencing; and
the punishments were, by the standards of the day, quite light. Un-
deterred by popular opposition, Norfolk boards of guardians proceeded
steadily with the erection of workhouses and the revision of relief
lists.

   Direct action against workhouse buildings or poor law administrators was only the most obvious indication of the fear and hostility
with which the Norfolk poor regarded the 1834 act and the changes
in relief practices that it had brought about. During 1835-8 the
Norfolk countryside was alive with suspicion and rumour about im-
pending changes in poor relief. Stories about the deaths of paupers
through ill-treatment echoed the earlier murder allegations that had
circulated when the Old Poor Law incorporations had been set up. A
child was allegedly starved to death in the Gressenhall workhouse in
the Mitford and Launditch Union during 1837, and in 1838 an outdoor
pauper in Welney, on the Norfolk—Cambridgeshire border, was supposed to have met with the same fate. Neither story had any factual

foundation. Earlier, in the Wayland Union the outdoor paupers went about in mortal terror that they were to be branded with a P for Pauper, and that their scanty possessions were to be confiscated, after threatening statements by the union's relieving officer in 1835. In the Docking Union, where there had been the most serious rioting against the New Poor Law, 800 poor people preferred to migrate or emigrate between 1835 and 1837 rather than endure the new relief policies. The able-bodied poor found the workhouse especially repugnant, and despite low wages or under-employment few would accept indoor relief during the late 1830s or early 1840. Labourers in Norfolk in 1844 were said to prefer to live off near-starvation wages rather than enter the workhouse.(16)

II   'FOR THE LABOURER IS WORTHY OF HIS HIRE'

'Who can we go to but to the gentlemen of the county if our farmers refuse us relief? We cannot starve.'(17) This heartfelt cry from Norfolk labourers at the period of transition from Old to New Poor Law reflected their desperation when the Poor Law Amendment Act of 1834 had cut their judicial life-line to the gentry. No longer could they appeal against the judgements of poor law officials to the magistrates. Although the justices could sit as ex officio members of the new rural boards of guardians, their more liberal viewpoint was increasingly swamped by the miserly attitudes and policies of the elected farmer-guardians. This would not have aroused such bitterness among the rural labourers were it not that they felt themselves to be held mercilessly in a pincer grip; the farmers, as employers, reduced the real value of their wages, but when they sought poor relief to alleviate their condition they found that the poor law guardians who administered a harsh system of relief were drawn from this same body of penny-pinching farmers. The New Poor Law seemed to the poor to have placed the coping stone on the economic ascendancy of the farmer, and to have torn away the crumbling facade of patronage and protection traditionally given by the propertied classes to the poor.   A petition from Suffolk agricultural labourers pinpointed the feelings of the East Anglian poor at this time. It said that the labourers had always thought that their social superiors considered it 'one of their first duties to guard and protect the rights and interests of the poor', but that they now considered that their rights were taken from them and their interests 'woefully neglected'.(18)
    East Anglia had been an exceptionally disturbed part of the country in the early nineteenth century when violence had become endemic. The Norfolk countryside became a battleground of conflicting interests in which the abdication from social responsibility of the propertied was matched by the alienation from duty and loyalty of the poor. Stealthy retaliation against agricultural property was all too easy despite the introduction, first, of rural watchmen and, later of a rural police force. In 1839 William Watts was transported for life for killing cattle at Buxton in north-east Norfolk. His defence in court was that having to pay poor rates and other taxes had led his family to starvation. Not every case of cattle-maiming or arson can be construed as social protest, and some was a matter of the paying off of individual grievances. But covert protest in the

form of incendiarism could follow open rioting, as in 1830-1, and
be directed to secure the same social ends. Mr William Green, a
farmer and poor law administrator of Walpole St Peter in west Norfolk, received a letter in 1831 which threatened him for his harsh
administration of poor relief: 'You may thank yourself for the
attending at the committee house so often and speaking against the
poor that you are trettened to be burned.' The fires of East Anglia
during 1843-4 lit up the condition of the rural labourer there and
warmed public opinion on his behalf. A special correspondent of
'The Times', John Campbell Foster, wrote a series of articles in
the spring and summer of 1844 in which he analysed the causes of
this widespread incendiarism. He attributed the fires to the mal-
administration of the New Poor Law in the use of the ticket system,
a form of labour allocation, which has been discussed in Chapter 6
above. Incendiarism was virulent in the areas of east Norfolk that
operated the ticket system and many ricks were fired which belonged
to farmers who also acted as poor law guardians. The New Poor Law
was a major target for the discontented labourer. The union workhouses symbolized his deteriorating condition and in the Depwade
and Aylsham Unions there were attempts to set the workhouses on
fire at this time.(19)

Riot, arson and cattle-maiming meant that an undeclared civil
war was waged in rural Norfolk for much of the nineteenth century.
The sullen resentment of the labourer erupted into direct action
if his already depressed condition suffered further deterioration.
The enclosure of land aroused an acute feeling of dispossession in
the labourer which was similar to that provoked by the reform of
poor relief. Much land was enclosed late in Norfolk; between 1801
and 1870 17 per cent of its acreage was affected in this way. The
land concerned was often commons and wastes which had given the
poor man a valuable supplement to his income in the way of grazing
rights and fuel collection.(20) The extent of this enclosure suggests that property-owners' attitude to their land was changing, and
that an increasing stress was being placed on its economic value for
the private individual rather than on its social value to the community. This view of the landed estate as a source of profit was
associated with an increase in absenteeism among the landed gentry
in Norfolk. For the poor this was one more indication of an abdi-
cation from social responsibility by the propertied classes.

Enclosure was particularly rapid at the beginning of the century
and elicited a notable protest from the poor of Ashill in central
Norfolk in 1816 to the gentlemen of the parish. They were accused
of putting the poor under a hard yoke by robbing them of their
commons.(21) Enclosure was a continual reminder to the labourers
that they were being disinherited from their traditional rights.
By 1870 the enclosure of land had provoked an organized resistance
by the labourers in several parts of Norfolk. The Defence of the
Poor Association, which was formed in Fakenham in north-west Norfolk,
petitioned Parliament against the local enclosure of commons. Sensitivity about their rights over common land helped to radicalize
the Norfolk labourer, and the Association for the Defence of the
Poor evolved into the first trade union for agricultural labourers
in the county, Flaxman's short-lived Eastern Counties Union.(22)
The Norfolk farm labourer was helped in these trade union acti-

vities by artisans, tradesmen and, later, by schoolteachers.

A central preoccupation of the radical labourer in Norfolk was
the necessity of being paid a living wage. This demand had begun
in the late eighteenth century when poor relief first began to be
used as a more permanent supplement to the farm labourers' wages:(23)

> That — *The labourer is worthy of his hire,* and that the mode
> of lessening his distresses, as hath lately been the fashion,
> by selling him flour under the market price, and thereby ren-
> dering him an object of the parish rate, is not only an indecent
> insult on his lowly and humble situation (in itself sufficiently
> mortifying from his degrading dependence on the caprice of his
> employer) but a fallacious mode of relief, and every way inade-
> quate to a radical redress of the manifold distresses of his
> calamitous state.

This statement by the labourers of Heacham, Snettisham and Sedgeford
in north-west Norfolk in 1795 had been intended as a curtain-raiser
for a national petition of agricultural labourers to Parliament, but
this did not take place because of the enactment of the Treason and
Sedition Acts. However, sporadic action continued to take place in
Norfolk villages in which labourers attempted to achieve a subsistence wage. In 1800 the Feltwell labourers in south-west Norfolk
threatened a strike if their demands for higher wages were not met,
and five years later labourers in the south Norfolk town of Diss
refused to work for their existing low wages but were unsuccessful
in their attempt to increase them. In Marsham, in the north-east
of the county, labourers demanded more work and wages in 1833 and
again used the words from St Luke's Gospel, 'the labourer is worthy
of his hire', as their justification.(24)

The Norfolk countryside in the 1850s and 1860s was very discontented, and a social upheaval was imminent, according to George
Edwards, who was to become a leader in the National Agricultural
Labourers Union and later a Member of Parliament. His father,
Thomas Edwards, had been among the Marsham protesters and had been
victimized for his insubordination by local farmers who became
reluctant to give him work. George Edwards knew at first hand that
the farm labourer was not sharing in the increased prosperity of
Norfolk agriculture in the 1850s and 1860s. He commented that the
chasm between the farmer and labourer was unprecedentedly wide at
this time.(25) Farmers dominated rural boards of guardians in
Norfolk, and they controlled the labour market both through col-
lusion in fixing the rate of wages and through labour allocation
schemes. One form of allotting labour was the ticket system, which
gave the farmers a stranglehold over the local labour market through
their control of both wages and poor relief. The ticket system had
been operated for several decades in the Newmarket Union, which
straddled an area of east Cambridgeshire and west Suffolk, and it
was in this poor law union that the East Anglian lock-out began in
1872.(26) This conflict broadened into the first large-scale confrontation between farmers and labourers in the eastern counties.
It accelerated the unionization of the Norfolk agricultural labourer,
who for the first time was drawn into a national agitation. Earlier,
the protests of the Norfolk poor against the New Poor Law in the
1830s had been quite separate from the organized resistance of the
anti-poor law movement on the North of England, while chartism had

barely touched the lives of the rural labourer in Norfolk.
    Mark, farmers and squires, 'ere I finish;
    If you give but to labour its due,
    Your unions will greatly diminish
    For the old will give place to the new!
This popular labourers' song in the 1870s(27) expressed the heartfelt hope that agricultural trade unions would secure a living wage
which would make the relief of the poor law union a thing of the
past. By 1874 successful recruitment of farm labourers by the
Eastern Counties Union, the Lincolnshire Labour League and the
National Agricultural Labourers Union had resulted in Norfolk becoming the most heavily unionized county as far as union membership
was concerned. At last, 'collective bargaining by riot' had been
replaced by organized, non-violent methods to achieve economic objectives. The bargaining power of the unions was helped by the
tighter labour market in Norfolk by the 1870s and notable successes
were secured in raising wage rates, reducing hours and getting over-
time payments. The Norfolk labourer was cushioned for a long time
from the effect of the deepening agricultural depression in local
agriculture and his real income remained much more buoyant than
other groups who drew their income from the land.(28) Able-bodied
pauperism in Norfolk was therefore no longer a major matter of
concern by the last quarter of the nineteenth century. But the
relief of the labourer when age and infirmity had overtaken him
became a burning issue.
    That old people had to go on the parish was one of the commonest
complaints aired by agricultural labourers at trade union meetings.
Edwards said that the 'aged people have a great liking to remain in
their own village in which they have worked and lived, and brought
up their families ... when poor people are put in the workhouse
they are a great way from their friends.'(29) The shadow of the
workhouse still threatened the lives of old people who had to seek
poor relief when their physical strength failed them and their
earning capacity dwindled. Even at the end of the nineteenth century there was an enduring distrust of the workhouse by the Norfolk
poor.(30) It was not just that relief inside the workhouse suggested that you were not one of the respectable poor and so conferred a social stigma, but that in the Norfolk countryside the
workhouse was still to some extent regarded as a prison, as it had
been in the 1830s or, indeed, the 1770s. Outdoor relief to old
people was given on a parsimonious scale, however, and only after
rigorous inquiry as to whether their children could afford to support them. Norfolk farm labourers with elderly parents fiercely
resented this policy. They asked how a man with a large family and
a wage of 13s per week could possibly support his parents? They
argued that the same class who paid low farm wages were by their
actions as miserly poor law guardians seeking to place additional
financial burdens on the labourer. Class antagonisms in the countryside made it seem that deliberate injustices were being done when a
small outdoor allowance was given or an old labourer was sent into
the workhouse. The board rooms of the Norfolk workhouses became
the focus of the class struggle between farmers and labourers. This
struggle was bitter and protracted, since in the 1870s the Norfolk
farmers had denied the right of the labourer to organize himself,

20   Freebridge Lynn Union Workhouse, c. 1930

and it was not until 1915 that the farmers conceded the right of
collective bargaining to the Norfolk labourer.(31)   But the farmer-
guardians of Norfolk did not always have things their own way. Two
incidents from the later history of Norfolk workhouses may illustrate this.

Indoor paupers inside the workhouse were showing an independent
attitude by the 1870s.   In the Wicklewood House, in the Forehoe
Incorporation, William Secker succeeded in having the workhouse
master reprimanded by the board of guardians.   He achieved this by
exercising every pauper's right to have his food weighed to see
whether it corresponded with the official workhouse dietary, and on
this occasion his ration was two and a half ounces of potatoes short.
Outside the workhouse the labourers in this incorporation showed
their spirit and their contempt for the Poor Law by exploiting the
routine of the workhouse in order to get a free meal.   They knew
that Saturday was a day on which a meat dinner was served and guessed
that officials would be too busy serving it to have the time to go
through the time-consuming procedures of receiving them into the
workhouse.   So they presented themselves at the workhouse at Saturday dinner time in the guise of destitute persons, filled their
bellies with a substantial hot meal, discharged themselves and
rapidly returned home.(32)   They had a good tale to tell, and one
that was enhanced by its rarity value.   It was not often that the
able-bodied Norfolk labourer won a victory over the administrators
of poor relief.

EPILOGUE

The complex realities of relief administration in nineteenth-century
Norfolk do not confirm the simple stereotypes of poor law mythology,
since in this area the workhouse was compatible with welfare, and the
guardians were more than just grinders of the poor. Documentary
evidence indicates that Norfolk paupers might benefit from a social
administration that conferred a better standard of living than that
of the independent labourer. Poor law archaeology suggests that the
popular conception of a workhouse as a barbarous, barrack-like
institution bore small resemblance to the more civilized arrangements
of the East Anglian pauper palaces.

Distinctive ideals of social welfare, which were encapsulated
within the pauper palace tradition, had their foundations in the
prosperity of eighteenth-century Norfolk. In the nineteenth century
the local economy faltered under periodic agrarian depression and
the decline of the Norwich textiles industry. Readjustments in
social policy followed in order to accommodate the resultant surplus
labour problem. Although a minority of paupers inside the workhouse
continued to benefit from customary generosity in indoor relief, the
majority of paupers found that the necessity for financial stringency
had curtailed their outdoor allowances. Social policy was influenced
by sectional economic interests since local farmers administered poor
relief to further their own ends as employers. Regarded from this
perspective, it might be thought that the farmers played the role of
villains in the local poor law drama. An alternative interpretation
might see them as heroes, since they were the actual ratepayers who
handed over the money for the poor rates that financed relief. But
this alternative view would fail to take account of the underlying
economic relationship between the farmer and his landlord in which
changes in the level of poor rates paid by the farmer would eventually be reflected in the rent exacted by the landowner. In reality,
the tenant farmer and the landowner, as well as the pauper, were the
victims of an unreformed system of poor law finance, which continued
to tax local poverty rather than national prosperity. Standards in
social welfare were circumscribed by the economic resources that were
available to sustain them. While the system of poor relief rested on
a local financial basis, a national reform of the poor law stood
little chance of success. Central initiatives in social policy

tended to founder on local economic interests.

The impact of the national reform of the Poor Law after 1834 was conditioned not only by the economic circumstances of Norfolk and by the existence of an established regional pattern of relief, but also by the evolving relationship of local and central administrators. At first, the newly created central administration had been responsive to the ideas of its regional inspectors and ready to promote at the national level the practices of progressive localities. In this same honeymoon period Norfolk guardians looked favourably on the centrally determined policies of the New Poor Law in the hope that they might succeed where the local remedies of the Old Poor Law had failed. By the 1840s local administrators had become disillusioned with London's panaceas while the central administration was becoming sluggish at learning from local experiment. The unpopularity and political weakness of the Poor Law Commission, and the bureaucratization of the Poor Law Board, resulted in a blanket condemnation of local innovation as harmful abuse. In mid-century the central administration attempted to stultify progressive developments made by Norfolk administrators (as in the Docking rating reform or the Norwich children's homes), and tried unsuccessfully to impose a uniform mediocrity in poor law practice. Even the advent of the more vigorous Local Government Board after 1871 failed to dent substantially the well entrenched relief system of Norfolk, and considerable deviations from national policy continued. The central bureaucracy tolerated this situation, where local relief practice remained stubbornly independent of central theory, because of the geographical remoteness and political insignificance of Norfolk and its surrounding region. Its lack of status in the eyes of central government was indicated by the habit of promoting a successful poor law inspector from the eastern region to the more strategic metropolitan area (as in the case of Kay-Shuttleworth), or of exiling to the eastern counties a troublesome London inspector (as in the case of Farnall).

The ineffectuality of central bureaucracy resulted in considerable autonomy for Norfolk administrators so that the local Poor Law was shaped to an unusual degree by the context in which it operated. Poor relief in the county was a sensitive indicator of changing social relationships and reflected the way in which older ideas about the paternalistic protection that was owed to the labourer retreated before a newer desire to enforce social discipline on him. Selective adoption of measures within the New Poor Law suggested the extent to which social welfare was being subordinated to social control. Pauper education in the mid-nineteenth century provided the clearest illustration of the underlying assumption that the Poor Law could be made to convert the feckless poor into hardworking, useful subordinates. A spectrum of local relief policies reflected moral values in Norfolk society. They ranged from generosity to the impotent poor inside the pauper palaces, to harsh deterrence in the relief offered to the unmarried mother or the vagrant, and a refusal of relief to the poacher or drunkard. The changing structure of Norfolk society meant that traditional ideas of social responsibility by the propertied towards the poor gave way to sectional economic interests in the administration of poor relief. The growing power of the farmers in local society extended

their influence over the Poor Law and resulted in a confusion of the
privately financed farm labour bill with the publicly funded Poor
Law. This involved a widespread use of outdoor allowances to relieve the able-bodied labourer because of the farmers' reluctance
to pay a subsistence wage to him. It was on the harshness of this
refusal to give a living wage, rather than on the relief system
itself, that the Norfolk labourer focused most of his hostility.

High levels of pauperism in Norfolk society during the nineteenth
century suggest the exceptional importance of the Poor Law for the
county's inhabitants. The lives of individuals intersected with the
administrative processes of the Poor Law. The use of poor law records strips paupers of their usual anonymity within social history,
and an emotive but blind sympathy is revealed as an inadequate historical reaction to their condition. While the case studies cited
in this volume reveal the significance that the Poor Law could have
in human lives, they also expose the complexity of the pauper's
situation in relation to society. In responding to the complicated
requirements of Norfolk pauperism, poor law administrators in the
county showed considerable versatility. But limitations in financial resources, in administrative processes and in ideology restricted the liberality of social policy.   For the outdoor poor, relief
in the freedom of their own homes was often associated with material
deprivation, while for the indoor poor, the psychological hardships
of institutional life made dreary a material standard of living
that was superior to that of the independent labourer. Indeed, the
independent poor might be harmed by over-generosity in the administration of the Poor Law since even the labourer could find himself
contributing to the poor rates that financed poor relief. The
administrators of the poor law had always to balance their financial
accountability to the ratepayer against their social responsibility
to the poor. Although the compromises that resulted did lead to
some hardship, the standard of relief administration in Norfolk was
generally humane, when judged by contemporary ideals of social
welfare.

This detailed analysis of the interaction between poor law administration and its socioeconomic context in one locality has revealed
a distinctive pattern. This pattern may not be representative of
the historical experience of other areas, since in nineteenth-century
Norfolk national poor law policies were modified to an unusual extent, both because of very high levels of pauperism and because of
the continuation of extremely strong regional traditions on the relief of the poor. As a result there was a complex and changing relationship between theory and practice in the administration of the
Norfolk Poor Law. A substantial difference existed in most years
between the theoretical framework of relief administration (as laid
down by national legislation or central regulation), and the actual
relief of poverty at the local level. In shaping local relief policies alterations in the economic dimensions of poverty and concomi-
tant changes in social attitudes were of more significance than was
national legislation. In the past these national reforms have appeared to historians to act as convenient signposts to the general
map of poor law studies. But their inadequacy as authoritative
guidelines is suggested by the results of recent research in several areas, which have revealed the existence of substantial regional

variations in relief administration. It is clear that more
detailed local perspectives — such as this study of Norfolk —
could supply valuable additional information on poor law topo-
graphy. Ultimately this would enable an adequate guide to be
constructed for the historical landscape of the national poor law.
Image and reality would be more clearly separated in poor law
studies and Oliver Twist could then be assigned an honourable place
in classic mythology.

ABBREVIATIONS USED
IN THE NOTES

BM	British Museum
LGB	Local Government Board
NRO	Norfolk Record Office
PLB	Poor Law Board
PLC	Poor Law Commission
PL Cat	Poor Law Catalogue
PP	Parliamentary Papers
PRO	Public Record Office
RC	Royal Commission
SC	Select Committee

Unless otherwise stated in the references the place of publication is London.

NOTES

CHAPTER 1   PERSPECTIVES

1   'The Borough' XVIII, 109-17.
2   Crabbe was born in Aldeburgh in 1754 and lived in Suffolk until
    his departure for London in 1780. Residing in Aldeburgh in
    1765 it is likely that he heard much about the rioting by the
    Suffolk poor at the Melton, Bulcamp, and Nacton Houses of
    Industry some 15 miles away. From 1771 to 1775 he was an ap-
    prentice in Woodbridge and must have been familiar with the
    Melton House of Industry on the outskirts of the town.
3   'Second Report of PLC', PP 1836, XXIX, Pt 1, 154.
4   'The Borough', XVIII, 119-22, 201-4. R. Huchon, 'George Crabbe
    and his Times 1754-1832', trans. F. Clarke, 2nd edn (1968), 64.
5   J.P. Kay to PLC 8 November 1835, MH 32/48, PRO.
6   PLC to Marquess of Normanby 31 July 1840, HO 73/56, PRO.
7   N. McCord, The Implementation of the 1834 Poor Law Amendment
    Act on Tyneside, 'International Review of Social History', 14
    (1969), 93-5, 99-104. A. Brundage, The Landed Interest and the
    New Poor Law: a reappraisal of the revolution in government,
    'English Historical Review', LXXXVII (1972), 31-41.
8   J.D. Marshall, The Nottinghamshire Reformers and their Contri-
    bution to the New Poor Law, 'Economic History Review', 2nd
    ser. XIII (1961), 382-96.
9   P. Dunkley, The Landed Interest and the New Poor Law: a critical
    note, 'English Historical Review', LXXXVIII (1973), 838. A.
    Brundage, The Landed Interest, 33, 42-6. A. Brundage, The
    English Poor Law and the Cohesion of Agricultural Society,
    'Agricultural History', XLVIII (1974), 408.
10 U. Henriques, How Cruel was the Victorian Poor Law?, 'Historical
    Journal', XI (1968), 371. H.L. Beales, The New Poor Law, re-
    printed in E.M. Carus-Wilson (ed.), 'Essays in Economic History'
    (3 vols, 1962), III, 185.
11 A. Digby, The Labour Market and the Continuity of Social Policy
    after 1834: The Case of the Eastern Counties, 'Economic History
    Review', 2nd ser. XXVIII (1975), 69-83.
12 M. Blaug, The Myth of the Old Poor Law and the Making of the
    New, 'Journal of Economic History', XXIII (1963), 176-7; The

Poor Law Report Re-examined, 'Journal of Economic History', XXIV (1964), 229, 241-3.

13 D. McCloskey, New Perspectives on the Old Poor Law, 'Explorations in Economic History', X (1973), 419-35. D.A. Baugh, The Cost of Poor Relief in South-East England, 1790-1834, 'Economic History Review', 2nd ser. XXVIII (1975), 50-68.

14 B.A. Holderness, 'Open' and 'Close' Parishes in England in the Eighteenth and Nineteenth Centuries, 'Agricultural History Review', 20 (1972), 134-6. M.E. Rose, The New Poor Law in an Industrial Area in R.M. Hartwell (ed.), 'The Industrial Revolution' (Oxford, 1970), 136-9.

15 N. McCord, The Government of Tyneside 1800-50, 'Transactions of the Royal Historical Society', 5th ser. 20 (1970), 9, 13.

16 M.E. Rose, Poor Law Administration in the W. Riding of Yorkshire 1820-55 (University of Oxford, D. Phil. thesis, 1965), 370-3. E.C. Midwinter, 'Social Administration in Lancashire 1830-1860' (1969), 60-1.

17 P. Searby, The Relief of the Poor in Coventry, 1830-60, forthcoming article in 'Historical Journal'.

18 V.J. Walsh, Old and New Poor Laws in Shropshire, 'Midland History', II (1974), 235. A. Digby, The Rural Poor Law in D. Fraser (ed.), 'The New Poor Law in the Nineteenth Century' (1976), 157-60.

19 M.E. Rose, The Allowance System under the New Poor Law, 'Economic History Review', 2nd ser. XIX (1966), 611-13. P. Dunkley, The 'Hungry Forties' and the New Poor Law: A Case Study, 'Historical Journal', XVII (1974), 330, 334-40.

20 Norwich Minutes 1 September 1835, N/TC 3/1, NRO.

21 M.E. Rose, 'The Relief of Poverty 1834-1914', Economic History Society publication (1972), 15-16.

22 N.C. Edsall, 'The Anti-Poor Law Movement 1833-44' (Manchester, 1971). M.E. Rose, The Anti-Poor Law Agitation in J.T. Ward (ed.), 'Popular Movements c. 1830-50' (1970).

23 P. Dunkley, The 'Hungry Forties', 342-6. D. Roberts, How Cruel was the Victorian Poor Law?, 'Historical Journal', IV (1963), 97-107.

CHAPTER 2   ECONOMIC AND SOCIAL LIFE IN NORFOLK

1 A. Young, 'General View of the Agriculture of the County of Norfolk', reprint of 1804 edn (Newton Abbot, 1969), 2-14. W. Marshall, 'The Rural Economy of Norfolk', 2nd edn (2 vols, 1795), II, 276-83. R.N. Bacon, 'The Report on the Agriculture of Norfolk' (1844), 13-19. C.S. Read, Recent Improvements in Norfolk Farming, 'Journal of the Royal Agricultural Society', XIX (1858), 265-73.

2 A. Cossons, The Turnpike Roads of Norfolk, 'Norfolk Archaeology', XXX (1951), 190-2, 208. C.J. Allen, 'The Great Eastern Railway', 4th edn (1967).

3 N. Kent, 'General View of the Agriculture of the County of Norfolk', see p. 377, reprint of 1845 edn (Newton Abbot, 1969), 520-3, 682-3, 734, 737.

4 One of 'the Squad', 'The Plot Counterplootted etc.' (Lynn,

1839). D. Fraser, The Poor Law as a Political Institution in
D. Fraser (ed.), 'The New Poor Law', 122-6. G. Clive to PLC
27 April 1839, N. Palmer to PLC 20 May 1839, MH 12/8630, PRO.

5   G. Ewart Evans, 'The Days That We Have Seen' (1975), Chapter 9
passim. W. White, 'Directory', 250-2.

6   P. Mathias, 'The Brewing Industry in England 1700-1830'
(Cambridge, 1959), 287-8, 293, 296-7. W.H. Bidwell, 'Annals
of an East Anglian Bank' (Norwich, 1900), 11, 287.

7   J.H. Clapham, The Transference of the Worsted Industry from
Norfolk to the West Riding, 'Economic Journal', XX (1910),
197-210. J.K. Edwards, The Decline of the Norwich Textiles
Industry, 'Yorkshire Bulletin of Economic and Social Research',
XVI (1964), 39-41.

8   H. Martineau, 'Autobiography' (3 vols, 1877) I, 127-9, 141-2,
184-5, 218-19. Court Book of Norwich Guardians (1828-33),
Case 20 shelf e, NRO.

9   W.L. Sparkes, 'The Story of Shoemaking in Norwich' (North-
ampton, 1949). C.B. Hawkins, 'Norwich. A Social Study' (1910),
17-18, 44, 65.

10 A.L. Bowley, Rural Population in England and Wales. A Study
of the Changes of Density, Occupations, and Ages, 'Journal of
the Royal Statistical Society', LXXVII (1914), 605. J. Saville,
'Rural Depopulation in England and Wales 1851-1951' (1957),
48-51, 54-5. D. Friedlander and R.J. Roshier, A Study of
Internal Migration in England and Wales, Part 1: Geographical
Patterns of Internal Migration 1851-1951, 'Population Studies',
XIX (1966), 253-4, 265. 'R.C. on Agriculture', PP 1895, XVII,
363. G.E. Evans, 'Where Beards Wag All' (1970), 241-5, 251-7.

11 For supporting evidence see A. Digby, The Operation of the Poor
Law in the Social and Economic Life of Nineteenth-Century
Norfolk (University of East Anglia PhD thesis, 1972), 224-30,
250-60, 349.

12 E. Chadwick, 'Report of an Inquiry into the Sanitary Condition
of the Labouring Population of England' (2 vols, 1842), II,
135-9. 'Report on the Employment of Children, Young Persons,
and Women in Agriculture', PP 1867-8, XVII, 95-9.

13 W. Marshall, 'Rural Economy', II, 177-8.

14 For a discussion on the complexity of establishing wage rates
and for figures on Norfolk wages see A. Digby, The Operation of
the Poor Law, 132-6, 148-57, 334-44.

15 'Sixth Report of the Medical Officer of the Privy Council',
PP 1864, XXVIII, 264, 298-301, 316-17. Chadwick, 'Sanitary
Condition', 241.

16 Return from Flegg relieving officer to Sir J. Walsham, BM Add.
MS 40587 fo. 193.

17 P.H.J.H. Gosden, 'The Friendly Societies in England 1815-75'
(Manchester, 1961), 22, 31, 42, 53, 200-3. P.H.J.H. Gosden,
'Self Help. Voluntary Associations in the 19th Century' (1973),
12-13, 46-7, 69-71, 112, 187, 246. L.M. Springall, The Norfolk
Agricultural Labourer 1834-84 (University of London, PhD thesis,
1935), 186. Hawkins, 'Norwich', 277-8. 'Abstract of Answers
and Returns on the Expense and Maintenance of the Poor', PP
1803-4, XIII, 715. 'Abridgement of Abstracts and Returns Relative to the Expense and Maintenance of the Poor, 1813, 1814,
1815', PP 1818, IX, 302.

18 Flegg Minutes 3 October 1860, PL Cat. NRO. 'Sixteenth Report
    of LGB', PP 1887, XXXVI, 24, 233-4.
19 'General Digest of Endowed Charities', PP 1867-8, LII, Pt II,
    34, 110-27, 152-5.
20 'R.C. on Poor Law. Report on Endowed and Voluntary Charities',
    PP 1909, XLII, 891-3.
21 B. Almack, The Agriculture of Norfolk, 'Journal of the Royal
    Agricultural Society', V (1845), 356. 'Norwich Mercury', 31
    October 1835.
22 D.C. Barnett, Allotments and the Problem of Rural Poverty 1780-
    1840 in E.L. Jones and G.E. Mingay (eds), 'Land, Labour and
    Population in the Industrial Revolution' (1967), 163, 172, 178.
    'S.C. on Inclosure Act', PP 1868-9, X, QQ. 1797-8.
23 'Census. Religious Worship', PP 1852-3, LXXXIX, ccxiv. O.
    Chadwick, 'Victorian Miniature' (1960), 19, 39.
24 For example, Walsingham Minutes 20 July 1836, PL Cat. NRO.
25 The Humbugg about Emigration or the Farmer's Lamentation in
    Norwich Election Squibs 1786-1857, Rye and Colman Library,
    Norwich. C.D. Brereton, 'The Subordinate Magistracy' (Norwich,
    1827); 'A Letter on the Proposed Innovation in the Rural
    Police' (Swaffham, 1830); 'A Refutation of the First Report of
    the Constabulary Force' (n.d.).
26 A. Jessopp, 'The Trials of a Country Parson' (1909), 52-3. L.M.
    Springall, 'Labouring Life in Norfolk Villages' (1936), 114-15.
27 O. Chadwick, 'Victorian Miniature', 16, 40-1, 54, 57-9, 62,
    71-4, 87-8.
28 F.M.L. Thompson, 'English Landed Society in the Nineteenth
    Century' (1963), 32, 113, 117. 'Return of Owners of Land',
    PP 1874, LXXII, Pt 1.
29 'The Agricultural State of the Kingdom. Replies to the Board
    of Agriculture' (1816), 185-227. 'S.C. on State of Agriculture',
    PP 1821, IX (evidence of R.C. Harvey and G.B. George); PP
    1833, V (evidence of R. Wright), PP 1836, VIII, Pt 2 (evidence
    of J. Fison); PP 1837, V (evidence of J.T. Carter). 'R.C. on
    Agriculture', PP 1882, XV (report by S.B.L. Druce); PP 1895,
    XVII (report by H. Rew). 'R.C. on Labour, The Agricultural
    Labourer', PP 1893-4, XXXV (report by A. Wilson Fox).

CHAPTER 3 LOCAL REFORM BEFORE 1834

 1 J. Beresford (ed.), 'The Diary of a Country Parson: The Rev.
    James Woodforde' (5 vols, Oxford, 1924), I, 305.
 2 'Abstract of Answers and Returns on the Expense and Maintenance
    of the Poor', PP 1803-4, XIII. These returns are imperfect
    and have been cross-checked with other contemporary evidence.
 3 V.J. Walsh, Old and New Poor Laws in Shropshire, 'Midland
    History', II (1974), 225-7. S. and B. Webb, 'English Poor Law
    History' (reprint, 1963), Part 1, 126-8. Bulwer Papers, MS
    11928, NRO. 'Journal of House of Commons', XXXIII (1770-2), 104,
    164-5. 'Norwich Mercury', 19 January, 2 March, 9 March 1771.
 4 T. Ruggles, 'The History of the Poor' (2 vols 1793-4), II, 286,
    288. A. Young, 'General View of the Agriculture of Suffolk'
    (1804), 272-3. F.M. Eden, 'The State of the Poor' (3 vols,

1797), II, 453-76, 678-92. E. and W. Flegg Minute Book
5 October 1776, C/GP7/1, NRO.

5   15 G.3 c.13. M.F. Lloyd Prichard, The Treatment of Poverty
in Norfolk 1700-1850 (University of Cambridge, PhD thesis, 1949),
70.

6   E. and W. Flegg Minute Book 1775-6.

7   Ibid., 22 June 1776.

8   Forehoe Treasurer's Account Books (2 vols) 1776-1836, Forehoe
Shareholders Dividends (2 vols) 1776-1835, Mitford and Launditch
Indentures for Loans 1776-96, PL Cat. NRO. Eden, 'State of the
Poor', II, 471.

9   Smallburgh Workhouse Plans, WD 117, NRO. Smallburgh House of
Industry Book 9 September 1793, MS 4497, NRO.

10 Ibid., 9 September 1793.

11 Ibid., 15 August 1793.

12 Parry to PLC 12 October 1835 MH 12/8455, PRO, 10 June 1835
MH 32/60 PRO. Kay to PLC 20 March 1836, 3 September 1836
MH 32/48, 5 May 1836 MH 12/8578. Heckingham Committee Book
1769-70, Weekly Reports 1773-4, Weekly Disbursements 1773-4,
Admission Book 1772-86 PL Cat., NRO. 'Abstract of Returns on
Poor', PP 1776, 1st ser., IX, 252-5. 'Second Report PLC',
PP 1836, XXIX, Pt 1, 161.

13 Ibid., 57, 155. C. Dickens, 'Oliver Twist' (Penguin edn,
Harmondsworth, 1966), 93. Eden, 'The State of the Poor', II,
473.

14 10 Ann c 15. 42 G. 3 c. 57. E. Rigby, 'Reports of the Special
Provision Committee' (1788), 39, 41. E. Rigby, 'Further Facts
Relating to the Care of the Poor' (Norwich, 1812), 18-31, 34-51.

15 'Norwich Mercury', 7 February 1829, 7 March 1829. 7 and 8
G.4. c.29. 1 and 2 W.4. c.li. Norwich Court Book 31
December 1831, 3 March 1832, NRO. J.S. Taylor, The Unreformed
Workhouse 1776-1834 in E.W. Martin (ed.), 'Comparative Devel-
opment in Social Welfare' (1972), 71-4.

16 22 G.3. c.83. 46 G.3. c.xliv. M.F. Lloyd Prichard, The
Treatment of Poverty in Norfolk, 129-30.

17 'Returns of Dates of Incorporation of all Gilbert Unions', PP
1844, XL. Orders on Poor Law Unions (4 vols), Norfolk CC catalogue, NRO.

18 James Gay to PLC 17 Septermber 1834, MH 12/8474.

19 M.F. Lloyd Prichard, The Treatment of Poverty, 110, 82-4.

20 Ibid., 155-6. 15 G.3. c.59. 41 G.3. c.lxiii. Eden, 'The State
of the Poor', II, 456. Loddon and Clavering Committee Book
18 October 1831, PL Cat., NRO.

21 'An Act to Repeal the Two Acts Relating to the Hundreds of Loes
and Wilford and to Disincorporate the Said Hundreds', SO/30/31.1:
(4), Suffolk Record Office (Ipswich branch). Eden, 'The State
of the Poor', II, 692. A. Young, 'General View of the Agriculture of Suffolk' (1804), 248.

22 5.G.4. c.i. 3 and 4 W.4. c.cvii. G.E. Francis, A Notice,
7 December 1830 in Miscellaneous Cuttings from Periodicals,
Newspapers etc. 1737-1890, Colman Collection, Norwich Central
Library. East and West Flegg Minutes 11 January 1831, C/GP
7/9, NRO. Loddon and Clavering Committee Book 24 February 1834,
PL Cat., NRO. Sir E. Parry to PLC 10 June 1835, MH 32/60.

23 'Poor Rate Returns' 1820-34. 'Rural Queries', PP XXX-XXXIV
    (E. Rudham and S. Walsham returns). 'Report of Select Vestry
    of Great Yarmouth' (Great Yarmouth, 1835). M.F. Lloyd Prichard,
    The Treatment of Poverty, 120. E.M. Hampson, 'The Treatment of
    Poverty in Cambridgeshire 1597-1834' (Cambridge, 1934), 254-5.
    'Report on the Administration of the Poor Laws', PP 1834,
    XXVIII, 600-1.
24 'Second Report of PLC', PP 1836, XXIX, Part I, 151.
25 S. and B. Webb, 'The Parish and the County' (1906), 30-1, 301,
    420, 544-7. S. and B. Webb, 'Poor Law History', Part 1, 129-33,
    147.
26 'Norwich Mercury', 29 October 1831.
27 'Census', PP 1834, XXXVI, 77-80. Shipdham Town Books 1829-35
    (4 vols); Weekly Allowance Books 1821-31 (2 vols), Temporary
    Relief Books 1830-6 (2 vols), Surveyors Account Book 1822-32;
    Names of Persons Employed by Overseers 1830-5 (2 vols), Money
    Lent to Poor 1830-6; temporary deposit, NRO. I am grateful to
    the Rev. H.G.B. Folland for arranging this, and other, deposits.
28 'Census', PP 1834, XXVI. G.B. Ballachey, 'A Letter on a Reduc-
    tion of Wages in the Parish of Edgefield' (Norwich, 1833).
    G. Ballachey to PLC 12 June 1835, Edgefield Return of Emigrants,
    29 February 1836, MH 12/8293.
29 S. and B. Webb, 'Poor Law History', Part 1, 148. S. and B.
    Webb, 'Statutory Authorities for Special Purposes' (1922), 109.
30 PLC to C. Mott, 12 December 1834, MH 32/56.
31 Mott to PLC, December 1834, MH 32/56. Parry to PLC, 25 April
    1835, 20 June 1835, MH 32/60.

CHAPTER 4   THE IMPACT OF NATIONAL REFORM AFTER 1834

1 J.P. Kay to PLC, 1 May 1836, MH 32/48, PRO.
2 A. Brundage, The Landed Interest, 'English Historical Review',
   LXXXVII (1972), 35, 41. A Brundage, The English Poor Law,
   'Agricultural History', XLVIII (1974), 406.
3 Parry to PLC, 16 May 1835, MH 12/8249, PRO.
4 Parry to PLC, 2 May 1835, MH 32/60.
5 Kay to PLC, 17 March 1836, MH 12/8185. Parry to PLC, 4 September 1835, MH 12/8429. Parry to Sir W.J.H.B. Folkes, 21
   October 1835, NRS 7958, NRO.
6 Parry to PLC, 3 August 1835, MH 32/60.
7 Kay to PLC, 17 March 1836, MH 12/8185.
8 Parry to PLC, 9 September 1835, MH 12/8208.
9 Kay to PLC 20 March, 22 March, 23 July, 29 July, 3 September
   1836, MH 32/48.
10 Orders of PLC for Norfolk Unions (4 vols), Norfolk CC Cat., NRO.
    Twisleton to PLC, 30 March 1840, MH 32/72.
11 Kay to PLC, 15 February 1837, MH 32/49. J. Walsham to PLB, 30
    May 1856, MH 32/83. Walsingham Minutes, 3 March 1869. PL Cat.,
    NRO.
12 Parry to PLC, 13 May, 4 September 1835; Parish Officers of All
    Saints in S. Lynn to PLC, 22 July 1835, MH 12/8429.   Kay to
    PLC, 23 August 1836, Clive to PLC, 15 December 1838, Petition
    of Yarmouth Ratepayers, 2 April 1839, MH 12/8630. Kay to PLC,

24 September, 13 October, 1836, MH 32/48. The silver badges
are displayed in the King's Lynn Museum.

13 M.E. Rose, Poor Law Administration in the W. Riding of Yorkshire, 1820-55 (University of Oxford D.Phil. thesis, 1965), 109,
116, 142. E.C. Midwinter, 'Social Administration in Lancashire,
1830-1860' (1969), 16-20, 28, 33-5.

14 Parry to PLC, 30 October 1835, MH 12/8502. Power to PLC 18
March 1836, MH 12/741.

15 N. Pevsner, 'North-West and South Norfolk' (Harmondsworth,
1962). N. Pevsner, 'North-East Norfolk and Norwich' (Harmondsworth, 1962). H. Colvin, 'Biographical Dictionary of English
Architects 1660-1840' (1934). Workhouse Plans consulted in the
Architect's Department, Norfolk County Hall, Norwich. I am
grateful for the assistance of Mr G.C. Haydon, Mr J.R. Leeks
and Mr D. Harding. Minutes of Norfolk Unions, 1835-9 in PL Cat.,
NRO. Field work on existing workhouse buildings. 'Report on
Provincial Workhouses by Dr. E. Smith', PP 1867-8, LX, 448.

16 Sir Charles Chad to PLC, 6 December 1836, Kay to PLC, 10 December 1836, MH 12/8596. Walsingham Minutes, 14 September, 19
October, 1 November 1836, PL Cat., NRO.

17 Aylsham Minutes, 3 December 1850, PL Cat., NRO.

18 Parry to PLC, 9 January 1836, MH 32/60.

19 H.J. Hillen, 'History of the Borough of King's Lynn' (2 vols,
Norwich, 1911), 594-5. 'Lynn Advertiser and West Norfolk
Herald', 26 August 1854. King's Lynn Minutes 20 August, 28
August 1854, PL Cat., NRO.

20 Flegg Minutes, 11 October 1836, PL Cat., NRO. '2nd Report of
PLC', PP 1836, XXIX, Pt 1, 569. '4th Report of PLC', PP
1837-8, XXVIII, 345-6.

21 '1st Report of PLC', PP 1835, XXXV, 170.

22 Expenses of Erecting Walsingham Union House, MS 20281, NRO.
Docking Union Ledger and Exchequer Loan Account; PL Cat., NRO.

23 Walsham to PLB 22 October 1860, MH 32/84.

24 Based on the correspondence of the inspectorate with the central
board in the MH 32 class at the Public Record Office and on the
inspectors' reports published in Parliamentary Papers.

25 Walsham to PLB 24 August 1866, MH 32/84.

26 A. Brundage, The Landed Interest, 28-30, 43-7. P. Dunkley, The
Landed Interest and the New Poor Law: a critical note, 'English
Historical Review', LXXXVIII (1973), 836-41. Norfolk figures
are based on analysis of attendances given in the Guardians
Minutes of Norfolk Unions, PL Cat., NRO.

27 St Faith's Minutes 30 October 1844, Elected Guardians of the
Erpingham Union 1836-1910, PL Cat., NRO. 'SC on Irremoveable
Poor', PP 1859 (2nd sess.), VII, 175.

28 Docking Minutes, 14 December 1836; Loddon and Clavering
Minutes, 26 December 1842; Erpingham Minutes, 14 March 1842,
PL Cat., NRO.

29 'Twelfth Report PLC', PP 1846, XIX, 120-1. 'Third Report PLB',
PP 1851, XXVI, 168-9.

30 Walsham to PLB, 22 October 1860, MH 32/84.

31 'Norfolk Chronicle', 13 November 1875. 'Norwich Mercury',
17 October 1883.

32 H. Preston-Thomas, 'The Work and Play of a Government Inspector'

(1909), 235. G. Edwards, 'From Crow-Scaring to Westminster.
An Autobiography' (1922), 68-74. 'Royal Commission on the Poor
Law. Evidence on Rural Centres', PP 1910, XLVII, Q. 73148.
33 'Evidence on Rural Centres', PP 1910, XLVII.
34 H. Rider Haggard, 'A Farmer's Year, Being His Commonplace Book
for 1898' (1899), 428-9. Loddon and Clavering Minutes
1884-6, PL Cat., NRO.

CHAPTER 5   POOR RATES AND SETTLEMENT

1 Detailed statistics of Norfolk poor rates and relief expenditures are given in A. Digby, The Operation of the Poor Law
(University of East Anglia, PhD thesis, 1972), 357-9.
2 'Abstracts of Returns on the Poor', PP 1803-4, XIII, 714-15.
'Poor Rate Returns', PP 1824, VI, 383; 1826-7, XX, 670; 1834,
XLIII, 404-5. 'R.C. on Local Taxation', PP 1901, Cd. 638,
XXIV, 424. M.E. Rose, The New Poor Law in an Industrial Area
in R.M. Hartwell (ed.), 'The Industrial Revolution' (Oxford,
1970), 137-9.
3 R.H. Howes to PLC, 18 April 1837, MH 12/8356, PRO. E. Cannan,
'The History of Local Rates in England', 2nd edn (1912), 80,
97, 100. 54 G.3. c.170. 'Rural Queries', PP 1834, XXXI, Q.21.
G.A. Body, The Administration of the Poor Laws in Dorset 1760-
1834 (University of Southampton PhD thesis, 1965), 111.
4 E. Chadwick, 'Report on Sanitary Condition', II, 143-5. Henstead
Minutes, 22 March 1837, PL Cat., NRO. Guiltcross Union to PLC,
2 March 1837, T. Wornack to PLC, 10 February 1837, J.P. Kay to
PLC, 17 May 1837, MH 12/8394, PRO.
5 59 G.3. c.12. s.19. 13 and 14 V. c.99. Swaffham Union to PLC,
4 February 1836, MH 12/8539, PRO. Return of Docking Ratepayers,
MH 12/8253. Returns on Adoption of Small Tenements Act, PP
1852, XLV 575; 1859, XXIV, 591-3; 1866, LXI, 25-52. H.
Barrett, 'A Letter to Robert Peel' (Yarmouth, 1829), 9. J.P.
Kay to PLC 28 February 1838, MH 12/8630.
6 Quoted in G. Clive to PLC, 23 April 1839, MH 32/12, PRO.
7 Ibid. 'SC on Settlement and Poor Removal', PP 1847, XI,
Q.3377-83.
8 'Returns on Poor Rates', PP 1850, L, 53-61; 1863, Lll, 102.
'Report on Poor Laws' 5th edn (1905), 152-4, 342-3.
9 4 and 5 W.4. c.76. s.64-7.
10 'SC on Settlement and Removal' PP 1847, XI, Q.3235. Docking
Minutes, 2 December 1846, PL Cat., NRO. 'Report on Settlement
and Removal', PP 1850, XXVII, 263, 266, 268. B.A. Holderness,
'Open' and 'Close' Parishes, 'Agricultural History Review',
20 (1972), 134-5.
11 Bonds to Prevent Larling Settlements BRA 328 51/7-10, NRO.
Barton Collection BAR 73, NRO.
12 A. Young, 'Political Arithmetic' (1774), 93-4.
13 Thetford Minutes, 9 June 1848; Docking Minutes, 15 March 1846,
PL Cat., NRO. 'Report on Settlement and Removal', PP 1850,
XXVII, 137, 258, 305. 'Census', PP 1822, XV, 211.
14 'First Report of the Royal Sanitary Commission', PP 1868-9,
XXXII, Q. 6567a.

15   4 and 5 W.4. c.76. s.34. Memorial to PLC, 28 April 1844, MH
     12/8252, PRO. Blyth to PLC, 19 July 1847, MH 12/8253. A Digby,
     The Labour Market, 'Economic History Review', 2nd ser. XXVIII
     (1975), 82-3. 'SC on Settlement and Poor Removal', PP 1847,
     XI, QQ 2026-7, 2362-3. 'Report on Settlement and Removal',
     PP 1850, XXVIII, 306-8.
16   Ibid., 306.
17   Report on Union Settlement, 11 December 1850, MH 12/8253. Dock-
     ing Minutes, 24 October 1860, PL Cat., NRO; 'SC on Irremovable
     Poor' PP 1859, 2nd ser. VII, QQ 1839-41.
18   Mitford and Launditch Minutes, 10 February 1851, PL Cat., NRO.
     'Report on Settlement and Removal' PP 1850, XXVIII, 308.
19   E. Parry to PLC, 10 June 1835, MH 32/60. Loddon and Clavering
     Committee Book, 24 February 1834, PL Cat., NRO.
20   'SC on Parochial Assessments', PP 1850, XVI, QQ 1181-3. Norwich
     Relief Committee Minutes, 23 November 1835, N/TC3/20, NRO.
     'Norwich Mercury', 7 February 1846. E. Bailey to Sir J.
     Walsham, 5 June 1865, MH 32/84.
21   'Seventh Report of Medical Officer on Public Health', PP 1865,
     XXVI, 235.
22   Parry to PLC, 5 August 1835, 11 November 1835, MH 32/60, PRO.
     Twisleton to PLC, 4 November 1839, MH 32/70. Blyth family to
     PLC, 9 September 1834, MH 12/8249. T.B. Beevor to PLC, 31 July
     1835, MH 12/8616. Parry to PLC, 28 November 1835, MH 12/8415.
23   'Report on Poor Laws', 5th edn (1905), 178-80. Webb, 'Poor Law
     History', Part 2, I, 421-4. 'Report on Settlement and Removal',
     PP 1850, XXVII, 257-73.
24   Walsham to PLB, 5 January 1865, MH 32/84, PRO.
25   Wisbech Minutes, 7 June 1866, not catalogued, Cambs. RO.
26   'Abstracts of Reports by Union Assessment Committees', PP 1863,
     LII, 870-987; 1866, LXI, 73-4.
27   'Reports to RC on Agricultural Depression', PP 1895, XVII,
     342-3, 444-5.
28   Cannan, 'Local Rates', 133, 138, 154-5.
29   'Poor Rate Returns', PP 1824, VI, 383; 1826-7, XX, 670-1; 1834,
     XLIII, 404-5. 'SC on State of the Poor Laws', PP 1831, VIII,
     566-9.
30   'The Agricultural State of the Kingdom. Replies to the Board
     of Agriculture 1816' (1816), 197.
31   Ibid., 185-227. 'SC on Depressed Agriculture', PP 1821, IX,
     34-5, 90. A Norfolk Yeoman, 'A Letter on the Present Prospects
     of Agriculturalists' (Norwich, 1826). B.D. Hayes, Politics in
     Norfolk, 1750-1832 (University of Cambridge PhD thesis, 1957),
     302, 308, 341-2.
32   R.N. Bacon, 'Report on Agriculture', 79, 410. E.J. Hobsbawm
     and G. Rudé, 'Captain Swing' (1969), 153-4, 157-9.
33   Quoted in R.M. Bacon, 'A Memoir of Baron Suffield' (Norwich,
     1838), 336.
34   'SC on State of Agriculture', PP 1833, V, Q. 2265.
35   Ibid. Q. 2150. Bacon, 'Report on Agriculture', 39-40.
36   R.A.C. Parker, 'Coke of Norfolk. A Financial and Agricultural
     Study, 1707-1842' (Oxford, 1975), 149.
37   Ibid., 150-2. Bacon, 'A Memoir of Suffield', 288. W. Gunn,
     'Remedial Measures Suggested in Alleviation of Agricultural
     Distress' (1834), 2.

CHAPTER 6   POOR RELIEF IN RURAL NORFOLK

1 'Report', 5th edn (1905), 71, 354. Chadwick's Memorandum, 20
   May 1847, MH 32/81, PRO. J. Caird, 'English Agriculture in
   1850-1, 2nd edn (1968), 515.
2 'Norwich Mercury', 29 October 1831. 'Returns Relating to the
   Acreage of Land under Crops', PP 1866, LX, 6.
3 H. Lee-Warner to Sir E. Parry, 8 August 1835, MH 12/8596, PRO.
4 A. Redford, 'Labour Migration in England', 1800-50, 2nd edn
   (Manchester, 1964), 109.
5 Forehoe Minutes, 16 March 1837, PL Cat., NRO.
6 Attleborough Petition, 4 May 1836, MH 12/8616, PRO.
7 'Report from the Agent-General for Emigration from the United
   Kingdom', PP 1838, XL, 36. Report of A.C. Buchanan to Colonial
   Office, 1837, CO 384/43, PRO.
8 Redford, 'Labour Migration', 105-8. Kay to PLC, 13 February
   1836, MH 32/48. Undated Report on the Agricultural Labourer,
   MH 32/49. B.C. Bloomfield (ed.), 'The Autobiography of Sir
   James Kay-Shuttleworth', Education Libraries Bulletin Supplement No. 7 (1964).
9 Blofield Minutes, 20 October 1835, PL Cat., NRO. R.M. Muggeridge to PLC, 19 October 1836, MH 12/11762, 5 September 1835, MH
   32/58. 'Return of Persons who were Removed from Agricultural
   Districts to Manufacturing Districts', PP 1843, XLV, 123-68.
   'SC on the Administration of the Relief of the Poor', PP 1837-8,
   XVIII, Pt 1, 533-9.
10 Ibid., 537. Evidence of Sir T.B. Beevor.
11 H. Blyth, 'Report of the Chairman of the Docking Union' (Wells,
   1836). H.F. Day to PLC, 21 November 1835, MH 12/8539.
12 A. Digby, The Labour Market, 'Economic History Review', 2nd ser.
   XXVII (1975), 81.
13 J.R. Poynter, 'Poverty and Pauperism: English Ideas on Poor
   Relief, 1795-1834' (1969), 77-8. Webb, 'Poor Law History', I,
   176-8.
14 Smallburgh House of Industry Account Book 1793-4, MS 4497, NRO.
15 Notice of the Directors and Acting Guardians of the Poor in
   E. and W. Flegg 26 January 1795 in Misc. Newspaper Cuttings,
   Colman Library, Norwich. R. Taylor, The Development of the Old
   Poor Law in Norfolk, 1795-1834 (University of East Anglia MA
   thesis, 1970), 153-4. Lloyd Prichard, The Treatment of Poverty
   (University of Cambridge PhD thesis, 1949), 116-17.
16 W. Fawsett to R. Howard, 14 January 1789, 4 March 1795, 25
   December 1795, 6 March 1800; How 758, Howard Collection NRO.
17 Replies on Relieving Poor, 'Annals of Agriculture', XXIV (1795),
   141-2, 145, 169-72, 297-300; XXV (1796), 501; XXVI (1796),
   140, 157.
18 'SC on the Poor Laws', PP 1817, VI, 166-7. 'Reports of Assistant Commissioners', PP 1834, XXVIII, 346-9. Walsham to R. Peel,
   BM Add. MS. 40587.
19 'Abstract of Return on Labourers Wages', PP 1825, XIX, QQ 2-3.
   W. Copland, 'A Letter to the Rev. C.D. Brereton in Reply etc.'
   (Norwich, 1824), 94-5. P.S. Wood, 'A Letter in Reply to the Rev.
   C.D. Brereton's Censure' (Cambridge, 1825). 'Rural Queries',
   PP 1834, XXXI, QQ 24-5. D.A. Baugh, The Cost of Poor Relief in

South-East England, 1790-1834, 'Economic History Review' 2nd ser. XXVIII (1975), 50-68.

20 'Report', 5th edn (1905), 54. M. Blaug, The Poor Law Report Re-examined, 'Journal of Economic History', XXIV (1964), 231, 233-8.

21 'Rural Queries', PP 1834, XXXIII, QQ 39-40. C.D. Brereton, 'A Practical Inquiry into the Number, Means of Employment, and Wages of Agricultural Labourers' (Norwich, 1825), 6-7. 'Reports of Assistant Commissioners', PP 1834, XXVIII, 599-600. Loddon and Clavering Committee Books, 27 December 1830, 24 December 1835, PL Cat., NRO.

22 Kay to PLC, 19 February 1837, MH 32/49. PLC to Marquess of Normanby, 31 July 1840, HO 73/56, PRO. Twisleton to PLC, 24 April 1841, MH 32/72.

23 Loddon and Clavering Minutes, 14 November 1836, 23 January 1837; Aylsham Minutes, 1 November 1836, PL Cat., NRO. Clive to PLC, 23 April 1839, MH 32/12.

24 Walsingham Minutes, 9 April 1845, PL, Cat., NRO.

25 Quoted in R.N. Bacon, 'The Report on the Agriculture of Norfolk' (1844), 148.

26 J.A.H. Brocklebank, The New Poor Law in Lincolnshire, 'Lincolnshire Historian', 2 (1962), 32.

27 Report, 22 October 1860, MH 32/84.

28 Hartt, Q. 155 Material for a Report on Norfolk Agriculture, MS 4363, NRO.

29 M.E. Rose, The Allowance System under the New Poor Law, 'Economic History Review', 2nd ser. XIX (1966), 615-16.

30 Walsham to PLB, 7 January 1856, MH 32/83. 'Twenty-third Report of PLB', PP 1871, XXVII, 204-5.

31 SC on Settlement and Poor Removal', PP 1847, XI, Q. 2109.

32 Ibid., Q. 2104.

33 'Abstract of Poor Rate Returns', PP 1833, XXXII, 349-50. 'Returns on Expenditure on Highways', PP 1841, XXVII, 81; 1849, XLVI, 156. P. Dunkley, The Hungry Forties, 'Historical Journal', XVII (1974), 340.

34 Clive to PLC, 23 April 1839, MH 32/12.

35 Names of Persons Employed by Shipdham Overseers, 1830-5 (2 vols), temporary deposit NRO. D. Wallace (ed.), 'Waveney Valley Studies' (Diss, n.d.). 'Return of Labourers Wages', PP 1825, XIX, Q. 4. 'Rural Queries', PP 1834, XXXI, Q. 27.

36 Ibid., QQ 27-8. 'Report on the Practical Operation of the Poor Laws', PP 1834, XXVIII, 80-1. G. Johnson, 'A Plan to Regulate the Employment of the Labouring Poor etc.' (Swaffham, 1828). 'Norwich Mercury', 11 December 1830, 18 December 1830, 9 July 1831.

37 A. Digby, The Labour Market, 'Economic History Review', 2nd ser. XXVIII (1975), 75-8.

38 'The Times', 4 July 1844.

39 Blofield Minutes, 26 January 1836, 26 April 1836, PL Cat., NRO.

40 Walsham to PLC, 11 and 17 July 1844, MH 32/80. 'The Times', 4 July 1844.

41 Blofield Minutes, 20 July 1841, PL Cat., NRO. Twisleton to PLC, 26 August 1840, MH 12/8416. Walsham to PLC, 14 July 1844, MH 32/80.

42 Kay to PLC, 1 April 1837, MH 12/8293. A. Digby, The Labour
    Market, 74-5.
43 Loddon and Clavering Committee Books 1830-5, PL Cat., NRO.
    J. Yelloly, 'Some Account of the Employment of Spade Husbandry
    etc.' (1838), 5, 12.
44 Kendle, Q. 157, MS 4363, NRO.
45 'SC on Administration of Poor Relief', PP 1837-8, XVIII, Pt 1,
    QQ 4572, 4581. Report on the Agricultural Labourer, MH 32/49.
    Walsham to Peel, 18 March 1846, BM Add. MS 40587.
46 Hobsbawm and Rudé, 'Captain Swing', 360-3. S. MacDonald, The
    Progress of the Early Threshing Machine, 'Agricultural History
    Review' 23 (1975), 69-70, 76.
47 'Poor Rate Returns', PP 1825, IV, 58.
48 Attleborough Poor to PLC, 25 March 1837, MH 12/8616.
49 Tunstead and Happing Minutes, 14 May 1839, PL Cat., NRO.
50 QQ 13, 18, MS 4363, NRO.
51 'SC on the Burthens Affecting Agriculture', PP 1846, VI, Pt 1,
    QQ 708-9, 738.
52 W. Marshall, 'The Rural Economy of Norfolk' (2 vols, 1795) II,
    44. N. Kent, 'General View of the County of Norfolk' (1796), 211.
53 Marshall, 'Rural Economy', I, 219, 222; II, 36-8, 41-4, 53.
    Kent, 'Agriculture of Norfolk', 202, 204, 206, 211-2. 'Bury
    and Norwich Post', 19 October 1836. R.N. Bacon, 'The Report
    on the Agriculture of Norfolk', 337-8.
54 'Sixth Report of Children's Employment Commission', PP 1867,
    XVI, 76-7, 185, 203. 'Report on the Employment of Women and
    Children in Agriculture', PP 1843, XII, 292-3. 'Report on the
    Employment of Children, Young Persons, and Women in Agriculture',
    PP 1867-8, XVII, 66-7.
55 'Report on Employment in Agriculture', PP 1843, XII, 238.
    W. Hasbach, 'A History of the English Agricultural Labourer',
    trans. R. Kenyon (1908), 196-7. N. Riches, 'The Agricultural
    Revolution in Norfolk', 2nd edn (1967), 144.
56 F. de la Rochefoucauld, 'A. Frenchman in England', 1784, trans.
    S.C. Roberts (Cambridge, 1933), 216. 'Report on Employment',
    PP 1843, XII, 23.
57 A. Digby, The Operation of the Poor Law (University of East
    Anglia PhD thesis, 1972), 270-2, 355.
58 Report on Agricultural Labourer, MH 32/49. 'SC on Relief to
    Poor', PP 1837-8, XVIII, Pt 1, QQ 4572-80, 4835-51.
59 Q 157, MS 4363, NRO. Walsham to Peel, 18 March 1846, BM Add.
    MS 40587.
60 N. Kent, 'General View', 156. Walsham to Peel, 18 March 1846,
    BM Add. MS 40587. M. Blaug, The Myth of the Old Poor Law and
    the Making of the New, 'Journal of Economic History', XXIII
    (1963), 167-70.

CHAPTER 7   POOR RELIEF AND THE POLITICAL ECONOMY OF NORWICH 1834-63

1 'Inquiry into the State of Large Towns', PP 1845, XVIII, 641.
2 'Report on Hand-loom Weavers', PP 1840, XXIII, 149, 151. 'Norfolk Chronicle', 25 January 1845.
3 'Report on Hand-loom Weavers', 146-7.

4   10 Ann c.15. s.1-2.   7 and 8 G.4. c.29. s.3,4,10.   1 and 2 W.4.
    c.li. s.2-3.   Petitions against the Poor Law Bill, Case 15
    Shelf 6, NRO.   Hayes, Politics in Norfolk, 323-30.
5   'Report on Hand-loom Weavers', 182.
6   Norwich Election Squibs 1786-1857, Norwich Election Broadsides
    1835-6, Rye and Colman Library, Norwich.   Norwich Minutes,
    6 February 1844, 2 October 1860, 4 December 1860, 6 May 1861,
    6 August 1861, 7 January 1862, N/TC 3/2, 5-6, NRO.   Parry to PLC,
    13 July 1835 MH 12/8502, 14 November 1835, MH 32/60.   D. Fraser,
    Areas of Urban Politics, in H.J. Dyos and M. Wolff (eds),
    'The Victorian City: Images and realities' (2 vols, 1973), II,
    770-1.
7   'Report on Hand-loom Weavers', 182.   J. Athow to Sir E. Parry,
    7 January 1835, MH 32/60, PRO.
8   Kay to PLC, 22 March 1836, MH 32/48.
9   A.D. Bayne, 'A Comprehensive History of Norwich' (1869), 381-
    400.   'Hansard', 3rd ser. 1834, XXIII, 842, 1001, 1340-8.
10 Parry to PLC, 3 June, 16 June, 12 October, 1835, MH 32/60; 30
    October 1835, MH 12/8502, PRO.   'Norfolk Chronicle', 20 June
    1835.   'Norwich Mercury', 5 December 1835.   'Ninth Report of
    PLC', PP 1843, XXI, 14.
11 Municipal Characters or Waggeries for Whigs No. 11 in Norwich
    Election Broadsides, 1835-36.   W. Day to PLC, 26 November 1836,
    MH 12/8502.
12 Kay to PLC, 7 October 1836, MH 12/8502.
13 Kay to PLC, 28 November 1838, MH 12/8502.
14 Parry to PLC, 6 August 1835, MH 32/60.
15 'Norwich Mercury', 5 December 1835, 9 December 1848. 'Tenth
    Report of PLC', PP 1844, XIX, 145.
16 Parry to PLC, 13 July 1835, MH 12/8502.   Swaffham Minutes, 17
    September 1849, PL Cat., NRO.
17 M.E. Rose, The New Poor Law in an Industrial Area in R.M.
    Hartwell (ed.), 'The Industrial Revolution', 125, 130-6. 'Tenth
    Report of PLC', 142.   Norwich Minutes, 2 November 1852, N/TC
    3/4, NRO.   M.E. Rose, The Allowance System, 'Economic History
    Review', 2nd ser. XIX (1966), 610.
18 Norwich Minutes, 6 May, 3 June, 5 August 1834, N/TC 3/1; 7
    November 1848, N/TC 3/3; 4 August 1857, N/TC 3/5, NRO.   'Tenth
    Report of PLC', 142.
19 Ibid., 142.
20 'Norwich Mercury', 7 February 1846, 13 January 1849.
21 Ibid., 11 May 1844, 25 May 1844, 11 March 1848.   Norwich Minutes,
    7 September 1847, 5 February 1850, 4 February 1851, 5 August
    1851 N/TC 3/3, NRO.   Norwich Workhouse, Infirmary and Visiting
    Committee Minutes, 9 March 1853, N/TC 3/58, NRO.   'Tenth Report
    of PLC', 149-50.
22 'Report on Settlement and Removal', PP 1850, XXVII, 261-2.
23 'Norwich Mercury', 16 December 1843, 22 February 1845, 4 December
    1847, 16 January 1850.   'Rural Queries', PP 1834, XXX, Q 11.
    'Report on Hand-loom Weavers', 168-74, 177.   H. Davey, 'Poor
    Law Settlement and Removal' (1913), 11-12.
24 Ibid., 11-12.   Norwich Minutes, 16 November 1847, 5 November
    1857, N/TC 3/3,5, NRO.
25 Norwich Minutes, 5 November 1857.

26   'Report on Settlement and Removal', 261-3, 266, 268, 301.
     'Norwich Mercury', 20 November 1847. 'Norfolk News', 17
     October 1863. 'Census' 1801-51. W. White, 'History, Gazeteer
     and Directory of Norfolk, 1845' (reprint, Newton Abbot, 1969).
27   Norwich Minutes, 10 February 1846, N/TC 3/2, NRO.
28   'Report on Endowed and Voluntary Charities', PP 1909, Cd. 4593,
     XLII, 687-93. 'General Digest of Endowed Charities', PP 1867-8,
     LII, Part II, 110-27. C.B. Hawkins, 'Norwich. A Social Study'
     (1910), 225-6, 240, 244. Norwich Minutes, 4 December 1847,
     N/TC 3/3. 'Norwich Mercury', 13 January 1844, 2 January 1847,
     30 January 1847, 22 January 1848, 13 January 1849.
29   'Norwich Mercury', 22 January 1848.
30   Ibid., 12 November 1842. 'Inquiry into Large Towns', PP 1845,
     XVIII, 645-6. 'Report on Hand-loom Weavers', 161.
31   Norwich Minutes, 7 October 1834, 6 February 1844, N/TC 3/1-2;
     Norwich Relief Committee Minutes N/TC 3/20-2; NRO. 'Morning
     Chronicle', 29 January 1850. 'Norwich Mercury', 11 March 1848.
32   M.E. Rose, The Allowance System, 'Economic History Review',
     2nd ser. XIX (1966), 619. Norwich Court Book, 29 August,
     3 September, 3 December 1833, Case 20 Shelf C, NRO. E. Steward,
     'A Letter to the Ratepayers of Norwich etc.' (Norwich, 1833).
33   Norwich Minutes, 6 May 1834, N/TC 3/1, NRO.
34   'Norwich Mercury', 9 December 1848.
35   Ibid., 22 January 1848, 13 January 1849.
36   Norwich Minutes, 3 April 1855, N/TC 3/4, NRO.
37   'Norwich Mercury', 2 March 1861.
38   Ibid., 20 November 1847. Norwich Relief Committee Minutes 1832-
     49, N/TC 3/20, 20-2, NRO. Census Enumeration, 1841 and 1851.
39   'Norwich Mercury', 2 March 1861.
40   'Tenth Report of PLC', 138-9. P. Searby, Weavers and Freemen
     in Coventry, 1820-61 (University of Warwick, PhD thesis, 1972),
     613.
41   Minutes of Parochial Delegates, MS 8834, NRO.
42   C.B. Hawkins, 'Norwich. A Social Study', 136, 153. 'The
     Destitute of Norwich and How they Live', 3rd edn (1913), 16,
     25, 64-5.

CHAPTER 8   PAUPERS: I, THE ABLE-BODIED

 1   The changes in the policy of the central poor law administration
     after 1834, referred to in Chapters 8 and 9, are based on infor-
     mation in S. and B. Webb, 'English Poor Law Policy' (1910) and
     S. and B. Webb, 'English Poor Law History Part 2 (2 vols, re-
     print, 1963). References would be too numerous to cite indi-
     vidually.
 2   'RC on the Aged Poor', PP 1895, XIV, Q 6570.
 3   'Twenty-first Report of L.G.B.', PP 1892, XXXVIII, 157.
 4   For example, Henstead Minutes, 11 November and 24 November 1845,
     PL Cat., NRO.
 5   St Faith's Minutes, 4 February 1846, PL Cat., NRO.
 6   'Second Report of PLC', PP 1836, XXIX, Pt 1, 56-9, 155. 'Sixth
     Report of M.O. of the Committee of Council on Public Health',
     PP 1864, XXVIII, 289-9, 316-7.

7   Oral evidence of Oliver Meek, b. 1895. 'Reports on Vagrancy',
    PP 1847-8, LIII, 243-8; 1866, XXXV, 659-65. R. Hodgkinson,
    'The Origins of the National Health Service: The Medical Ser-
    vices of the New Poor Law 1834-71', Publications of Wellcome
    Historical Medical Library, XI (1967), 48, 469. 'Within Living
    Memory. A Collection of Norfolk Reminiscences' (Boydell Press,
    Ipswich, 1973), 29. I am grateful to Dr M.A. Crowther for let-
    ting me consult her unpublished paper, Vagrants and the Poor
    Law, 1882-1929.
8   Tables of County Expenditure 1826-33, Norfolk CC Records, NRO.
    'Returns of Vagrants Relieved', PP 1872, LI, 520-1; 1884,
    LXVII, 848; 1884-5, LXVII, 400; 1895, LXXXIV, 1173. 'Norwich
    Mercury', 19 February 1848. G. Edwards, 'From Crow-Scaring
    to Westminster' (1922), 83.
9   Aylsham Union Vagrants Admission and Discharge Books, 1867-
    1900 (interrupted series), PL Cat., NRO.
10 Holkham, Warham and Wighton Union Workhouse Books, 1789-96, 1796-
    1814; Wighton Parish Chest, Norfolk. I am grateful to the Rev.
    J. Holmes, Mr I. Whitworth and Mr W.O. Hassall for help on this
    Gilbert Union.
11 St Faith's Minutes, 13 July 1836, PL Cat., NRO. Norwich
    Guardians Minutes, 1 October 1850, N/TC 3/3, NRO. 'R.C. on the
    Aged Poor', PP 1895, XIV, Q 6496, Q 6500 (Evidence of G.
    Edwards).
12 Blofield Minutes, 17 December 1867, Freebridge Lynn Minutes,
    23 January 1836, PL Cat., NRO.
13 Wayland Minutes, 1 September 1836, 13 March 1837; Flegg
    Minutes, 12 April 1836; PL Cat., NRO. Yarmouth Minutes, 1
    January 1838, WE 69, NRO. Norwich Relief Committee Minutes,
    April-June 1834, N/TC 3/20, NRO. 'Fourth Report of PLC',
    PP 1837-8, XXVIII, 288-9. Wighton Workhouse Books, 1796-1814,
    Wighton Parish Chest. A Digby, The Operation of the Poor Law
    (University of East Anglia, PhD thesis, 1972), 227-30, 349.
14 Pamphlet by A. Goode included in correspondence of Sir E. Parry
    MH 32/60, PRO. King's Lynn Minutes, 12 February 1841, Swaffham
    Minutes, 18 June 1838, Docking Minutes, 1 December 1841, PL
    Cat., NRO. G. Edwards, 'From Crow-Scaring', 82-3.
15 Forehoe Minutes, 22 January 1844, Docking Minutes, 1 December
    1869, PL Cat., NRO. 'Return on Bastardy 1845-59', PP 1861,
    LV, 38.
16 For example, King's Lynn Minutes, 16 March 1849, 23 July 1852,
    PL Cat., NRO. Norwich Workhouse, Infirmary and Visiting Com-
    mittee Minutes, 4 January 1854, N/TC 3/58, NRO.
17 Tunstead and Happing Minutes, 11 September 1844, PL Cat., NRO.
18 A. Digby, The Operation of the Poor Law, 345-6. 'Twenty-Eighth
    Report of LGB', PP 1899, XXXVII, 111. 'Twenty-Ninth Report
    of LGB', PP 1900, XXXIII, 91-2.
19 'Fourth Report of PLC', PP 1837-8, XXVIII, 288-9. 'First
    Report of PLC', PP 1835, XXXV, 170. Wayland Minutes, 1 August
    1836, Thetford Minutes, 3 November 1837, Guiltcross Minutes,
    30 November 1836, PL Cat., NRO.
20 I am very grateful for this information to Dr Ronald MacKeith
    and the Historians Medical Information Bureau.

21 Downham Market Minutes, 4 and 18 February 1841, Forehoe Minutes,
    20 December 1858, Flegg Minutes, 24 June 1856, PL Cat., NRO.
22 H. Preston-Thomas, 'The Work and Play of a Government Inspector'
    (1909), 233.
23 S. and B. Webb, 'English Poor Law History', Pt 2, 310-11.
    M. Hewitt, 'Wives and Mothers in Victorian Industry' (1958),
    139-40. Docking Minutes, 1 December 1869, St Faith's Minutes,
    26 December 1844, PL Cat., NRO. R. Hodgkinson, 'The Origins
    of the National Health Service', 540-9.
24 Freebridge Lynn Union to PLB, 4 October 1856, Freebridge Lynn
    Letter Book, PL Cat., NRO. 'Within Living Memory', 106. Oral
    evidence of Mr O. Meek, b. 1895, Mr Hardingham, b. 1889. I am
    grateful to Miss B. Yates of the Norwich Museum's service for
    help on oral history.
25 'Within Living Memory', 134-7.

CHAPTER 9 PAUPERS: II, THE OLD AND THE SICK

 1 'Report of RC on Poor Laws', 1834, Cd. 2728, 5th edn (1905),
    307. Annual Reports of PLC gave a detailed breakdown of pauper-
    ism for the quarters ending 25 March from 1839 to 1846. 'Twenty-
    second Report of LGB', PP 1893-4, XLIII, lxiii. 'RC on Aged
    Poor', PP 1895, XIV, 84. 'SC on Aged Deserving Poor', PP 1899,
    VIII, 194. 'Report of RC on Poor Laws', Cd. 4499, quarto edn
    (1909), 222-3.
 2 'RC on Aged Poor' (evidence of G. Edwards, Z. Waller, H. Howell).
 3 'Twenty-fourth Report of LGB', PP 1895, L, 29.
 4 'Return on Aged Married Couples in Workhouses', PP 1863, LII,
    86, 91. H. Preston-Thomas, 'The Work of a Government Inspector',
    238-9. 'RC on Aged Poor', Q 8017.
 5 'Return of Adults in Workhouses', PP 1861, LV, 337-9. H. Rider
    Haggard, 'A Farmer's Year, Being His Commonplace Book for 1898'
    (1899), 427-8. Norwich Workhouse, Infirmary and Visiting
    Minutes, 27 February 1856, N/TC 3/59; Aylsham Minutes, 6
    December 1836; PL Cat., NRO.
 6 'Second Report of PLC', PP 1836, XXXIX, Pt 1, 56-9. Loddon
    and Clavering Minutes, 17 April 1843; Forehoe Minutes, 13
    April 1857; 22 February 1841; 10 December 1855; St Faith's
    Minutes, 4 May 1853; PL Cat., NRO. Yarmouth Minutes, 27 May
    1839, 9 March 1840, 6 December 1838, WE 69, NRO. H. Preston
    Thomas, 'The Work of a Government Inspector', 230.
 7 'Tenth Report of PLC', PP 1844, XIX, 148. Norwich Workhouse,
    Infirmary and Visiting Minutes 1849-58, N/TC 3/58-9, NRO.
    C.B. Hawkins, 'Norwich. A Social Study', 147.
 8 R. Hodgkinson, 'National Health Service', 105, 109, 269. 'Re-
    port on the Continuance of the PLC', PP 1840, XVII, 324-6.
    'Return on Medical Officers under the Poor Law', PP 1852-3,
    LXXXIV, 334, 361-3.
 9 J. Yelloly, 'Observations on the Arrangements Connected with
    the Relief of the Sick Poor' (1837), 33-4. E. Copeman, 'Remarks
    on The Poor Law Amendment Act with Reference to Pauper Medical
    Clubs' (Norwich, 1838), 18.
10 Hodgkinson, 'National Health Service', 58, 303, 336. Henstead

Minutes, 7 March 1836, PL Cat., NRO.
11 R. Bond, 'Familiar Narrative of Facts etc.' (Norwich, 1838).
    J. Banks, 'Letter to R. Bond etc.' (Norwich, 1839).
12 Forehoe Minutes, 22 February, 1 March, 8 March 1841; PL Cat.,
    NRO.
13 Depwade Minutes, 18 February, 25 February 1839; Henstead
    Minutes, 25 July 1843; 26 May 1855; Forehoe Minutes, 9
    February, 16 February, 25 March 1846; 28 February, 13 March,
    31 July 1848, 9 July 1849; PL Cat., NRO. Action for Damages
    against Mr Tunaley, MS 4304, NRO.
14 Henstead Minutes, 7 December 1869, Forehoe Minutes, 5 November
    1866, PL Cat., NRO. 'Return on Workhouse Infirmaries', PP
    1890-1, LXVIII, 685-6. H. Preston-Thomas, 'The Work of a
    Government Inspector', 228.
15 Ibid., 237.
16 St Faith's Minutes, 25 May 1843, 19 May 1847, PL Cat., NRO.
    J.E. Thorold Rogers (ed.), 'Joseph Rogers M.D. Reminiscences of
    a Workhouse Medical Officer' (1889).
17 H. Preston-Thomas, 'The Work of a Government Inspector', 228-9.
18 'Returns on Workhouse Infirmaries', PP 1890-1, LXVIII, 685-6;
    1896, LXXII, 672. R. Hodgkinson, 'National Health Service',
    58, 105, 572. 'Twenty-seventh Report of LGB', PP 1898,
    XXXIX, 83. 'Twenty-ninth Report of LGB', PP 1900, XXXIII, 93.
19 'Return on Insane Paupers', PP 1843, XXI, 276-7. 'Twenty-sixth
    Report of the Commissioners in Lunacy', PP 1872, XXVII, 93.
    'Return of Adults in Workhouses', PP 1861, LV, 335-9. St Faith's
    Minutes, 19 May 1858; Blofield Minutes, 30 November 1869; PL
    Cat., NRO.
20 Norwich Guardians Minutes 1841-64, N/TC 3/1-7, NRO. 'Tenth
    Report of PLC', 139, 144. 'Twenty-Sixth Report of the Commis-
    sioners in Lunacy, PP 1872, XXVII, 37.
21 Cholera posters, uncatalogued, King's Lynn Museum. I am grateful
    to Miss A.S. Mottram for locating this, and other, posters for
    me.
22 H. Preston-Thomas, 'The Work of a Government Inspector', 146.
23 Loddon and Clavering Minutes, 24 October 1836, PL Cat., NRO.
24 O. Chadwick, 'Victorian Miniature', 86-7.
25 R. Hodgkinson, 'National Health Service', 252, 274, 408. 'SC
    on Medical Relief', PP 1854, XII, Q 1875-92.
26 J. Riches, 'The Death of Jemima Livock in Depwade Workhouse'
    (Norwich, 1839).

CHAPTER 10 PAUPER EDUCATION

1 'Report on the Employment of Women and Children in Agriculture',
   PP 1843, XII, 263.
2 J.P. Kay, On the Establishment of Pauper Schools, 'Journal of
   the Royal Statistical Society', 1 (1838), 23. 'Fourth Report of
   PLC', PP 1837-8, XXVIII, 288. 'SC on the Administration of the
   Relief of the Poor', PP 1837-8, XVIII, Pt 1, Q 4406.
3 'Rules in St. James Workhouse' (King's Lynn, 1819), 5-6. F.
   Adams, 'An Essay on the Effects of Education in the Smallburgh
   House' (Norwich, 1812), 12-13, 23.

4   J. Neild, Remarks on Norwich Workhouse, 'Gentleman's Magazine'
    75 (1805), 892-4. D. Salmon, 'The Practical Parts of Lancaster's
    Improvement and Bell's Experiment' (Cambridge, 1932), 45-6.
5   F. Eden, 'The State of the Poor', II, 466.
6   Loddon and Clavering Committee Books 1834-5, PL Cat., NRO.
    'Second Report of PLC', PP 1836, XXIX, Pt I, 167-77.
7   'Fourth Report of PLC', PP 1837-8, XXVIII, 290.
8   Wayland Minutes, 22 May 1837, 19 June 1837, Blofield Minutes,
    17 November 1840, 16 February 1841, PL Cat., NRO. B.C. Bloom-
    field (ed.), 'The Autobiography of Sir James Kay-Shuttleworth',
    Education Libraries Bulletin Supplement No. 7 (1964), 28-9.
9   Yarmouth Minutes, 18 February 1839, 8 April 1839, WE 69, NRO.
    Forehoe Minutes, 27 June 1836, PL Cat., NRO.
10 'Fourth Report of PLC', PP 1837-8, XXVIII, 288-9.
11 Walsingham Minutes, 2 March 1837, Mitford and Launditch Minutes,
    20 January 1840, Loddon and Clavering Minutes, 25 September
    1837, Aylsham Minutes, 27 June 1837, Thetford Minutes, 21 July
    1838, Docking Minutes, 13 December 1837, PL Cat., NRO.
12 Docking Minutes, 6 June 1838, PL Cat., NRO.
13 Guiltcross Minutes, 26 April 1837, 25 April 1838, PL Cat., NRO.
    'Minutes of the Committee of Council on Education', PP 1851,
    XLIV, 75 (hereafter referred to as 'Minutes').
14 Walsingham Minutes, 26 December 1838, PL Cat., NRO.
15 'Minutes', PP 1862, XLII, 507.
16 St Faith's Minutes, 3 May 1843, Henstead Minutes, 1 November
    1853, Blofield Minutes, 7 May 1842, PL Cat., NRO.
17 A.M. Ross, The Care and Education of Pauper Children in England
    and Wales 1834-96 (University of London PhD thesis, 1955),
    262-3.
18 Aylsham Minutes, 7 November 1837; St Faith's Minutes, 13
    December 1837; Guiltcross Minutes, 1 November 1837, 15 Novem-
    ber 1837; Swaffham Minutes, 9 April 1838; Docking Minutes,
    6 June 1838; PL Cat., NRO.
19 Kay-Shuttleworth, 'Autobiography', 53.
20 Ibid., 53-4. J. Kay-Shuttleworth, 'Four Periods of Public
    Education' (1862), 287-8, 312.
21 'Minutes', PP 1852, XXXIX, 199; 1849, XLII, 284. Freebridge
    Lynn Minutes, 11 May 1849, 23 May 1851, PL Cat., NRO. Ross,
    Education of Pauper Children, 217.
22 'Minutes', PP 1849, XLII, 396-403; 1854, LI, 618. 'Return
    of Salaries of Teachers in Workhouse Schools', PP 1847-8, LIII,
    363-4. Downham Minutes, 3 May 1838, PL Cat., NRO.
23 'Minutes', PP 1847-8, L, 5-6; 1852-3, LXXIX, 585; 1862, XLII,
    507.
24 Ross, Education of Pauper Children, 63-4, 100, 114-5. For a
    useful discussion of the district school movement see F. Duke,
    Pauper Education in D. Fraser (ed.), 'The New Poor Law in the
    Nineteenth Century' (1976).
25 Twisleton to PLC, 24 March 1840, MH 32/72, PRO.
26 J.P. Kay, On the Establishment of Pauper Schools, 19-23. 'RC on
    Popular Education in England', PP 1861, XXI, Pt VI, QQ 3025-6.
27 W.A.C. Stewart and W.P. McCann, 'The Educational Innovators'
    (2 vols, 1967), I, 142-5, 155-6. H.M. Pollard, 'Pioneers of
    Popular Education, 1760-1850' (1956), 220-1. Walsingham

Minutes, 2 May 1838, 4 October 1837, PL Cat., NRO.

28 Downham Market Minutes, 5 April 1838; Loddon and Clavering
    Minutes, 30 October 1837, PL Cat., NRO.

29 'Minutes', PP 1848, XLII, 374.

30 Reports on Schooling by Walsham, 29 March 1847, 16 January
    1851, 29 December 1854, MH 32/81-3, PRO. 'Minutes', PP 1851,
    XLIV, 74-5; 1863, XLVII, 404-6.

31 Norwich Minutes, 1834-63, N/TC 3/1-6; Boys Home Minutes 1847-
    55, MS 4356; Boys Home Minutes 1855-62, N/TC 3/87; Girls
    Home Minutes N/TC 3/88; NRO. 'Third Report of LGB', PP 1874,
    XXV, 274-5. 'Twenty-seventh Report of LGB', PP 1898, XXXIX, 82.

32 Norwich Minutes, 3 January, 5 September, 3 October, 7 November,
    5 December, 1854, N/TC 3/4; Boys Home Minutes, 6 January 1857,
    N/TC 3/87; Girls Home Minutes, 1 December 1859, N/TC 3/88; NRO.
    'RC on Popular Education', PP 1861, XXI, Pt V, 436.

33 Undated report by J.P. Kay on apprenticeships, MH 32/50, PRO.
    'Reports by Inspectors on the Education of Pauper Children',
    PP 1862, XLIX, Pt 1, 562.

34 'Twenty-third Report of PLB', PP 1871, XXVII, 278.

35 Ibid., 278-81. 'Second Report of LGB', PP 1873, XXIX, 161-4.
    F. Mouat, On the Education and Training of the Poor, 'Journal
    of the Royal Statistical Society', XLIII (1880), 215.

36 Boys Home Minutes, 7 February 1854, MS 4356, NRO. 'Norwich
    Mercury', 17 September 1842. Mitford and Launditch Minutes,
    8 January 1844, 20 July 1846, PL Cat., NRO. 'Twenty-third
    Report of PLB', PP 1871, XXVII, 278.

37 'SC on the Administration of the Relief of the Poor', PP 1837-8,
    XVIII, Pt 1, Q 4438.

38 'Minutes', PP 1849, XLII, 396-403.

39 'Report on the Employment of Women and Children in Agriculture',
    PP 1843, XII, 264.

40 'Returns of Children Chargeable to the Poor Rates', PP 1854,
    LV, 560-1, 587; 1870, LVIII, 65-9, 561.

41 Report by Walsham, 25 March 1855, MH 32/83, PRO. W.H. Henslowe,
    'The Magistrate and his Minion etc.' (King's Lynn, 1850). W.
    Bates to PLB, October 1853, MH 12/8254, PRO.

42 'Returns of Children Chargeable to the Poor Rates', PP 1854,
    LV, 560-1, 587; 1870, LVIII, 65-9, 561.

43 Swaffham School Attendance Minutes, 27 November 1882, Docking
    School Attendance Minutes, 19 September 1877, PL Cat., NRO.

44 'Reports of LGB', PP 1895, L, 31; 1898, XXXIX, lxxv; 1899,
    XXXVII, iii; 1900, XXXIII, 91-2 'Norwich Mercury', 17 October
    1883. L.E. Jones, 'A Victorian Boyhood', (1955), 40.

CHAPTER 11 THE PROPERTIED AND THE POOR

1 F.M.L. Thompson, 'English Landed Society in the Nineteenth Century' (1963), 113-17. Junius, 'A Letter to Lord Brougham on
   the Magistracy of England' (1832), 15-16.

2 N. Kent, 'Hints to Gentlemen of Landed Property' (1775), 229-30.
   'Norfolk News', 12 September - 19 December 1863.

3 S. Wade-Martins, The Holkham Estate in the Nineteenth Century:
   with Special Reference to Farm Building and Agricultural

Improvement (University of East Anglia PhD thesis, 1975), 207-9, 215-17, 221-2. H.W. Keary, Report on Holkham Estates 1851 (2 vols), Micro Methods Microfilm no. 96708.

4 E. Chadwick, 'Report on an Inquiry into the Sanitary Condition of the Labouring Population of Great Britain (2 vols, 1842), II, 136.

5 F.M.L. Thompson, 'English Landed Society in the Nineteenth Century' (1963), 157, 187, 195-6, 231-7, 240. Wade-Martins, The Holkham Estate, 207-9, 216-17, 221-2. 'Sixth Report of the Commissioners of the Employment of Children', PP 1867, XVI, 88.

6 B.D. Hayes, Politics of Norfolk 1750-1832 (University of Cambridge PhD thesis, 1957), 302, 308, 314.

7 J. Waller, Hunstanton Hall (1846-53) 112, MS 21219, NRO. L.M. Springall, 'Labouring Life in Norfolk Villages' (1936), 58. 'Reports of Assistant Commissioners on the Employment of Women and Children in Agriculture', PP 1843, XII, 285.

8 Springall, 'Labouring Life', 58. Correspondence of R. Howard 1785-1801, 1798-1817, How 758, 750; Vouchers re Money Distributed to Poor 1816-17, How 595, NRO.

9 Account Book of Charities to the Sick and Poor, Le Strange Collection, NRO. J. Waller, Hunstanton Hall, 128-34.

10 E.J. Hobsbawm and G. Rudé, 'Captain Swing' (1969), 153-8. Springall, 'Labouring Life', 58, 76-7, 90, 112.

11 'Norwich Mercury', 17 May 1834. Editorial by R.M. Bacon.

12 R. Potter, 'Observations on the Poor Laws, on the Present State of the Poor, and on Houses of Industry' (1775), 37, 45, 54-5. T. Mendham, 'A Dialogue Intended as an Answer to a Pamphlet Published by the Rev. Mr Potter Intitled Observations on the Poor Laws' (Norwich, 1775).

13 'Norfolk Chronicle', 22 October 1774, 24 December 1774. C. Dickens, 'Oliver Twist', Penguin edn (Harmondsworth, 1966), 55.

14 A.W. Coats, Economic Thought and Poor Law Policy in the Eighteenth Century, 'Economic History Review', 2nd ser. XIII (1960), 39-51.

15 'The True Alarm! An Essay Showing the Pernicious Influence of Houses of Industry on the Political Interests of this Country' (1787), 3, 47.

16 E. Rigby, 'Further Facts Relating to the Care of the Poor' (Norwich, 1812), 9. J. Grisenthwaite, 'Remarks on the Political Economy and Management of the Poor in the Borough of King's Lynn', 2nd edn (Lynn, 1811), 15. T. Ruggles, 'The History of the Poor' (2 vols, 1793-4), Letters XLIV-VIII passim. F.M. Eden, 'The State of the Poor' (3 vols, 1797) II, 456, 471, 473, 684, 687, 692. E. Parry, 'An Account of an Incorporated House of Industry for two United Hundreds in the County of Norfolk' (1797), 19, 22-4.

17 A. Young, 'General View of the Agriculture of the County of Suffolk', 2nd edn (Newton Abbot, 1969), 256. 'Annals of Agriculture' XXIV (1800), 188-9.

18 C.D. Brereton, 'Observations on the Administration of the Poor Laws in Agricultural Districts' (Norwich, 1824), 13, 26-7, 38. 'A Practical Inquiry into the Number, Means of Employment, and Wages of Agricultural Labourers', 2nd edn (Norwich, 1825(?)), 85-6, 97, and 3rd edn (Norwich, 1826(?)), 6-7. 'The Subordinate

Magistracy' (Norwich, 1827), 7, 27. C.D. Brereton to Sir W.B.
Folkes, 7 March 1826, NRS 7958, NRO.

19 W. Copland, 'A Letter to the Rev. C.D. Brereton in Reply to
his "Observations on the Administration of the Poor Laws in
Agricultural Districts"' (Norwich, 1824), 8. P.S. Wood, 'A
Letter in Reply to the Rev. C.D. Brereton's Censure' (Cambridge,
1825), 3-4.

20 'Norwich Mercury', 13 March 1830.

21 Lord Melbourne to J. Wodehouse, 17 December 1830. HO 41/9, PRO.

22 J. Richardson, 'A Letter to Lord Brougham on an Alteration in
the Poor Laws', 2nd edn (1831), 4, 5, 7. J.R. Poynter, 'Poverty
and Pauperism: English Ideas on Poor Relief, 1795-1834' (1969),
177-8. J. Weyland, 'Thoughts Submitted to the Employers of
Labour in the County of Norfolk, with a few Words to the employed' (Norwich, 1830). R.M. Bacon, 'A Letter to Lord Suffield Upon the Distress of the Labourers and its Remedy'
(Norwich, 1831), 9-10, 39-42, 58.

23 T. Drummons, 'A Practicable Plan for the Benefit of Agricultural
Labourers' (——, 1830(?)). R. Calver, 'A Plan for the Relief
of the Country in a Letter to Earl Grey' (Norwich, 1830). T.
Watts, 'The Present Evils and Alarming Prospects of the Agricultural Population in a Letter to Lord Brougham' (Norwich,
1831) 20-4. S. Adams, 'A Letter to Lord Suffield Recommending
the Adoption of a Labour Rate' (Norwich, 1831) 6-10, 42-3. G.
Glover, 'Observations on the Present State of Pauperism in
England in a Letter to T.W. Coke Esq.' (1817), 36.

24 H. Bathurst, 'Practical Suggestions to Promote Clerical Resi-
dence and to Ameliorate the Habits and Conditions of the Poor'
(Wells, 1825), 37-44. W.H. Meteyard, 'Some Remarks on a Pam-
phlet Intitled Thoughts Submitted to the Employers of Labour'
(Norwich, 1830). H. Barrett, 'A Letter on the Subject of the
Poor's Laws to Robert Peel' (Yarmouth, 1829).

25 J.R. Poynter, 'Society and Pauperism', 310. J.D. Marshall,
The Nottinghamshire Reformers and their Contribution to the
New Poor Law, 'Economic History Review', 2nd ser. XIII (1961),
382-96.

26 P.S. Wood, 'Outline of a Plan for the Melioration of the Lower
Orders' (Downham Market, 1828), 33-43. J.T. Becher, 'The
Antipauper System' (1828), 1-20. W. Gunn, 'Remedial Measures
Suggested in Alleviation of Agricultural Distress' (1834).

27 Municipal and Provincial Correspondence, 1830; HO 52/9, PRO.
Miscellaneous Disturbances Entry Book, September - December
1830; HO 41/8,PRO. Lady Catherine Boileau to Lady A.M.
Elliott, 24 November 1830, Boi 62/1, NRO.

28 Returns from Local Guardians to the Constabulary Commission,
Q 6, HO 73/6 Pt 1; Q 9 HO 73/6 Pt 2, PRO.

29 Sir E. Parry to PLC, 7 June 1835, MH 32/60, PRO. J. Weyland
and H. Dover to Lord J. Russell, 17 June 1835; Docking justices
to Lord J. Russell, 29 July 1835; HO 52/26, PRO.

30 Aylsham Minutes, 21 February 1837; Depwade Minutes, 9 January
1837; Swaffham Minutes, 13 February 1837; Erpingham Minutes,
6 March 1837; Freebridge Lynn Minutes, 27 January 1837, PL
Cat., NRO.

31 Docking Minutes, 4 January 1837; Henstead Minutes, 8 February

1836;   Blofield Minutes, 19 January, 8 February 1836;   PL Cat., NRO.
32 Sir E. Parry to Sir W.B. Folkes, 21 October 1835, NRS 7958, NRO. J.P. Kay to PLC, 8 November 1836 MH 12/8474, PRO. Kay to PLC, 30 November 1836, MH, 12/8394. Kay to PLC, 17 March 1836, MH 12/8185. Kay to PLC, 23 February 1836, MH 32/48.
33 J. Fellowes, 'To the Inhabitants of the Parishes of Shotesham in the Henstead Union' (Norwich, 1836). A Norfolk Clergyman, 'The Nature and Design of the New Poor Laws Explained in an Address to the Labouring Classes' (Norwich, nd.),   67.
34 T.B. Morris to PLC, 23 September 1836, MH 12/8394. Guiltcross Minutes, 1 February 1837, 15 March 1837, PL Cat., NRO. Kay to PLC, 19 October 1837, MH 32/49.
35 F.H. Maberley, 'To the Poor and their Friends' (1836), 11. Lord John Russell to Bishop of Ely, 13 October 1836, HO 41/12, PRO.
36 Morris to PLC, 23 September 1836, MH 12/8394. A Goode, 'Substance of a Speech Prepared for the First Meeting of his Majesty's Commissioners, under the New Poor Law Amendment Bill' (Lynn, 1835). T. Cresswell to PLC, 27 November 1835; J. Coulton to PLC, 3 December 1835; J. Godfrey to PLC, 29 November 1835; MH 12/8429. King's Lynn Minutes, 22 July 1836, PL Cat., NRO.
37 J. Godfrey to PLC, 26 October 1835, MH 12/8429. Goode's broadsheets are included in MH 12/8429 and MH 12/8249. 'The Poor Man's Friend or a Few Plain Words from a Plain Man', 3rd edn (Lynn, 1835). T. Masters, 'Reform and Workhouses!' or Considerations Suggested by what is called the Poor Law Amendment Bill', 2nd edn (Lynn, 1835), 3.
38 Kay to PLC, 11 October 1836, MH 12/8208.
39 'Hansard's Parliamentary Debates', 3rd ser. 1839, L, 99-101. Kay to PLC, 24 September 1836, 13 October 1836, MH 32/48. Blofield Minutes, 15 October 1839, 5 November 1839, PL Cat., NRO. Clive to PLC, March 1839, MH 32/12. J. Cator to E. Twisleton, 21 April 1842, MH 32/72.
40 King's Lynn Minutes, 12 February 1841, PL Cat., NRO. Clive to PLC, December 1838, MH 32/12.
41 Yarmouth Minutes, 29 November 1838, WE 69, NRO.

CHAPTER 12   REVOLT BY THE POOR

1 'Norfolk Chronicle', 4 February 1775.
2 S. and B. Webb, 'Poor Law History', Pt 1, 141-2. R. Wearmouth, 'Methodism and the Common People of the Eighteenth Century' (1945), 31-2, 60.
3 Memorial Against the Erection of a House of Industry, Windham Papers vol. XLVIII, BM Add. MS 37889. E. and W. Flegg Minutes, 7 October 1775, C/GP7/1, NRO.
4 Lloyd Prichard, The Treatment of Poverty (University of Cambridge PhD thesis, 1949), 70-2. J. Matchett, 'The Norfolk and Norwich Remembrancer and Vade Mecum', 2nd edn (1822). R. Hindry Mason, 'A History of Norfolk' (1884), 478. R.B. Rose, Eighteenth Century Price Riots and Public Policy in England, 'International

Review of Social History', VI (1961), 277-92.
5   A.J. Peacock, 'Bread or Blood: A Study of the Agrarian Riots
in East Anglia in 1816' (1965), 78-81, 89.
6   E.J. Hobsbawm and G. Rudé, 'Captain Swing' (1969), 84, 152-9.
7   'Norwich Mercury', 4 December 1830. 'Rural Queries', PP 1834,
XXXIV, Q 53. J. Weyland and H. Dover to Lord Melbourne, 17
June 1835, HO 52/26, PRO. E.P. Thompson, The Moral Economy of
the English Crowd in the Eighteenth Century, 'Past and Present',
5O (1971), 136.
8   'Norwich Mercury', 26 December 1835. N. Edsall, 'The anti-
Poor Law movement, 1834-44' (Manchester, 1971), 34-7.
9   Kay to PLC, 23 July 1837, MH 32/49. 'Draft of a Petition to
Parliament from agricultural labourers of Suffolk against the
Poor Law Amendment Act' (Woodbridge (?), n.d.). Petition from
Agricultural Labourers in Wickham Market and District for
Repeal of Poor Law Amendment Act, HA 11/B5/25, Suffolk RO
(Ipswich branch).
1O   'Second Report of PLC', PP 1836, XXIX, Pt 1, 155, 161. G.J. Kett
to Frankland Lewis, 11 April 1836. J.P. Kay to PLC, 14 April
1836, 28 April 1836, MH 12/8455. 'Norwich Mercury', 6 August
1836. Kay to PLC, 26 March 1837, MH 12/834O.
11   John Collison to Sir W.B. Folkes, 1 August 1837, NRS 8742, NRO.
12   'Norwich Mercury', 18 July 1835. Docking magistrates to Lord
John Russell, 1 July, 4 July, 13 July 1835, HO 52/26, PRO. Sir
E. Parry to PLC, 2 July 1835, MH 12/8249. 'SC on Agriculture',
1837, V, Q 2971-4.
13   Sir E. Parry to PLC, 2 July 1835, MH 32/6O. Freebridge Lynn
Minutes, 12 February 1836, 11 March 1836, PL Cat., NRO.
14   'Norwich Mercury', 12 March 1836, 18 July 1836. Guiltcross
guardians to PLC, 16 February 1836, MH 12/8393.
15   Return from Great Massingham Q 17 to Constabulary Commission,
HO 73/7, Pt 1, PRO. Swaffham Minutes, 1O October 1835, Henstead Minutes, 15 June 1836, St Faith's Minutes, 26 July 1837,
PL Cat., NRO. Henstead guardians to PLC, 11 June 1836, MH
12/8415. 'Norwich Mercury', 2 July 1836.
16   Memorial against the Erection of a House of Industry, Windham
Papers, vol. XLVIII, BM Add. MS 37889. Mitford and Launditch
Minutes, 11 September 1837; Wayland Minutes, 22 October 1835;
Docking Minutes, 15 February 1836, 26 July 1836; PL Cat., NRO.
A. Birrell to PLC, 9 April 1838, MH 12/741, PRO. 'The Times',
6 July 1844, 16 July 1844.
17   James Gay to PLC, 17 September 1834, MH 12/8474.
18   Petition from Agricultural Labourers, HA 11/B5/25, Suffolk RO,
(Ipswich branch).
19   J.P.D. Dunbabin (ed.), 'Rural Discontent in Nineteenth Century
Britain' (1974), 59. R. Hankinson to Lord Melbourne, 31
August 1831, HO 4O/29, PRO. 'The Times', 14 June 1844, 4 July
1844. Aylsham Minutes, 2 May 1843; Depwade Minutes, 2 September
1844 PL Cat., NRO.
2O   R.N. Bacon, 'Report on the Agriculture of Norfolk', 83. N.
Riches, 'The Agricultural Revolution in Norfolk', 2nd edn (1967),
59.
21   A.J. Peacock, 'Bread or Blood', 65-6.
22   L.M. Springall, The Norfolk Agricultural Labourer 1834-84

(University of London PhD thesis, 1935), 238.

23 'Annals of Agriculture', XXV (1796), 504.

24 C.S. Orwin and B.I. Felton, A Century of Wages and Earnings in Agriculture, 'Journal of Royal Agricultural Society of England', 92 (1931), 231. C. Mackie, 'Norfolk Annals' (2 vols, Norwich, 1901) I, 42. G. Edwards, 'From Crow-Scaring to Westminster' (1912), 17.

25 G. Edwards, 'Crow-Scaring', 18-23, 37.

26 A. Digby, The Labour Market, 'Economic History Review', 2nd ser. XXVIII (1975), 74-80.

27 F. Clifford, 'The Agricultural Lockout' (Edinburgh, 1875), 364.

28 J.P.D. Dunbabin, The Incidence and Organization of Agricultural Trades Unionism in the 1870s, 'Agricultural History Review', 16 (1968), 115. 'RC on Agricultural Depression', PP 1882, XV, 106, 'RC on Labour', PP 1893-4, XXXV, 387.

29 A. Clayden, 'The Revolt of the Field' (1874), 87. J. Arch, 'The Autobiography of Joseph Arch', abridged edn (1966), 57. 'RC on Aged Poor', PP 1895, XIV, Q 6570.

30 H. Rider Haggard, 'A Farmer's Year' (1899), 429-30. 'RC on Aged Poor', PP 1895, XIV, QQ 7077, 7194.

31 'RC on Aged Poor', PP 1895, XIV, QQ 6454, 6471.

32 Forehoe Minutes, 14 March 1870, 7 March 1870, PL Cat., NRO.

BIBLIOGRAPHICAL NOTE

Attention is here confined only to the principal primary sources on the Poor Law since a brief note cannot do justice to the wide range of sources which have been consulted for this book.

The wealth of archival material on the Poor Law to which reference has been made in the Norfolk Record Office included interesting material on the urban Poor Law in the Yarmouth Borough Archives, and more particularly in the Norwich City Archives, with its excellent series of court and committee books for the Norwich guardians. The rural poor law in the county was defined by reference to the Parish Records Collection and the Poor Law Catalogue. The parochial machinery of the Old Poor Law in the Norfolk countryside was revealed in the many overseers' accounts, settlement and removal documents and emigration papers in the former collection, while the latter included the books and returns of the contemporary, local, poor law incorporations. The backbone of the material in the Poor Law Catalogue consisted of the minute books, registers and rate books of the new poor law unions, and these records of a standardized administration were found to have a less immediate interest than the lively idiosyncracies of the records of the preceding era.

There is a mass of correspondence on the New Poor Law to be read at the Public Record Office in the MH 32 class (which comprised the general correspondence of the assistant commissioners or inspectors with the central administration), and also in the MH 12 class (which dealt with the letters and returns of individual poor law unions). The latter gave a good insight into the socioeconomic circumstances within each area and the war of attrition waged by central bureaucracy to subdue local independence in poor relief policy. The letters and returns in the former gave insight into the importance that the personalities of administrators had on the Poor Law, as well as giving a good indication of the practical progress of the national reform of poor relief after 1834.

Selective quotations from these inspectors' papers were included in the annual series of Reports by the Poor Law Commission, Poor Law Board and Local Government Board which were published in Parliamentary Papers. These were a major source of information on the New Poor Law, and one in which it was found that complacent conclusions in general reports were often undercut by detailed

statistical returns in appendices. More detailed information on
specialized poor law topics was gained by looking at allied material
in the Reports of Select Committees which periodically examined
topics such as medical relief or settlement and removal. More
regular returns on other aspects of poor law administration, such
as finance or workhouse administration, were consulted in Accounts
and Papers. The Royal Commissions on the Poor Law of 1832-4 and
1905-9 produced a wealth of fascinating material which was also
published in Parliamentary Papers.

The reform of the Poor Law was featured in the vigorous local
press, and newspapers such as the 'Norwich Mercury' or 'Norfolk
Chronicle' were found to be a useful source of information when
changes in the Poor Law occurred, and also gave some indication of
contemporary attitudes to reform. Much more evidence on the local
debate on the Poor Law was to be gleaned from the astonishingly
rich pamphlet literature which was found in local library collec-
tions in East Anglia, and most notably in the Rye and Colman Collection in the Central Library, Norwich. While some indication of
the wealth of this material can be gained from the footnotes in
this volume, a fuller list is included in the bibliography of the
thesis that formed the starting point for this book — The Operation
of the Poor Law in the Social and Economic Life of Nineteenth-Century
Norfolk (University of East Anglia PhD thesis, 1972).

INDEX